7200
75u

D1529123

POWER REVOLUTION IN THE INDUSTRIALIZATION
OF JAPAN: 1885–1940

POWER REVOLUTION IN THE INDUSTRIALIZATION OF JAPAN: 1885–1940

BY

RYOSHIN MINAMI

ECONOMIC RESEARCH SERIES
NO. 24
THE INSTITUTE OF ECONOMIC RESEARCH
HITOTSUBASHI UNIVERSITY
KUNITACHI TOKYO 186

KINOKUNIYA COMPANY LTD.
Tokyo, Japan

Printed in 1987

Published by Kinokuniya Company Ltd.
17-7 Shinjuku 3-chome, Shinjuku-ku,
Tokyo 163-91, Japan

(In U.S.A.)
Distributed by New York Kinokuniya Bookstores
10 West 49th Street,
New York, NY 10020
U.S.A.

ISBN 4-314-00472-X

Printed by
Kokusaibunken Insatsusha
Tokyo, Japan

PREFACE

Industrialization or the growth of manufacturing industry proceeded in Japan for the prewar period at a higher rate than in earlier developed countries. This fact was closely associated with the marked power revolution—an increase in the capacity of mechanical power with a change in its sources. This association is mutual; the industrialization has promoted the power revolution and the power revolution has supported an expansion of manufacturing activities. In this sense the industrialization in Japan can be fully clarified only with a study of the power revolution and its significance. This study is a subject of the present volume.

Chapter 1 is an introduction, which presents the framework of the study and its significance, and a survey of the history of the Japanese industrialization.

Prior to the study of the power revolution in the process of industrialization, we discuss a history of various engines or sources of mechanical power in Part I. First in chapter 2 we survey and evaluate the utilization of the traditional engine, the water wheel for the pre-industrialization period and the early phase of industrialization. In chapter 3 we survey a history of an invention of modern engines—steam and internal combustion engines, water and steam turbines, and electric motors in the West and of adoption of these engines in Japan.

Part II contains statistical analyses of the process of power revolution in Japan for 1885–1940. In chapter 4 an introduction of engines or the mechanization of nonpowered factories is surveyed. In chapter 5 we examine the growth of total power capacity of all kinds of engines. In chapter 6 we argue a change in the composition of total power capacity by type of engines. Chapter 7 clarifies factors for the electrification, the most sweeping among many technological advances in the prewar Japanese manufacturing.

Six chapters of Part III clarify an impact of the power revolution on the industrial growth in six selected industries; silk reeling, cotton spinning, weaving, lumbering, match making and printing (chapters 8–13). Depending on these studies we discuss about the general impact of the electrification in chapter 14.

In chapter 15 of Part IV, we will summarize major findings in the previous chapters concerning the history of the power revolution and discuss about the characteristics of Japanese technological progress.

The main part of this book was previously published as a mimeograph with the same title as this volume (Discussion Paper Series, Nos. 56 and 57, Institute of Economic Research, Hitotsubashi University, 1982). Based on new works performed after 1982 the mineograph was fully revised and a new chapter (chapter 11) was added to make the present volume.

In carrying out these studies I have been indebted to many people. I would like to express much thanks to Profs. Kazushi Ohkawa (International Development Center of Japan), Mataji Umemura (Sōka University), Takafusa Nakamura (University of Tokyo), Hugh Patrick (Columbia University) and Kozo Yamamura (University of Washington) for their encouragements. Also thanks are due to Prof. Fumio Makino (Tokyo Gakugei University) for his collaboration in studying the technology of the silk-reeling, weaving and lumbering industries. Studies on the first two industries are partly adopted in this volume and a study on the last industry is included as chapter 11. Finally I like to express gratitude to Prof. Mahmoud Motavasseli (Tehran University) and Mrs. Donna Vandenbrink for editing the English in this volume, and to the Esso Standard Oil Foundation for giving finantial aids to this study.

June 1986

RYOSHIN MINAMI
Institute of Economic Research
Hitotsubashi University

CONTENTS

CONTENTS

viii

CONTENTS

LIST OF TABLES

LIST OF TABLES

LIST OF TABLES

LIST OF FIGURES

One *koku* = 180 liters
One *monme* = 3.76 grammes
One *kan* = 1,000 *monme* = 3.76 kilogrammes
One yen = 100 sen

INTRODUCTION

This volume examines the diffusion of mechanical power in Japan and its significance to her industrialization. The broader purpose in undertaking this analysis is to clarify the connection between developments in power utilization and the processes of industrialization and economic growth.

The first section of this introductory chapter outlines the coverage of the study, sets forth the conceptual framework, and demonstrates the significance of the analysis of power utilization. For the convenience of readers who are not familiar with Japanese economic history, the second section contains a brief discussion of Japan's modern economic performance and important factors in her industrialization.

Coverage, Framework of Analysis, and Significance

Coverage

This study is focused on the utilization of mechanical power in the private manufacturing sector during the period between 1885 and 1940. There are two reasons why it begins in 1885. The first is that modern economic growth in Japan commenced in the middle of 1880s.[1] Substantial industrialization had its inception at about the same time as the establishment of modern cotton-spinning factories. The second reason for beginning the study in 1885 is a practical one. Official

---

[1] Minami 1986, pp. 10–14; Ohkawa and Rosovsky 1965, p. 66.

statistics for horsepower capacity are only available from that date. Data on power capacity by type of engine and on the number of powered and nonpowered factories are the basis for the quantitative analysis of the diffusion of mechanical power. For this study, estimates by sub-industry groupings and by scale of firms have been made from official statistics. (The data and estimation procedure are described in full in the Appendix.) The time span covered differs with the availability of data by these classifications. Some statistics have been calculated for the period 1884 to 1940 while others were made available only for the period 1909 to 1940.

The decision to exclude the years after 1940 from this study is that mechanization and electrification were almost completed by 1940; there has been no significant change in the sources of manufacturing power thereafter.

Framework

The conceptual basis of this study is that mechanical power utilization and industrialization are mutually reinforcing phenomena. (1) The growth of manufacturing industry has indeed created the need for mechanical power sources. (2) Developments in power sources and power capacity have supported the expansion of manufacturing and they have helped to shape the path of industrial progress. When David S. Landes claimed that "the story of power is the story of industrialization,"[2] he referred to these mutual relationships. These relationships may be described in the following way.

Power revolution as a result of industrialization. The relationship of power revolution as a response to industrialization (1) is revealed in some parts of this volume. Above all a quantitative study on the changes in horsepower capacity of manufacturing and mining in chapter 5 clearly shows that an increase in power capacity is explained by indexes of profit, that is, by the volume and rate of return on capital. This implies that an industry tends to expand its power capacity (and also other types of production facilities) when it expects to have high profit. The level of

[2]   Landes 1969, p. 293.

profit depends on various factors such as demand for products, technological progress, and costs of raw materials and wages.

Some case studies on individual industries also furnish useful information on this relationship. Prior to 1885, Japanese manufacturing was less dependent on nonhuman power (i.e., water wheels and animal power) than Western countries at similar stages of economic development. Japan's historically greater reliance on human power was basically due to an insufficient overall demand for mechanical (and animal) power (chapter 2). Eventually, the development of the manufacturing industry and the accompanying expansion of output markets during the Meiji period stimulated producers to turn to mechanical power sources. Furthermore, the subsequent transition from water wheels to more expensive and powerful steam engines in the cotton-spinning industry was made necessary in part because of the expansion of cotton manufacturing itself (chapter 9). In short, industrialization created a need for mechanical power.

Power revolution as a cause of industrialization. Mechanical power utilization should not, however, be viewed simply as a consequence of industrial growth. What is overlooked is the fact that the diffusion of mechanical power has been a significant force of industrial development (2). The power revolution—the expansion of power capacity, the mechanization of manufacturing, and the transition to newer power sources—motivated modern manufacturing growth. Moreover, the utilization of power motivated improvements in production technology and thereby stimulated further industrial development.

(a) Impact of Expansion of Power Capacity

As is shown in chapter 5, expanding power capacity is necessary to sustain industrialization. Manufacturing growth depends on increasing capital stock, and greater power capacity must accompany additions to the capital stock. This is not simply because equipment for power generation and transmission is one component of the capital stock. The great bulk of capital stock consists of energy-using equipment, and installation of such equipment requires, along with it, an increase in power capacity.

Different types of impacts of the mechanization and the transition to newer power sources are studied in seven chapters of part 3. Following is a summary of these studies.

(b) Impact of Mechanization

The introduction of engines to nonpowered factories was one of the most epochal events in economic history. This event was closely related with the transition from hand-held tools to machinery. In the West, the invention of cotton-spinning machinery by James Hargreaves, Richard Arkwright, and Samuel Crompton made it possible to utilize animal and water power. Later the invention of the steam engine by James Watt promoted the mechanization of cotton-spinning. This mechanization is usually considered as the foundation of the Industrial Revolution in England.

In Japan, too, modern manufacturing had its roots in the mechanization of spinning, and, as in England, the initial source of mechanical power to this industry was the water wheel. The introduction of the *gara* spinner which employed water power to operate traditional machinery raised labor productivity in cotton spinning in early Meiji Japan well beyond that of the traditional (hand-powered) spinning technique. Modern spinning technology introduced from the West also relied initially on water power, and until the beginning of the 1880s almost all spinning mills in Japan were operated by water wheels (chapter 9).

Silk reeling was the most typical industry which relied on water power in the early Meiji period. Machine filature technology, combined with water power, was substituted for the traditional sedentary reeling method (chapter 8).

The introduction of mechanical power to the lumbering and the printing industries was of revolutionary importance because lumbering by hand saw and printing by hand press required considerable physical effort. Lumbering represents an industry whose mechanization was made by water wheels, while printing is a typical industry in which water wheels were rarely used and steam engines were the first mechanical power source (chapter 13).

For the most part, mechanization in Japan occurred first in large-scale textile factories. Small-scale plants could not afford the initial capital outlay and the operating expense of steam power. But with the mass production of standard-type small motors and the decrease in electric power rates realized in the 1910s and 1920s, small-scale plants could switch from human to mechanical power. The introduction of electric power modernized production technology in various industries. For example, the substitution of power looms for hand looms in small-scale weaving plants depended largely on electrification (chapter 10). Also the introduction of electric motors in match-making plants made possible the shift from less efficient treadle machines to modern machines invented in Germany (chapter 12).

The mechanization of manufacturing technology depending on water wheels, steam engines, and electric motors, which was referred to in the above, increased labor productivity of manufacturing and promoted industrialization.

(c) Impact of Transition to Newer Power Sources

Adoption of newer power sources stimulated further growth of manufacturing. The transition from water wheels to steam engines and the transition from steam engines to electric motors have had far-reaching consequences for the progress of industrialization.

As for the transition from water power to steam power (steam revolution), Japan and England are really different cases. In England water wheel was a major source of power in the early stage of the Industrial Revolution, and maintained its significance during the later stage. Even in cotton manufacturing, a typical industry characterized by the steam revolution, "massive growth of steam power occurred in the later nineteenth century, not in the heroic age of the early industrial revolution."[3]

In Japan the progress of the modern spinning industry depended eventually on the adoption of steam power. For a number of reasons, the water-powered cotton-spinning plants established before the 1880s never became viable commercial operations. The establishment of the Osaka Spinning Mill in 1883, equipped with an imported steam engine,

[3] Musson 1976, p. 436.

was the first successful use of modern technology in Japan and paved the way for the development of a modern textile industry based on large-scale, steam-powered spinning mills (chapter 9). Thus it may be said that the relative importance of steam power compared with water power was greater in Japanese industrialization than in the English Industrial Revolution.

The transition from steam engines to electric motors has had an equally significant impact on the progress of industrialization. Displacement of steam engines by electric power purchased from public utilities brought about a fundamental change in the production system of factories. The group-drive system was replaced by a unit-drive system, in which each individual machine was run directly by small motor. The shift to the unit-drive system generated great savings in capital costs and energy consumption. In addition, a complete reorganization of factory layout and design, which had been hindered by the shafts and belts necessary for the group-drive system, became possible with electrification and introduction of the unit drive (chapter 14). The transition to electric motors was thus an important event in the development of manufacturing.

(d) Power Revolution and Production Technology

The power revolution not only provided the capacity for sustaining manufacturing growth and development but it also contributed to shaping that development by inducing improvements in production technology. The best example of the impact of the power revolution on production technology may be the shift from the group-drive to the unit-drive system which occurred with electrification. Another example can be found in the effect of the transition to steam power on machinery in the silk-reeling industry. In Japan, machinery of traditional wooden construction was employed in the silk-reeling industry even after the introduction of water wheels. But the shift from water power to steam power gave rise to improvements in silk-reeling machinery because wooden machinery tended to wear out and break down rather easily under the greater speed and engine vibration of steam engines. Consequently, all-wooden machinery was first replaced by equipment combining wood and iron, and later by much more efficient machinery of iron construction (chapter 8).

Such progress in production technology is perhaps the most essential feature of industrialization and modern economic growth. By examining developments in power utilization we can understand the motivations for such innovations. But economic historians have tended to neglect this relationship or to view the chain of causation in the opposite direction. For example, in discussing technology in *Das Kapital*, Marx argued that it is improvements in production machinery which stimulate developments in power technology.[4] His evidence was that the development of cotton-spinning machinery motivated the introduction of steam engines at the start of the Industrial Revolution. In the framework of this study, which is to view power utilization and industrialization as mutually reinforcing phenomena, it is argued that the diffusion of power itself also induces progress in production technology and we focus on this impact of the power revolution in several key industries in Japan's economic development.

Significance

There are two ways in which the study of the diffusion of power contributes to understanding economic growth. First, analysis of power capacity provides a means to investigate capital accumulation and second, investigation in power utilization provides a means to clarify technological change.

Horsepower statistics and capital stock. Horsepower statistics provide a means to analyze the growth of the capital stock by sub-industry group and by the size of firms, because power capacity is closely correlated with the size of the capital stock.[5] Indeed, horsepower statistics have in the past been used as a proxy index for capital stock in some countries,

[4] Marx 1954, p. 375.

[5] Estimating a correlation coefficient of the relation between horsepower capacity (H) and capital stock (K) in manufacturing and mining for 1907–40, we obtain 0.984. Also it is 0.985 for the relation between primary horsepower capacity (H') and K in the same industry for 1917–40. Figures for H and H' are our estimates (see Table 5-3) and those for K are the same as those used in Table 1-3.

including Japan. For instance, Miyohei Shinohara relied on horsepower data to estimate production functions for Japanese manufacturing for the period from 1929 to 1940.[6]

In recent years, however, the significance of horsepower statistics has decreased with the greater availability of capital stock data. Estimates of Japan's capital assets for primary and nonprimary sectors appeared in 1966 as part of *Chōki Keizai Tōkei* (Estimates of long-term economic statistics of Japan, henceforth LTES).[7] In 1968 capital stock estimates for the nonprimary sector were further divided into four industry groups: manufacturing and mining, construction, facilitating, and services.[8] Estimation by sub-industry group in manufacturing, however, has never been attempted and appears to be almost impossible because of the paucity of data. Thus, in spite of the recent appearance of capital stock data, horsepower statistics are necessary for the disaggregated analysis of capital assets.[9]

Power diffusion and technological change. The existence of a relationship between changes in power utilization and developments in production technology suggests that the study of the diffusion of

[6]   Shinohara 1949, sect. 5 of chap. 4. Ron Napier made an attempt to estimate manufacturing capital stock by sub-industry group and by scale of establishments depending on power capacity (1981, pp. 223–29).

[7]   Ohkawa *et al.* 1966.

[8]   Chōki Keizai Tōkei Iinkai 1968, part 4.

[9]   There are a few problems, however, in employing horsepower statistics for this purpose. First, although power capacity may express the capacity of machines which directly save human labor, it does not provide a measure of equipment used for heating, cooling, and chemical reaction or of machines operated by hand. This deficiency is most significant in the case of chemical and related industries. Second, data on power capacity of stationary engines do not express the capacity of moveable transport equipment, whether used inside or outside of factories. Third, building and structures, one component of capital assets, are not necessarily closely related with horsepower measures. This final limitation of horsepower statistics is the least serious. Figures excluding structures are appropriate for the purpose of estimating changes in production capacity (e.g., for estimating production functions). Production capacity does not necessarily increase with an expansion of buildings, but it can be expected to increase with additions to machinery and power equipment. See Economic Commission for Europe, Research and Planning Division 1951, p. 24 and Thorp 1929.

mechanical power may throw some light on technological progress and economic growth. Assuming that technological progress is expressed by the growth of total factor productivity, it can be measured as the "residual" increase in output after accounting for the contribution of growth in individual factor inputs. The analysis of economic growth and the growth of specific industries has been stimulated and developed to a great extent by such "growth accounting". But, even if growth in total factor productivity does provide an approximate measure of technological progress, growth accounting does not give any information about the kind of technological change which has occurred. The study of the diffusion of power and its impact on production equipment is one way to make up for this deficiency in our understanding of technological progress.

In the second section of this introductory chapter growth accounting is applied to examine Japanese manufacturing and mining from 1911 to 1940. This brief analysis explains the important role of rapid technological progress in the growth of these industries. The borrowed technology argument proposed by Alexander Gerschenkron is an explanation for rapid technological progress in Japan.[10] As a late comer, Japan had the advantage of exploiting modern technologies developed in more advanced countries. This study provides some evidence for the Gerschenkron hypothesis.

International significance. In addition to the study's significance cited above this study includes an international significance. First it facilitates an international comparison of economic history among developed countries. Recently several important studies have been made on the history of power utilization in England and the United States which have contributed greatly to an understanding of the economic history of these countries.[11] Since present study provides historical data of mechanization of factories and of power capacity in Japan and examines Japanese industrialization based on these data, thus a comparison

[10]   The applicability of the full Gerschenkron model to Japan is examined in chap. 15.
[11]   For instance Byatt 1979, Hills 1970, Musson 1976 and von Tunzelmann 1978 for England, and Du Boff 1967, Fenichel 1966, and Hunter 1979 for the Unites States.

between the Japanese experience with the experiences of the earlier developed countries is possible. Although this volume does not explicitly aim to make such comparison, some references comparing Japan with England and the United States will be made in various parts of this volume.

Second, our study on Japanese history may provide some lessons to developing countries. Since Japan had succeeded in industrialization by exploiting the backlog of modern technology in the West, a study on the technological progress in Japan is expected to provide some useful information on exploiting modern technology. An attempt to tackle this important but difficult problem will be made in chapter 15.

Overview of Japan's Industrialization

Record of Industrialization

Growth of manufacturing. It is a well-documented fact that the economic growth of Japan since the Meiji era has depended decisively on industrialization.[12] The expansion of real manufacturing output explained 34.1% of the growth in real Net Domestic Products (NDP) between 1888 and 1937. Moreover, manufacturing played an increasingly larger role in overall economic growth over this period. Manufacturing growth comprised 13.2% of the increase in real NDP for the earliest years, 1888–1900. But this rate almost doubled to 23.9% for the years 1900–20 and doubled again to 46.7% for the period 1920–37. Consequently, the proportion of manufacturing output in nominal NDP, which was merely 11.4% in 1888, increased to 21.2% in 1920 and to 30.9% in 1937.[13]

The contribution of industrialization to Japan's economic growth is much more significant than what is conveyed by these figures. A growing

---

[12] See Minami 1986, chap. 5 for a quantitative study of Japanese industrialization.

[13] Both real and nominal output figures are based on seven-year averages centered on the indicated years (Ohkawa *et al.* 1974, pp. 202, 205, 226, 229). Real output is at 1934–36 prices.

manufacturing sector could provide consumer and producer goods in sufficient supply to meet increasing demand from rising per capita income and increasing population. Industrialization permitted import substitution and later supported export expansion. With the development of manufacturing, then, the country with scarce resources could import the raw materials indispensable to economic growth without deteriorating her balance of payments position.

The speed with which Japan achieved industrialization has been the subject of many empirical research. The Nagoya Index of Manufacturing Output, the first long-term estimates, gave the impression that Japanese industrialization occurred at a rate unparalleled in the world. Three more recent studies by Yasukichi Yasuba, Yuichi Shionoya, and Miyohei Shinohara have revealed that the high rate of growth observed in the Nagoya Index stemmed from underestimation of output in the early years. These later studies found a rather more moderate rate of growth. The most recent study, the Shinohara Index, for example, estimated the annual rate of growth at 5.6% for the years 1881 to 1938.[14] Although lower than previous estimates, these figures show that the rate of growth of manufacturing in Japan was still much higher than in earlier developed countries. The annual rate of growth for 1881–1940 was 4.2% in the United States, 3.9% in Sweden, 3.4% in Germany (1881–1935), 2.5% in Italy, and only 2.2% in United Kingdom (1881–1935).[15] Furthermore, the Shinohara Index revealed an upward trend in the rate of manufacturing growth in Japan. A simple regression of the rate of growth of manufacturing (g) on time (t) for 1878–1938

---

[14]   The annual rate of growth in real manufacturing output, Y is calculated as an average of $(Y_t - Y_{t-1})/Y_{t-1} \times 100$ for this period. Y is seven-year moving average of the figures in Shinohara 1972, pp. 145, 147.

[15]   Minami 1986, table 5-2 on p. 103.

A gap between Japan and the earlier developed countries should be smaller for the period corresponding to the same stage of economic development in respective countries. For instance, the growth rate in the United Kingdom is 2–4% for the first half of the nineteenth century.

Table 1-1. Annual Rate of Growth of Real Output by Industry
Group

(percent)

Industry Group	1878–1900	1901–1920	1921–1938
All manufacturing	4.38	5.41	6.53
Light industry[a]	4.51	4.25	4.01
Heavy industry[b]	4.93	9.92	9.83
Textiles	6.93	5.88	5.59
Metals and metal products	3.98	14.82	10.23
Machinery	11.36	14.01	9.40
Ceramics	4.23	7.30	7.51
Chemicals	3.98	5.39	10.31
Wood and wood products	3.89	2.53	7.26
Food	3.64	3.13	2.16
Miscellaneous	3.13	4.33	5.01

Sources: Shinohara 1972, pp. 144–47.

Notes: Figures in this table are the annual rate of growth of real output, O (1934–36
prices). Figures for O are seven-year moving averages (five-year average for 1938).
Rate of growth is an average of $(O_t - O_{t-1})/O_{t-1} \times 100$ for each period.

[a] Total of textiles and food.

[b] Total of metals and metal products, machinery, and chemicals.

confirms the upward trend in g.[16]

$$g = -130.03 + 0.0709t \qquad r = 0.524 \quad F = 22.28$$

Correlation coefficient (r) is statistically significant, which indicates the
existence of the increasing trend in g.

Structure of manufacturing. The rapid growth of manufacturing industry
was accompanied by a remarkable change in its structure. Table 1-1 and

[16] Data used here is the same as that in n. 14. The acceleration in the growth of
manufacturing output was largely responsible for the increasing economic growth rate, a
phenomenon which was termed "trend acceleration" by Ohkawa and Rosovsky (1975, pp.
196–200). See also Minami 1986, pp. 50–58.

Table 1-2. Relative Contributions to Total Increase in Real Output by Industry Group

(percent)

Industry Group	1877–1900	1900–1920	1920–1938
All manufacturing	100.0	100.0	100.0
Light industry	75.2	50.5	28.4
Heavy industry	13.0	39.6	61.4
Textiles	34.9	28.9	21.6
Metals and metal products	1.5	11.3	17.5
Machinery	4.0	19.4	23.6
Ceramics	1.2	2.5	2.8
Chemicals	7.5	8.9	20.3
Wood and wood products	2.5	1.4	2.8
Food	40.3	21.6	6.8
Miscellaneous	8.1	6.0	4.6

Sources: Same as Table 5-1.
Notes: Relative contribution of industry (i) is calculated as $(O_{i,t} - O_{i,t-n})/(O_t - O_{t-n})$ $\times 100$, where n denotes length of period. $O = \sum_{i=1}^{8} O_i$.
Also see the notes to Table 1-1.

Table 1-2 provide informations on this change. In these tables the manufacturing sector is divided into eight sub-industry groups, in which textiles and foods are grouped as light industry, while metals, machinery and chemicals are grouped as heavy industry.

In 1877–1900 the relative contribution of light industry to manufacturing growth (percentage of the increase in real output of this industry in the increase in total manufacturing output) amounted to 75%, compared with the 13% contribution of heavy industry, indicating that manufacturing growth in the early phase was dependent decisively on light industry. This signifies that Japanese industrialization repeated the traditional pattern of industrialization from textiles to metals and machinery observed in the English Industrial Revolution, and can be contrasted with the experiences in other developed countries like Germany, in which the heavy industry was a leading sector.[17] The choice of light industry as the leading sector in the early industrialization in Japan seemed to be appropriate; that is, labor intensive textiles had relative advantage over capital intensive heavy industry in this country with abundant labor and scarce capital.

The relative contribution of heavy industry did increase in later years especially after WWI; in 1920–38 it amounted to 61%, compared with 28% of light industry. This change came from a rise in the rate of growth of heavy industry (from 5% in 1878–1900 to 10% in 1901–20 and 1921–38). As a result of this change, the share of light industry in total manufacturing output decreased and that of heavy industry increased. In 1887 the shares of these industry groups were 72% and 17%, while in 1937 they were 37% and 52% respectively. Heavy industry surpassed light industry in terms of output between 1930 and 1938.[18] Among the three components of heavy industry, machinery was the most important; it showed the largest relative contribution in this century and occupied the largest share of output of heavy industry as a whole.

Factors for Rapid Industrialization

Growth of industry depends on three factors, the supply of labor, capital accumulation, and technological progress.

Supply of labor. From the beginning of industrialization until the late 1950s, Japanese manufacturing had the advantage of a pool of surplus labor. Unlimited supplies of labor were available to manufacturing from the "traditional sector" (agriculture, commerce, and services).[19] It has been argued that the marginal productivity of labor in the traditional

[17] Shionoya 1968, pp. 77–78.

[18] See Table 5-5, panel C. This is calculated from nominal output data.

[19] My studies on marginal labor productivity and wages in agriculture, and on wage differentials between agriculture and manufacturing lead to the conclusion that an unlimited supply of labor existed in agriculture until the end of the 1950s or the beginning of the next decade (Minami 1973, pp. 225–36). Although no comprehensive studies have been attempted for the commerce and service sector, surplus labor seems also to have existed in this sector (Minami and Ono 1978b, pp. 19–21).

sector was lower than the subsistence level of wages, and therefore the wages in the traditional sector were determined by the subsistence level. In this situation "capitalist sector" in manufacturing could employ as much labor as it needed without bidding up wages. One of the most important consequences of the existence of unlimited supplies of labor, then, was the existence of the lag in wage increases in manufacturing behind the increase in labor productivity which brought about a decrease in the relative income share of labor.[20]

Two additional comments about the supply of labor during Japan's industrialization should be made here. First, although the workers coming from the traditional sector were unskilled, they were eligible for participation in the modern sector. These workers quickly became an excellent manufacturing labor force after some on-the-job training. Second, a part of the work force in manufacturing was comprised of skilled workers whose supply was limited. Therefore, increase in the wages of these workers accounts for the increase in average manufacturing wages over the period of industrialization.[21]

Capital accumulation. Japanese capital assets in manufacturing increased rapidly. The mean annual rate of growth of real gross capital stock in manufacturing and mining was 6.6% for the period 1906 to 1940.[22] Vigorous investment activity occurred largely because of the high expected rate of return on capital. The high rate of return was in turn attributed to factors such as the expansion of output markets, the rapid introduction of modern technology from developed countries, and the increasing trend in the relative income share of capital.

The steady rate of capital accumulation in Japan permitted rapid mechanization of production processes. From 1908 to 1938 the mean annual rate of growth in the ratio of capital stock to employed workers (seven-year moving averages) in manufacturing and mining was 3.5%.[23] Table 1-3 shows the average annual rates of growth in output and labor

[20] Minami and Ono 1981.
[21] Minami and Ono 1978b, pp. 21–23.
[22] The capital stock figures used here are the same as those used in Table 1-3.
[23] The labor force figures used here are those used in Table 1-3.

productivity (seven-year moving averages) in Japanese manufacturing and mining and components of these growth rates. This table demonstrates that the increasing capital-labor ratio, $G(\rho K/hL)$, was responsible for about one third of the total increase in labor productivity, $G(O/hL)$, for the period 1908 to 1938.

Technological progress. Technological progress in Japanese manufacturing was also remarkable, and it relied mainly on the introduction of modern technology from the United States and European countries. Modern technology was introduced mostly by importing foreign-made machinery, and to the less extent by imitating imports, by relying on the guidance of foreign engineers, and by arranging for technical cooperation with large foreign companies.[24]

According to Table 1-3, the growth rate of total factor productivity (the "residual" estimate of technological progress) $G(T)$, was 2.9% for the period 1908–38.[25] This rate was higher than the 2.5% rate of growth of American manufacturing from 1909 to 1937.[26] The growth in total

[24]   Imports from the West provided the models for the oil engine made by the Tokyo Artisan School in 1895, for the gas engine made by the Tokyo University of Engineering in 1896 (chap. 3) and also for the rotary press built by the Asahi Newspaper Company in 1904 (chap. 12). The Kobe Factory of the Japanese National Railways produced the first Japanese locomotive with the assistance of an English engineer in 1893 (chap. 3). Cooperation with foreign manufactures began in the late Taishō period in the electric machinery industry (chap. 7).

[25]   Our estimates for $G(T)$ do not differ much from the estimates by Ohkawa and Rosovsky (1973, table 4-2 on p. 73) for the observation years as a whole. The mean of our estimates for 1908–38 is 2.92% and that of Ohkawa and Rosovsky for 1912–38 is 3.38%. However, there is a significant difference between the two sets of estimates in the pattern of changes in $G(T)$. That is, our estimations show that $G(T)$ was highest in the 1920s, whereas according to the estimations of Ohkawa and Rosovsky it was lowest during this decade. (In this respect our estimates are similar to Napier's estimates which depend on quite different sources of data. Napier 1981, table 1 on p. 221.) Based on the following differences in estimation procedures, it seems that our result is much more realistic. First, the changes in labor hours and capital utilization have not been taken into consideration by Ohkawa and Rosovsky. Second, they employ tentative estimates for relative income shares, based on postwar information, while the relative income shares used in Table 1-3 are the results of our newer estimates of factor incomes for nonprimary industries (Minami and Ono 1978a; 1981).

[26]   Kendrick 1961, p. 136. This comparison involves a problem similar to that pointed out in n. 14.

factor productivity in Japan explained almost two-fifths of the rate of growth in real output, $G(O)$, and almost three-fifths of the rate of growth of labor productivity, $G(O/hL)$. The decomposition of manufacturing growth, or growth accounting, suggests that technological progress played a very important role in Japanese industrialization and that the rapid growth of Japanese manufacturing compared with other countries was largely dependent on the rate of technological progress.

It is also interesting to take note of the change in the rate of growth of total factor productivity, $G(T)$, over time. $G(T)$, which was only 0.3% for 1908–10, increased to 2.6% in the 1910s, and to 4.3% in the 1920s. This was responsible for an increase in the growth rate of labor productivity, $G(O/hL)$, for 1908–30. (The growth rate accounted for by an increase in capital-labor ratio, $E_K G(\rho K/hL)$, showed a decreasing trend for this period.) For the 1930s, $G(T)$ decreased to 2.6%. But $G(O/hL)$ continued to increase for this decade, because $E_K G(\rho K/hL)$ increased significantly to cancel out a decrease in $G(T)$.

It is appropriate to make two comments here. The first comment is on the high value of $G(T)$ in the 1920s. This reflects the fact that big enterprises, faced with a business depression, made great efforts to improve labor productivity by means of borrowed technology. Furthermore, it should be noted that electrification was most pronounced in the 1920s, which suggests the important role of electrification in the technological progress occurring in manufacturing (chapter 6). The second comment is about the high value of $E_K G(\rho K/hL)$ in the 1930s. This was due to a large figure of $E_K G(\rho K)$; $E_K G(\rho K)$ turned to increase in the 1930s from a decreasing trend for the previous periods. The rapid expansion of capital asset in the 1930s may have been a result of the decision making of enterprises to cope with a notable expansion of demand in the boom years since 1932.[27]

International comparison of labor productivity. To close this section we make a comparison of the level of labor productivity between Japan and

---

[27] This explanation confirms the view expressed by R. Napier that short-term fluctuations in the growth rate of labor productivity are a result of a response of entreprenuers to changes in demand (1981, p. 222).

Table 1-3. Decomposition of Output and Labor Productivity
Growth in Manufacturing and Mining

(percent)

	Rate of Growth				
	1908 –1938	1908 –1910	1911 –1920	1921 –1930	1931 –1938
Growth in output, $G(O)$	6.94	4.47	7.36	5.00	9.78
Labor input, $E_L G(hL)$	1.34	1.01	1.83	0.06	2.20
Capital input, $E_K G(\rho K)$	2.68	3.16	2.95	0.66	4.97
Total, $E_L G(hL) + E_K G(\rho K)$	4.02	4.17	4.78	0.72	7.17
Residual, $G(T)$	2.92	0.30	2.58	4.28	2.61
Growth in labor productivity, $G(O/hL)$	4.53	2.85	4.00	4.91	5.34
Capital-labor ratio, $E_K G(\rho K/hL)$	1.61	2.55	1.42	0.63	2.73
Residual, $G(T)$	2.92	0.30	2.58	4.28	2.61

earlier developed countries. The gap which have been enormously large
when Japan started to industrialize, decreased during the process of
industrialization. Figure 1-1 provides a comparison of labor productivity (O/L) and per capita primary power capacity (H'/L) of
manufacturing in Japan and 18 Western countries in the 1930s.[28]
Although differences in data coverage and in years of observation make
it difficult to attain definite conclusions, we may argue as follows. Both
per capita net output (an index of labor productivity) and per capita
power capacity (an index of capital-labor ratio, one of the determinants
of labor productivity) are the lowest in Japan. Per capita output of
Japan ($283) was only 40% of the mean level in the advanced countries

[28] Small establishments with less than five workers are included in O and L, but not in
H'. Because power equipment in these establishments was rather negligible in comparison
with that for larger establishments, however, this problem does not seem to be serious.

Table 1-3. (continued)

(percent)

	Relative Contribution				
	1908 −1938	1908 −1910	1911 −1920	1921 −1930	1931 −1938
Growth in output, $G(O)$	100.0	100.0	100.0	100.0	100.0
Labor input, $E_L G(hL)$	19.3	22.6	24.9	1.2	22.5
Capital input, $E_K G(\rho K)$	38.6	70.7	40.1	13.2	50.8
Total, $E_L G(hL) + E_K G(\rho K)$	5.79	93.3	65.0	14.4	73.3
Residual, $G(T)$	42.12	6.7	35.0	85.6	26.7
Growth in labor productivity,					
$G(O/hL)$	100.0	100.0	100.0	100.0	100.0
Capital-labor ratio,					
$E_K G(\rho K/hL)$	35.5	89.5	35.5	12.8	51.1
Residual, $G(T)$	64.5	10.5	64.5	87.2	48.9

Sources: Minami 1986, table 5-3 on p. 105.
Notes: Figures are for the private sector only.
 $G(\ )$ denotes mean annual rate of growth for the respective period.
 O = gross domestic product at 1934–36 prices.
 L = number of labor force.
 K = gross capital stock at 1934–36 prices.
 h = labor hours.
 ρ = rate of capital utilization.
 E_K = output elasticity of capital.
 E_L = output elasticity of labor = $1 - E_K$.
 $G(T)$ = rate of growth in total factor productivity
  = $G(O) - E_L G(hL) - E_K G(\rho K)$.

($711), while its per capita power capacity (1.1 hp) was 44% of the mean
in the advanced countries (2.5 hp). This implies that mechanization of
Japanese manufacturing was still underdeveloped compared with that of
developed countries in the 1930s. This fact seemed to be partly as a result
of the existence of surplus labor, which discouraged substitution of

19

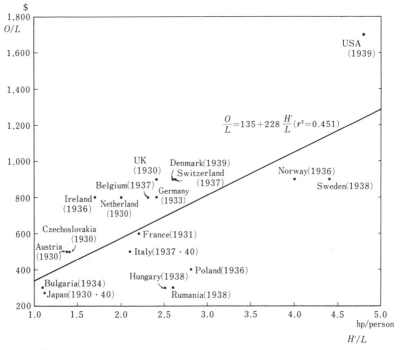

Fig. 1-1. International Comparison of Labor Productivity (O/L)
and Primary Power Capacity Per Capita (H'/L)

Sources: Japan (private manufacturing industry): O (net domestic product) is calculated from NDP including the government sector, which is converted to U.S. dollars by using the exchange rate. NDP is from Ohkawa *et al.* 1974, p. 203 and the exchange rate is from Nippon Ginkō, Tōkei Kyoku 1966, p. 320. See Table 1-1 for the procedure to exclude the government sector from the original NDP figure. L is obtained from Minami and Ono 1978a, p. 168. H' refers to our estimates (see Appendix). Means of 1930 and 1940 are used in O/L and H'/L.
Other countries: Economic Commission for Europe, Research and Planning Division 1951, pp. 27 and 31.

capital for labor, and a cause for the relatively low level of labor productivity. Catching up with industries in advanced countries was not attained until the post WWII period.

Figure 1-1 also demonstrates the estimated correlation between per capita primary power capacity and manufacturing productivity. In this figure Japan is located not far from the regression line. It appears that by the 1930s the state of technology in Japanese manufacturing did not differ greatly from the state to be expected from its degree of mechanization based on the international production function. This conclusion is quite reasonable considering that almost all technology prevailing in Japanese industry at that time had been introduced from these other countries.

PART I

TRADITIONAL AND MODERN SOURCES OF POWER

The next two chapters set the stage for the study of the power revolution in Japan. First, in chapter 2 we discuss the traditional source of mechanical power, the water wheel. Some reasons for the low level of power utilization in Japanese manufacturing at the outset of industrialization can be found in historical and economic conditions which restricted the application of water power and in deficiencies in domestic water wheel technology. Then, in chapter 3 we briefly trace the appearance of modern sources of power—the steam engine, the internal combustion engine, and the electric motor—both in the West and in Japan. These two chapters provide a historical perspective for part 2 where we show that in Japan, in contrast to the West, it was modern engines and not the water wheel which were largely responsible for the initial mechanization of manufacturing.

Chapter 2

WATER WHEELS IN THE

TRADITIONAL ECONOMY

In this chapter we examine the utilization of the water wheel, a traditional source of mechanical power prior to industrialization. Water wheels were the primary source of mechanical power in pre-industrial Japan. In fact, before the end of the Tokugawa period (1603–1867), the water wheel was the only widely used source of power other than human power. Animal and wind power were rarely utilized in Japan, unlike in the West.[1]

---

[1]   The use of animal power in Japanese industry was limited to sugar manufacturing. Cows were used from the late eighteenth century in the Ryūkyū Islands and Kagoshima Prefecture to turn the *sakusha*, a rotary cylinder used to crush sugar cane. In 1883 at Amami Ōshima in Kagoshima Prefecture there were 6,574 cow-operated *sakusha* compared with only 552 water-powered machines. It was only after 1902 with an invention of Shikakichi Okuyama that hullers and threshers were operated by animals in some regions, especially Okayama Prefecture, Kyūshū, and Shikoku. Lack of utilization of animal power in Japan is partly attributable to the existence of an abundant labor force and partly to the fact that scarce land and dense population were not conducive to animal husbandry. Wind power was used for irrigation and rice cleaning only in very limited areas because Japan is frequently hit by typhoons. Meiji-Zen Nippon Kagakushi Kankōkai 1973, pp. 17, 88–90.

   In the Western countries the utilization of animal and wind power was rather common (Forbes 1956; Derry and Williams 1960, chap. 8). Richard L. Hills and A. E. Musson emphasized importance of animal power utilization in the early Industrial Revolution in England. Hills argues that animals formed an important source of power for Arkwright's frames and for the carding engines (1970, p. 89). And Musson claims as follows: Horses were much more widely used in industry than has been generally realized. Especially in the industries other than textiles horses were utilized well into the nineteenth century. Windmills, horse-mills and water-mills were more important than steam engines in the early nineteenth century (Musson 1976, pp. 419–20).

In Japan before the end of the Tokugawa period the utilization of water wheels was limited almost entirely to a few agricultural activities, such as rice cleaning and milling, and application to proper manufacturing activities was rare. Although the main focus of this study is on power utilization in manufacturing, we survey the early use of water power both in manufacturing and in agricultural activities in this chapter. There are two reasons for including such agricultural activities in our study. First, grain processing although carried out in the agricultural sector is technologically similar to manufacturing. In fact the commercial grain processers which appeared mainly in urban areas in the nineteenth century are classified as manufacturers. Second, the earlier use of water wheels in agriculture was basically responsible for the introduction of water power to manufacturing activities, and sometimes water wheels in agriculture were converted to manufacturing activities.

The first section of this chapter takes up the use of the water wheel in rice polishing and flour milling. Although this survey is focused on the traditional economy, reference will be made also to the early phase of industrialization, the years before the 1910s. The second section surveys the history of water wheels in proper manufacturing activities. The third section examines the technology of the water wheel. The fourth section discusses some implications to be drawn from this analysis. These implications concerns how the early use of water power affected development of manufacturing and the level of technology of machinery production before industrialization. In other words, this study helps to describe the initial conditions of industrialization in Japan.

Water Wheels for Processing Grain

Water Wheels before the Meiji Period
Rice cleaning. Before the Meiji period the main use of water wheels in Japan, outside of irrigation, was for processing grain, primarily for

cleaining or polishing rice and to a lesser extent for milling wheat.[2] Japanese farmers' widespread use of water for irrigation purposes, however, had several significant effects on the diffusion of water power to these activities.

The use of water wheels for rice processing in Japan dates back to the seventh century. One of the earliest Japanese historical records, says that in 610 the priest Don Cho from Korea constructed a quern operated by a water wheel. A second reference to the water-powered quern is found in a legal code promulgated in 718.[3] Among the laws laid down in this document is the stipulation that the water-powered quern could be used only when it did not disturb public and private irrigation. The use of water wheels for rice processing, however, did not become widespread and virtually disappeared after the early eighth century. This fact can be explained by the dietary preferences of the times. Unpolished rice was generally preferred, and the demand for rice cleaning was small.[4]

The water-powered quern reappeared early in the Tokugawa period. Historical records show that one such quern was operated at Yamada near the Aikawa Mine on Sado Island during the Genroku era (1688–1703) and another one was erected at Takasaki Shuku in Kōzuke around the beginning of the eighteenth century.[5] There are two hypotheses to explain the revival of the water-powered quern. The first claims that use of the water wheel for irrigation eventually led to the reapplication of water power for rice cleaning. This hypothesis has been developed from references to the fact that in 1726 Ichiroemon erected a water-powered quern at Sano in Shimotsuke. Ichiroemon used a water wheel employed to draw irrigation water from the Yodo River, as a model for this quern. The second hypothesis is that the water-powered quern was reintroduced from abroad. It is argued that the technology either came directly from China and Korea or was developed in Japan

[2]   We have relied on Meiji-Zen Nippon Kagakushi Kankōkai 1973, pp. 1–28, 84–97, 269; Saigusa 1973, pp. 106–10, 194–202; and Yoshida 1974, pp. 1–40 for the history of water wheels in Japan.

[3]   These documents stand for *Nippon Shoki* and *Yōryō Ritsuryō* respectively.

[4]   Nōgyō Hattatsushi Chōsakai 1954, p. 93.

[5]   Tamura 1943a, p. 731.

relying on Chinese agricultural textbooks in the seventeenth century.[6]

During the Tokugawa period the water-powered quern gradually came to replace the foot-powered quern which had become popular in the early seventeenth century. But at the time of its reintroduction the demand for water power in rice processing was still quite small. Outside of the court and the aristocracy, people ate unpolished or at most semipolished rice, and semipolishing could be accomplished easily with human power. However, the increasing popularity of polished rice among the common people after the eighteenth century stimulated the spread of the water-powered quern.[7]

Flour milling. Milling grain was the only other use of the water wheel in Japan before the Meiji period. But, unlike in the West, water wheels were only rarely used for milling wheat and other grains.[8] This was true in spite of the fact that milling requires much greater energy than rice cleaning. In order to separate and remove the hard skin of wheat, the grain must be ground into a fine powder. The difference in diet and the greater difficulty of wheat processing account for the wider utilization of water power for milling in the West.[9] However, even in Japan, water power was used for this purpose in some areas where double-cropping was common. For instance, in the Tokugawa period vermicelli manufacturers in Hyōgo Prefecture drew water from the Kako River to power water wheels used for grinding wheat.

The fact that Japanese agriculture depended heavily on water had two opposing impacts on the diffusion of water wheels for grain processing. On the negative side, the water concession of farmers restricted water power utilization for non-irrigation purposes. The clause from the legal code in 718 cited earlier suggests that the conflict between purely agricultural and "manufacturing" uses of water existed as far back as the eighth century.

This conflict can be seen much more in recent times. For example, in

---

[6]   These are *Tenkō Kaibutsu* (1637) and *Nōsei Zensho* (1639).

[7]   Nōgyō Hattatsushi Chōsakai 1954, pp. 93–96.

[8]   As for the history of water power utilization in milling in the West, there are a number of literature; for instance, Derry and Williams 1960, pp. 250–53; Forbes 1956.

[9]   Miwa 1975, p. 226.

1744 permission was given to install a water wheel at a mill in the Minami Kōchi District of Osaka Prefecture only on the condition that the mill be closed during the growing season, from spring to autumn. Struggles between millers and farmers in this district became more serious with the construction of another four water wheels between 1751 and 1763. In 1764 the millers finally had to agree to remove the water wheels within the subsequent five years. During the Tokugawa period millers were restricted from operating water wheels during the rainy season from spring to summer throughout Japan. And in winter, when they were allowed to operate, sufficient water was not available. This conflict with agricultural interests for access to water disturbed the development of water-powered grain processing as a business independent of agriculture.

On the positive side, the importance of water in Japanese agriculture, quite apart from the restrictions it imposed, also created a situation favorable to the diffusion of water power for non-irrigation purposes. The highly developed irrigation system, which extended to most of the arable land, made it possible to install water wheels throughout the country. In other words, grain processors were not limited to locations near principal rivers or streams. This positive impact has been largely neglected in appraising the early development of Japanese manufacturing.[10]

Water Wheels in the Meiji Period

Rice cleaning. During the Meiji period (1868–1911) the importance of water wheels for grain processing gradually diminished as new sources of power became available.[11] It is possible to trace this trend in some

[10] We are indebted to Professor Hiroshi Shinpo of Kobe University for making this point.

[11] In spite of the diminishing importance of water wheels in rice cleaning, an interesting innovation appeared in this field. It was rice cleaning in a boat on the Tenryū River, which commenced in 1893–94 and became most developed during the late 1910s. Six to twelve (usually eight) querns were run by water wheels installed on both sides of a boat. Tamura 1943a, pp. 735–36. This technique calls to mind the "floating mill" which was widely seen in Europe. Derry and Milliams 1960, p. 252.

Table 2-1. Number of Water Wheels for Rice-Cleaning and Their Capacity Compared with Rice Production: 1882–1910

Year	Number of Water Powered Mills	Total Capacity for Rice Cleaning a	b	Rice Production	Ratio (2)/(4)	(3)/(4)
	(1)	(2)	(3)	(4)	(5)	(6)
		(1,000 *koku*)		(1,000 *koku*)	(%)	
1882	62,879	8,803	13,205			
1883	56,507	7,911	11,866	27,481	28.7	43.2
1884	55,692	7,797	11,695	23,583	33.1	49.6
1885	59,264	8,297	12,445	25,673	32.3	48.5
1886	47,048	6,587	9,880	35,797	18.4	27.6
1887	48,649	6,811	10,216			
1889	52,924	7,409	11,114	30,121	24.6	36.9
1890	47,776	6,689	10,033	41,082	16.3	24.4
1891	52,130	7,298	10,947	39,656	18.4	27.6
1896	52,710	7,379	11,069	38,261	19.3	28.9
1900	38,983	5,458	8,186	41,441	13.2	19.8
1902	42,823	5,995	8,993	37,278	16.1	24.1
1904	43,047	6,027	9,040	49,773	12.1	18.2
1906	44,100	6,174	9,261	46,231	13.4	20.0
1908	43,705	6,119	9,178	51,322	11.9	17.9
1910	43,876	6,143	9,213	46,316	13.3	19.9

Sources: See Text.

a Estimation under the assumption that the rice-cleaning capacity of a water wheel is 140 *koku*.

b Estimation under the assumption that the rice-cleaning capacity of a water wheel is 210 *koku*.

detail because statistics on water wheels are available for the Meiji period.

Nationwide statistics on water wheels used for rice cleaning for the years 1822 to 1910 are available from the survey by the Rikugunshō

(Ministry of War).[12] This survey was conducted to determine the national capability to provide goods and resources in time of emergency. It records the number of water-powered rice-cleaning mills in operation, which can also be taken as an estimate of the number of water wheels employed for this activity. Table 2-1, which is taken from this survey, shows that a great number of water wheels were in operation and their number was rather constant from 1882 to 1910 (column 1). (The decline between 1896 and 1900 is attributable to a change in the coverage of the survey.[13])

The significance of water power in rice cleaning during the Meiji period can be judged further by comparing the capacity of water-powered mills with total rice production. Columns 2 and 3 of Table 2-1 present estimates of rice-cleaning capacity under the assumptions that a water wheel can process 140 or 210 *koku* of rice per year.[14] Total rice production is shown in column 4, and the ratio of capacity to production is indicated in column 5 or 6 depending on the capacity assumption. Two important observations can be made from these statistics. The first is the overall low level of dependence on water power in rice cleaning early in the Meiji period. As shown in columns 5 and 6, only 30–50% of total rice production in 1883–85 was cleaned by water power. In other words, since other sources of mechanical power were negligible, these figures indicate that 50–70% of the rice produced in Japan at that time was polished by human power.[15] This surprisingly low level of mechani-

[12] This survey is the *Chōhatsu Bukken Ichiran Hyō*. pp. 735–36. The earlier version of this survey by the Rikugunshō, the *Kyōbu Sei Hyō*, also contains statistics on the number of water powered rice cleaning mills. There were 9,200 in 1878; 9,516 in 1879; and 10,010 in 1880. The average number of water wheels in these three years, 9,575, was only about one seventh of the number recorded in the *Chōhatsu Bukken Ichiran Hyō* for 1882 (Table 2-1, column 1). One of the reasons for this underenumeration in the former survey is that this survey covers only towns and cities with 100 or more inhabitants.

[13] Since 1900 the survey has been limited to water-powered mills which can clean more than one *koku* of rice per day and which are used continuously throughout the year.

[14] These assumptions are taken from Yoshiyuki Sueo's study (1980, p. 94).

[15] Sueo's estimates for rice cleaning capacity of Nara Prefecture, depending on the number of water wheels in the *Suisha Shirabe* (Survey on water wheels) in 1881, shows that only one-ninth to one-sixth of rice produced in Nara Prefecture was cleaned with the water wheeels (1980, p. 94).

zation in rice cleaning can be explained by two factors: the small power requirements of the rice-polishing process and the restrictions imposed by the farmer's water concession system. In addition, low wages may also have discouraged the mechanization of rice polishing.

The second observation to be made from these statistics is the decreasing dependence on water wheels for rice cleaning over the Meiji period. The percentage of total rice production cleaned in water-powered mills fell to 13–20% by 1910. This trend is attributable to the substitution of other sources of power—steam engines, internal combustion engines, and electric motors—for the water wheel in rice cleaning.[16] This substitution was closely associated with the development of rice cleaning as a commercial activity in urban areas.

Flour milling. It is more difficult to examine the utilization of the water wheel for milling because there are no nationwide statistical data for this examination. Nevertheless, some indication of the importance of water-powered milling in the early Meiji period can be gained from the survey on water wheels in Nara Prefecture in 1881.[17] According to this survey, out of 556 water wheels operating in Nara prefecture in 1881 only 38 (6.8%) were employed for milling wheat compared with the 296 (53.2%) employed for cleaning rice. Although relative use of water wheels for milling and rice cleaning certainly differed among prefectures, it would be safe to conclude that throughout Japan milling wheels were far outnumbered by rice-cleaning wheels during the Meiji period, just as they had been during the Tokugawa period.

Not only flour milling was a relatively insignificant activity, but also the dependence on water power in milling decreased over the Meiji period with the establishment of large-scale mills employing steam engines. As shown in Table 2-2, the percentage of total flour consumption processed by water wheels fell rapidly from its 97% share in

---

[16] Although there are no nationwide data on the number of water wheels after 1910, it is believed that it decreased rapidly since the 1920s depending on the substitution by internal combustion engines and electric motors. Kuroda, Tamaoki and Maeda 1980, p. 150.

[17] Sueo 1980, p. 89.

Table 2-2. Wheat Flour Consumption by Source: 1878–1912

(%)

| Year | Imports | Processed by: | |
		Water Wheels	Other Engines
1878	1	97	2
1884	1	97	2
1896	7	89	4
1897	6	89	5
1898	6	88	6
1899	7	87	6
1900	16	78	5
1901	12	79	9
1902	16	76	8
1903	35	56	9
1904	33	57	10
1905	32	56	12
1906	29	59	12
1907	20	47	33
1908	10	41	49
1909	5	37	58
1910	5	41	54
1911	5	43	52
1912	4	36	60

Sources: Meiji Kōgyōshi Hensan Iinkai 1930, pp. 199–200, 222–23.

1878 to 36% in 1912, while wheat flour processed by other engines reached to 60% in 1912.

During the Meiji period grain processing came to rely less and less on the water wheel as a source of power. This trend was seen both in rice polishing and in wheat milling. The declining trend of water wheel usage is believed to have continued in the post Meiji years and can be inferred from the spread of other power sources to this traditional, rural-based manufacturing activities. For example, the total number of rice-

33

cleaning machines powered by internal combustion and electric engines almost tripled from 25,153 in 1927 to 72,597 in 1939.[18] In addition, milling machines powered by 1-2.5 hp engines became popular during the 1920s.[19] Consequently, their numbers increased to 3,265 in 1927 and four times as many in 1939.[20]

Water Wheels for Industrial Use

Historical Observations before the Late Tokugawa Period

The use of water power for "proper" manufacturing dates back to the eighteenth century. However, until the late Tokugawa period, water wheels were, with few exceptions, found only in lower levels of manufacturing processes. Nevertheless, a wide range of industries had realized the advantages of mechanization by water power at that time.

Sake brewing was an early typical industry which benefited from the introduction of water wheels.[21] Sake brewing consists of two processes, rice cleaning and brewing itself. Although brewing, which required technical skill and long experience, could not be mechanized, labor-saving mechanical devices could be applied to rice cleaning, which was a very simple process. Brewers in Nadagogō were the first to successfully employ water wheels for rice cleaning at the beginning of the eighteenth century. Nadame, a section of Nadagogō, situated on the so-called fall-line starting at the Rokkō Dislocation, was a particularly favorable location for water power utilization. The number of water wheels employed by sake brewers increased from 4 in 1718 to 66 in 1810.

Introducing water power brought considerable positive benefits to sake brewers. It reduced labor cost, increased output and improved the output quality remarkably. Tarozaemon Yamamura utilized water wheels to produce a special brand of sake from rice cleaned continuously

[18] Nōgyo Hattatsushi Chōsakai 1955, table 15 of chap. 3 of part 3.
[19] Hashimoto 1937, pp. 41–46.
[20] See n. 18.
[21] Kawamura 1952, pp. 23–36.

for 72 hours. Incessant cleaning for such a long time with constant speed and power had been impossible with only human labor. As a result of this innovation and the quality improvement, the sake of Nada earned a high reputation and overwhelmed all other brands sold in Edo (Tokyo).

There are numerous other examples of the advantages of water power to manufacturing. In the eighteenth century oil manufactureres in Settsu, Kōchi, and Izumi introduced water wheels to grind toasted rape and cotton seeds.[22] Record of oil manufactures in 1836 documents that grinding efficiency doubled with this innovation.[23] Once the seeds were ground, they were then pressed by wedge press and lever press to release their oil.[24] Although the grinding process was successfully mechanized with the water wheel, no attempts were made to apply mechanical or animal power to the latter pressing process.

In sugar cane processing technical progress occurred first with the introduction of animal power, but eventually these processors also employed water power.[25] Substitution of cows for men to operate the rotary machine increased the amount of sugar cane processed per day from 135–136 *kan* to 250–1,000 *kan*.[26] Then, in 1717 Sabuni Tabata in Amami Ōshima introduced a water wheel, as a result the output of raw sugar which had been 1 *chō* per day with animal power, doubled to 2 *chō*.[27]

Ceramic manufacturers and ore processors also realized the advantages of water power for crushing materials.[28] It is known, for example, that a water wheel was installed on a boat on the Nishiki River at Iwakuni to crush potter's clay since the early nineteenth century. And at Arita and Seto, the two centers of porcelin production in the Tokugawa period, water wheels were used to crush subsoil at least since the late

[22] Meiji-Zen Nippon Kagakushi Kankōkai 1973, pp. 9–10.

[23] This record stands for *Seiyu Roku* written by Nagatsune Okura.

[24] These presses are *sa* and *nakagi* respectively.

[25] Meiji Kōgyōshi Hensan Iinkai 1925, pp. 777–78; and Meiji-Zen Nippon Kagakushi Kankōkai 1973, pp. 84–92.

[26] This machine stands for *sakusha*.

[27] A *chō* is a measure of a barrel of sugar, the size of which is unknown.

[28] Yoshida, 1974, pp. 15–21.

eighteenth century. During the Bunka era (1804–17), a gold mine in Sado employed a water wheel with nine pounders to crush ore into much finer powder than was possible by human power using iron hammers.

The industrial application of water wheels during the early Tokugawa period occurred almost solely at the primary level of manufacturing. As the above examples shows, utilization of water power was most common in activities which involved processing or crushing materials (rice, wheat, rape seeds, sugar cane, soil, and ore). Water wheels were used only rarely at higher levels of production processes. One example of the more advanced application of water wheels occurred in yarn production. Water power had been used in twisting silk yarn at Ashikaga from about 1800. And in 1859 Shigeichiro Numaga at Fujitsuka Village in the Usui District connected several sets of *zakuri* (sedentary reeling machine) together like machine filatures and powered them with a water wheel. This unique structure was washed away by a flood in 1861.[29] There were no imitators of this technique.

In spite of its advantages water power was not widely applied to industrial activities until the end of the Tokugawa period. The water concession system, discussed earlier as a restriction on the application of water wheels to grain processing, undoubtedly was a factor limiting the use of water power in manufacturing activities as well. But it does not seem to have been the decisive factor, because it does not explain the expansion of water power utilization to industrial uses which began at the end of the Tokugawa period. It is our hypothesis that the low level of demand for mechanical power played a significant role in limiting the diffusion of water power. That is to say, until the end of Tokugawa, manufacturing industries had not been developed enough to make mechanical power a necessity.

[29] Meiji-Zen Nippon Kagakushi Kankōkai 1973, pp. 12–13.

Historical Observations in the Late Tokugawa and the Early Meiji Periods

Over the later part of the Tokugawa and early Meiji periods water power was increasingly applied to a number of more sophisticated manufacturing processes. The spread of water power to these industrial activities occurred both with the introduction of Western technology and with the wider use of the traditional Japanese water wheel.

Modern water power technology imported from the West in the late Tokugawa period offered advantages to a number of industries.[30] The Saga Clan installed a water wheel in 1852 and used it to bore a cannon in the next year. By this innovation they reduced labor inputs and increased the accuracy of the cannon. In 1853 the Satsuma Clan made the same innovation. Water power was also used to operate bellows at the Kamaishi Iron Mine in 1857, and in the middle 1850s the Tokugawa Shogunate established several gun powder plants powered by water wheels. A notable example of water power utilization was the water-powered factory at Tagami Village in the Satsuma daimyo's territory.[31] Here imported weaving machines were run by water power for about ten years starting in 1857.

Water wheels became a substantial source of power for manufacturing in the early Meiji period. The government policy to encourage water power utilization in place of steam power was somewhat responsible for the spread of water wheels. A government report on the International Exhibition in Vienna in 1873 was a declaration of that policy. The report emphasized the advantages of water power over steam power in Japan, a country with abundant water resources. Under the so-called *Shokusan Kōgyō Seisaku* (Policies to promote industrialization) the government encouraged the use of the Western water wheel and water-powered turbine.[32] These engines were widely adopted in modern industries like

[30] Meiji-Zen Nippon Kagakushi Kankōkai 1973, pp. 8–9, 13–14, and Saigusa 1973, pp. 106–108.

[31] This factory was called *Suisha Kan*.

[32] This energy policy of the Meiji government was intended to save on domestic coal consumption and to promote coal exports. Okamoto 1975, pp. 55–64; Yoshida 1974, pp. 28–29.

37

spinning, weaving, paper manufacturing, metal mining, and so forth.

However, substantial growth in water power utilization also occurred with the application of the traditional Japanese water wheel in traditional industries.[33] The textile industry is the foremost example of this phenomenon. The traditional water wheel was the primary source of power in the silk-reeling industry, which developed in Nagano Prefecture during the early Meiji period (1877–86). This technique gradually spread to silk-reeling establishments in other regions (chapter 8). Water power was also used in connection with traditional technology in cotton spinning. For example *gara* spinners, a development of the older hand spinners, were run by water wheels from the second decade of the Meiji period (chapter 9).

The significance of the application of water power to the traditional textile industry can be understood by comparing power capacity in this industry with that of other manufacturing industries in the early Meiji period. Table 2-3 shows the mean power capacity of water wheels and water turbines in various manufacturing industries for 1884–90. (These machines were largely of the Japanese type and turbines were not yet widely used.) The textile industry as a whole used almost 90% of total manufacturing water power capacity. Furthermore, silk reeling alone employed over 70% of the water power capacity of the manufacturing sector and was thus the principal industrial user of water power in Japan during 1880s. Spinning also employed a quite large share of total water power compared to other industries. This share was far below that of silk reeling, however, because spinning was accomplished to a large extent in modern factories which were powered by steam engines. Among industries other than textiles, metals and metal products, chemicals, and wood and wood products were the most important users of water power, though their share of total water power capacity was quite small in comparison to textiles.

Not only total water power capacity was heavily concentrated in the textile industry, but also water was a more important source of power to

[33] Yoshida 1974, p. 23 and Gendai Nippon Sangyō Hattatsushi Kenkyūkai 1967b, p. 114.

Table 2-3. Power Capacity of Water Wheels and Water Turbines: 1884–1890

Industry	Horsepower[a] of Water Wheels and Turbines	Share of Total
		(%)
All manufacturing	2,447[b]	100.0
Textiles	2,144	87.6
Silk reeling	1,809	73.9
Spinning	320	13.1
Others	15	0.6
Metals and metal products	131	5.4
Machinery	2	0.1
Ceramics	21	0.9
Chemicals	73	3.0
Wood and wood products	54[c]	2.2
Printing and binding	0[c]	0.0
Food	22	0.8
Miscellaneous	0[c]	0.0

Sources: Our estimates. See Appendix for estimating procedure.

Notes: Figures are for the private establishments with 10 or more production workers.

[a] Mean power capacity in seven years, 1884–90.

[b] Total of the nine industry groups.

[c] Mean power capacity in five years, 1886–90.

textile production than to other manufacturing activities. Table 2-4 provides a comparison between the share of water power out of total power capacity (water and steam) in textiles and in all manufacturing. In 1884 water power comprised over 75% of total power capacity in textiles compared with a little over 60% in manufacturing as a whole. In other words, during the early Meiji period, textile production was much more dependent on water power than other industries; other industries were heavily relied on steam power.

Table 2-4 also documents the declining importance of water power

Table 2-4. Power Capacity of Water Wheels and Water Turbines and Share of Water Power in Total Power Capacity in All Manufacturing and Textiles: 1884–1890

	All Manufacturing			Textiles		
	Power Capacity of		Share of	Power Capacity of		Share of
	All Engines[a]	Water Wheels and Turbines	Water Power	All Engines[a]	Water Wheels and Turbines	Water Power
			(%)			(%)
1884	2,064	1,274	61.7	1,437	1,088	75.7
1885	2,026	1,020	50.3	1,408	906	64.3
1886	4,796	2,519	52.5	3,624	2,421	66.8
1887	8,915	2,793	31.3	6,407	2,642	41.2
1888	13,414	3,176	23.7	9,515	2,910	30.6
1889	25,072	2,515	10.0	17,738	2,025	11.4
1890	29,948	3,425	11.4	21,795	3,015	13.8

Sources: Same as Table 2-3.
[a] Water wheels and turbines, and steam engines and turbines.

and the rise of steam power during the early years of the Meiji period. By
1887, water power's share of total power capacity had fallen below 50%
both in all manufacturing combined and in textiles alone. Thus, the
place of water power in all manufacturing fell dramatically as the textile
industry, the predominant industrial user of water power capacity,
switched over to steam power. In other words, because the textile
industry had been the largest manufacturing activity to rely heavily on
water power, the transition from water to steam power in Japan was
confined largely to the textile industry.[34]

[34] In small establishments, which are not covered in Table 2-4, tools and machines
were operated by both human and water power. Human and water power were replaced by
electric motor in the 1920s (chaps. 4, 6 and 14). There was no age of steam power.
Therefore, inclusion of these establishments does not alter our conclusion in the text that
the transition from water to steam power was virtually limited to a few industries like
textiles and lumbering.

Western Experience

In contrast to the Japanese experience water power was widely used in European manufacturing since the tenth century and well into the age of steam power. A number of water-mills were erected for various kinds of production; tanning, fulling, cutley grinding, sawing, forging and others even before the Industrial Revolution.[35] Also in the early phase of the revolution water was a main source of power. This fact has been emphasized by many authors in recent years. For instance A. E. Musson says:

"It is also evident that although steam power had become predominant in textile mills, water power was by no means insignificant in the mid-nineteenth century, still providing about a fifth of total power in 1850."[36]

In the first half of the nineteenth century "in the whole wide range of other industries (coal-mining, cotton and iron) it (steam power) was still of comparatively minor importance."[37]

And he concluded:

"It seems clear that really massive growth of steam power occurred in the later nineteenth century, not in the heroic age of the early Industrial Revolution."[38]

A similar argument is made by Phillis Deane: she states

"outside the textile factories and the mines, iron-works and railways, steampower was still a rarity in the mid-nineteenth century."[39]

American manufacturing in the early years relied more heavily on water power than in English manufacturing. The census of 1870 revealed that the ratio of water power to the total power capacity in manufacturing was 48%, a bit smaller than that of steam power (52%).[40] Water power utilization was most evident in New England. Especially the Merrimack River was the most noted water power river, which supplied

[35] Derry and Williams 1960, pp. 250–53; Forbes 1956; Lilley 1965, pp. 46–48.
[36] Musson 1976, p. 424
[37] Musson 1976, p. 434.
[38] Musson 1976, p. 436.
[39] Deane 1979, pp. 132–33.
[40] Hunter 1975, p. 170.

about 900 mills and factories with an aggregate of nearly 80,000 horsepower in 1880.[41] (This figure is comparable to the total power capacity of all engines in the Japanese manufacturing at the beginning of this century.)

The Technology of Water Wheels

Traditional Technology

The development of water wheel technology in Japan—both the design of the wheel itself and the transmission mechanism—lagged far behind that in Europe.

The design of water wheels, overshot and undershot, remained almost unchanged from the earliest water-powered querns.[42] Until the late Tokugawa period, all water wheels in Japan were wooden, and they were made by wheel carpenters.[43] Relying on instructions passed on from their masters and on their own experience, and considering the size and speed of the stream, these craftsmen determined the diameter of the wheel and the number of paddles so that the wheel would rotate ten to fifteen times a minute. This traditional method of construction continued unaltered throughout the Tokugawa period.[44] In contrast, in Europe in the middle of the eighteenth century several experiments revealed the greater efficiency of the overshot against the undershot type water wheel. For instance, John Smeaton of England contributed a paper to the Royal Society in 1759 showing the superiority of the

[41]   Hunter 1975, p. 181.

[42]   There are no historical records which refer to the horizontal water wheel (Greek or Norse mill) having been used in Japan. This fact seems to be attributable to a technical condition. The horizontal wheel with vertical shaft was easily used for operating wheat mills because the shaft of the mill was also vertical. But rice cleaning, which was more important than milling in Japan, depended on the up-and-down movement of pounders, and this motion was not easily achieved with a horizontal wheel. With the vertical wheel, on the other hand, rotation of the horizontal wheel shaft was converted to up-and-down movement simply by placing lugs on the shaft.

[43]   They were *kuruma daiku* in Japanese.

[44]   Maruyama 1956, p. 6.

overshot water wheel.[45] Such scientific investigations into the efficiency of the water wheel were never conducted in Japan, and this was perhaps one reason why technological development of water wheels remained stagnant.

The application of the water wheel to manufacturing depends not only on the design of the wheel itself, but also on the mechanism by which power is transmitted to accomplish the final task. In this respect, too, Japan lagged behind Europe. Rice cleaning, ore crushing, and other typical uses of the water wheel in Japan depended on the up-and-down movement of pounders. Power was transmitted to the pounders by lugs attached to the rotating wheel shaft. In addition, a gear system which converted the rotation of the shaft to vertical movement was employed to run the rotary quern used for milling wheat and rape seeds and to run the rotary machine used for crusing sugar cane. Both of these mechanisms, which were widely used in Japan, are rather simple to construct.

A more complicated transmission mechanism was necessary to employ the water wheel for general, industrial activities. For example, a combination of two gears of different sizes or two pulleys of different sizes connected by belts is necessary in order to change the speed of rotation and transmit power from the wheel shaft to a parallel shaft which runs machinery. In Europe cutlery grinding machines and lathes employing these kinds of mechanisms were operated by water wheels from the thirteenth or fourteenth century.[46] But this type of apparatus was rarely seen in Japan before the Meiji period. Japanese craftsmen had developed a primitive machine tools, lathe and potter's wheel which had two pulleys of different sizes connected by belts.[47] However, these tools were operated by human power until about 1887 before an attempt was made to connect the machine to a water wheel.[48]

A crank and cum transmission system converts the rotating motion of

---

[45]   Hills 1970, p. 98.
[46]   Information on transmission technology in Europe comes from Lilley 1965, p. 46.
[47]   These tools were called *rokuro*.
[48]   Meiji-Zen Nippon Kagakushi Kankōkai 1973, p. 269.

the water wheel to reciprocating motion. In Europe bellows and sawing machines equipped with such a system were developed in the eleventh and thirteenth centuries respectively. In the United States water powered sawing mills were rather more popular than water powered flour mills in the 17–19 centuries.[49] In Japan, however, water power was rarely employed for sawing, and the traditional iron manufacturing technique, usually depended only on human power.[50] In Izumo, one of the representative places for this production, it was not until the third decade of the Meiji period (1887–96) that water-powered bellows were first employed. Water-powered bellows, which were built betwen 1851 and 1961, were utilized, however, in a few places such as Nejime in Kagoshima Prefecture.

Influences of Western Technology

Western technology relating to the water wheel was not introduced in Japan until the end of the Tokugawa period. The wooden water wheel with wooden gears installed in the Satsuma Clan's factory in 1857 is believed to have been brought from the Netherlands.[51] In addition, modern water wheels were imported from the West in the Meiji period. For instance, an iron water wheel from England was installed at the Kashima Spinning Mill in 1872.[52] The modern technology also motivated an improvement in the traditional water wheel, which still comprised the majority of the water wheels in use during the Meiji period.[53] Masataka Tazawa and Keijiro Kishi of Dengyō Company produced small-capacity iron water wheels from 1910 until about 1917. These machines were about twice as efficient as the wooden wheels which were still being produced in the rural areas by traditional

[49] Water powered sawing mills amounted to 31,650, compared with 22,661 of water powered flour mills in 1840. Hunter 1979, table 2 on p. 38.
[50] This technique stands for *tatara*. For a discussion of water power utilization with the *tatara*, see Kuroiwa and Tamaoki 1978, pp. 102–109; Okumura 1973, p. 138; Saigusa 1973, p. 212.
[51] Meiji-Zen Nippon Kagakushi Kankōkai 1973, p. 14.
[52] Gendai Nippon Sangyō Hattatsushi Kenkyūkai 1967b, p. 117.
[53] Meiji-Zen Nippon Kagakushi Kankōkai 1973, p. 15.

techniques.[54]

The Diffusion of Water Wheels as a Basis for Industrial Development

This examination of water wheels and the unique characteristics of the diffusion of water power in the pre-industrial economy of Japan has at least three implications relating to the preconditions for modern economic growth. First, the introduction of mechanical power to manufacturing activities has as a prerequisite a certain level of development of these activities themselves. The limited application of water wheels to industrial uses in Japan during the Tokugawa period indicates that manufacturing had not yet generated a significant demand for mechanical power. Had the need for power existed, water wheels, which had been available long before steam engines, would have been more widely exploited. In fact, it was the growth of the textile industry in the early Meiji period which led to the heavy reliance of this industry on the water wheel, the only accessible source of mechanical power.

Second, Japan's experience indicates the role of the availability of technology in determining the process of the transition to modern industrial production. The classic transition from traditional water wheels to modern steam engines was virtually limited to a small number of industries like textiles and lumbering. Western-type water wheels had been used by some modern industrial factories during the early Meiji period on the advice of the government. But utilization of the water wheel in such modern plants was not widespread because the steam engine, which was already available at that time, was much more powerful. Even in the textile industry, the first successful introduction of modern cotton-spinning technology at the Osaka Spinning Mill depended on steam power. Because modern technology became available simultaneously with the steam engine most industries never relied on

[54] Tamura 1943b, pp. 286–88.

water power. More generally, it can be concluded that as a late-comer to industrialization, Japan had the advantage of introducing highly advanced technology at a very early stage of development, and thus, her modern industries virtually bypassed traditional technology and traditional sources of mechanical power (chapter 15).

The final implication of this analysis relates to the role of the level of development of machine technology as a condition for modern industrialization. On the one hand, the large number of wheel carpenters dispersed in the rural areas of Japan and the development of clock making before Meiji were to some extent responsible for the successful application of modern machinery technology.[55] It may be important to examine the availability of such skilled crafts in order to appraise the initial conditions of Japanese industrialization compared with present developing countries (chapter 15).

On the other hand, by and large the technology of machine production in Japan on the verge of modern industrialization was at a low level. Clock making had suffered during the closing of Japan in the Tokugawa period, because the long prohibition on ocean navigation limited the need for accurate time keeping.[56] In addition, the scarcity of livestock and the poor condition of the roads meant that vehicles, especially animal-powered ones, were rarely used.[57] These two factors were unfavorable to the development of a machinery industry.[58]

[55] For instance, Hisashige Tanaka, the most prominent clockmaker in the Tokugawa period, became an electric engineer. In 1875 he established the Tanaka Factory, the first electric machinery producer in Japan and the forerunner of the present-day Tōshiba Electric Company.

[56] Imazu 1964, p. 45.

[57] Two factors were responsible to the poor conditions of the roads in Japan. First, because of the frequent rainfall the land was often muddy. Second, a number of rivers flow from the mountain ranges at the center of the mainland to either the Pacific Ocean or the Japan Sea. Therefore the roads through the island frequently encounter rivers which had to be forded or crossed by boat. Yoshida 1974, pp. 93–94.

[58] In Europe, in contrast, the production of water wheels, clocks, and vehicles led to the development of a machinery industry prior to industrialization. The machinery industry became the basis for the modern engineering which characterized industrialization in the West. According to Samuel Lilley, "modern engineering is the child of a

Besides clocks and vehicles, the water wheel was the major mechanical apparatus developed in the traditional economy. But the facts that a large percentage of rice was polished by human power and also water power was rarely applied to milling of manufacturing indicate that both the capacity and the number of water wheels in Japan were far below their levels in the West. Furthermore, before the late Tokugawa period the technology of the water wheel had been stagnant, and the means had not been developed to adapt water power to the advanced transmission needs of manufacturing. Thus, one may state that the use of the water wheel had not contributed significantly to the domestic development of adequate machine technology, as it had prior to the Industrial Revolution in the West.

In general, then, the level of technology of machine production inherited from the pre-industrial economy in Japan was quite underdeveloped. The deficiency in machine technology may partly account for the slow progress of the machine industry in Japan during the early stage of industrialization up to World War I.[59]

marriage between the clock-maker's skill in fine workmanship and the techniques of heavy engineering that were used by the millwrights and builders of other power-driven machinery." Lilley 1965, p. 56.

[59]   Arisawa 1960b, pp. 11–22.

INVENTION, IMPORT, AND

PRODUCTION OF

MODERN ENGINES

As a background for the examination of the diffusion of power to Japanese industry, this chapter briefly describes the power sources—steam and internal combustion engines, water and steam turbines, and electric motors—on which the growth of Japanese industry depended in the late nineteenth and early twentieth centuries. The first section of the chapter, which discusses the invention of these engines in the West and their industrial applications, will acquaint the reader with the characteristics of each type of power source. The second section then reviews the ways in which the modern engines became available to Japanese manufacturing—their importation from the West, the beginning of domestic production, and eventual import substitution. This survey describes one means by which Western technology was introduced to Japanese manufacturing and reveals the extent to which Japan lagged behind the West in the usage of modern power sources.

Invention in the West

Steam Engines
The introduction of the steam engine was critical to the development

of modern manufacturing.[1] Although traditional power sources, especially water power, played an important role in the early phase of the Industrial Revolution of England (chapter 2), by the 1770s the rapidly expanding cotton-spinning industry was pushing against the limitations of traditional power sources. The number of horses which could be used at one time was limited and the water wheel, although much more powerful than the horse, was limited both in capacity and by local conditions. It was the invention of the steam engine which enabled the cotton-spinning industry in England to overcome the power shortage and meet increasing demand for output. Indeed, the steam engine found its first manufacturing application in English cotton-spinning plants where it was employed to circular water over the water wheel, thereby increasing production capacity. In 1712 Thomas Newcomen designed a steam engine to pump water from the lower mill pond back to the upper pond so that it could run over the water wheel again and again. Early Watt engines, which became much more efficient than Newcomen engines with the invention of a separate condenser in 1769, were used in a similar manner.

The spread of steam power to other industrial uses required further refinements in the steam engine. James Watt's invention of the sun and planet gear (1782) and of the parallel motion (1784) solved the problem of converting the oscillation of the beam into rotary motion. The rotating steam engine created an entirely new field of application for steam power. These engines were immediately adopted in a wide range of manufacturing plants. Steam power became even more suited to manufacturing uses with the invention of the compact high-pressure engine by an Englishman Richard Trevithick in 1802 and an American Oliver Evans in 1804.

Steam power facilitated the development of cotton textile industry and other industries in the later phase of the Industrial Revolution. But by the mid-nineteenth century it had become evident to the early in-

---

[1] The survey in this section is based on Hills 1970, chaps. 8 and 9; Derry and Williams 1960, chaps. 11, 21, and 22; Lilley 1965, chaps. 6–8; Singer *et al.* 1958, chaps. 5 and 6 of vol, 4, chaps. 6, 8–10 of vol. 5; Usher 1954, chaps. 13 and 15.

dustrialists that the steam engine also had its limitations. The boilers and condensers needed to generate the steam prevented the production of lightweight, small-sized engines, and the great bulk of steam engines made them unable to attain high speed.

Water and Steam Turbines

Turbine engines satisfied the growing need during the nineteenth century for higher speed than the steam engine could generate. The invention of the water turbine, by Benôit Fourneyron in 1832, came in response to the demand for a more powerful water wheel in the south part of France, a region abundant in streams but lacking in coal to feed steam engines. Before the age of electric power the water turbine was used primarily in factories to run machinery, but since the end of the nineteenth century it has been most widely used, because of its high speed, to generate electricity. The steam turbine was developed from the water turbine by Charles A. Parsons in 1884. Steam turbines were gradually substituted for steam engines to generate electricity and run ships and eventually steam turbines with much greater capacity and much higher engine speed were developed to meet the power requirements of these principal users.

Internal Combustion Engines

The internal combustion engine filled the need for a light weight, small-sized power source, and dates from the four-cycle engine developed by the German inventor Nikolaus A. Otto in 1878. This engine was widely adopted to manufacturing uses, especially in smaller-scale plants. However, because of its greater mobility than either the steam engine or the turbine, the internal combustion engine came to play its greatest role in transport. The appearance of automobiles and aircraft depended on gasoline-powered internal combustion engines.

Electric Motors

The electric motor had a significance in the history of industrialization and power utilization unparalleled by the turbine or the internal combustion engine and equaled only by the invention of the Watt's steam engine. The electric motor had two distinct advantages over all other earlier mechanical power sources. First, a motor of any capacity, large or small, was easy to produce and small capacity motors were nearly as efficient as large ones. Second, the electric motor was simple to operate by just turning a switch and required little maintenance (chapter 7). Because of these advantages, the electric motor was used in industry to a much greater extent than any other engine. Furthermore, electrification of industrial plants had far-reaching impacts on manufacturing technology (chapter 14).

The first motor of commercial importance was demonstrated in Vienna in 1873 by Zénobe Théophile Gramme, a Belgian engineer. Gramme's innovation was to combine two direct-current dynamos, either one of which operated as a generator to provide electricity to the other as a motor. Finally, with the invention in 1888 of the polyphase alternating-current electric motor by Nikola Tesla, a Croatian-born engineer, electrification took root in industrial operations. The Tesla motor, a prototype for the modern one, had several characteristics which made it more applicable to industrial uses than the direct-current motor. Because of its simple structure without a commutator it did not need special care, and because it could be sealed it could withstand humidity and dust.

In addition to the advantages of the motor itself, availability of cheap electric power was another factor which stimulated the wide diffusion of the electric motor. By the end of the nineteenth century large power plants equipped with large capacity water and steam turbines could supply power cheaply through long distance distribution lines. These economies of scale in electric power generation were not realized until the introduction of the alternating-current motor because long distance transmission had been technically impossible with the direct-current system. As a result of these developments, during the twentieth century electric motors came to dominate over all other types of engines in providing power to manufacturing.

Import and Production in Japan

Steam Engines

The first visit of Commodore Perry and the steam powered "black ships" to Uraga in June 1853 was one of the most dramatic events in Japanese history.[2] It awakened Japan from her long isolation of more than two centuries and motivated the Meiji Restoration of 1868, the transition from the Tokugawa feudal system to modern centralized government. The arrival of Commodore Perry was also significant to the development of modern industry because it marked the initial face-to-face encounter of the Japanese with the steamship and, more important, the steam engine.

The steam engine was the first modern engine to be employed in Japan, and in the early Meiji era both import and domestic production of the steam engine developed for steamships. The first steamer operating in Japan was the Kankō Maru, a warship which was donated by the Netherlands to the Tokugawa Shogunate in 1855. In the same year, the first Japanese-made steam engine was installed on a ship, the Unkō Maru.

The import of stationary steam engines for industrial use began in 1861 when the Nagasaki Ironworks, owned by the Tokugawa Shogunate, imported production equipment from the Netherlands. This equipment included three steam engines; a 6-hp engine was installed in the foundry, an 8-hp engine was used for running a steam hammer, and a 15-hp engine was employed to operate lathes and other machine tools. During the next two decades imported steam engines were set up in a number of manufacturing plants. The steam engines installed in the two pioneering cotton-spinning mills operated by the Satsuma Clan—the Kagoshima Mill (1867) and the Sakai Mill (1870)—were imported from

---

[2]   These ships were called *kuro fune* in Japanese.

For this survey of the steam engines and steam and water turbines we relied on Arisawa 1960b, part 1; Gendai Nippon Sangyō Hattatsushi Kenkyūkai 1967b, pp. 114–26; Watto Tanjō 200-Nen Kinenkai 1938, chap. 4 and chronological table.

Manchester, England. In 1871 Tomioka Filature, a model plant established by the Meiji government, was equipped with machine filatures operated by a 17.5-hp steam engine. Both the engine and the filatures were imported from France. Other representative plants which introduced steam power in the early Meiji period are listed below along with the year the engine was installed: Takashima Coal Mine (1869); Osaka Paper Mill (1874); Yūkō Company, a paper manufacturer (1874); Tokyo Paper Manufacturing Company (or Ōji Paper Manufacturing Company, 1875); and Taiwan Sugar Manufacturing Company (1900). These engines were all imported from England.

Experimental production of the steam engine was inaugurated in the later Tokugawa period. The Satsuma Clan translated a Dutch book on steamer technology in 1849, and commenced to produce the first Japanese engine in 1851.[3] This engine was completed in 1855 and, as was mentioned earlier, was installed on a paddle steamer, the Unkō Maru. After the arrival of the black ships the Japanese turned more seriously to producing their own steam-powered ships. The Saga Clan completed a 10-hp paddle steamer, the Ryōfū Maru, in 1865. The Ishikawajima Shipyard, established by the Mito Clan, produced a 158-ton warship in 1866. This ship, the Chiyoda Gata, was powered by a 60-hp steam engine made by the Nagasaki Iron Works. The fact that production of steam engines in Japan began as a means to provide steam engines to steamers, especially to warships, signifies that the interest in steam power exhibited by both the Tokugawa and Meiji governments arose from their serious concern with strengthening national defense.

Production of stationary steam engines followed the production of engines for steamers sometime during the first decade of the Meiji period (1877–87). By the 1890s Japanese shipyards had succeeded in producing large capacity engines for industrial use. In 1892 for instance, the Kawasaki Shipyard produced a 300-hp engine for the Yodobashi Water Purification Plant operated by the city of Tokyo and in 1896 the Ishikawajima Shipyard provided six 330-hp engines for the Asakusa

---

[3]   This book refers to *Suijōsen setsuryaku* (Short explanation of steamships).

Power Plant of Tokyo Electric Light Company.[4]

Water and Steam Turbines

Water turbines installed in Japan during the early Meiji period were mostly imported from the West. A 75-hp German-made engine fixed in the Umezu Paper Plant in 1876 was one of the earliest such imports. Domestic production of water turbines started in the 1870s mainly in shipyards. In 1879, for instance, the Yokosuka Shipyard provided an engine to the Aichi Spinning Mill. In 1892 the Ishikawajima Shipyard produced two Pelton wheels which were installed in the Keage Power Plant of Kyoto City to generate electricity.

Both import and domestic production of the steam turbine started at the beginning of the twentieth century. In 1904–05 the Fukagawa Power Plant of Tokyo Street Railways, the Senju Power Plant of Tokyo Electric Light Company, the Miike Coal Mine of Mitsui Mining Company, the Osaka Armory all installed imported steam turbines to generate electricity. In 1908 two turbo-steamers made in England, the Hirafu Maru and the Tamura Maru, began ferry service on the Aomori-Hakodate Line of the Japanese National Railways, and the Tenyō Maru, a ship equipped with an English-made turbine, was completed by the Mitsubishi Nagasaki Shipyard. In 1904 the Mitsubishi Shipyard began commercial production of the Parsons turbine for steamers and industrial use.

Internal Combustion Engines

Internal combustion engines first appeared in Japan in the 1880s. In 1884 the Tokyo Artisan School (later Tokyo University of Engineering)

---

[4] In this connection it may be appropriate to refer briefly to the history of the steam locomotive in Japan. The steam locomotive was first operated in 1872 on the Shinbashi–Yokohama line of the Japanese National Railways (JNR). Locomotives, rolling stock, and other equipment were all imported from England. The Kobe Factory of JNR produced the first locomotive in Japan with the assistance of an English engineer in 1893. In 1896 the Locomotive Manufacturing Company was established and in 1907 the Kawasaki Shipyard began to produce locomotives and rolling stock. These two companies produced locomotives copied from English and German models respectively. Since 1912 all JNR orders for locomotives have gone to domestic producers. Watto Tanjō 200-Nen Kinenkai 1938, pp. 172–74.

imported an oil engine from England.[5] A copy of this engine was exhibited at the Fourth Industrial Exhibition in 1895. The gas engine was first imported in 1882–83 by the Kōbu University for experiments. In 1896 the Tokyo University of Engineering introduced a 5-hp gas engine. Students at the school managed to duplicate this engine and eventually sold several of their copies to newspaper companies.

Commercial production of these kinds of internal combustion engines started at the turn of the century. In contrast to the production of steam engines and turbines, small- and medium-scale manufacturers, such as Ikegai Iron Works (1890) and Niigata Iron Works (1895), were important manufacturers of internal combustion engines. The engines produced by such firms were sold to a variety users including small factories and small fishing boats, and they were also employed in irrigation and rice cleaning.

Import Substitution: Steam Engines, Turbines, and Internal Combustion Engines

Demand for steam engines, turbines, and internal combustion engines grew steadily during and after the Meiji period. As shown in Table 3-1, this demand was met by increasing both imports and domestic output of modern engines. Annual data on the value of imports and domestic output, from which the averages shown in Table 3-1 are calculated, indicate the timing of import substitution. Import substitution was achieved in 1927 in the case of water turbines, and in 1928 in the case of steam engines and turbines. The value of domestic output of internal combustion engines had exceeded that of imports in 1923, the year when the output statistics are first available. Thus, import substitution of this engine was achieved sometime before 1923. Earlier import substitution in the case of internal combustion engines may be partly due to the fact that the production of these engines technologically much easier than that of turbines and steam engines.

---

[5] Our discussion of the internal combustion engine relies on Meiji Kōgyōshi Hensan Iinkai 1930, pp. 54–57.

Table 3-1. Average Annual Value of Import and Domestic
Output of Engines: 1884–1940

(1,000 yen)

Year	Steam Engines and Turbines		Water Turbines		Internal Combustion Engines	
	Import	Output	Import	Output	Import	Output
1884 – 89	236					
1890ᵃ–1900	505				87	
1901 – 10	1,346				344	
1911ᵇ– 20	767		569		1,087	
1921ᶜ– 30	1,429	1,440	1,426	1,639	7,244	18,064
1931 – 40	436	12,013	180	4,391	12,250	711,478

Sources: Imports: Figures for 1884–1933 are taken from Tōyō Keizai Shinpōsha 1935,
pp. 319–20. Figures for 1934–40 are taken from Nippon, Ōkurashō 1934, vol. 3, pp.
224–25; 1935, vol. 3, pp. 250–51; 1936, vol. 3, pp. 220–21; 1937, vol. 3, pp. 234–35;
1938, vol. 3, pp. 236–39; 1939, vol. 1, p. 920; 1940, vol. 1, pp. 828–29.
Domestic output: 1923–25: STF 1926, pp. 512–13. 1926–35: STF 1935, pp. 837–38.
1936–40: STF 1940, vol. 1, pp. 325–27. See Table A-2.
ᵃ   1896 for internal combustion engines:
ᵇ   1912 for water turbines.
ᶜ   1923 for production.

Electric Motors

The use of electric motors for industrial production depends first of all
on the availability of electric power.[6] In Japan electricity was first
supplied to a limited number of firms and later it became available on a
wider scale to the general public. Electric power was initially used only
for lighting, but a short time later electricity was applied to drive motors
for manufacturing and transportation.

The utilization of electricity in Japan began with the establishment of

⁶   This survey of the history of the electric utilities and the electric machinery industry is
a summary of the full discussion in chap. 7.

Tokyo Electric Light Company (TELC) in 1883. The company installed a dynamo to light arc lamps at the Yokosuka Shipyard in 1883 and built an independent electric power plant for lighting incandescent electric lamps at the Sangenya Plant of Osaka Spinning Company in 1886. Supply of electricity to the public started in 1887 when the Nihonbashi Station of TELC began providing electric lighting to the offices in its vicinity. In all of these cases, thermal power generators produced direct-current electricity. Alternating-current was first provided by Osaka Electric Light Company in 1889 and TELC changed from direct to alternating-current in 1895. The first recorded use of electric power for manufacturing production was at the Tokyo Asahi Newspaper Company in 1888 (chapter 13). The first application of electric power to transportation was made by the Kyoto Electric Railways in 1895.[7]

Hydro-electric power generation was inaugurated in 1890 at Shimotsuke Hemp Spinning Company and at Ashio Copper Mine. In both of these firms the electricity was generated solely for internal use. Hydro-electric power was initially provided to public users by the Keage Power Plant of Kyoto City in 1892. The Keage Plant generated power not only for lighting but also to operate electric railways, spinning equipment, machinery plants, and various other types of industrial equipment. Improvement in transmission technology, especially during the 1910s and 1920s, made it possible to transmit hydroelectric power generated from remote places to urban areas. With this development hydro-generation became dominant over thermal-generation and re-alized a plentiful, low-cost supply of electric power to Japanese industry in the 1920s.

The production of electric motors and equipment developed more slowly than the electric utilities. The electric machinery manufacturing industry dates back to 1884 and the establishment of the Miyoshi Electric Factory which provided dynamos and motors to TELC. This factory and another early electric machinery producer, Meiden Sha (established in 1897), were small in scale. In the 1890s big enterprises like

---

[7] Yoshida 1977, pp. 251–52.

the Ishikawajima Shipyard and Shibaura Factory (or Tokyo Shibaura Electric Company) entered into the electric machinery business. The electric motors produced in Japan, even in these large-scale factories, were merely copies of imports. Production technology for electric machinery made progress by means of an accumulation of experience and, in the large firms, with technical cooperation from foreign enterprises. Eventually, import substitution was achieved by this industry, first in the production of small capacity machinery and spreading to larger-scale machinery.

The development of electric utilities and electric machinery industry supported the rapid electrification of manufacturing in Japan. The total power capacity of electric motors (including secondary motors) in Japan exceeded that of the water wheel by 1908 and that of the steam engine by 1917 (chapter 6).

Timing of Diffusion of Modern Technology

The survey in this chapter has emphasized the considerable time lag between the development of modern power technologies in the West and their application in Japan. For instance, the stationary steam engine was first imported to Japan in 1861, and domestic production began between 1877 and 1886. These events occurred respectively 79 years and 95 to 104 years after Watt's invention of the steam engine in 1782. However, a closer look at the timing of the utilization of modern power technologies in the West and in Japan reveals two more significant points. First, the lag tended to be shorter for the newer engines, like turbines and electric motors, because all the various technologies developed in the West over years of the Tokugawa period were introduced almost simultaneously in Japan with the opening of the country. This argument is developed more fully in chapter 15. Second, the lag between importation and imitation in Japan was surprisingly short. For instance, this lag was only 16 to 25 years in the case of stationary steam engine. This phenomenon reveals the great enthusiasm shown by the Meiji Japanese to modernize their long isolated nation.

It should be noted, however, that these initial attempts at domestic production were sometimes experimental, and substantial engineering production started much later. Import substitution of engineering products in general was not realized until WWI, when import of these products from the Western countries involved in the warfare was inhibited. Furthermore it was only after WWII that machinery industries like automobile manufacturers succeeded in import substitution and export expansion. Substantial development of engineering industry came into existence by means of a full-scale expansion of domestic demand and accumulation of capital and technology.

PART II

THE POWER REVOLUTION

In part II we follow the history of power utilization during Japan's industrialization. The first three chapters of this part rely on long-term statistics on all manufacturing factories and power capacity to trace various developments in the use of power after 1885. These three chapters together describe the power revolution in Japan—the shift from human to mechanical power, the great increase in total power capacity, and the rapid shift from water to steam and subsequently from steam to electric power.

The feature of the power revolution in Japan unlike that in the West was the relatively early and extensive use of electric motors as a source of power. The final chapter in this part is devoted to examining the reasons for this special feature of power utilization in Japan.

Chapter 4

THE MECHANIZATION OF
NONPOWERED FACTORIES

In order to begin the analysis of the dimensions of the power revolution in Japan, we examine the mechanization of nonpowered factories regardless of engine type or capacity. In the first section of this chapter we survey changes in the number of factories as a whole and in the number of powered factories. In the following sections we examine the process of mechanization more closely by studying the changes in the proportion of powered factories by industry group and by factory scale.

We denote the proportion of powered factories out of the total number of factories by α. This proportion is a measure of the degree of mechanization, one of the major components of technological progress. Therefore, through the analysis of mechanization we may come up to some conclusions on the effect of the power revolution on manufacturing technology.

Factory Statistics

Factory Statistics for All Manufacturing

Statistical comparison on the number of factories and powered factories is one means to examine trends in the mechanization of nonpowered factories. The total number of factories and powered factories for all manufacturing industries combined is depicted in Fig. 4-1 for the periods 1896–1940 and 1898–1940 respectively. These figures

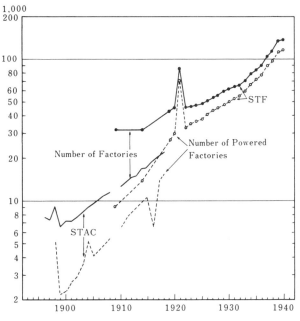

Fig. 4-1. Number of Factories

Sources: Minami 1976b, pp. 222–25.
Notes: STAC figures are for the private factories with ten or more production workers, while STF figures are for the private factories with five or more workers. Figures in 1921 include private powered factories with four workers or less.

are derived from two sets of official statistics: *Nōshōmu Tōkei Hyō* (Statistical tables for agriculture and commerce), henceforth referred to as STAC, and *Kōjō Tōkei Hyō* (Statistical tables for factories), henceforth called STF. STAC covers the period up to 1918 and STF the period from 1909 to 1940. Two problems encountered in using these sources are as follows. First, there is a large discrepancy between the STAC and STF figures for the overlapping period 1909-18. This is due to differences in the coverage of the two sources. Second, a big jump in STF for 1921 comes from a change in the coverage of data and the abnormal changes in STAC for 1898, 1904, and 1916 should be viewed as a data problem.

In spite of these problems, Fig. 4-1 reveals a definite overall increasing trend of mechanization. The total number of factories increased remarkably as Japan industrialized between the end of the nineteenth century and 1940. But the growth rate in the number of powered factories exceeded that in the total number of factories up to 1930. The faster growth of powered factories indicates the increasing degree of mechanization (increasing α) in manufacturing as a whole.

Factory Statistics by Industry Group

Additional insight into trends in mechanization can be gained by further comparison between the total number of factories and powered factories. First, we break down the manufacturing factory statistics into industry groups. Table 4-1 presents this breakdown calculated from the STAC figures for 1900 and 1915. The table shows the industrial composition of factories and powered factories as a percentage of the manufacturing total.

This table reveals several noteworthy characteristics of the early period of industrialization. First is the predominance of textiles as a frontrunner in mechanization as well as industrialization. In 1900 over half of all manufacturing factories and almost two-thirds of powered factories were producing textiles. Moreover, the fact that the textile industry had a greater share of powered factories than of total factories (65.4% versus 59.2% in 1900 and 55.4% versus 50.4% in 1915) indicates that α was much higher in textiles than in other industry groups. The second feature is the relative decline in the place of the textile industry between 1900 and 1915. The textile industry's share of both total factories and powered factories fell over these fifteen years with the growth of other manufacturing industries and their introduction of mechanical power.

Table 4-2 presents the breakdown of manufacturing factory statistics by industry group calculated from the STF figures for 1909, 1919, and 1940. Panel A of the table shows the number of factories and powered factories by industry group and panel B shows the percentage com-

65

Table 4-1. Composition of Factories by Industry Group

(percent)

Industry Group	All Factories		Powered Factories	
	1900	1915	1900	1915
All manufacturing	100.0	100.0	100.0	100.0
Textiles	59.2	50.4	65.4	55.4
Metals and metal products	4.5	3.4	4.4	4.3
Machinery	4.8	5.4	8.2	7.2
Ceramics	5.1	4.9	1.6	2.7
Chemicals	6.0	5.8	5.5	5.9
Wood and wood products	1.5	3.9	1.4	4.5
Printing and binding	2.6	4.0	3.5	5.2
Food	11.6	14.3	8.3	10.4
Miscellaneous	4.6	7.9	1.7	4.3

Sources: Same as Fig. 4-1.
Notes: Figures are for the private factories with ten or more production workers.

position of manufacturing factories and powered factories by industry group. These STF figures depict the textile industry in the same way as the STAC figures. Textiles' position as a leader in industrialization and mechanization continued to erode from 1909 to 1940. In 1940, among all nine industry groups, textiles still had the largest share of total factories, 25.2%, even though this share was 45.9% in 1909. Similarly, the percentage of all powered factories in textiles fell from 51.9% in 1909 to 25.4% in 1940.

On the other hand, Table 4-2 shows the emergence of the metals, machinery, and wood groups during this later period. The trend in the machinery group is especially conspicuous. The percentage of all manufacturing factories producing machinery more than tripled from only 4.8% in 1909 to 18.2% in 1940. The machinery industry's share of powered factories grew from 8.4% to 20.8% over the same period. The emergence of these three industry groups was due to the remarkable

66

Table 4-2.   Number and Composition of Factories by Industry
Group

Industry Group	All Factories			Powered Factories		
	1909	1919	1940	1909	1919	1940
A. Number of Factories						
All manufacturing	32,124	43,723	137,142	9,059	26,729	115,285
Textiles	14,753	17,954	34,595	4,692	11,364	29,290
Metals and metal products	1,035	2,542	11,470	435	2,049	10,869
Machinery	1,535	3,490	24,997	763	2,753	23,943
Ceramics	1,902	2,728	6,638	156	868	5,258
Chemicals	1,403	2,537	8,664	401	1,674	6,585
Wood and wood products	1,531	2,610	13,836	671	1,912	12,673
Printing and binding	962	1,240	3,596	408	1,010	3,489
Food	6,202	6,801	22,578	1,302	3,613	16,133
Miscellaneous	2,801	3,821	10,768	231	1,486	7,045
B. Composition by Industry Group (%)						
All manufacturing	100.0	100.0	100.0	100.0	100.0	100.0
Textiles	45.9	41.1	25.2	51.9	42.4	25.4
Metals and metal products	3.2	5.8	8.4	4.8	7.7	9.4
Machinery	4.8	8.0	18.2	8.4	10.3	20.8
Ceramics	5.9	6.2	4.8	1.7	3.2	4.6
Chemicals	4.4	5.8	6.3	4.4	6.3	5.7
Wood and wood products	4.8	6.0	10.1	7.4	7.2	11.0
Printing and binding	3.0	2.8	2.6	4.5	3.8	3.0
Food	19.3	15.6	16.5	14.4	13.5	14.0
Miscellaneous	8.7	8.7	7.9	2.5	5.6	6.1

Sources: Same as Fig. 4-1.
Notes: Figures are for the private factories with five or more production workers.

increase both in the total number of factories and in the number of powered factories. The contrast between the relative decrease in the number of factories and powered factories in textiles and food and the relative increase in machinery and metals indicates the development of industrialization in favor of heavy industry during the twentieth century (chapter 1).

Factory Statistics by Factory Scale

The breakdown of manufacturing factory statistics by factory scale also uncovers some important characteristics of the process of mechanization. Table 4-3 summarizes the number and percentage composition of total factories and powered factories by scale for 1909, 1919, and 1940.

The table reveals that the percentage of small-scale factories did not decrease during this period of industrialization. Special attention should be paid to this rather surprising fact. Small-scale factories, those with 5 to 29 employees, comprised 85.7% of all factories in 1909 and a slightly larger percentage, 87.2%, in 1940. This is explained by the large increase in the number of small-scale enterprises between 1909 and 1940. Thus, although the rapid growth of manufacturing was brought about mainly by the expansion of large enterprises, the contribution of the steady growth of small enterprises to industrialization should not be overlooked.[1]

Table 4-3 also shows that, although manufacturing was dominated by small-scale factories, smaller enterprises initially lagged behind larger-scale factories in mechanization. Factories with 5–29 employees comprised only 62.4% of powered factories in 1909 compared with their 85.7% share of all factories. It appears that α was lower in small establishments than in other scale categories. But, by 1940 85.3% of powered factories were small enterprises employing 5–29 workers. This development implies a faster rise in α among small establishments than in larger manufacturing establishments. Thus, in order to identify clearly

[1]   See Chap. 5 for a discussion of the change in the composition of output by factory scale.

Table 4.3. Number and Composition of Factories by Factory
Scale

Scale (persons)	All Factories			Powered Factories		
	1909	1919	1940	1909	1919	1940
A. Number of Factories						
All factories	32,124	43,723	137,142	9,059	26,729	115,285
5– 9	16,780	20,034	76,433	2,413	9,213	60,029
10– 29	10,760	15,556	43,233	3,242	10,107	38,225
30– 49	2,016	3,447	8,210	1,285	2,954	7,867
50– 99	1,452	2,455	4,767	1,133	2,278	4,681
100–499	976	1,869	3,599	850	1,816	3,583
400–999	82	202	506	78	202	506
1,000 or more	58	160	394	58	159	394
B. Composition by Scale (%)						
All factories	100.0	100.0	100.0	100.0	100.0	100.0
5– 9	52.2	45.7	55.7	26.6	34.4	52.1
10– 29	33.5	35.6	31.5	35.8	37.8	33.2
30– 49	6.3	7.9	6.0	14.2	11.1	6.8
50– 99	4.5	5.6	3.5	12.5	8.5	4.1
100–499	3.0	4.3	2.6	9.4	6.8	3.1
500–999	0.3	0.5	0.4	0.9	0.8	0.4
1,000 or more	0.2	0.4	0.3	0.6	0.6	0.3

Sources: Minami 1965, pp. 228–31.
Notes: Figures are for the private factories with five or more production workers

the important trends in mechanization our study must go on to a direct
examination of changes in α, which is undertaken in the following two
sections.

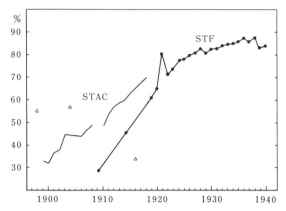

Fig. 4-2.   Proportion of Powered Factories (α)

Sources: Same as Fig. 4-1.
Notes: For an explanation of △ for the text and for the definition of STAC and STF, see the notes to Fig. 4-1.

Mechanization by Industry Group

Mechanization in Manufacturing as a Whole

In order to analyse mechanization of manufacturing we first consider changes in the proportion of powered factories in manufacturing as a whole. The proportion of powered factories, α, is depicted in Fig. 4-2. This proportion was calculated from the STAC and STF data presented in Fig. 4-1. The abnormal years in the STAC data (1898, 1904, and 1916) are marked by a △. By excluding these years two observations can be made about mechanization in manufacturing during the years covered by STAC. The first observation concerns the low level of mechanization at the beginning of the period. In the years just preceding and following the turn of the century, α was only 32–34%. In other words, about two-thirds of manufacturing establishments were not equipped with mechanical power. The second observation concerns the trend in mechanization during the early years of the twentieth century. By 1918 α reached 70%; the proportion of powered factories in manufacturing rose

70

by a 40 percentage points over the first two decades of this century.

The proportion of powered factories calculated from the STF data shows a steadily increasing trend from 1909 to 1940. (The jump in α between 1920 and 1921 reflects only the fact that coverage of STF statistics for 1921 differed from other years.) The pace of mechanization was quite rapid during the ten years following 1909. After this overall advances in the proportion of powered factories the trend tended to occur more slowly. For the years when the STF and STAC statistics overlap (1909–18) the STF figures show a higher rate of increase in α. This difference is attributable to the fact that smaller-scale enterprises (5–9 persons), which are not included in the STAC figures, were mechanized more quickly than large-scale factories. Together, these two surveys make clear that mechanization of manufacturing proceeded rapidly during the twentieth century, although the rate of change tended to dampen as time passed.[2]

Mechanization by Industry Group

The manufacturing factory statistics indicate large differences among industry groups in the share of powered factories. Examination of the proportion of powered factories by industry reveals further differences in the degree and timing of mechanization among industries.

Table 4-4 presents a breakdown of α by industry group calculated from the STAC data for 1900 and 1915, and Table 4-5 presents similar values calculated from STF data for various years between 1909 and 1940. These breakdowns show the wide range among industry groups in the proportion of powered factories during the early years. In 1900, for example, according to Table 4-4 α varied from its highest value 55.4% in

[2]   Mechanization of the Japanese manufacturing proceeded much faster than that in the United States manufacturing. The proportion α in the United States was 64.0% in 1899, 68.7% in 1909 and 97.5% in 1939. Du Boff 1967, table 1 on p. 515. The increase was 28.8 percentage point for 30 years between 1909 and 1939, compared with 55.9 percentage point increase for 21 years between 1909 and 1940 in Japan (Table 4-5). The faster increase in mechanization in Japan was partly attributable to the fact that small-scale plants, almost unmechanized at the beginning of this century, occupied a larger portion of the manufacturing plants in Japan than in the United States.

Table 4-4. Proportion of Powered Factories (α) by Industry
Group

(percent)

Industry Group	1900	1915
All manufacturing	32.3	63.4
Textiles	35.7	69.7
Metals and metal products	31.5	81.2
Machinery	55.4	84.1
Ceramics	10.0	35.5
Chemicals	29.3	35.5
Wood and wood products	30.2	73.3
Printing and binding	44.3	82.0
Food	23.1	46.0
Miscellaneous	11.7	34.5

Sources: Same as Fig. 4-1.
Notes: Figures are for the private factories with ten or more production workers.

machinery to its lowest value 10.0% in ceramics. Similarly, Table 4-5 indicates that in 1909 α was highest in machinery (49.7%) and lowest in the ceramics and miscellaneous groups (8.2%).[3] Over time, α increased in all industry groups, but the increase tended to be greater for industries with smaller α in the early years. Between 1909 and 1940 the increase in α was largest in the ceramics and miscellaneous groups; these industries recorded 71.0 and 57.2 percentage point increases, respectively.[4]

The printing industry, which recorded the third largest increase in α

[3] The low α in ceramics in 1909 is mainly attributable to the low α in pottery making (5.0%) and brick making (5.3%). Factories in these two categories comprised 77.5% of all ceramics factories. STF 1909. See Table A-2. The low α in the miscellaneous group was due to the low α in paper-products (wall papers, fans, and so forth) (5.4%); straw-mats, strawwork, and chipwork (0.6%); jewerywork, hornwork, bonework and shellwork (2.2%). These three categories accounted for 27.1% of the factories in the miscellaneous group. STF 1909. See Table A-2.

[4] Among the ceramics group, between 1909 and 1940 α increased 69.3 percentage points in pottery making and 81.9 percentage points in brick making. STF 1909 and 1940. See Table A-2.

Table 4-5. Proportion of Powered Factories (α) by Industry Group

(percent)

Industry Group	1909	1914	1919	1930	1935	1940
All manufacturing	28.2	45.6	61.1	82.5	86.0	84.1
Textiles	31.8	51.9	63.3	89.6	91.6	84.7
Metals and metal products	42.0	57.7	80.6	92.2	93.0	94.8
Machinery	49.7	64.4	78.9	89.0	94.3	95.8
Ceramics	8.2	19.2	31.8	65.2	72.1	79.2
Chemicals	28.5	52.5	66.0	82.8	86.7	76.0
Wood and wood products	43.8	50.5	73.3	81.9	85.1	91.6
Printing and binding	42.4	65.3	81.5	96.3	97.0	97.0
Food	21.0	38.1	53.1	76.9	81.3	71.5
Miscellaneous	8.2	17.7	38.9	57.8	63.6	65.4

Sources: Same as Table 4-3.
Notes: Figures are for the private factories with five or more production workers.

between 1909 and 1940, is worthy of special attention. Printing was mechanized most rapidly between 1909 and 1914 as shown by the 22.9 percentage point jump in α over these five years. In 1914, with almost two-thirds of printing plants operating with mechanical power (α of 65.3%), printing became the most highly mechanized of all industry groups, and it continued its position until 1940. Thus, the printing industry must be taken as a leader in mechanization.[5]

Mechanization in the Earliest Years of Industrialization

The earliest factory data available from STAC are for the year 1896,

[5] Because the data on α in Table 4-5 may also reflect changes in industrial composition by scale, they may present a biased picture of real inter-industry differences in mechanization. To examine this possibility we calculated hypothetical figures for α under the assumption that the composition of industry groups by scale up to 1940 remained constant at the level in the manufacturing sector as a whole in 1909. The pattern of changes in the degree of mechanization according to these estimates does not differ greatly from the pattern in Table 4-5. These estimates are shown in Minami 1976b, table 2-4 on p. 39.

Table 4-6.   Number of Factories and Type of Power by Industry Group

	1881–87					
Industry Group	Number of Factories[a]	Type of Power (%)				α[b]
		Human	Water	Steam	Other	
All manufacturing	1981	44.2	47.3	3.6	4.9	55.8
Textiles	1206	28.9	65.8	2.2	3.1	71.1
Metals	159	84.9	0.6	1.9	12.6	15.1
Machinery	38	78.9	0.0	21.1	0.0	21.1
Ceramics	238	92.9	0.4	0.8	5.9	7.1
Chemicals	91	74.7	1.1	9.9	14.3	25.3
Food	184	8.2	76.1	11.4	4.3	91.8
Miscellaneous	65	87.7	1.5	3.1	7.7	12.3

	1889–94					
Industry Group	Number of Factories[c]	Type of Power (%)				α[b]
		Human	Water	Steam	Other	
All manufacturing	2971	38.2	13.9	17.6	30.3	61.8
Textiles	1531	33.7	22.9	24.5	18.9	66.3
Metals	215	44.2	14.4	11.6	29.8	55.8
Machinery	71	25.3	1.4	23.9	49.4	74.7
Ceramics	292	48.6	1.4	4.8	45.2	51.4
Chemicals	264	48.9	3.4	10.2	37.5	51.1
Food	313	31.6	2.9	17.9	47.6	68.4
Miscellaneous	285	47.7	3.2	3.5	45.6	52.3

Sources: Yamaguchi 1956, tables 17 and 20 in chap. 5.
[a]   Total for the seven years 1881–87.
[b]   Sum of water, steam, and other categories.
[c]   Total for the six years 1889–94.

at least a decade after the start of Japan's industrialization. In order to examin the degree of mechanization at the outset of the modern period we must turn to another source of data. The *Fuken Tōkei* (Prefectural statistics, henceforth referred to as PS) provide estimates of the number of manufacturing factories prior to 1895. Kazuo Yamaguchi has used these data to estimate the proportion of factories employing different types of power for production. These estimates for 1881–87 and 1889–94 are summarized in Table 4-6.[6] We have taken his estimates and assumed that the factories classified as "others and unknown" are equipped with some type of mechanical power, in order to calculate the proportion of powered factories which appears in the table as α.

For the entire manufacturing industry α stands at 55.8% in 1881–87 and at 61.8% in 1889–94. The fact that these proportions are much higher than the figures from STAC for 1900 may be due to a bias in the PS data toward large-scale enterprises. Nevertheless, the PS data reveal an overall increase in the degree of mechanization in manufacturing between the 1880s and the early 1890s.

This breakdown by industry group reveals that among the seven industry groups food has the highest α in the 1881–87 period and the second highest α in the 1889–94 period. This position is not consistent with the STAC figures in Table 4-4, which indicate that food was one of the least mechanized industry groups in 1900. A tentative explanation for the discrepancy is that the food factories surveyed in PS are biased toward rice-polishing and milling enterprises, which have a higher α than other food processors. This explanation is developed from our analysis of more detailed STAC data which show that in 1900 the α for grain processing was 89.3%, more than five times the level for other food processors.[7] STF figures for 1909 show a similar disparity between the degree of mechanization in grain processing and in other food industries with an α of 96.9% and 15.0% respectively.[8]

[6] The survey covered forty-three prefectures for 1881–87 and forty-four prefectures for 1889–94. Yamaguchi 1956, pp. 89, 109.

[7] STAC 1900. See Table A-1.

[8] STF 1909. See Table A-2.

The PS data for the early years of industrialization do present a picture of mechanization in other industry groups which is consistent with the observations made from STAC data. For example, according to Table 4-6 ceramics was the least mechanized of all seven industry groups in the 1881–87 period with an α of only 7.1. Although α in ceramics increased drastically by the 1889–94 period this industry group still had one of the smallest proportion of powered factories before the turn of the century. Thus the PS data support the earlier observation that ceramics was an industry which lagged behind in mechanization. In contrast, α for textiles in the PS data, 71.1% in the 1881–87 period and 66.3% in the 1889–94 period, is higher than the STAC figures. This strengthens our previous finding that the textile industry was a pioneer in mechanization.[9]

Factors Responsible for Industrial Differentials in Mechanization

While the overall statistics underscored the steady trend and the rapid pace of mechanization in manufacturing from the late 1880s to 1940, inter-industry comparisons revealed the uneven pattern of mechanization among industries. Three factors which affect the introduction of mechanical power appear to have contributed to differences in the timing of mechanization by industry. The first factor is the suitability of mechanical power to the production requirements of a given industry. The high degree of mechanization in rice polishing and milling, especially in the early stage of industrialization, depended basically on the fact that these production processes were quite simple. Water wheels were easily introduced and the quality of the product was not affected by their uneven speed.[10] The same argument applies to the relatively early mechanization of the wood and wood products industry. Also laborious work of sawing had the great demand for mechanical power.[11] Similarly,

[9] When we divide textiles into subgroups, the PS data show that α is high in spinning and low in weaving; α in silk reeling lies in between these two. For 1881–87, for instance, α is 92.6% in cotton spinning, 75.8% in silk reeling, 13.6% in silk weaving, and 5.6% in cotton weaving. Yamaguchi 1956, table 17 of chap. 5.

[10] Yamaguchi 1956, p. 97.

[11] See chap. 11.

the emergence of machinery as a highly mechanized industry in the second decade of the twentieth century depended on the particular characteristic of machinery production. Operation of machine tools such as lathes and milling machines required both greater amounts of energy than could be provided by human power and a steadier source of power than could be provided by the water wheel. Thus, machinery producers quickly adopted modern sources of power. Small-scale machine factories turned to internal combustion engines and the larger ones employed steam engines and electric motors.[12]

A second factor influential in the introduction of mechanical power is the degree of industrial development. In other words, industrial differences in the timing of mechanization appear to be associated with differences among industries in their level of development. For instance, the textile industry was a pioneer in mechanization because textile producers (mainly silk reelers and particularly spinners) had begun to employ modern production equipment much earlier than other industries—spinning and reeling production had expanded sufficiently, even by the 1880s, to demand mechanical power.[13] The third factor concerns the effect of factor prices on the substitution of capital for labor together with the timing of the substitution of mechanical for human power. The delayed mechanization of pottery making, and hence ceramics, can be explained largely by the argument that the low wages of the women operating pottery wheels discouraged this substitution.

---

[12]   In 1909 α was quite large in small-scale machinery factories. It was 32.8% in factories with 5–9 persons and 63.5% in those with 10–29 persons. These figures for small machinery factories are much larger than comparable figures for small-scale factories in manufacturing as a whole (14.4% and 30.1%) (Table 4-7). The relatively high α in the smaller machinery factories resulted from the wide utilization of internal combustion engines and contributed to the comparatively high degree of mechanization in the machinery industry as a whole. In 1909 α was 49.7% in this industry as a whole, compared with only 28.2% in manufacturing as a whole. For details see Minami 1976b, n. 10 on p. 45.

[13]   In 1909 α was 67.4% in silk reeling (Table 8-3) and 93.7% in spinning (Table 9-2), compared with 31.8% in textiles as a whole and 28.2% in the entire manufacturing sector (Table 4-5). The silk-reeling and spinning industries are studied in chaps. 8 and 9.

Mechanization by Factory Scale

The factory statistics examined in the first section of this chapter pointed to the continued importance of small enterprises throughout the period of industrialization as well as to the delayed mechanization of small-scale factories. In this section we examine mechanization by factory scale in somewhat greater detail.

Changes Over Time

Table 4-7 presents the breakdown of the proportion of powered factories by scale for several years between 1909 and 1940, and Fig. 4-3 depicts the same information graphically. Differences in levels and trends in α by factory scale indicate three significant characteristics of mechanization.

First, there was a marked scale differential in mechanization, particularly in the early years; α is consistently higher for the larger factory size. Scale differentials have been found to be a persistent and salient feature of Japanese industrialization. The existence of the correlation between wages and labor productivity, and factory scale are referred to as "dual structure" or "differential structure".[14]

Second, there was a drastic advance in the mechanization of small-scale factories between 1909 and 1930. During these two decades α increased 62.2 percentage points in the smallest factories (5-9 persons) and 57.1 percentage points in the next smallest scale (10-29 persons). As will be shown in chapter 14, this rapid mechanization of small-scale factories was realized mainly by electrification. Table 4-7 also shows that between 1909 and 1930 advances in α were inversely related to the size of factory. The consequent narrowing of the scale differential over these decades can be seen as a third significant characteristic of mechanization

---

[14] Ohkawa and Rosovsky 1973, pp. 198–201.

Table 4.7. Proportion of Powered Factories (α) by Factory
Scale

(percent)

Scale (persons)	1909	1914	1919	1930	1935	1940
All factories	28.2	45.6	61.1	82.5	86.0	84.1
5– 9	14.4	28.5	46.0	76.6	80.4	78.5
10– 29	30.1	48.8	65.0	87.2	90.5	88.4
30– 49	63.7	75.9	85.7	93.8	95.5	95.8
50– 99	78.0	87.7	92.8	97.3	98.0	98.2
100–499	87.1	92.8	97.2	99.1	99.7	99.6
500–999	95.1	96.8	100.0	100.0	99.7	100.0
1,000 or more	100.0	97.6	99.4	100.0	100.0	100.0

Sources: Same as Table 4-5.
Notes: Figures are for the private factories with five or more production workers.

in Japanese manufacturing.[15]

Scale Differentials in Later Years

In spite of the great advances in the mechanization of small-scale factories after 1909, some scale differential persisted even in the 1930–40 period. In 1930 the difference in α between the smallest and the largest factory scales was 23.4 percentage points, and this difference had only been reduced to 21.5 percentage points in 1940.[16] Smaller enterprises

[15] The scale differential in mechanization exists independent of industrial differences in mechanization by factory scale. We have estimated α by factory scale under the assumption that the industrial composition of the factories in each scale category was equal to the industrial composition of all manufacturing factories as a whole in 1909. The resulting figures confirms our previous conclusions that a factory scale differential existed in the mechanization of manufacturing up to 1940 and that this differential decreased drastically between 1909 and 1930. These estimates of α are given in Minami 1976b, table 2-8 on p. 47.
[16] According to a 1934 survey on manufacturing plants in Tokyo, α was only 1.6% in the smallest-scale plants (those with total capital assets of ¥99 or less) and it was 8.4% in the second smallest-scale (capital of ¥100–499). For details, see Minami 1976b, n. 2 on pp. 48–49.

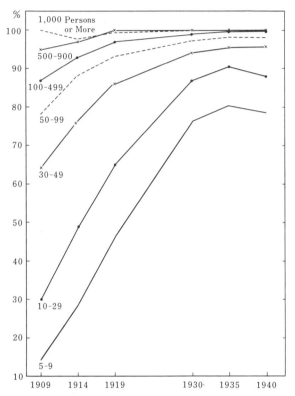

Fig. 4-3. Proportion of Powered Factories (α) by Factory Scale

Sources: Table 4-7.

remained significantly less mechanized than larger factories.

In 1940, among the factories in the smallest-scale category, the miscellaneous industry group was the least mechanized (α of 58.8%), followed by chemicals (63.6%) and food (67.4%). According to a further breakdown of the miscellaneous industry group, α was especially low in the following industries: leather shoes (20.5%), lacquerware (21.7%), nonfelt hats (30.7%), bamboo products (35.0%), and ropes and nets (46.0%). Animal fertilizer processing (14.6%) and Japanese paper making (51.7%) were the least mechanized among chemical industries, and sugar refining (3.6%) and marine products processing (48.2%) were typical non-mechanized food industries.[17]

Both the failure of these industries to mechanize and the predominantly small scale can be attributed to the fact that their production processes were mostly traditional and quite simple, and therefore they did not need much power. Bamboo products and animal fertilizer processing are typical examples. Baskets, a common bamboo product, were manually produced by weaving bamboo strips which were themselves provided by hand. Processed animal fertilizer was made from dried sardines and from the dried wastes remaining after removing oil from sardines and herring. The processes of drying, boiling, and pressing required no mechanical power.

Differences in mechanization by factory scale can be summarized rather simply. The utilization of modern production equipment, including that to generate mechanical power, has been a feature of large-scale enterprises since the earliest years of industrialization. In contrast, small-scale enterprises, in which traditional production technologies were predominant, relied heavily on human power for a long time and did not turn significantly to mechanical power until the 1910s and 1920s. Without the eventual mechanization of small enterprises, however, the productivity differential between large and small-scale factories would have been certainly much greater than it was.

[17] STF 1940. See Table A-2.

Chapter 5

THE GROWTH OF POWER CAPACITY

Having considered the introduction of mechanical power, we now examine the growth of manufacturing power capacity during the industrialization period. In this chapter the only concern is the overall change in horsepower as a measure of power capacity. In the first section we begin with a discussion of the horsepower statistics used to estimate power capacity. In the second section, the growth of power capacity in the manufacturing sector as a whole as well as by industry group and by factory scale are described. Finally, in the third section the ratio of power capacity to production-related variables such as output, capital stock, and labor force are examined. Industrial and scale differences in these ratios provide some indication of the contribution of expanding horsepower capacity to manufacturing growth.

The Measurement of Power Capacity

Horsepower Statistics

We have estimated the horsepower capacity of manufacturing engines by industry group for the period 1884 to 1940 based on STAC and STF.[1] For the benchmark years of 1909, 1914, 1919, 1930, 1935, and 1940, we also estimated power capacity by factory scale. The types of engines covered in our estimation include water wheels and turbines, steam engines and turbines, internal combustion engines, and electric motors. The sum of horsepower capacity of all these engines and motors is

---

[1] The estimation procedure is described in the Appendix.

denoted here by H, and our estimates of total horsepower capacity in different years are used to express changes in production power capacity.

This total horsepower measure is not, however, the best index of power capacity for our purposes. The problem arises because of the inclusion of electric motors. Of course, if we are to examine changes in production power capacity we must include the horsepower of electric motors because these motors serve precisely the same function as the other engines—they drive production machines.[2] But, while some (primary) electric motors are powered by purchased electricity, others (secondary electric motors) are operated by electricity generated within the firm by steam engines or water or steam turbines. The total horsepower measure H includes both secondary electric motors and the engines employed to drive them, and therefore this measure overstates the power capacity directly available for production.

In order to gauge changes in production power capacity more accurately we have estimated another horsepower series which excludes the capacity of secondary electric motors.[3] This series is denoted here by H' and is a measure of primary power capacity, power capacity for production. However, the basic data classifies electric motors into the two categories, primary and secondary motors, by factory scale only for a limited number of years. For this reason in this study we follow both horsepower series H and H' in order to examine changes in power capacity.

The Share of Primary Electric Power

Before employing the horsepower estimates to investigate the growth

[2] Fenichel 1966, p. 443.

[3] Another method for calculating primary power capacity is to measure the capacity of engines used to drive machinery directly *plus* the capacity of all electric motors. The problem with this method lies in the difficulty of classifying engines into two categories; those directly driving machinery and those driving generators. However, the statistical differences between the two methods seem to be negligible. In censuses taken in the United Kingdom in 1930 and in Denmark in 1946, for instance, the differences amounted to only a fraction of one percent (Economic Commission for Europe, Research and Planning Division 1951, p. 26). The validity of using horsepower statistics as an index of power capacity was discussed by William L. Thorp (1929, pp. 376–85).

Table 5-1. Share of Primary Electric Power in Total Electric
Power by Industry Group

(percent)

Industry Group	1900	1905	1909	1914	1919	1930	1935	1940
All manufacturing	46.1	35.0	38.8	54.5	74.2	89.6	80.1	85.7
Textiles	0.0	42.8	30.3	65.4	63.4	94.0	95.2	97.9
Metals and metal products	39.3	38.7	38.8	57.8	88.7	99.0	79.2	86.2
Machinery	0.1	12.8	17.9	34.4	65.8	98.3	82.2	99.8
Ceramics	0.0	47.1	66.2	66.5	87.6	47.4	27.6	31.9
Chemicals	0.0	31.3	46.0	52.0	75.4	89.1	77.7	76.2
Wood and wood products	—	81.0	84.6	94.3	94.2	98.4	98.8	99.3
Printing and binding	100.0	100.0	99.6	93.3	99.2	100.0	99.0	99.8
Food	—	73.3	80.4	91.2	92.0	96.8	96.4	97.0
Miscellaneous	—	88.1	88.3	92.0	94.3	99.9	99.5	99.9

Sources: See Appendix.
Notes: Figures are for the private factories with five or more workers.

of power capacity, it is worthwhile to compare primary electric power with total electric power capacity. Examining variations in the share of primary electric power over time, among industry groups, and by factory scale reveals several important dimensions of electric power utilization in manufacturing.

The ratio of primary electric power to total electric power is presented in Table 5-1 for selected years. For the manufacturing sector as a whole, the share of primary electric power increased from 35.0% in 1905 to 89.6% in 1930. This trend reflects the transition from the generation of electricity within the firm to the purchase of electricity from public utilities (chapter 7). Within the manufacturing sector, however, the ratio varied widely among industry groups. The share of primary electric power was relatively large in the wood, printing, foods, and miscellaneous groups. Indeed the printing industry consistently relied on public utilities to supply almost all of its electric power. Textiles, metals, and machinery, on the other hand, apparently satisfied a large proportion of their electric power needs by generating electricity within the firm. This situation was especially pronounced in the machinery industry during the early years.

It might be expected that as electric power from public utilities became more generally available, the need for secondary electric power would diminish and primary electric power would consequently comprise a larger and larger share of total electric power. As the table shows, however, the share of primary electric power did decrease for several years. The fall in the share for all manufacturing between 1900 and 1905 is due to a problem in the original data, STAC. However, other delines in later years in the share of primary electric power, in metals, machinery, chemicals, and ceramics as well as in manufacturing as a whole, seem to be attributable to technological progress in the generation of power within the plant.

During the 1930s firms in the metals, machinery, and chemicals industries began to utilize the waste steam, gas, and heat which were necessarily created during the production process, to generate electricity. As a result of this innovation firms in these industries decreased their reliance on electric power purchased from public utilities. For example, in the metals industry iron mills began to utilize exhausted gas from blast furnaces to generate electric power. Thus the utilization of secondary electric motors to operate production machinery thus increased.[4] A similar innovation occurred in the chemicals industry where the production of fertilizer, synthetic textiles, and so forth required great quantities of steam. After 1928 the number of large-scale firms making these products expanded. In order to save on energy costs these factories used the waste steam to power turbines and generate electricity.[5] Consequently, in this industry too, the share of secondary electric power

[4] Watto Tanjō 200-Nen Kinenkai 1938, p. 287. In the iron and steel industry the share of total electric consumption purchased from public utilities decreased from 98.8% in 1930 to 82.0% in 1940. STF 1930, 1940. See Table A-2.

[5] Watto Tanjō 200-Nen Kinenkai 1938, p. 286. From 1930 to 1940 the share of purchased electricity in total electric consumption decreased rapidly in the chemical fertilizer industry (from 92.0% to 88.9%), and in chemical textiles (from 85.3% to 49.6%). STF 1930, 1940. See Table A-2.

increased relative to primary electric power.

The ceramics industry also experienced a shift away from purchasing electric power through this sort of technological innovation. The large decline in the share of primary electric power in ceramics between 1919 and 1935 can be accounted for by developments in two industries in this group. First, the number of glass-making plants to use waste steam to generate electric power for production purposes increased.[6] Second, in 1921 cement makers began to utilize exhaust heat and gas to produce electricity within the factory. In this year, at plants in Taiwan and Kawasaki, the Asano Cement Company started generating its own electricity by using the heat given off by rotary kilns. The success of this innovation, which revealed the possibility of self-sufficiency in electricity generation, motivated the wide diffusion of the technique in the ceramics industry.[7]

Examining the share of primary electric power by factory scale, which is shown in Table 5-2, also reveals a significant characteristic of electric power utilization in manufacturing. According to the table, the smaller the factory the more primary electric power tended to outweight secondary power in importance. In small enterprises the preponderant share of electric power was supplied from public utilities rather than being generated within the plant as in very large factories. This tendency was especially marked in 1909 when, among the smallest scale factories (5-9 employees) primary electric power comprised almost 100% of total electric power capacity in these enterprises. This situation underscores the importance of the development of electric utilities in realizing the mechanization of small enterprises (chapter 14). Between 1909 and 1919 scale differences narrowed as the share of primary electric power in very

[6] Watto Tanjō 200-Nen Kinenkai 1938, p. 286. In glass manufacturing the share of purchased electricity decreased from 100.0% in 1930 to 94.9% in 1940. STF 1930, 1940. See Table A-2.

[7] Watto Tanjō 200-Nen Kinenkai 1938, p. 287. In cement making the share of purchased electricity decreased from 75.3% in 1930 to 16.4% in 1940 (STF 1930, 1940. See Table A-2). At Asano Cement the share of purchased electricity dropped from the 20–30% range in the 1921–25 period almost zero in the mid-1930s. Asano Semento K.K. 1940, pp. 671–73.

Table 5-2. Share of Primary Electric Power in Total Electric
Power by Factory Scale

(percent)

Scale (persons)	1909	1914	1919
All factories	38.8	57.5	74.2
5– 9	99.7	96.9	88.0
10– 29	84.7	97.3	95.5
30– 49	85.9	98.6	88.3
50– 99	77.1	90.7	93.4
100–499	50.5	77.1	85.8
500–999	44.6	38.8	89.4
1,000 or more	1.8	31.9	51.3

Sources: Minami 1965, pp. 232–37; 1976b, pp. 236–37.

large factories rose drastically and approached that in small-scale
factories. This development reflects the fact that as public utility rates
declined, large-scale factories shifted from internally generated to purchased electricity. Unfortunately, it is not possible to examine the share
of primary electric power by factory scale after 1919.

The Growth of Horsepower Capacity

Entire Manufacturing Sector

Total power capacity (H) and primary power capacity (H') in
manufacturing increased rapidly from the late 19th century up to 1940.[8]

[8] The growth in power capacity was much faster in Japan than in the United States.
The ratio of H' between two selected years is calculated as follows:

	Japan	United States
1939/1899	124.2	4.9
1939/1909	27.1	2.7

Figures for H' in the United States manufacturing are from U.S. Dept. of Commerce 1913,
p. 507; 1942, p. 278 (Unsmoothed figures are used).

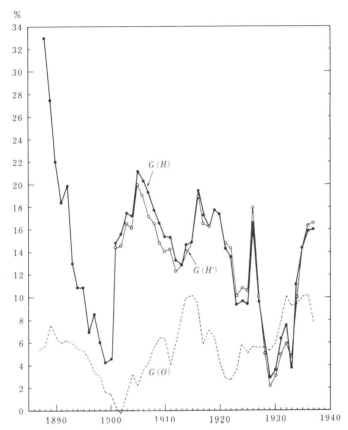

Fig. 5-1. Annual Rates of Growth of Power Capacity (H, H')
and Real Output (O)

Sources: H, H': See Appendix.

O: Calculated by subtracting output of government enterprises from Shinohara's total output estimates (1972, pp. 145–46). Output of government enterprises is estimated by adjusting Shinohara's estimates for the composition of NDP between the private and government sectors. See Table 1-3.

Notes: All figures are for the private sector only.

Output O is in 1934–36 prices.

Figures for H, H', and O are seven-year moving averages.

Between 1887 and 1937 H grew at an average annual rate of 13.8%, and H' grew at a similarly rapid annual rate of 13.5%. The rate of growth of power capacity was more than twice as high as the rate of growth in real manufacturing output, 5.6%.[9]

Examining the series on annual growth rates of total power capacity, $G(H)$, and primary power capacity, $G(H')$, clarifies the way in which manufacturing power capacity expanded as the manufacturing sector developed. These series are depicted graphically in Fig. 5-1 along with the growth rate of real manufacturing output, $G(O)$. The distinct fluctuations in the horsepower series show clearly that expansion of manufacturing power capacity proceeded at an uneven pace. In the figure, $G(H)$ and $G(H')$ show troughs in 1899, 1913, and 1929 and peaks in 1905, 1916, and 1937.

It is interesting to note the relationship between fluctuations in the rate of growth of power capacity and movements in the rate of growth in real manufacturing output, $G(O)$. In Fig. 5-1 swings in $G(O)$ appear to occur in 20-year cycles with troughs in 1902 and 1922 and peaks in 1915 and 1936.[10] Peaks in $G(H)$ and $G(H')$ correspond to those in $G(O)$, and troughs in $G(H)$ and $G(H')$ correspond to those in $G(O)$ with a few years' difference. One exception to this rule is that there is no obvious swing in $G(O)$ correspondent to the swing in $G(H)$ and $G(H')$ with a peak in 1905 and a trough in 1913. Rather, we should state that it is the small change in $G(O)$ with a peak in 1909 and a trough in 1911 which corresponds to the swing in $G(H)$ and $G(H')$ under consideration.

It is also interesting to compare $G(H)$ and $G(H')$ with the rate of growth in the capital stock. Fig. 5-2 depicts the annual growth rates of power capacity, output, and capital stock for manufacturing and mining combined, because capital stock data is not available for manufacturing alone.[11] The capital stock series, $G(K)$, has troughs in 1912 and 1929 and

[9]   See Fig. 5-1 for the sources for H, H' and real manufacturing output.
[10]   The long swings in manufacturing have been fully studied by M. Shinohara (1972, chap. 2).
[11] $G(H')$ is calculated only from 1921, because H' series for mining is available since 1917.

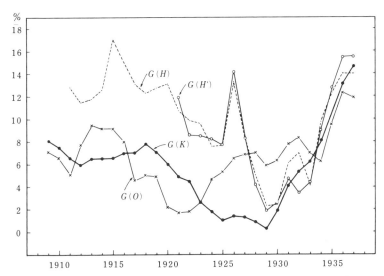

Fig. 5-2. Annual Rates of Growth of Power Capacity (H, H'),
Real Gross Value Added (O), and Real Gross Capital
Stock (K) in Manufacturing and Mining

Sources: H, H': See Appendix.
O, K: Same as Table 1-3.
Notes: All figures are for the private sector only.
Figures for O and K are in 1934–36 prices.
Figures for H, H', O and K are seven-year moving averages.

a peak in 1918. These turning points correspond more closely to those in
the $G(H)$ and $G(H')$ series than to the output series. This relationship
substantiates the notion that the expansion of production equipment
must necessarily be accompanied by growth in power capacity (chapter
1).

Power Capacity by Industry Group

The rate of growth of power capacity varied widely among industry
groups. The industry breakdown of the average annual growth rate in
total power capacity for various time periods is presented in Table 5-3.

Table 5-3. Annual Rate of Growth of Power Capacity (H, H') by Industry Group

(percent)

Industry Group	Rate of Growth in H					
	1888 –1937	1888 –1900	1901 –1910	1911 –1920	1921 –1930	1931 –1937
All manufacturing	13.8	14.3	17.6	15.9	9.4	10.7
Textiles	10.8	11.4	14.7	12.2	10.0	3.1
Metals and metal products	19.1	29.8	11.9	22.6	7.1	21.8
Machinery	17.7	22.7	23.5	21.7	8.3	7.7
Ceramics	17.4	17.6	28.2	13.7	15.6	9.6
Chemicals	15.6	15.6	21.1	16.2	8.2	17.8
Wood and wood products	18.5	20.9	37.7	15.0	9.6	4.4
Printing and binding	18.6	38.9	13.7	9.6	17.0	3.3
Food	13.0	13.3	19.2	14.6	13.0	1.0
Miscellaneous	15.5	17.8	24.5	16.6	8.6	6.4

For each industry the rate of growth of horsepower also differed greatly among sub-periods. Over the entire period 1888 to 1937 total horsepower capacity grew most rapidly in the metals group, followed by printing, wood, and machinery. Table 5-4 shows the contribution of each industry to the overall increase in manufacturing power capacity for the same period of Table 5-3. For the entire 50-year period, the relative contribution was highest in chemicals and metals. Similar observations can be made in terms of primary power capacity, which is shown in Tables 5-3 and 5-4.

One way to summarize industrial differences in manufacturing is to compare the group of heavy manufacturing industries, including metals, machinery, and chemicals, with light manufacturing, such as textiles and

Table 5-3. (continued)

(percent)

Industry Group	Rate of Growth in H'					
	1888 –1937	1888 –1900	1901 –1910	1911 –1920	1921 –1930	1931 –1937
All manufacturing	13.5	14.3	16.2	15.6	9.9	10.0
Textiles	10.7	11.4	13.9	11.3	11.1	3.3
Metals and metal products	18.8	29.7	9.6	23.5	8.5	20.2
Machinery	17.5	22.6	18.0	25.1	9.9	7.5
Ceramics	15.9	17.6	27.0	13.5	10.9	7.8
Chemicals	15.2	15.6	19.7	15.4	8.4	17.4
Wood and wood products	18.5	20.9	37.5	14.9	9.4	4.9
Printing and binding	18.6	38.9	13.4	9.7	17.1	3.3
Food	12.9	13.3	19.0	14.5	13.2	0.7
Miscellaneous	15.5	17.8	24.2	16.3	9.1	6.4

Sources: See Appendix. The horsepower series by industry group and by type of engines contain some abnormal figures. In a place of such figures we used estimates arrived at by simple interpolation.

Notes: Figures for H and H' are seven-year moving averages. Rate of growth is an average of $(H_{i,t} - H_{i,t-1})/H_{i,t-1} \times 100$ for each period.

food. The difference in the growth of power capacity among these groups seems to be fundamentally linked to the process of industrialization. The relative contribution of metals, machinery, and chemicals to the increase in both H and H' between 1887 and 1937 was 64.5%. In contrast textiles and food accounted for only 21.6% of the increase in H and 24.4% of the increase in H' during the same period. In other words, expanding power capacity in heavy industries accounted for almost three times the contribution of light industries to the overall increase in manufacturing power capacity. Furthermore, as Table 5-4 shows, the

Table 5-4. Relative Contributions to Total Increase in Power
Capacity (*H*, *H'*) by Industry Group

(percent)

Industry Group	Relative Contributions to *H*					
	1887 −1937	1887 −1900	1900 −1910	1910 −1920	1920 −1930	1930 −1937
All manufacturing	100.0	100.0	100.0	100.0	100.0	100.0
Light industry	21.6	51.5	42.7	30.4	39.0	6.8
Heavy industry	64.5	41.7	41.2	57.9	41.2	82.3
Textiles	17.6	45.8	35.8	24.7	30.1	6.5
Metals and metal products	23.3	18.1	7.6	16.9	9.7	34.5
Machinery	13.2	8.3	12.7	20.9	14.9	10.0
Ceramics	9.1	3.2	7.8	5.3	12.5	8.4
Chemicals	28.0	15.3	20.9	20.1	16.6	37.8
Wood and wood products	3.0	1.2	5.7	4.3	4.5	1.5
Printing and binding	0.6	1.4	0.8	0.4	1.2	0.2
Food	4.0	5.7	6.9	5.7	9.0	0.3
Miscellaneous	1.2	1.0	1.8	1.7	1.5	0.8

gap between light and heavy manufacturing tended to widen as time
went on. The predominant position of metals, machinery, and chemicals
in the growth of total power capacity reflects the bias of industrialization
towards heavy industry.

Changes in the industrial composition of manufacturing power
capacity further substantiate the argument that industrialization was
biased toward heavy industry. Panels A and B of Table 5-5 present the
composition of *H* and *H'* by industry group. In 1887 textiles and foods
combined accounted for 77.5% of both total manufacturing power
capacity and primary power capacity. The share of light manufacturing
far exceeded the combined share of metals, machinery, and chemicals,

Table 5-4.   (continued)

(percent)

Industry Group	Relative Contributions to H'					
	1887 –1937	1887 –1900	1900 –1910	1910 –1920	1920 –1930	1930 –1937
All manufacturing	100.0	100.0	100.0	100.0	100.0	100.0
Light industry	24.4	51.7	46.4	30.4	42.3	8.5
Heavy industry	64.5	41.4	35.9	56.9	43.3	83.5
Textiles	19.9	46.0	38.6	24.0	32.7	8.3
Metals and metal products	23.9	17.9	6.2	17.1	11.3	35.7
Machinery	13.9	8.2	8.4	20.5	16.7	10.5
Ceramics	5.5	3.2	8.2	5.5	6.7	4.7
Chemicals	26.7	15.3	21.3	19.3	15.3	37.3
Wood and wood products	3.5	1.2	6.6	4.9	4.7	2.0
Printing and binding	0.7	1.5	0.9	0.4	1.3	0.3
Food	4.5	5.7	7.8	6.4	9.6	0.2
Miscellaneous	1.4	1.0	2.0	1.9	1.7	1.0

Sources: Same as Table 5-3.

Notes: Figures for H and H' are seven-year averages centered on indicated years. Relative contribution is calculated as $(H_{i,t} - H_{i,t-n})/(H_t - H_{t-n}) \times 100$, where n denotes length of period. $H = \sum_{i=1}^{9} H_i$.

See the notes to Table 1-1 for definition of light and heavy industries

which was only 18.8% of both H and H'. But in the years after 1887 the share of light industries decreased while that of heavy industries increased and in 1937 the position of the two groups was reversed. Power capacity of light industries had fallen to 21.7% of H and 24.5% of H', while heavy industries accounted for almost two-thirds of manufacturing power capacity (64.4% of H and of H'). This swelling of power capacity in the heavy industries is consistent with changes in the industrial composition of manufacturing output during these same

Table 5-5. Composition of Power Capacity (H, H') and Output
by Industry Group

(percent)

Industry Group	1887	1900	1910	1920	1930	1937
A. Composition of H						
All manufacturing	100.0	100.0	100.0	100.0	100.0	100.0
Light industry	77.5	56.4	45.5	33.9	36.9	21.7
Heavy industry	18.8	37.5	40.4	53.9	46.4	64.4
Textiles	70.8	50.5	38.8	28.0	29.2	17.7
Metals and metal products	3.1	15.4	9.1	15.1	11.9	23.3
Machinery	2.9	7.3	11.6	18.8	16.5	13.2
Ceramics	2.1	3.0	6.8	5.6	9.7	9.1
Chemicals	12.8	14.8	19.7	20.0	18.0	27.9
Wood and wood products	0.5	1.0	4.8	4.4	4.5	3.0
Printing and binding	0.2	1.2	0.9	0.5	0.9	0.6
Food	6.7	5.9	6.7	5.9	7.7	4.0
Miscellaneous	0.9	0.9	1.6	1.7	1.6	1.2
B. Composition of H'						
All manufacturing	100.0	100.0	100.0	100.0	100.0	100.0
Light industry	77.5	56.5	48.6	34.7	39.3	24.5
Heavy industry	18.8	37.3	36.3	52.0	46.8	64.4
Textiles	70.8	50.6	41.2	28.1	30.9	20.0
Metals and metal products	3.1	15.2	8.2	15.0	12.8	23.8
Machinery	2.9	7.2	8.2	17.6	17.1	13.9
Ceramics	2.1	3.0	7.0	5.8	6.4	5.5
Chemicals	12.8	14.9	19.9	19.4	16.9	26.7
Wood and wood products	0.5	1.1	5.4	5.0	4.8	3.5
Printing and binding	0.2	1.2	0.9	0.6	1.0	0.7
Food	6.7	5.9	7.4	6.6	8.4	4.5
Miscellaneous	0.9	0.9	1.8	1.9	1.7	1.4

Table 5-5. (continued)

(percent)

Industry Group	1887	1900	1910	1920	1930	1937
C. Composition of Output						
All manufacturing	100.0	100.0	100.0	100.0	100.0	100.0
Light industry	72.4	73.0	67.4	58.6	57.1	36.8
Heavy industry	16.5	15.9	21.7	31.1	30.9	52.2
Textiles	34.3	37.2	33.0	35.8	33.3	22.9
Metals and metal products	1.3	1.9	3.5	7.8	8.7	16.1
Machinery	1.6	3.0	6.7	13.1	9.8	20.3
Ceramics	1.8	1.9	2.5	2.8	2.8	2.3
Chemicals	13.6	11.0	11.5	10.2	12.4	15.8
Wood and wood products	3.3	3.8	2.9	2.6	3.1	3.3
Printing and binding	0.4	0.6	1.1	1.4	2.8	1.9
Food	38.1	35.8	34.4	22.8	23.8	13.9
Miscellaneous	5.6	4.8	4.4	3.5	3.3	3.5

Sources: *H*, *H'*: Same as Table 5-3. Output: Shinohara 1972, pp. 140–43.

years. As panel C of Table 5-5 shows, between 1887 and 1937 light industries' share of total manufacturing output decreased from 72.4% to 36.8%, while that of heavy industries increased from 16.5% to 52.2%.

Power Capacity by Factory Scale

Table 5-6 depicts the annual rate of growth in power capacity by factory scale for various time periods. According to the table, power capacity grew somewhat more rapidly in larger-scale factories than in smaller enterprises. For the years 1909 to 1940, the average annual rate of growth in *H* ranged between 14 and 17% in the categories of factories with 5-99 workers, but it exceeded 20% in factories with 100 or more employees. These figures indicate the existence of a scale differential in the growth rate of power capacity.

In drawing such a conclusion, however, one should be careful not to

Table 5.6. Annual Rate of Growth of Power Capacity (H, H') by Factory Scale

(percent)

Scale (persons)	Rate of Growth of H					Rate of Growth of H'		
	1909 –1940	1909 –1914	1914 –1919	1919 –1930	1930 –1935	1935 –1940	1909 –1914	1914 –1919
All factories	18.5	19.7	27.5	19.5	4.4	20.6	17.6	26.2
5– 9	16.5	13.9	20.7	23.1	2.0	15.3	13.6	18.3
10– 29	13.6	13.2	23.4	11.1	5.5	17.6	13.4	22.6
30– 49	14.2	20.4	25.1	9.6	3.8	17.7	20.7	22.4
40– 99	13.5	20.9	18.5	12.3	2.2	14.9	20.9	17.8
100–499	20.1	10.8	27.3	35.4	−1.3	9.8	10.9	26.1
500–999	29.2	54.0	3.2	43.7	−4.7	32.7	42.0	7.1
1,000 or more	22.0	19.1	51.6	9.0	19.4	26.4	15.7	49.6

Sources: Minami 1965, pp. 232–45; 1976b, pp. 236–37.
Notes: Figures are the rate of growth between two indicated years.

ignore the significance of the growth of power capacity among small-scale enterprises. As Table 5-6 shows, in the period 1914-19 the rate of growth in H was above 20% per year in the three smallest-scale categories. And between 1919 and 1930 power capacity increased at a faster rate in the smallest-scale factories than in manufacturing as a whole. Moreover, as will be shown later in this chapter, power capacity in small-scale enterprises expanded more rapidly than did the labor force. From these observations one must conclude that small-scale factories were also affected by the power revolution.

In spite of the fact that small-scale factories experienced a significant growth in power capacity, the expansion of manufacturing power capacity was concentrated in large-scale factories. Table 5-7 shows the contribution to the increase in total manufacturing power capacity by plant size. The three largest-scale categories, comprising factories with

Table 5-7. Relative Contributions to Total Increase in Power
Capacity (H, H') by Factory Scale

(percent)

Scale (persons)	Relative Contributions to H						Relative Contributions to H'	
	1909 −1940	1909 −1914	1914 −1919	1919 −1930	1930 −1935	1935 −1940	1909 −1914	1914 −1919
All factories	100.0	100.0	100.0	100.0	100.0	100.0	100.0	100.0
5– 9	3.4	3.8	3.5	4.7	2.1	3.0	4.6	3.7
10– 29	5.5	7.3	7.8	4.7	7.3	5.2	8.9	9.0
30– 49	3.1	5.9	5.3	2.7	3.1	3.0	7.1	5.6
50– 99	4.2	9.6	6.2	4.7	2.8	3.7	11.4	7.1
100–499	20.0	16.4	23.2	41.9	− 10.3	13.2	18.9	25.0
500–999	15.3	30.0	2.4	22.3	− 19.6	18.1	26.9	5.0
1,000 or more	48.5	27.0	51.6	19.0	114.7	53.8	22.2	44.6

Sources: Same as Table 5-6.

100 or more workers, accounted for 83.8% of the increase in total
manufacturing power capacity between 1909 and 1940. Furthermore,
the subperiod figures in the same table show that the contribution of
these largest factories to the expansion of total horsepower increased
over time, from 73.4% in 1909-14 to 85.1% in 1935-40. This trend is also
evident, over a much shorter period of time, in the figures for primary
power capacity.

Table 5-8 presents a similar picture of the expanding position of large-
scale firms in terms of the composition of manufacturing power
capacity. As shown in panel A, factories in the three largest-scale
categories increased their share of total manufacturing horsepower from
68.8% in 1909 to over 80% in 1940. These factories also accounted for an
increasingly large percentage of primary power capacity between 1909
and 1919 as shown in panel B. This trend in the composition of

Table 5-8. Composition of Power Capacity (*H*, *H'*) and Output
by Factory Scale

(percent)

Scale (persons)	1909	1914	1919	1930	1935	1940
A. Composition of Total Power Capacity (*H*)						
All factories	100.0	100.0	100.0	100.0	100.0	100.0
5– 9	5.5	4.7	4.0	4.5	4.0	3.5
10– 29	11.0	9.1	8.4	5.9	6.1	5.7
30– 49	5.7	5.8	5.5	3.6	3.5	3.2
50– 99	9.0	9.3	7.5	5.6	5.1	4.4
100–499	30.0	23.3	23.2	36.0	27.6	20.3
500–999	11.0	20.4	10.0	18.4	11.5	14.9
1,000 or more	27.8	27.4	41.4	26.0	42.2	48.0

	B. Composition of Primary Power Capacity (*H'*)			C. Composition of Output		
All factories	100.0	100.0	100.0	100.0	100.0	100.0
5– 9	5.9	5.3	4.4	9.0	6.2	8.0
10– 29	11.7	10.4	9.6	13.4	12.1	13.4
30– 49	6.1	6.6	6.0	7.9	7.4	7.7
50– 99	9.6	10.4	8.5	12.0	9.7	9.0
100–499	30.5	25.1	25.0	28.2	25.0	21.1
500–999	11.3	18.6	10.9	12.9	12.6	10.1
1,000 or more	24.9	23.6	35.6	16.6	27.0	30.7

Sources: Same as Table 5-6.

manufacturing power capacity is consistent with the changes in the composition of manufacturing output by factory scale. The breakdown of manufacturing output by factory scale, which is possible only from 1930 on, is presented in panel C of Table 5-8. It shows the growing contribution of large-scale firms to total manufacturing output.

Table 5-9. Estimates of Functions Explaining Expanding Power
Capacity in Manufacturing and Mining

Variable	Constant	Parameters of		r^2	d
		R	R/K		
ΔH	-70.041	0.307		0.602*	0.87
ΔH	-514.345		20.760	0.280*	0.57

Sources: H: Same as Table 5-3. R is calculated as real GDP (Table 1-3) multiplied by
the relative income share of capital (Table 1-3). R/K is obtained by dividing nominal
rate of return (Minami and Ono 1978a, appendix table 4) by the NDP deflator for this
industry (calculated from Ohkawa *et al.* 1974, pp. 202 and 226).

Notes: All figures are for the private sector only. Observation period is 1911–37.
Figures for R and K are in 1934–36 prices. Figures for H (thousand hp), R (million
yen), and R/K (%) are seven-year moving averages.

* signifies that r (correlation coefficient) is statistically significant at 99% level.

Factors Responsible for Expanding Power Capacity

In order to explore factors responsible for expanding power capacity
one must try to explain the industrialization process, because expansion
of power capacity is one of the major factors responsible for this
phenomenon. In other words, industrial growth depends on the increase
in energy-using equipment which in turn necessitates the expansion of
power capacity (chapter 1).

Our hypothesis is that the expansion of power capacity (ΔH) depends
on the expected return on capital. This hypothesis is derived by analogy
from the theory of fixed investment, because ΔH seems to be positively
associated with fixed investment.[12] Shigeru Ishiwata and myself have
shown separately that real fixed investment in private non-primary
sector is explained largely by the real return on capital (R) and its rate to

[12] A correlation coefficient of the relation between ΔH and the real fixed investment
both in the manufacturing and mining sector is 0.876. Data and estimating period are the
same as Table 5-9. Fixed investment is from Chōki Keizai Tōkei Iinkai 1968, p. 163.

Table 5-10. Input-Output and Factor Ratios in Manufacturing
and Mining

Ratio	1910	1920	1930	1937
H/K (hp/1,000 yen)	0.492	0.891	1.518	1.595
H'/K (hp/1,000 yen)		0.763	1.288	1.328
K/L (1,000 yen/person)	0.411	0.562	0.650	0.887
H/L (hp/person)	0.202	0.501	0.987	1.414
H'/L (hp/person)		0.429	0.837	1.177
O/L (1,000 yen/person)	0.339	0.456	0.691	0.956
K/O	1.212	1.234	0.941	0.927
H/O (hp/1,000 yen)	0.596	1.100	1.429	1.479
H'/O (hp/1,000 yen)		0.941	1.212	1.232

Sources: H, H', K and O: Same as Fig. 5-2. L: Same as Table 1-1.

Notes: Factories with four or less workers are not included in H and H'. Seven-year averages centered on the indicated years. L, K, and O stand for employment, real gross capital stock, and real gross value added respectively.

capital stock (R/K).[13] Now we set forth following functions:

$$\Delta H = a + bR + u$$

and

$$\Delta H = a + bR/K + u,$$

where u stands for a random variable. The results of estimating these functions for 1911–37 which are presented in Table 5-9 substantiate our hypothesis.

We may conclude that enterpreneurs tended to decide the capacity of power equipment relying largely on the expected return on capital. From this conclusion it may be inferred that the rapid increase in power capacity in Japan was attributable to the high rate of return on capital. The high rate of technological progress (coming basically from the huge backlog of unexploited modern technology), the rapid expansion of home market, the decreasing trend in the labor share of income

[13] Ishiwata 1975; Minami 1986, chap. 6.

Table 5-11. Input-Output and Factor Ratios by Industry Group: 1935

Industry Group	H/L	H'/L	O/L^a	H/O^a	H'/O^a
	(hp/person)		(1,000 yen/ person)	(hp/1,000 yen)	
All manufacturing	1.99	1.31	4.13	0.48	0.32
Textiles	1.00	0.80	3.08	0.33	0.27
Metals and metal products	4.49	2.93	7.83	0.57	0.37
Machinery	1.32	1.02	3.27	0.40	0.31
Ceramics	4.84	0.91	2.76	1.76	0.33
Chemicals	4.92	3.12	6.82	0.72	0.46
Wood and wood products	1.78	1.27	2.51	0.71	0.51
Printing and binding	0.51	0.49	3.04	0.17	0.16
Food	1.30	1.03	6.33	0.20	0.16
Miscellaneous	0.96	0.92	2.58	0.37	0.36

Sources: H, H': Same as Table 5-3. L, O: Nippon, Tsūshō Sangyōshō 1961, pp. 180–98.

Notes: All figures are for the private factories with five or more production workers.
[a] In this table O stands for nominal output.

(coming from the existence of surplus labor) and other factors must have been responsible for the high rate of return on capital.[14]

Power Capacity in Relation to Other Production Variables

Entire Manufacturing Sector

The significance of expanding power capacity to industrial growth can be seen by relating horsepower statistics to other production variables. Various indexes of the input-output ratios and ratios among inputs for the manufacturing and mining sectors combined are shown in Table 5-10.[15] The horsepower-capital stock ratios, H/K and H'/K, increased

[14] Minami 1986, p. 170.
[15] It should be noted that the coverage of the horsepower statistics and the other variables in this table differs. However, this difference does not affect our conclusions.

rapidly up to 1930 and then increased only slightly during the last prewar decade.[16] This trend was partly due to the increase in the share of producers' durable equipment in total capital sotck. The need for mechanical power was more closely associated with such equipment than with the other components of capital stock, buildings and structures.[17] Both the capital-labor ratio, K/L, and the horsepower-labor ratios, H/L and H'/L, showed increasing trends for the entire period, although these growth rates were smaller in the 1930s than in the earlier decades. These increases, which express the progress of mechanization, were one of the major factors contributing to the increase in labor productivity, O/L.

The capital-output ratio, K/O, was relatively constant during the 1910s and 1930s and decreased over the 1920s.[18] The decrease in the capital-output ratio during the 1920s occurred simultaneously with an acceleration in the rates of growth in labor productivity and technological progress (Table 1-3). The horsepower-output ratios, H/O and H'/O, increased for all periods, but in the 1930s the increase was very small. The decline in the growth rates in these ratios in the 1930s was a consequence of the aforementioned decrease in the growth rate of H/L and H'/L in that decade.[19]

Analysis by Industry Group

Comparing ratios in Table 5-10 among industry groups clarifies further the role of power capacity. Since capital stock figures are not

[16]   The increasing trend in H/K and H'/K is implied in Fig. 5-2 which depicts the rates of growth in H, H', and K.

In the manufacturing sector in the United States H'/K decreased until 1914, when it began to increase. Du Boff 1966, chart 1 on p. 428. Compared with the United States, then, the expansion of power capacity during industrialization in Japan was quite remarkable.

[17]   Capital stock figures by type have been estimated only for the nonprimary sector as a whole. According to these estimates the seven-year average share of producers' durable equipment increased from 7.1% in 1882/88 to 45.1% in 1934/40. Ohkawa *et al.* 1966, table 2-6 on p. 21. A similar phenomenon can be expected to have occurred in the manufacturing and mining sector.

[18]   Refer to the growth rates of K and O depicted in Fig. 5-2.

[19]   Refer to the relations $H/O=(H/L)/(O/L)$ and $H'/O=(H'/L)/(O/L)$.

available by industry group, we are limited to considering the relations among power capacity, labor force, and output. Table 5-11 presents the breakdown of these input-output ratios and factor ratios by industry group for 1935.[20] Examining this table reveals two ways in which power capacity contributes to labor productivity.

Comparison of the metals and chemicals industries with the textile and miscellaneous categories indicates the direct contribution of mechanization to labor productivity. The difference in labor productivity (O/L) between these two groups of industries is associated with a difference in power capacity per worker (H/L and H'/L), or a difference in mechanization.[21] That is, the comparatively low labor productivity in textiles and miscellaneous industries is associated with very low H/L and H'/L', while the high labor productivity in metals and chemicals is associated with comparatively greater power capacity per worker.[22] (Furthermore, metals and chemicals exhibit high labor productivity in spite of the fact that power capacity in these industries is relatively less efficient in terms of output produced; i.e., these industries have relatively high H/O and H'/O.[23]) Thus, one may state that differences in mechanization give rise to differences in labor productivity. In other words, it is expected that industries with relatively greater power requirements will benefit from a relatively more productive labor force.

The possible conclusion that industrial differences in horsepower capacity per worker are solely responsible for differences in labor productivity is contradicted, however, by the situation in the food industry. Labor productivity (O/L) is very high in this industry—at a

[20] An attention should be paid to a difference in coverage and definition of data between Table 5-10 and Table 5-11. That is, factories with four or less workers are included in the former table (L and O), but not in the latter table. And value added figures are used in the former table, while gross output figures are employed in the latter table.

[21] In our study mechanization is measured by the proportion of powered factories in total factories, α. H/L and H'/L seem to be closely related to this variable.

[22] For instance, the iron and steel industry needs huge amounts of power to operate the cranes which carry ore and coal and to operate bellows for the furnaces. Furthermore, a large amount of mechanical energy is necessary for rolling iron and transporting the final products. Tanaka 1917, p. 745.

[23] Refer to the relation $O/L=(H/L)/(H/O)=(H'/L)/(H'/O)$.

Table 5-12. Input-Output and Factor Ratios by Factory Scale: 1935

Scale (persons)	H/L	O/L	H/O
	(hp/person)	(1,000 yen/person)	(hp/1,000 yen)
All factories	1.99	4.13	0.48
5– 9	0.74	2.32	0.32
10– 29	0.71	2.91	0.25
30– 49	0.78	3.44	0.23
50– 99	0.94	3.70	0.25
100–499	2.47	4.64	0.53
500–999	2.23	5.05	0.44
1,000 or more	4.27	5.68	0.75

Sources: Same as Table 5-11.
Notes: Figures are for the private factories with five or more production workers.

level close to that of metals and chemicals—in spite of the fact that power capacity per worker (H/L and H'/L) is quite low, particularly in comparison with the level in metals and chemicals. Moreover, although labor productivity in the printing industry is low comparatively speaking, it is not as low as would be expected given the position of printing at the bottom of all industry groups in terms of power capacity per worker. The relative efficiency of labor in printing and foods can be explained by noting that these two categories have the lowest horsepower-output ratios among all the industry categories. The relatively greater efficiency of mechanical power in these two industries (in terms of output per horsepower), apparently made a significant contribution to labor productivity. We may conclude, then, that differences in the output efficiency of mechanical power as well as differences in mechanization (horsepower per worker) create differences in labor productivity among industries.

Analysis by Factory Scale

Table 5-12 presents the breakdown by factory scale of some output and factor ratios for 1935. In that table labor efficiency (O/L) increases steadily with the size of the factory. Just as striking, however, is the correlation between scale and mechanization, or power capacity per worker (H/L). Plants in the three largest-scale categories employ over twice as much power capacity per worker as smaller-scale factories. Thus, in spite of the fact that the power capacity of large plants is less output efficient than smaller factories (higher H/O with factory scale), large factories are able to achieve greater labor productivity because of their relatively greater mechanization. This observation indicates that previously mentioned scale differentials in wages and labor productivity may be explained in terms of scale differentials in capital-labor ratios.[24] That is, because power capacity is positively correlated with capital stock, and also power capacity to labor ratio increases with factory scale, therefore we may infer that similar scale differentials existed in capital-labor ratios.

Our study on the changes in power capacity in relation to other production variables in this section has revealed an important role of mechanization measured by power capacity per worker on labor productivity. It should be noted, however, that this conclusion does not deny a role of technological progress on improving labor productivity. It was already pointed out in Table 1-3 that technological change was an important factor for industrialization.

[24] This may support Shinohara's hypothesis concerning the dual structure. He claimed that the scale-differential in the capital-labor ratio was basically responsible for the differential in productivity and consequently in wages (1962, chap. 8).

Chapter 6

CHANGES IN SOURCES OF POWER

Analysis of the power revolution is not complete without taking into account the kinds of engines employed to generate power. During Japan's industrialization, not only did power capacity expand greatly, but there also occurred changes in the relative contributions of different types of engines to total power capacity. That is, expansion of power capacity was accompanied by a shift to newer and more efficient engines.

The nature of this transition is examined in this chapter by considering four broad categories of engines: water wheels and turbines, steam engines and turbines, internal combustion engines, and electric motors. The first section of this chapter provides an overview of the transition in the sources of power. It describes greatly the growth and composition of manufacturing horsepower in terms of these four engine types. The second section identifies industrial differences in the pattern of transition to different sources of power. These inter-industry differences are accounted for, in part, by differences in production technology. The third section examines the pattern of changes in horsepower composition by factory scale and identifies a significant scale differential. The final section reveals the distinctive characteristics of the changes in the composition of manufacturing power in Japan by comparing these changes to the transition in power generation in the United States.

The Transition in the Sources of Power

In this section we examine the changes in the sources of power in the manufacturing sector in two ways. First, we examin over time changes in the total power capacity of each of the four types of engines (water wheels, steam engines, internal combustion engines, and electric motors). Then we analyse the consequent changes in the overall composition of manufacturing power capacity by engine type. This analysis of the growth of power capacity by engine type clarifies the relative importance of new power technology versus old technology.

The Growth of Power Capacity

Fig. 6-1 depicts, for the years 1887–1937, the power capacity of various categories of engines employed in the manufacturing sector. Tables 6-1 and 6-2 present statistics on the growth of manufacturing power capacity by engine type during these years.[1] According to Fig. 6-1, power capacity of water wheels and water turbines continued to grow throughout much of the period of industrialization. However, the 6.9% average annual rate of growth in water power for the entire 50-year period was far below the over-all rate of growth in manufacturing power capacity (Table 6-1).

Increasing utilization of the water turbine was the main reason why water power capacity continued to grow even in the later phases of industrialization. Between 1908 and 1937 the power capacity of Western-type water wheels (mainly water turbines) increased 15,417 hp, while the capacity of the Japanese-type increased only 839 hp.[2] Expanding use of water turbines occurred primarily in connection with

[1] Unless stated otherwise all figures presented in this chapter are calculated from seven-year moving averages of raw power capacity estimates.

[2] Statistics on the horsepower of Japanese-type and Western-type water wheels are available only since 1905. See Appendix.

The increase in the capacity of Japanese-type water wheels was significant until the 1910s. It increased by 3,453 hp between 1909 and 1919, out of which the increase in the smallest-scale plants with 5–9 workers (2,924 hp) occupied 85%. Figures for the horse-power capacity in the two years (unsmoothed) are from Minami 1965, pp. 232, 236. The increasing trend in the 1910s may be taken as an extention of the same trend (presumably much steeper trend) before this period. It should not be neglected that the utilization of the traditional source of power in smaller-scale plants became more evident in the early phase of industrialization.

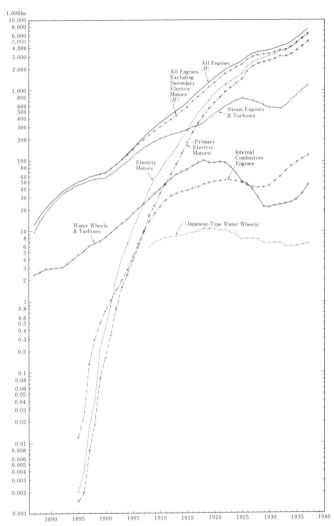

Fig. 6-1. Power Capacity by Engine Type

Sources: See Appendix. In place of abnormal figures estimates by interpolation are used.

Notes: Figures are for the private factories with five or more workers.

Table 6-1. Annual Rate of Growth of Power Capacity (H, H')
by Engine Type

(percent)

Engines	1888 –1937	1888 –1900	1901 –1910	1911 –1920	1921 –1930	1931 –1937
All engines (H)	13.8	14.3	17.6	15.9	9.5	10.7
All primary engines (H')	13.5	14.3	16.3	15.7	9.9	10.0
Water wheels and turbines	6.9	10.3	16.7	9.6	−12.9	11.2
Steam engines and turbines	10.4	15.0	13.6	8.6	2.4	11.4
Internal combustion engines	33.4[a]	162.7[b]	40.8	8.7	−1.3	15.2
Electric motors	46.5[a]	224.9[b]	71.3	28.1	13.3	10.5
Primary electric motors	46.3[a]	203.9[b]	73.5	34.6	14.9	10.4

Sources: Same as Fig. 6-1.
Notes: See the notes to Table 5-3.
[a] Mean for the period 1896–1937.
[b] Mean for the period 1896–1900.

the development of hydro-electric generation in the manufacturing sector, particularly after 1930.

Almost at the outset of Japan's industrialization water power was surpassed by steam power (power generated by steam engines and turbines). As is shown in Fig. 6-1 steam power capacity exceeded water power capacity in 1887. This demarcation is confirmed by the raw horsepower statistics (not the smoothed ones used in the figure) as well. This marks a significant point in the history of power utilization in the manufacturing sector (see chapter 2).

Over the next 50 years steam power grew at a rather moderate pace. Nevertheless, steam engines were an important source of expanding manufacturing power capacity. From 1888 to 1937 steam power capacity increased at an average rate of 10.4% per year. Only the capacity of water wheels grew at a lower rate during these years (Table 6-1). Despite the fact that steam power grew comparatively slowly, the increase in steam power contributed almost 16% to the overall growth of

Table 6-2. Relative Contribution to Total Increase in Power
Capacity (H, H') by Engine Type

(percent)

Engines	1887 –1937	1887 –1900	1900 –1910	1910 –1920	1920 –1930	1930 –1937
All engines (H)	100.0	100.0	100.0	100.0	100.0	100.0
Water wheels and turbines	0.6	10.8	11.2	4.8	−3.4	0.6
Steam engines and turbines	15.9	87.0	53.9	22.7	4.8	16.4
Internal combustion engines[a]	1.6	1.4	7.9	2.4	−0.3	2.0
Electric motors[a]	81.9	0.8	27.0	70.1	98.9	81.0
All primary engines (H')	100.0	100.0	100.0	100.0	100.0	100.0
Water wheels and turbines	0.7	10.9	13.1	5.7	−3.7	0.8
Steam engines and turbines	18.5	87.4	62.9	26.6	5.2	20.1
Internal combustion engines[a]	1.9	1.4	9.2	2.9	−0.3	2.4
Primary electric motors[a]	78.9	0.3	14.8	64.8	98.8	76.7

Sources: Same as Fig. 6-1.
Notes: See the notes to Table 5-4.
[a] Power capacity of these engines are assumed to be zero in 1887.

total power capacity (H) between 1887 and 1937, and it contributed 19%
to the growth of primary power capacity (H') (Table 6-2). These shares
were second only to those of electric motors and of primary electric
motors. Furthermore, for the years before 1900 increases in steam power
were a far more important factor in the growth of power capacity than
increases in electric power. That is, between 1887 and 1900 increases in
steam power accounted for 87% of the increase in both total power
capacity and primary power capacity. For 1900-10 steam engines
contributed more than 50% to the increase in H and more than 60% in
the increase in H'. Consequently, steam engines were the largest single
source of power in manufacturing up to the 1900s and they remained the
second most important source for the entire period up to 1937.

Although the power capacity of internal combustion engines increased almost continuously from 1895 to 1937, this type of engine made

113

a relatively insignificant contribution to total manufacturing power capacity. The large increase in the power capacity of the internal combustion engine during the 1900s and 1910s was mainly due to the development of the gas engine. From 1901 to 1920 gas engines increased 41,460 hp compared to the 8,368 hp increase of oil engines.[3] Decline in the utilization of the gas engine during the 1920s was responsible for the absolute fall in the power capacity of internal combustion engines during this decade. But, in the 1930s application of both gas and oil engines increased, and the power capacity of internal combustion engines again began to rise. Overall, however, between 1897 and 1937 increases in the power capacity of all internal combustion engines comprised only 2% of the total growth of manufacturing power capacity (H and H').

The electric motor was decisively the most important factor in the expansion of manufacturing power during Japan's industrialization. According to Fig. 6.1, electric power exceeded steam power in 1916 (in 1917 according to the raw horsepower estimates). Furthermore, both the rate of growth and the relative contribution of electric motors to the increase in manufacturing power capacity were overwhelmingly larger than those of the other types of engines. Between 1896 and 1937 electric power capacity in manufacturing increased at an annual rate of 47%. The increasing use of electric motors accounted for over 80% of the total growth in manufacturing power between 1887 and 1937. The rate of growth of electric power was very rapid throughout the whole period of industrialization, and, although it began to slacken after 1900, it remained consistently above the growth rates of the other engines. In addition, the relative contribution of electric motors to the growth of total power capacity increased over time, reaching its highest level during the 1920s. During this decade, almost the entire increase in manufacturing power capacity came from electric motors.

Considering primary electric power we arrive at the same conclusions, because primary electric power had almost the same rate of growth as total electric power and it made almost the same contribution to

[3] See Appendix for statistics on the power capacity of gas and oil engines.

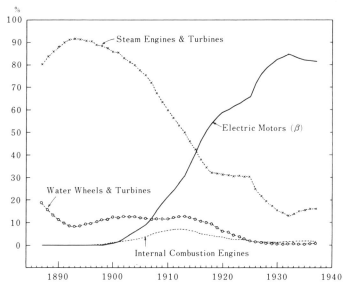

Fig. 6-2. Composition of Total Power Capacity (*H*) by Engine
         Type

Sources: Same as Table 6-1.
Notes: See the notes to Fig. 6-1.

increases in manufacturing power capacity. Primary electric power
capacity exceeded steam power capacity in 1917 according to seven-year
moving averages and in 1918 according to raw statistics. Thus, while the
eclipse of water power by steam power in 1887 was one milestone in the
history of power utilization, an equally significant transformation in the
sources of manufacturing power occurred in the years 1916–18 when
electric motors surpassed steam engines.

Composition of Power Capacity

Changes in the composition of power capacity by engine type express
even more clearly the timing of the transition in the sources of
manufacturing power. Fig. 6-2 depicts, for the period 1885 to 1937, the

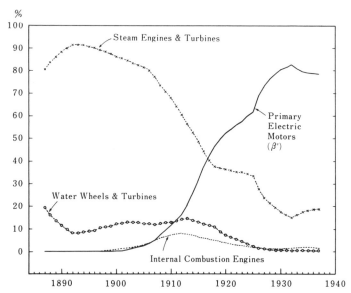

Fig. 6-3. Composition of Primary Power Capacity (H') by
Engine Type

Sources: Same as Fig. 6-1.
Notes: See the notes to Fig. 6-1.

share of total power capacity of each of the four engine types. From this
figure it appears that the first great change, the transition from water to
steam power, was completed before the turn of the century. The
contribution of water wheels to total power capacity followed a
generally declining trend. From a high level of 19.4% in 1887 it fell to
less than 1% in 1937. Prior to 1900, the decline in the share of water
wheels was accompanied by a rise in the share of steam engines. The
contribution of steam power grew from 80.6% in 1887 to a peak of
91.6% in 1893.

Following this peak, the share of steam engines fell almost continuously up to 1937. This decline was caused uniquely by the emergence
of electric motors. The share of electric power, which is denoted by β,

116

increased rapidly after the turn of the century. The early 1930s mark the end of this second great transformation in the composition of manufacturing power. β reached a peak of just under 85% in 1932 and then leveled off, because electrification of manufacturing was virtually completed.

Our conclusions about the timing of transition form steam to electric power are not altered if we look at the composition of primary power capacity, which appears in Fig. 6-3. During the first three decades of the twentieth century the position of steam engines eroded as the use of primary electric motors rose drastically. The share of primary electric motors, β' surpassed the share of steam engines in 1917 (in 1918 in terms of raw figures) and reached a peak of 82.7% in 1932.

Unlike water wheels, steam engines, and electric motors, internal

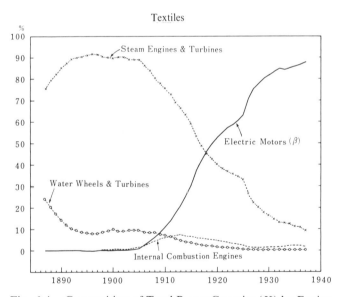

Fig. 6-4. Composition of Total Power Capacity (H) by Engine Type and by Industry Group

Sources: Same as Table 6-1.
Notes: See the notes to Fig. 6-1.

Metals and Metal Products

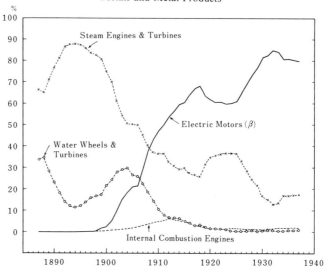

Machinery

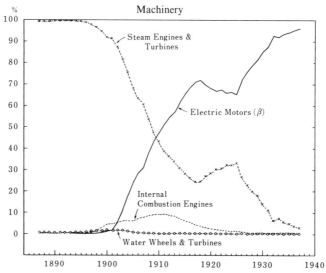

Fig. 6.4. (continued)

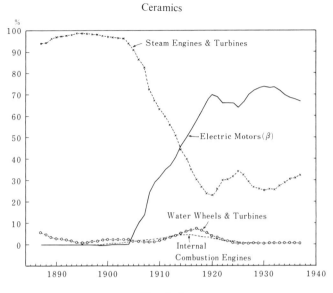

Ceramics

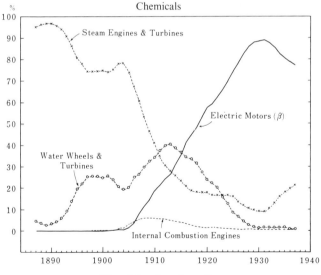

Chemicals

Fig. 6.4. (continued)

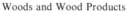

Woods and Wood Products

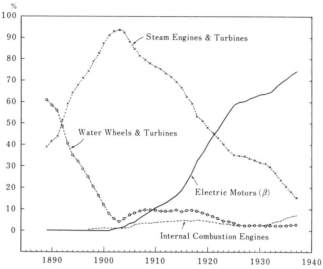

Printing and Binding

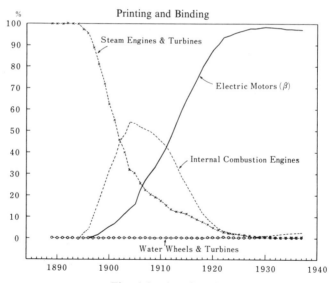

Fig. 6.4.   (continued)

Food

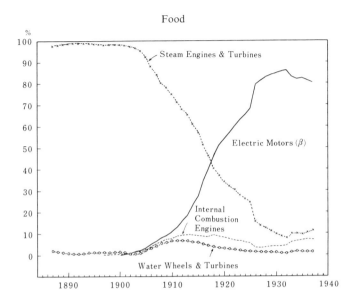

Miscellaneous

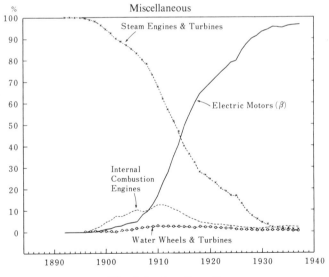

Fig. 6.4. (continued)

Table 6-3. Composition of Power Capacity (H) by Engine Type and by Industry Group: 1887–1937

(percent)

Year	Electric Motors (β)	Steam Engines and Turbines	Internal Combustion Engines	Water Wheels and Turbines	Electric Motors (β)	Steam Engines and Turbines	Internal Combustion Engines	Water Wheels and Turbines
	All Manufacturing				Chemicals			
1887	0.0	80.6	0.0	19.4	0.0	95.4	0.0	4.6
1900	0.6	85.9	1.1	12.4	0.0	75.0	0.3	24.7
1910	21.8	60.1	6.6	11.5	18.7	41.2	6.1	34.0
1920	58.9	31.3	3.4	6.4	57.6	17.0	1.7	23.7
1930	82.6	15.6	1.2	0.6	88.9	9.1	0.7	1.3
1937	81.8	16.0	1.6	0.6	77.3	21.3	0.5	0.9
	Textiles				Wood and Wood Products			
1887	0.0	75.8	0.0	24.2	0.0	39.2[a]	0.0	60.8[a]
1900	0.0	89.7	0.4	9.9	0.0	87.3	0.9	11.8
1910	11.0	75.9	6.0	7.1	10.4	76.6	3.8	9.2
1920	52.7	40.5	4.9	1.9	40.4	47.9	4.2	7.5
1930	81.8	16.5	1.4	0.3	63.5	31.9	2.3	2.3
1937	88.0	9.8	2.0	0.2	74.5	15.8	7.0	2.7

Metals and Metal Products

1887	0.0	66.1	0.0	33.9
1900	2.5	75.2	0.4	21.9
1910	47.5	36.9	4.9	10.7
1920	61.6	34.8	2.0	1.6
1930	81.7	17.1	0.8	0.4
1937	80.0	17.4	1.9	0.7

Printing and Binding

1887	0.0	100.0[a]	0.0	0.0
1900	5.2	62.6	32.2	0.0
1910	37.4	17.5	45.1	0.0
1920	87.8	5.0	7.1	0.1
1930	98.4	0.3	1.3	0.0
1937	97.4	0.0	2.6	0.0

Machinery

1887	0.0	99.4	0.0	0.6
1900	1.7	91.8	4.6	1.9
1910	47.3	43.3	9.2	0.2
1920	68.5	28.9	2.5	0.1
1930	85.1	14.3	0.6	0.0
1937	96.2	3.0	0.8	0.0

Food

1887	0.0	97.9	0.0	2.1
1900	0.1	98.4	0.4	1.1
1910	10.7	75.0	7.9	6.4
1920	54.4	34.3	8.1	3.2
1930	85.0	10.1	3.9	1.0
1937	80.4	11.3	7.0	1.3

Ceramics

1887	0.0	94.2	0.0	5.8
1900	0.0	97.4	0.3	2.3
1910	31.9	63.6	3.0	1.5
1920	69.8	23.1	2.9	4.2
1930	73.6	25.6	0.3	0.5
1937	67.0	32.4	0.4	0.2

Miscellaneous

1887	0.0	100.0[b]	0.0	0.0
1900	1.3	94.1	4.4	0.2
1910	17.6	67.3	12.7	2.4
1920	69.2	24.9	3.9	2.0
1930	93.3	4.4	1.8	0.5
1937	96.3	1.0	2.3	0.4

Sources: Same as Fig. 6-1. *Notes*: Figures are seven-year averages centered on indicated years.
[a] Figures for 1889. [b] Figures for 1892.

combustion engines never attained a position of significance as a source of manufacturing power. From 1895 to 1937 the share of internal combustion engines remained quite small; at its largest share, in 1912, was only 7%. The timing of this peak indicates, however, that the internal combustion engine did play a role as an intermediate source of power between the age of the steam engine and the ascendancy of the electric motor.

The Transition in Power Utilization by Industry Group

When the transformation in the sources of manufacturing power is examined by industry group, the picture is more varied than that described above. Fig. 6-4 depicts changes in the composition of power capacity by type of engine for each of the nine major industry groups between 1887 and 1937. Table 6-3 summarizes this information for selected years. While the transition from water wheels to steam engines and from steam engines to electric motors is generally evident in all industry groups, the extent and timing of these changes exhibit distinctive patterns in each industry.

From Water to Steam Power

If we consider first the substitution of steam for water power, we discover that the textiles, metals, and wood groups experienced a transformation distinct from the remaining industry groups. These three industries relied more heavily on water power at the outset of industrialization in the 1880s. In 1887 water wheels supplied almost one quarter of the power in textiles and one third in metals, and as late as 1889 they supplied 60.8% of power capacity in the wood and wood products industry.[4] However, in the late 1880s and throughout 1890s,

---

[4]   Although the percentage of water power in total power capacity was relatively high in metals and wood, just as it was in textiles, the water power used in these two industries was very small compared with that in textiles (Table 2-3). Therefore there is no need to change the conclusion that textiles was the only center of water power utilization (chap. 2).

the share of steam power in these industries increased, as steam engines were substituted for water wheels. The share of steam power reached peaks of about 90% in textiles and metals at the beginning of the 1890s. The largest proportion of steam power was reached at the beginning of the next decade in the wood industry.

By contrast, the other six industry groups (machinery, ceramics, chemicals, printing, food, and miscellaneous) utilization of the water wheel was negligible, even in the very early years of industrialization. The extreme case is the printing industry, where virtually no water wheels were ever employed. From 1887 to the early 1890s the share of steam power in this industry was 100%. The year in which the share of steam power began to fall off differed among these six industry groups. The decline of steam engines started in about 1890 in chemicals, in the mid-1890s in machinery, printing, and miscellaneous, and at the beginning of the 1900s in ceramics and food.

The decline in the share of steam power, a phenomenon common to all industries, was due mainly to the diffusion of the electric motor. But the metals, chemicals, and printing industries deserve to be mentioned as special cases in this respect. In metals and chemicals, decreasing utilization of steam power was accompanied for a time by an increase in utilization of the water wheel. In metals, the share of water power increased between 1894 and 1904. Evidently, this was due to the diffusion of water turbines for electric generation. In 1905 the share of the Western-type water wheels (which were largely turbines) in total water power was 94.5%, according to the raw figures. This trend occurred to a much greater extent in chemicals between 1889 and 1913, when the share of the water power rose from 2.7% to 40.5%. This recovery of water power was due to introduction of the water turbine for pulping in paper manufacturing, and to the spread of hydro-electric generation throughout the chemicals industry. Western-type water wheels comprised 99.6% of the increment in water power in the chemicals industry between 1909 and 1913. (The total increment in water power was 29,474 hp.)

In the printing industry, the substitution of the internal combustion

Table 6-4. Composition of Primary Power Capacity (H') by Engine Type and by Industry Group in Manufacturing: 1887–1937

(percent)

All Manufacturing

Year	Primary Electric Motors (β')	Steam Engines and Turbines	Internal Combustion Engines	Water Wheels and Turbines
1887	0.0	80.6	0.0	19.4
1900	0.6	85.9	1.1	12.4
1910	11.6	68.1	7.4	12.9
1920	52.3	36.3	4.0	7.4
1930	80.6	17.4	1.3	0.7
1937	78.7	18.7	1.9	0.7

Chemicals

Year	Primary Electric Motors (β')	Steam Engines and Turbines	Internal Combustion Engines	Water Wheels and Turbines
1887	0.0	95.4	0.0	4.6
1900	0.0	75.0	0.3	24.7
1910	9.0	46.1	6.8	38.1
1920	49.2	20.4	2.0	28.4
1930	86.8	10.8	0.9	1.5
1937	72.4	25.9	0.6	1.1

Textiles

Year	Primary Electric Motors (β')	Steam Engines and Turbines	Internal Combustion Engines	Water Wheels and Turbines
1887	0.0	75.8	0.0	24.2
1900	0.0	89.7	0.4	9.9
1910	5.3	80.7	6.4	7.6
1920	45.5	46.7	5.7	2.2
1930	80.9	17.4	1.4	0.3
1937	87.6	10.1	2.1	0.2

Wood and Wood Products

Year	Primary Electric Motors (β')	Steam Engines and Turbines	Internal Combustion Engines	Water Wheels and Turbines
1887	0.0	39.2[a]	0.0	60.8[a]
1900	0.0	87.3	0.9	11.8
1910	8.8	78.0	3.8	9.4
1920	38.6	49.2	4.4	7.8
1930	61.9	33.3	2.4	2.4
1937	74.3	15.9	7.1	2.7

Metals and Metal Products

Year				
1887	0.0	66.1	0.0	33.9
1900	2.5	75.2	0.4	21.9
1910	34.2	46.4	6.1	13.3
1920	55.0	40.8	2.3	1.9
1930	81.0	17.7	0.9	0.4
1937	77.2	19.9	2.1	0.8

Machinery

Year				
1887	0.0	99.4	0.0	0.6
1900	1.7	91.8	4.6	1.9
1910	15.2	69.8	14.8	0.2
1920	60.9	35.9	3.1	0.1
1930	84.0	15.3	0.7	0.0
1937	95.8	3.3	0.9	0.0

Ceramics

Year				
1887	0.0	94.2	0.0	5.8
1900	0.0	97.4	0.3	2.3
1910	25.5	69.6	3.3	1.6
1920	66.2	25.9	3.2	4.7
1930	55.2	43.4	0.6	0.8
1937	37.0	61.9	0.7	0.4

Printing and Binding

Year				
1887	0.0	100.0[a]	0.0	0.0
1900	5.2	62.6	32.2	0.0
1910	35.7	18.0	46.3	0.0
1920	87.7	5.1	7.2	0.1
1930	98.4	0.3	1.3	0.0
1937	97.4	0.0	2.6	0.0

Food

Year				
1887	0.0	97.9	0.0	2.1
1900	0.1	98.4	0.4	1.1
1910	8.7	76.8	8.0	6.5
1920	53.1	35.3	8.3	3.3
1930	84.7	10.3	4.0	1.0
1937	79.8	11.7	7.2	1.3

Miscellaneous

Year				
1887	0.0	100.0[b]	0.0	0.0
1900	1.3	94.1	4.4	0.2
1910	15.8	68.8	13.0	2.4
1920	67.7	26.1	4.1	2.1
1930	93.3	4.4	1.8	0.5
1937	96.3	1.0	2.3	0.4

Sources: Same as Fig. 6-1. Notes: See the notes to Table 6-3.
[a] Figures for 1889. [b] Figures for 1892.

engine for the steam engine is also noteworthy. The share of power capacity of the former engine in the printing industry increased very rapidly from 2.5% in 1895 to a peak of 54.1% in 1904. Most of this increase was due to the application of the gas engine. Out of 604 hp increment in the power capacity of internal combustion engines in printing between 1895 and 1904, 76.7% was supplied by gas engines.

From Steam to Electric Power

Generally speaking, the share of steam engines in Japanese manufacturing power capacity decreased as the share of electric motors (β) increased. But the speed of the transition from steam to electric power differed greatly among industry groups. For example, electrification was most conspicuous in printing. In this industry the share of steam power fell from 17.5% in 1910 to 5.0% ten years later, while β rose from 37.4% to 87.8%. On the other hand, electrification progressed more slowly in textiles and wood. In 1910 the share of steam power was a little over 75% in both industries, and, although utilization of steam engines declined over the next decade, in 1920 steam engines still supplied 40.5% of all mechanical power used in producing textiles and 47.9% of that used in producing wood and wood product. Over these ten years β rose from 11.0% to 52.7% in textiles and from 10.4% to 40.4% in wood, but electrification of these industries had not yet advanced to the same extent as it had in printing.[5]

Changes in the composition of primary power capacity reveal almost the same industrial differences in electrification. Table 6-4 presents for selected years the composition of H' by engine type for each industry

[5] One problem affecting our conclusions about industrial differences in the timing of electrification is that the actual figures in Table 6-3 may express not only real industrial differences in the composition of power capacity by engine type but also industrial differences in the composition of power capacity by factory scale. To take account of this possibility, we have calculated β for each industry for selected years under the assumption that the composition of power capacity by scale was equal to that in the manufacturing sector as a whole in 1909. Although there are some discrepancies between the actual and these estimated values of β, our previous conclusion that electrification of heavy industries preceeded that of light industries remains basically unaltered. Minami 1976b, table 4-5 on p. 102.

Table 6-5. Year in Which Electric Power Exceeded Steam
Power by Industry Group

Industry Group	Electric Power (1)	Primary Electric Power (2)
All manufacturing	1916 (1917)	1917 (1918)
Textiles	1918 (1918)	1921 (1920)
Metals and metal products	1909 (1910)	1913 (1910)
Machinery	1910 (1911)	1915 (1916)
Ceramics	1914 (1916)	—[a]
Chemicals	1914 (1914)	1916 (1917)
Wood and wood products	1922 (1921)	1922 (1921)
Printing and binding	1907 (1909)	1907 (1909)
Food	1918 (1918)	1918 (1919)
Miscellaneous	1915 (1915)	1915 (1916)

Sources: Same as Fig. 6-1.

Notes: Critical years were determined on the basis of seven-year moving averages of steam and electric power capacity. Years determined on the basis of non-smoothed data appear in parentheses.

[a] Primary electric motors exceeded steam engines in 1916, but fell behind steam engines again in 1932.

group. Only for ceramics do the trends in the composition of H' differ much from the trends in the composition of H. In this industry the share of primary electric motors (β') decreased during the 1920s and 1930s, while the share of electric motors (β) was constant during these periods. This difference in the trends in β and β' resulted from the development of techniques for generation of electricity within ceramic plants (chapter 5).

Industrial differences in the timing of electrification are more clearly revealed by comparing the critical years in which the share of electric power exceeded that of steam power. Column 1 of Table 6-5 lists these critical years by industry group. The figures are based on seven-year moving averages of power capacity. The years in parentheses are non-smoothed figures for the critical years. Electric power overtook steam power first in the printing industry, in 1907. The critical year for electrification followed shotly in metals, machinery, chemicals, and miscellaneous followed shortly after that of printing industry. Wood products was the last industry to experience electrification. The critical year for the wood industry was 1922, fifteen years after the critical year for the printing industry. Electrification was also delayed in the textiles and food industries. We can summarize these industrial differences in the transition from steam to electric power by stating, then, that electrification tended to occur earlier in printing and heavy industries and later in light industries.

The figures in column 2 of Table 6-5 indicate the year in which primary electric power exceeded steam power. For all industry groups with the exception of ceramics there are only very slight differences between the critical years indicated in columns 1 and 2. However, in ceramics steam power exceeded primary electric power again in the 1930s. This was due to the aforementioned rise in electric generation within ceramics plants.

Explanations for Industrial Differences

Generally speaking, two factors—the distinctive characteristics of production technology and the timing of industrial development—may account for differences among industries in the transformation of the sources of power. There are number of examples confirming the role of characteristics of technology unique to an industry in the transformation of the sources of power in that industry.

First, in the textile group the relatively slow electrification or long dependence on steam power occurred, because steam was used not only for operating steam engines but also for heating purposes in spinning and for boiling cocoons in silk reeling.[6] Electrification of production still left a need for equipment to generate steam for heating purposes. Based on raw figures, electric power did not exceed steam power until 1918 in spinning and until 1929 in silk reeling. The delayed electrification of

[6] Arisawa 1960a, p. 107.

130

spinning and silk reeling helped to make the critical year for the textile group as a whole the second latest among all industry groups.

A second example of the way in which production technology affected changes in the sources of power can be seen in the chemicals industry. The relatively high reliance on water wheels in the early years in the chemical group can be traced to the wide utilization of water power for Western-style paper manufacturing.[7] Initially, Western-style paper making was dependent on steam power for boiling, bleaching, and drying the rags and straw which were used as pulp.[8] However, the introduction of a new production technique using wood pulp, as well as a rise in coal prices, caused a shift from steam to water power.[9]

The shift from steam to water power accompanied the introduction of wood pulp as a raw material for paper production, because steam was no longer needed for the preparation of rags and straw and also almost all timber-grinding machines were operated with hydro-turbines.[10] Pulping relied mainly on water power for two reasons. First, most pulp mills were located in mountainous areas near logging operations, and such locations were favorable for using water power. Second, the simple process of timber grinding was well suited to the use of water wheels and turbines.

From the first decade of the twentieth century, however, the direct use of water power for pulping was gradually replaced by the indirect use of water power. Water turbines were employed to generate electricity to

[7] In 1909 in paper manufacturing in general the proportions of water and steam power in total power capacity were 47.9% and 36.6%, while in Western-style paper manufacturing alone they were 46.9% and 35.9%. STF. See Table A-2.

[8] For the history of paper manufacturing technology we rely on Gendai Nippon Sangyō Hattatsushi Kenkyūkai 1967a, pp. 66, 100–101, 165, 170.

The pioneers in this industry, Osaka Paper Mill, Yūkō Company, and Shōji Company (later Paper Manufacturing Company), all employed steam-powered machinery. Kanbayashi 1948, pp. 76–77.

[9] All engines used in paper manufacturing in 1884–85 were steam engines. The water wheel was first employed in this industry in 1886. STAC. See Table A-1.

[10] Ōji Paper's Second Kida Plant is a good example. This was the first wood pulp plant in Japan, erected in 1894. Five Pelton wheels (612 hp in total) were used to run timber grinding machines and to generate electricity for lighting.

operate the grinding machines. A typical example of this indirect use of water power in paper manufacturing was Ōji Paper's Tomakomai Plant established in 1909. All production in this plant was accomplished with internally generated hydroelectric power.

The distinctive characteristics of the wood products industry provide a third example of how industrial technology shaped changes in the sources of power. The rather heavy utilization of the water wheel in the wood industry group occurred for the same reasons as it did in pulping. These producers were generally located in mountainous areas and they employed relatively simple production techniques. Furthermore, this industry was the last to turn from steam to electric power in part because waste wood chips could be used as fuel for steam engines. Thus, the cost of operating with steam power in the wood industry was less than in other industries, where coal had to be purchased to fuel engines (chapter 11).

A fourth example of the effect of industrial technology can be found in the printing industry. The requirement of steady power for printing was a fundamental factor determining the type of engines used in this industry. The unique experience of the printing industry in its non-utilization of water wheels occurred, because steam engines could generate a more even supply of power than water wheels and also location of printing plants in urban areas was not conducive to water power utilization. Moreover, the early electrification of printing was stimulated by the great advantages which electric power offered to an industry requiring steady power, but at intermittent intervals (chapter 12).

Finally, the reasons for the decline in the share of primary motors in the chemical and ceramic industries during the 1930s are also to be found in the distinctive characteristics of production technology in these industries. The decline in β' was due to the increase in intra-plant thermal-electric generation which, as was described earlier, was accomplished by employing waste heat and steam extended in the primary production process.

These five examples all verifies the importance of differences in industrial technology in creating differences in the transformation of the sources of power among industries. In addition to this factor, however, differences in the timing of industrial development also can be considered for differences among industries in the pattern of changes in the sources of power. Light industries, such as food and textiles, developed rather early and made large investments in fixed capital during the age of steam power. Once these investments were made, the substitution of electric power for steam power was delayed, because replacement of old assets generally required a long time. On the other hand, the more modern heavy industries such as metals, machinery, and chemicals did not emerge until later and made their major investments in fixed capital during the age of electric power. Therefore old capital stock was not a hindrance and electrification proceeded rapidly in these industries.

The Transition in Power Utilization by Factory Scale

The composition of total power capacity by type of engine broken down by factory scale is given in Table 6-6 for six different years. (These figures are all based on non-smoothed power estimates.) In order to analyse the transition in the sources of power by factory scale, we first examine the composition of power capacity in 1909. In that year, smaller-scale plants relied more heavily than larger-scale plants on internal combustion engines. There was also a slight negative correlation between factory scale and the share of water wheels. By contrast, the share of steam power increased with factory scale. The share of electric motors was rather constant, increasing only slightly with plant size. It is worthwhile to note that among factories with fewer than 50 workers, the share of the internal combustion engine was greater than that of the electric motor. Thus, internal combustion engines appear to have played a significant role in mechanization of small-scale factories before the age of electric power. By far the most striking characteristic of the situation in 1909, however, is the great preponderance of steam power over all other types of power at all scale levels.

Table 6-6. Composition of Power Capacity (H) by Engine Type and by Factory Scale

(percent)

Scale (persons)	Electric Motors (β)	Steam Engines and Turbines	Internal Combustion Engines	Water Wheels and Turbines
		1909		
All factories	13.0	70.1	6.2	10.7
5– 9	10.6	49.6	19.2	20.6
10– 29	9.8	59.6	17.4	13.2
30– 49	7.0	63.4	11.4	18.2
50– 99	9.8	76.0	7.3	6.9
100–499	13.2	64.4	4.7	17.7
500–999	9.7	83.8	1.5	5.0
1,000 or more	18.3	78.1	1.4	2.2
		1914		
All factories	30.1	46.9	7.0	16.0
5– 9	27.4	41.9	17.5	13.2
10– 29	26.1	46.4	20.3	7.2
30– 49	20.5	47.2	13.0	19.3
50– 99	23.7	40.0	9.1	27.2
100–499	26.1	47.2	7.9	18.8
500–999	33.7	32.7	0.7	32.9
1,000 or more	36.7	60.2	2.9	0.2
		1919		
All factories	58.5	28.1	4.8	8.6
5– 9	56.9	19.7	10.8	12.6
10– 29	58.7	24.3	11.7	5.3
30– 49	55.1	33.9	8.0	3.0
50– 99	59.8	30.6	5.8	3.8
100–499	59.3	28.0	3.5	9.2
500–999	69.1	29.2	0.9	0.8
1,000 or more	55.7	28.1	4.1	12.1

Table 6-6. (continued)

(percent)

Scale (persons)	Electric Motors (β)	Steam Engines and Turbines	Internal Combustion Engines	Water Wheels and Turbines
1930				
All factories	86.7	11.4	1.2	0.7
5– 9	84.4	6.4	5.4	3.8
10– 29	86.3	9.2	2.5	2.0
30– 49	82.9	13.8	2.9	0.4
50– 99	88.0	9.8	1.4	0.8
100–499	87.2	11.2	1.2	0.4
500–999	95.8	3.9	0.1	0.2
1,000 or more	80.4	18.5	0.4	0.7
1935				
All factories	82.2	15.4	1.9	0.5
5– 9	85.5	4.2	7.5	2.8
10– 29	87.8	6.4	4.8	1.0
30– 49	87.8	6.8	4.8	0.6
50– 99	90.9	5.5	3.3	0.3
100–499	80.4	18.1	0.9	0.6
500–999	90.3	8.5	1.1	0.1
1,000 or more	78.6	19.6	1.4	0.4
1940				
All factories	81.5	16.4	1.2	0.9
5– 9	89.3	1.0	6.9	2.8
10– 29	92.4	2.7	3.9	1.0
30– 49	93.5	3.3	2.9	0.3
50– 99	94.9	3.3	1.6	0.2
100–499	84.8	14.1	0.8	0.3
500–999	86.2	12.1	0.3	1.4
1,000 or more	74.8	23.6	0.7	0.9

Sources: Minami 1965, pp. 232–45.

Table 6-7. Composition of Primary Power Capacity (H') by
Engine Type and by Factory Scale: 1909–1919

(percent)

Scale (persons)	Primary Electric Motors (β')	Steam Engines and Turbines	Internal Combustion Engines	Water Wheels and Turbines
1909				
All factories	5.5	76.2	6.7	11.6
5– 9	10.5	49.7	19.2	20.6
10– 29	8.4	60.6	17.6	13.4
30– 49	6.0	64.1	11.5	18.4
50– 99	7.8	77.7	7.4	7.1
100–499	7.1	69.0	4.9	19.0
500–999	4.6	88.5	1.6	5.3
1,000 or more	0.4	95.2	1.7	2.7
1914				
All factories	19.8	53.7	8.1	18.4
5– 9	26.7	42.2	17.7	13.3
10– 29	25.6	46.5	20.6	7.3
30– 49	20.3	47.3	13.1	19.3
50– 99	22.0	40.9	9.3	27.8
100–499	21.4	50.2	8.4	20.0
500–999	16.5	41.3	0.8	41.4
1,000 or more	15.6	80.2	4.0	0.2
1919				
All factories	51.5	33.0	5.7	10.2
5– 9	53.8	21.1	11.6	13.5
10– 29	57.6	24.9	12.0	5.5
30– 49	52.0	36.3	8.5	3.2
50– 99	58.2	31.9	6.0	3.9
100–499	55.6	30.5	3.8	10.1
500–999	66.6	31.5	1.0	0.9
1,000 or more	39.3	38.4	5.6	16.7

Sources: Minami 1965, pp. 232–37. Also see Appendix.

Comparing the composition of power capacity in 1909 with that in 1930, the year in which electrification was largely completed, reveals several significant changes. First, the tendency in 1909 for the share of each type of engine to increase or decrease with factory scale disappeared in 1930. Second, the share of electric motors reached a very high level in all scale classes, ranging between 80% and 96%.[11] These changes arose from the substitution of electric motors for steam engines in larger-scale factories and from the substitution of electric motor for water wheels and internal combustion engines in small-scale factories. In other words, while the transition from water to steam power occurred mainly among large-scale plants, electrification was realized evenly among all scale classes.[12]

A rather similar picture emerges if we examine the composition of primary power capacity, which is presented in Table 6-7. (Unfortunately, the breakdown of power capacity by factory scale is only possible up to 1919.) One difference between the composition of H and that of H' was that the share of primary electric motors (β') was negatively correlated with increasing factory scale while, as was mentioned previously, β tended to be slightly higher in larger-scale classes. In other words, there was a disparity between β and β' which tended to increase with factory scale. The decline of β' with increasing factory scale was due to the aforementioned fact that the proportion of primary motors in total electric motors was smaller in larger factory scale classes (Table 5-2).

---

[11]   Information on factories with four or fewer workers is available from a 1934 survey of Tokyo. The share of electric power (β) was almost 100% even in factories with only 1-4 workers. Minami 1976b, table F-4 on p. 109.

[12]   Observations based on Table 6-6 and Fig. 6-5 may be affected by differences among scale classes in the composition of power capacity by industry group. In order to investigate this possibility we have calculated the share of electric motors (β) for various years under the assumption that the industrial composition of power capacity in each scale class was equal to that prevailing in the manufacturing sector as a whole in 1909. Comparison of these estimates with the actual figures suggests no reasons for altering the observations made in the text. Minami 1976b, table 4-8 on p. 113.

Comparative Analysis with the United States

Before closing this investigation of the transition in the sources of manufacturing power it is worthwhile to relate the Japanese experience with that in another country. By examining briefly the transition from water to steam and from steam to electric power in the United States we can identify some of the unique features of the transition in Japan. The United States was chosen for comparison because of the availability of horsepower statistics comparable to our estimates.

Table 6-8 presents data on the composition of manufacturing primary power capacity by engine type in the United States manufacturing for selected years between 1879 and 1939. In 1879 almost two-thirds of the mechanical power used in U.S. manufacturing came from steam engines. By contrast, in 1884 (the earliest year for which Japanese data are available) steam engines supplied only 38.3% of the mechanical power used in Japanese manufacturing, and undoubtedly this figure was much lower in 1879. (Horsepower figures used here are non-smoothed ones.) However, the share of steam engines increased rapidly in Japan. By 1889 it had reached 90.0%, quite above the 78.4% share in the United States in that year. Thus, it can be stated that while the transition from water to steam power began much later in Japn, it also proceeded much faster there than in the United States.[13]

Water power in 1879 was still comprised over one-third of mechanical power in the Unites States. Water power was widely used in some industries, particularly in cotton-spinniing in the eastern states. But in Japan water power utilization for cotton-spinning was limited to small-scale plants employing traditional production techniques. These small plants were rapidly overwhelmed by large-scale, steam-powered plants after the middle of 1880s. In other words, in Japan the modern development of cotton spinning began with the age of steam power,

---

[13] The late start of Japan's revolution is also revealed by comparing Japan to Britain. The proportion of steam power in the British textile industry was already 72.6% in 1838 and had reached 93.6% in 1870. Musson 1976, pp. 424 and 437.

Table 6-8. Composition of Primary Power Capacity (H') by
Engine Type in U.S. Manufacturing: 1879–1939

(percent)

Year	Primary Electric Motors (β')	Steam Engines and Turbines	Internal Combustion Engines	Water Wheels and Turbines
1879		64.1		35.9
1889		78.4	0.1	21.5
1899	1.8	82.0	1.4	14.8
1904	3.3	81.9	2.2	12.6
1909	9.2	76.6	4.1	10.1
1914	17.2	69.9	4.5	8.4
1919	31.6	57.9	4.3	6.2
1925	44.0	47.3	3.4	5.3
1929	53.0	40.3	2.9	3.8
1939	57.6	35.6	3.5	3.3

Sources: Du Boff 1966, table 1 on p. 427. Du Boff's figures are calculated from the Census of Manufacturers.

skipping the age of water power (chapters 2 and 9).

Almost the same story can be said about other industries in Japan. When modern industries began, steam power technology was already available, therefore there was no need to employ the less efficient water wheel. Thus, water power utilization was eventually limited largely to traditional Japanese industries like silk reeling and *gara* spinning.

Just as the transition from water to steam power occurred more rapidly in Japan than in the United States, the change from steam engines to electric motors also occurred in the same way. According to Table 6-8 the share of primary electric motors (β') in U.S. manufacturing rose quickly from the start of the twentieth century. But the increase was even more drastic in Japan. For example, in Japan β' rose from 0.9% in 1904 to 51.1% in 1919 while in the United States it moved from

Table 6-9. Year in Which Electric Power Exceeded Steam
Power by Industry Group in U.S. Manufacturing

Industry Group	Electric Power (1)	Primary Electric Power (2)
All manufacturing	1919– 25	1919– 25
Textiles	1919– 25	1925– 27
Metals and metal products	1919– 25	1929– 39
Machinery	1909– 19	1909– 19
Ceramics	1909– 19	1919– 25
Chemicals	1909– 19	1925– 27
Wood and wood products	1929– 39	1939–
Printing and binding	1899–1909	1899–1909
Food	1919– 25	1919– 25

Sources: 1899: U.S., Census Office 1902, pp. 584–94.
1909: U.S., Dept. of Commerce 1913, pp. 522–40.
1919: U.S., Dept. of Commerce 1923, pp. 123–28.
1925: U.S., Dept. of Commerce 1928, pp. 1238–50.
1927: U.S., Dept. of Commerce 1930, pp. 1272–83.
1929: U.S., Dept. of Commerce 1933, pp. 113–18.

3.3% in 1904 to 31.6% fifteen years later. In the Unites States primary electric power surpassed steam power sometime during the latter half of the 1920s. However, the critical year in Japan was 1917 (Table 6-5). Thus, electrification started later but proceeded much faster in Japan.[14] The more rapid electrification in Japan was basically due to the fact that electric power became available to the manufacturing sector before mechanization had been completed. In particular, small-scale plants which had been largely untouched by the age of steam power, were

[14] The faster electrification in Japan was also a case in comparison with England. The share of primary electric power capacity in the total primary power capacity (H') is calculated as 4.2% in 1907, 9.7% in 1912 and 28.3% in 1924. H' is estimated as a total of power applied mechanically and of power applied electrically (Byatt 1979, pp. 74–76). This proportion is much smaller than that in both Japan (Table 6-4) and the United States (Table 6-8).

mechanized by means of electrification.

Table 6-9 gives for each industry group the year in which electric power and primary electric power exceeded steam power in the United States. The industrial differences in the speed of electrification which are shown in that table are similar to those found in Japan. For example, in both countries, electric power surpassed steam power first in printing and binding and last in wood and wood products. This similarity verifies our claim that the speed of electrication depends to a large extent on the characteristics of production technology distinct to each industry.

Chapter 7

ELECTRIFICATION

As was shown in the previous chapter, electrification proceeded very rapidly in Japan. Moreover, as will be seen in the seven chapters of part 3, electrification was the most influential among many technological advances in prewar Japanese manufacturing. To understand the nature of technological change in Japan, it is necessary, to explain the factors which led to electrification of manufacturing. There were essentially three main factors, which will be discussed in this chapter. First, electric motors offered specific advantages which other engines did not. Second, the development of electric utilities enabled electrification of manufacturing without resort to independent power plants. Third, import substitution of electric machinery including motors became possible with the growth of the domestic electric machinery industry.

The Advantages of Electric Motors

Divisibility of Power

There are two main distinguishing characteristics of electric motors: their variability in power capacity and their ease of operation. The former characteristic is known as "divisibility of power" and refers to the fact that electric motors can be produced with large or small power capacity, depending on the needs of the sources of demand. Other engines generally do not have this flexibility. For example, it is impractical to produce small steam engines because as engine capacity decreases, efficiency also decreases. For this reason, steam engines have not been employed outside of large-scale plants. Electric motors, however, remain highly efficient whatever their size.[1] Thus, divisibility of power gave the electric motor the advantage of unmatched versatility in competition with other motors. As Harold I. Sharlin has said,

> "Great electric motors can move mountains and miniscule motors can make fine adjustments on precision machinery, or cut whiskers."[2]

In Japan small electric motors became particularly widespread in two fields. The first was in small-scale plants, which had remained un-powered in the age of steam engines. The shift from human muscles to machines in these plants was made possible in part by the introduction of the internal combustion engine, but it was truly the versatility of the electric motor which was the most significant factor in the mechanization of these small plants. The second area of widespread application of the electric motor was in large plants which adopted the so-called unit-drive system. Rather than employing elaborate linkage systems to drive many machines from one power source they began using small electric motors to drive individual machines. The introduction of this unit-drive system was made possible precisely because of the divisibility of power of the electric motor.

The statistics on average power capacity by engine type shown in Table 7-1 demonstrate more concretely the consequences of divisibility of power. According to panel A, in manufacturing as a whole the average power capacity of the electric motor was always much smaller than that of the steam engine. After increasing from 1914 to 1930, the average size of electric motors showed a big decline between 1930 and 1935. If the data are reliable, this decline would be consistent with our argument that the diffusion of the unit-drive system in larger-scale plants and the electrification of smaller-scale plants were both carried out largely through the application of small electric motors. In contrast to the trend toward smaller-sized electric motors, average power capacity of gas engines increased between 1930 and 1935 and exceeded that of electric motors. The average size of oil engines was smaller than that of electric motors for 1909–30, but the subsequent decline in the average

[1] Mumford 1934, p. 223.
[2] Sharlin 1963, p. 171.

Table 7-1.   Average Power Capacity of Engines: 1909–1940

(hp)

Year Scale (persons)	Electric Motors	Steam Engines	Steam Turbines	Gas Engines	Oil Engines	Water Wheels
A. All Manufacturing, Average for All Scales						
1909	15	35	46	13	5	12
1914	14	41	84	19	5	35
1919	19	42	134	28	6	36
1930	22	44	844	38	14	15
1935	9	41	1,965	76	21	16
1940	8	64	3,888	70	14	41
B. All Manufacturing, by Factory Scale, 1940						
5– 9	4	17	9	21	8	7
10– 29	5	30	5	27	11	11
30– 49	7	35	150	42	17	16
50– 99	8	26	313	39	20	21
100–499	11	31	2,435	60	36	165
500–999	10	34	2,949	94	35	3,700
1,000 or more	7	297	5,456	1,777	66	2,512

Sources: Figures are power capacity divided by the number of engines. Figures for power capacity and the number of engines are from STF. See Table A-2.

power capacity of electric motors reversed this situation by 1935. Thus, by 1935 the electric motor was the smallest power source employed in manufacturing. (It does not make sense to compare here electric motors with water wheels, water turbines, or steam turbines, because these engines were used mainly for electric power generation.)

Panel B of Table 7-1 shows average power capacity by plant scale in the manufacturing sector in the year 1940. In the case of electric motors there is no striking correlation between motor size and factory scale. Average power capacity was 4 hp in the smallest-scale plants (5–9 persons) and 7 hp in the largest-scale plants (1,000 or more persons). For all other engines, however, the correlation is quite strong.

Table 7-2. Average Power Capacity of Electric Motors by Industry Group and by Factory Scale

(hp)

Industry Group Scale (persons)	1909	1914	1919	1930	1935	1940
A. By Industry Group						
All manufacturing	15	14	19	22	9	8
Textiles	17	11	17	20	8	6
Metals and metal products	9	18	22	21	23	20
Machinery	15	14	15	25	8	6
Ceramics	58	32	28	55	30	20
Chemicals	24	39	37	30	6	6
Wood and wood products	14	14	14	18	13	9
Printing and binding	4	3	3	7	3	3
Food	8	7	11	13	7	6
Miscellaneous	4	8	8	10	6	5
B. By Factory Scale						
All factories	15	14	19	22	9	8
5– 9	4	3	4	5	4	4
10– 29	5	5	7	8	6	5
30– 49	6	9	13	12	8	7
50– 99	11	13	18	16	10	8
100–499	20	18	26	32	16	11
500–999	19	53	29	38	12	10
1,000 or more	37	24	35	32	8	7

Sources: Same as Table 7-1.

Table 7-2 gives the time-series on average power capacity of the electric motor by industry group (panel A) and by factory scale (panel B). Two facts are revealed in panel A. First, average power capacity tended to decrease during the 1930s for all industry groups, and second, the industrial differential tended to narrow down as time passed. In 1909, for instance, the differential between the largest average power capacity (58 hp in ceramics) and the smallest (4 hp in both printing and

Table 7-3. Average Engine Prices: 1930–1945

Year	Electric Motors		Steam Engines		Steam Turbines		Internal Combustion Engines[a]	
	Ave. Price (yen)	Price Index	Ave. Price (yen)	Price Index	Ave. Price (yen)	Price Index	Ave. Price (yen)	Price Index
1930	128	1	3,951	31	58,476	457	217	2
1935	116	1	7,775	67	56,423	486	557	5
1940	354	1	8,894	25	106,549	301	1,033	3
1945	666	1	9,562	14	101,806	153	4,268	6

Sources: Value of output divided by the number of engines produced (Nippon, Tsūshō Sangyōshō 1962, pp. 193–96).
[a] Internal combustion engines include gasoline engines, oil engines, and heavy oil engines.

binding and miscellaneous) amounted to 54 hp. In 1940 the differential was only 17 hp (20 hp in both ceramics and metals and 3 hp in printing). This decrease in the differential occurred mainly because of a decrease in average power capacity in those industries which had large average power capacities in the early years of their development.

Panel B of Table 7-2 reveals two other facts. First, average power capacity tended to decline in large-scale factories in the 1920s and 1930s, whereas it was almost constant in smaller-scale factories. Second, there was a positive correlation between average power capacity and factory scale in the early years. In 1909, for instance, average power capacity ranged from 4 hp in the smallest-scale factories to 37 hp in the largest-scale factories. Thereafter this scale differential tended to narrow as a result of a decrease in average power capacity in the large factories.

Table 7-3 gives the average price of engines by type and a price index taking the price of electric motors as unity for the selected years. This table reveals that the motor was less expensive than either the steam engine or the internal combustion engine.

The findings from the above three tables may be summarized as follows. First, the electric motor was smaller in capacity and therefore less expensive on the average than all other engine types, especially the steam engine. Second, the average power capacity of the electric motor tended to decrease over time in almost all industry groups and in larger-scale plants. This decrease likely reflected the diffusion of the unit-drive system.

Ease of Operation

In addition to offering the advantage of divisibility of power, the electric motor is distinguished from other engines by its ease of operation. This motor can be started and stopped just by turning a switch, its speed is easily controlled, and it does not need skilled operators. In this respect, the electric motor contrasts sharply with the steam engine which needs to be operated by such special artisans as boilermen. Moreover, unlike all other types of engines the electric motor is rarely subject to engine trouble. If electric motors did not possess this characteristic, the unit-drive system might have never been developed in Japan, because the considerable difficulties involved· in maintaining a large number of unreliable motors would likely have proved to be prohibitive.

This operational convenience of the electric motor is, strictly speaking, the only characteristic of the three-phase alternating-current motor which was invented by Michael von Dolibo-Dobrowòlsky in 1889. This type of motor, compared with the earlier direct-current motor, was so simple in structure (it had no commutator) that it needed no special care. Also, it could easily be sealed and was therefore highly resistant to moisture and dust.[3] These advantages, coupled with the fact that alternating-current electricity was more suitable for transmission than direct-current, contributed to the wide diffusion of alternating-current motors in factories.[4] In short, the development of the alternating-current

[3] Bel'kind 1966, p. 610.
[4] Bel'kind 1966, p. 579.

technology was a decisive factor in the electrification of factories.[5]

The Growth of the Electric Utilities

Historical Background

Origin. The engineer Ichisuke Fujioka played an important role in the creation of electric utilities in Japan.[6] Fujioka, who had participated in the first lighting of electric lamps (arc lamps) in Japan in 1878, was at that time an Associate Professor at Kōbu University (University of Engineering). He proposed the establishment of an electric power company and tried to arrange financing for such a venture. Private enterprises at first were, however, sceptical of his proposition and were too timid to invest in this pioneering business. He therefore asked the help of Yasuzo Yamao, a high level government official who came from Fujioka's home province of Chōshū. Yamao recommended him to Sakuro Yajima, and the result was the establishment of the Tokyo Electric Light Company (TELC) in 1883 with the initial capital of 200,000 yen which was advanced by sixty four persons, among whom was Yajima himself as the largest shareholder. Other investors were of three types: aristocrats (for instance, Mochiaki Hachisuka and Muneki Date); businessmen with political affiliations (for instance, Eiichi Shibusawa and Kihachiro Okura); and wealthy rural merchants (for instance, Ichiroemon Kitani). Fujioka was appointed chief engineer and took charge of technical matters for the company. In other words, the electric industry is a typical case in which pioneering engineers and progressive government officials, in place of conservative capitalists, took an initiative in its establishment.

The business of TELC for 1883–86 was limited to construction of small-scale private facilities of generating and lighting electricity at

---

[5] Du Boff 1967, p. 509.

[6] For the history of electric utilities, we have referred to Arisawa 1960a, part 2; Gendai Nippon Sangyō Hattatsushi Kenkyūkai 1964a, part 1 and chronological table; and Tokyo Dentō K.K., 1936, pp. 1–224.

factories such as the Yokosuka Shipyard, the Bank of Tokyo, the printing office of the government, the Sangenya Plant of Osaka Spinning Company and others. It was in 1887 that TELC completed the Nihonbashi Power Plant and began to supply electricity to the public. In this plant a 25-kW direct-current dynamo was driven by a 30-hp steam engine. During 1888–90 four other generating plants were erected. Total power capacity of steam engines in these five plants amounted to 945 and theses plants lit 9,600 of incadescent lamps and 135 of arc lamps.[7]

Once TELC had shown the way, electric light companies began to appear in larger cities throughout Japan. For instance in 1887 electric light companies were erected in Kobe, Kyoto and Osaka, and in 1889 they appeared in Nagoya and Yokohama. As a result the number of electric companies reached to thirty three in 1896. The total number of electric lamps installed by these companies amounted to 116,406.[8]

Thermal generation. At first electricity in Japan was produced by burning coal to create heat to turn the generator. TELC in the early years, for instance, had individual small-scale thermal electric generation plants scattered in various districts. However, in 1895 TELC established the Asakusa Thermal Generation Plant as a central station. Plants that had previously generated electricity were then transformed into distribution stations. In the central station four one-hundred-cycle alternators made by the Ishikawajima Shipyard and six three-phase, fifty-cycle alternators from Germany were installed. Total capacity of these alternators was 2,400 kW. The alternators imported from Germany were the origin of the fifty-cycle alternating current standard in the eastern half of Japan. In western Japan, on the other hand, sixty-cycle current became standard after the Osaka Electric Light Company imported alternators from the United States in 1897.[9] The consequent coexistence of two different electric generation systems has caused considerable inconvenience and diseconomies for the country as a whole, and still

[7] Arisawa 1960a, p. 101.

[8] Gendai Nippon Sangyō Hattatsushi Kenkyūkai 1964a, table 16 on p. 35.

[9] It was in 1889 that Osaka Electric Light Company started alternating current generation with 125-cycle alternators imported from the United States.

does so today. Several attempts at integration have been made, but in vain.

Hydro-generation. Hydro-electric power was first generated in Japan in 1890 by Shimotsuke Hemp Spinning and Ashio Copper Mining, each of which established facilities for their own use. The first hydro-electric plant to supply the public was the Keage Power Plant of Kyoto City. The opening of this plant in 1891 was, along with the establishment of TELC, a momentous event in the history of electricity in Japan.

In 1883 Kyoto City issued a prospectus of constructing the aquaducts from the Lake Biwa to the city to facilitate water transportation, turn water wheels (616 hp in total), and supply water for daily use and agriculture.[10] In this prospectus relative advantages of water wheels over steam engines were emphasized. One of the most important advantage was, according to the prospectus, the savings in coal consumption. They estimated that the annual savings of coal would amount to more than 120,000 yen (coal needed to operate 616-hp steam engines). Other advantages listed were freedom from air pollution by smoke, ease and safety in operation and ready start (it took long time to boil water in the case of steam engines). This plan was along the energy policy of the Meiji government to save coal and to exploit abundant water resources (chapter 2). Kyoto City started the construction in 1885 and completed it in 1890.

In the process of construction Sakuo Tanabe, a graduate of Kōbu University and the initiator and chief engineer of this project, proposed that the aquaducts also be used for hydro-electric generation. His idea as well as the hydro-generation by Ashio Copper Mining was influenced by the hydro-generation at the Aspen Silver Mine in Colorado in the United States. After investigating the Aspen Silver Mine in 1888, Tanabe constructed the Keage Power Plant. This plant was much larger than the plant of Aspen (equipped with a 150-hp Pelton wheel); it was powered by two Pelton wheels and nineteen direct-current dynamos (1,785 kW in total). The electricity produced was used for electric lighting and to power industries such as weaving and an electric railway.

[10]   For the prospectus we owe to Yoshida 1974, p. 29.

Later substitution of alternators for direct-current dynamos enabled expanded coverage of transmission. The total capacity of electric motors run by this hydro-electric power plant increased from 36 hp in 1891 to 2,209 hp in 1899.[11]

Following the Keage Power Plant a number of small-scale hydro-generating plants were established in the mountainous districts with abundant water falls. For instance the Hakone Electric Light Generating Plant, the Nikko Electric Power Company, and the Maebashi Electric Light Company appeared during 1892–94. An epochal event at the end of the last century was the hydro-generation by the Hiroshima Hydro-Electric Company established by Shibusawa in 1897. Under the guidance of authorities on electric engineering like Tanabe and Fujioka the company erected the Hiro Generating Plant equipped with three Pelton wheels (300 hp in each) and three three-phase alternators (250 kW in each) succeeded in the long-distance (26 km) and high voltage (11 kV) transmission to Hiroshima City in 1899. This event is usually taken as the beginning of the long-distance transmission in Japn. The hydro-generating power of all electric utilities reached at 31% of total generating power in 1905 (column 11 of Table 7-4).

Demand for electricity. In the early Meiji period electricity was utilized exclusively for electric lighting. At first, even the demand for electric light was very limited; eventually in Tokyo it was limited to office buildings of the government and big enterprises, and to busy quarters of the city: *yūkaku* (red-light districts like Yoshiwara) and *hanamachi* (districts crowded with geisha-houses like Tsukiji). Yoshiwara especially was a good customer for electric companies. One of the aforementioned five generating plants of TELC was established in 1888 to supply electricity exclusively to Yoshiwara.

Because of the high economic efficiency of electric lighting compared with traditional lamps, however, electric lighting became popular gradually. A report in 1926 demonstrates that electric lighting was much more efficient than *tōmyō* (tapers), *andon* (paper-covered lamps), and Japanese lamps, in terms of both mean candlepower and the hourly cost

[11] Gendai Nippon Sangyō Hattatsushi Kenkyūkai 1964a, table 14 on p. 34.

Table 7-4.   Generating Power of Electric Utilities: 1905–1940

| Year | Generating Power | | | Ratio of Hydro to Total (%) |
	Total	Hydro (1,000 kW)	Thermal	
1905	39	12	27	30.8
1910	161	79	82	49.1
1915	569	395	174	69.4
1920	951	658	293	69.2
1925	2,167	1,562	605	72.1
1930	3,961	2,815	1,146	71.1
1935	5,137	3,309	1,828	64.4
1940	7,881	4,997	2,884	63.4

Sources: Minami 1965, p. 206.

per candlepower (Table 7-5). Consequently the number of electric lamps installed by public utilities increased rapidly in the 1890s (Table 7-6).

Also the demand for electric power seemed to increase remarkably in the course of industrialization, which created an increase in energy consumption. The increasing trend can be estimated from the increasing trend in the power capacity of primary electric motors (motors driven by electric power purchased from electric utilities) in the manufacturing sector (Fig. 6-1). As a result of this trend, in 1907 electric power consumption occupied 36% of total electric consumption (column 12 of Table 7-7).

Diffusion of hydro-generation. It was at the turn of the century that hydro-generation of electricity began to become widespread. Table 7-4 shows that the percentage of hydro-electric power in total generating power increased from 31 in 1905 to 70 in 1915–30. Furthermore, column 11 of Table 7-7 demonstrates that the percentage of hydro-electric power generated in total electric power generated reached about 90 in 1915–30.

The diffusion of hydro-generation was attributed to the higher

Table 7-5. Comparison of Economic Efficiency of Lamps by
Type: 1926

Lamps	Mean Candlepower (1)	Hourly Cost (2)	Hourly Cost per Candlepower (3)=(2)/(1)
Traditional		(sen)	(sen)
Tōmyō	0.25	0.50	2.000
Andon	0.2	0.50	2.500
Japanese candle	0.5	2.50	3.100
Modern			
Western candle	0.9	0.90	1.000
Lantern (with Western candle)	0.6	0.90	1.500
Kerosene lamp (15 mm wick)	3.2	0.38	0.120
Acetylene lamp	16.0	1.50	0.093
Gas lamp (rated 20 candlepower)	20.0	0.60	0.030
Carbon electric bulb (rated 10 candlepower)	8.5	0.57	0.067
Tungsten electric bulb (rated 24 candlepower)	18.0	0.45	0.025
Gas filled electric bulb (40 W)	30.0	0.65	0.021

Sources: Gendai Nippon Sangyō Hattatsushi Kenkyūkai 1964a, table 40 on p. 65.

economic efficiency than thermal-generation. This is evident from a
comparison of electric lighting rates and power rates between the two
methods of power generation in 1900.[12] The monthly electric lighting
rate for a 16-candlepower bulb was 1.00 yen (Kyoto) and 0.95 yen
(Fukushima) in hydro-generation, compared to 3.00 yen (Tokyo) and
1.70 yen (Osaka) in thermal-generation. Furthermore the monthly
electric power rate for a 30-hp motor was 115 yen (Kyoto) in hydro-
generation, while 420 yen (Tokyo) and 200 yen (Osaka) in thermal-

[12] Gendai Nippon Sangyō Hattatsushi Kenkyūkai 1964a, table 35 on p. 56.

Table 7-6.   Number of Electric Lights: 1890–1940

(1,000)

1890	21
1895	89
1900	217
1905	464
1910	1,949
1915	7,538
1920	16,138
1925	27,321
1930	36,840
1935	43,231
1940	54,083

Sources: Minami 1965, p. 69.
Notes: Figures are numbers of lights installed only by electric utilities.

generation. Such relative efficiency of hydro-generation seemed to have increased because of two factors: an increase in coal prices and technological progress in hydro-generation. These factors will be explained later.

Demand for electric lighting increased by means of the substitution for the other modern lighting; kerosene and gas lamps. Just after kerosene and gas lamps were introduced to Japan, they were mainly used respectively at home and in the streets. Furthermore the importation of gas mantles in 1896 realized a wide utilization of gas lamps at shops and residential houses. Thus gas lamps were predominant over kerosene lamps and electric lighting until the end of Meiji period.

However a decrease in electric lighting rates and an improvement of electric bulbs, especially with the appearance of tungsten bulbs, gave rise to a substantial diffusion of electric lighting. As is shown in Table 7-6 the number of electric lamps installed by public utilities increased very fast especially since the 1910s. Consequently the number of gas lamps began to decrease after a peak in 1917. The substitution of electric lights for the other modern lamps, was largely attributable to the higher economic

155

Table 7-7. Electric Power Generation and Consumption: 1907–1940

(million kWH)

Year	Electric Utilities and Industrial Plants		Electric Utilities						Ratio (%)			
	Genera-tion	Consump-tion	Generation			Consumption						
			Total	Hydro	Thermal	Total	Light	Power	(3)/(1)	(6)/(2)	(4)/(3)	(7)/(6)
	(1)	(2)	(3)	(4)	(5)	(6)	(7)	(8)	(9)	(10)	(11)	(12)
1907	277	233	193		211	149	95	54	69.7	63.9		63.7
1910	621	523	427			329	227	102	68.8	62.9		69.0
1915	2,217	1,802	1,811	1,600	211	1,396	800	596	81.7	77.5	88.3	57.3
1920	4,669	3,795	3,815	3,166	649	2,941	1,548	1,393	81.7	77.5	83.0	52.6
1925	9,093	7,322	7,735	6,742	993	5,964	2,341	3,623	85.1	81.5	87.2	39.3
1930	15,773	12,618	14,034	12,525	1,509	10,878	2,780	8,098	89.0	86.2	89.2	25.6
1935	24,698	19,393	22,155	18,454	3,701	17,389	2,800	14,589	89.7	89.7	83.3	16.1
1940	34,566	28,576	30,603	23,646	6,957	24,614	2,900	21,714	88.5	86.1	77.3	11.8

Sources: Columns 1, 3, 4 and 5: Minami 1965, pp. 196–97.
Columns 2, 6, 7 and 8: Minami 1965, pp. 198–99.

156

efficiency of electric lighting. According to Table 7-5 electric bulbs are more efficient than kerosene and gas lamps both in mean candle power and in the hourly cost per candle power.

Demand for electric power increased much faster than that of electric light. As columns 7 and 8 of Table 7-7 show, electric consumption for lighting increased thirty-fold from 1907 to 1940, while consumption of electric power per se, excluding electric lighting, increased by a tremendous four-hundred-fold. Consequently the share of electric power consumption increased from 36% in 1907 to 88% in 1940 (column 12 of the same table). The increasing trend in electric power consumption is correspondent to the increasing trend in the power capacity of primary electric motors in manufacturing industries (Fig. 6-1).

In short, the demand shift from electric lighting to electric power and the technological shift from thermal-generation to hydro-generation combined to stimulate rapid development of electric utilities in Japan. Thus, the relative contribution of electric utilities in total power generated (kWH), shown in column 9 of Table 7-7, reached about 70% in the first decade of the 1900s and about 90% in the 1930s. Due to the progress made by the utilities, electric power became available to factories throughout the country; this in turn stimulated the substitution of electric power for other sources of power in production.

Electric power and lighting rates. The substitution of electric power for other sources of power was also encouraged by a relative decline in the electric power rate compared with other power costs. In order to substantiate this argument we must first examine the changes in the electric power rate itself, in comparison with electric lighting rate. Prior to 1932 electric light and power rates were not under government control but were determined by generating costs and supply-demand conditions. Table 7-8 shows the average rates of electric lighting and power.[13] It

[13]   Indexes of electric light and power estimated from electric rates tables of individual electric utilities are conceptually superior to these average-rates estimates. The reason for not using the former is that in the period of oversupply after World War I, electric power was sold at much lower rates than indicated in the table of charges, so indexes based on the tables would probably substantially overestimate the actual rates during this period.

Table 7-8. Electric Utility Rates and Coal Prices: 1905–1940

Year	Average Electric Light Rate (yen/1,000 kWH)	Average Electric Power Rate	Wholesale Price Index of Coal (1934–36 = 1)
1905	85.1[a]	20.2[a]	0.42
1910	69.4	30.0	0.42
1915	50.5	30.0	0.44
1920	72.4	66.3	1.44
1925	88.9	55.6	1.00
1930	98.8	38.0	0.86
1935	105.9	29.4	1.00
1940	112.4	37.6	1.48

Sources: Electricity rates: Minami 1965, p. 222. Coal price: Arisawa 1960a, pp. 10–11 of appendix tables.
[a]   Data for 1907.

appears from these figures that in the period between 1907 and 1915 the average rate for electric lighting decreased, while the power rate increased. However, this increase in power rates was a superficial trend resulting from statistical and methodological problems in estimation. In reality, the rate for electric power seems also to have declined during this period.[14] The fall in power rates was the result of a decrease in generating costs accompanying the introduction of hydro-generation and the success of high-voltage transmission after the Russo-Japanese War. In 1908 TELC cut lighting rates by 12% and power rates by 22% because of a sharp drop in generating costs which in turn was due to the completion of the Komabashi Power Plant in 1907. Aggressive competition among utilities accelerated the decline in all electric rates. In Tokyo, for instance, in 1907 there were three competing suppliers of electric power: TELC, Tokyo City government, and the Tokyo Electric Railways Company.

[14]   The index for electric power rates estimated by Fujino (1965, statistical note 4) did show a decline during this period.

Table 7-9. Comparison of Electric Utility Rates to General
Price Indexes: 1907–1940

(1934–36 = 1)

Year	Ratio of Electric Lighting Rate[a]	Ratio of Electric Power Rate[b]
1907	1.38	0.25
1910	1.21	0.40
1915	0.87	0.37
1920	0.50	0.34
1925	0.68	0.38
1930	0.95	0.39
1935	1.06	0.30
1940	0.86[c]	0.23

Sources: Electricity rates: Table 7-8. Consumer price index: Ohkawa *et al.* 1967, pp. 135–36. Manufacturing output price index: Ohkawa *et al.* 1967, pp. 192–93.
[a] Average electric lighting rate divided by consumer price index.
[b] Average electric power rate divided by manufacturing output price index.
[c] 1938 data.

TELC reduced its rates when the Yatsuzawa Power Plant started operating in 1912. After a trough in 1915 (at which time the average electric power rate was 30 yen per 1,000 kWH), rates began to rise in response to strong demand caused by the economic boom during and after World War I. The upward trend of power rates during these inflation years (1915–19) was much larger than the increase in lighting rates. As a result, the ratio of the electric power rate to the manufacturing output price index shown in Table 7-9 remained almost constant, while the ratio of the lighting rate to the consumer price index decreased for 1915–20.

During the recession years after the war boom lighting and power rates showed different patterns of change. The lighting rate continued to rise during this period. It went from 72 yen per 1,000 kWH in 1920 to 99 yen in 1930. Consequently, the ratio of the lighting rate to the consumer price index increased. The power rate on the other hand declined from a peak in 1923 (69 yen per 1,000 kWH) and returned to its 1916 level in 1932. This decline was caused by aggressive price cutting by electric utilities trying to dry up excess supply.[15]

There were two reasons for this oversupply of electric power. The first was a technical one: hydro-electric plants at that time did not have dams and thus could not control seasonal variations in water flow. Consequently, the need to have sufficient generating capacity to meet peak loads in periods of water shortage necessarily gave rise to oversupply under normal conditions. The second reason was a decrease in the growth of industrial demand during the depression of the 1920s and early 30s.[16] The oversupply of electricity reduced prices, which created new sources of demand. More small factories in manufacturing began using electric power and electrochemical industries producing ammonium sulphate and employing electrolysis were originated at that time. The appearance of these new users lessened the financial difficulties of the electric utilities.

Differences in pattern of changes between the lighting rate and the power rate are explained by differences in the price elasticities of demand. Electric lighting consumption, which is inelastic, does not decrease much in response to a rise in its rate contrary to the price elastic consumption of electric power. Therefore the pricing policies of the utilities were to stimulate demand for electric power by reducing its price and to compensate for the loss of profits by increasing the lighting rate. In this way a large difference between the two rates appeared in the

[15]   There was also competition among electric suppliers in Nagoya. Thus, electric rates were much cheaper in Tokyo and Nagoya than in other areas. Tsunehiko Watanabe has pointed out that this may explain the unusually high number of small-scale enterprises in these two cities. The hypothesis that geographical differences in the price of electricity were related to the geographical distribution of small firms merits empirical testing.

[16]   Of these two oversupply factors, the first seems to have been much more influential. Electric light and power generated, shown in Table 7-7, column 3, continued to increase during the years after the war boom. But electric generating capacity, shown in Table 7-4, increased even faster. Consequently, the ratio of generating capacity to power generated, a proxy for the capital-output ratio in the electric utilities, increased from 1920 to 1930. This ratio changed with movements in economic activity. A study on the capital-output ratio in the electric utilities has been made in Minami 1965, pp. 81–82.

1920s.[17]

Since 1932, the year in which the electric power cartel was established, rates have been under government control. Under this control, rates for electric lighting and power were not permitted to increase out of line with other price indexes. In fact the ratio of the electric lighting rate to the consumer price index decreased from 1935 to 1940, and the ratio of the electric power rate to the manufacturing output price index also declined from 1930 to 1940 (Table 7-9).

While differences in the relative price of electric lighting and electric power led to differences in demand between these two uses of electricity, the price of coal was also an important factor in the overall demand for electric power. Changes in the price of coal affected the substitution of electric power for steam. The coal price index in Table 7-8 shows a sharp increase after 1915. Consequently, the ratio of the electric power rate to the coal price, shown in Table 7-10, began to decline remarkably in the middle of 1920s. One of the basic causes of this decline seems to be that technological progress was much faster in the electric utilities than in coal mining. Relative labor productivity, calculated in Table 7-10, rose continually from 1910 to 1940. Thus, the difference in the rate of technological progress between electric utilities and coal mining accelerated the substitution of electric power for steam power.[18]

Technological progress. Technological progress in the electric utilities was vitally important in Japanese economic development by stimulating the electrification of the manufacturing sector which in turn generated further technological advances. This technological progress in electric

---

[17]   It should be emphasized that this difference has continued even to the present day for number of reasons. First, there was a difference in transmission cost coming from differences in voltage requirements. (Large users take high voltages and are often closer to the thermal power stations.) Second, large companies often consume most of their electricity late at night. Third and most important was the intention of the government to stimulate industrial development. Such an energy policy is possible basically because of the difference in the price elasticity between electric light and power.

[18]   The substitution of electric power for steam power did not necessarily mean a reduction in the use of coal, since thermal generation of electricity depended heavily on coal. Such a transformation in energy sources is worth further study.

Table 7-10. Comparison of Prices and Labor Productivity in
Electric Utilities and Coal Mining: 1907–1940

(1934–36 = 1)

Year	Price[a] Ratio	Productivity[b] Ratio
1907	1.56	
1910	2.43	0.22
1915	2.32	0.40
1920	1.61	0.71
1925	1.89	0.76
1930	1.50	0.96
1935	1.00	1.00
1940	0.86	1.33

Sources: Electric power rate, coal price: Table 7-7. Electric power generated per
employee: Minami 1965, p. 207. Number of employees in coal mining and coal
output: Arisawa 1960a, pp. 10–11 of appendix tables.
[a] Average electricity power rate divided by wholesale price index of coal.
[b] Electric power generated per employee divided by coal produced per employee.

utilities was entirely dependent on borrowed technology. Electric generation and transmission techniques were introduced from abroad, and tools and machinery were all imported. Two TELC plants provide examples of the extent of reliance on foreign technology. The Komabashi Power Plant (15,000 kW), completed in 1907, employed water wheels, generators, and transformers, and distributing boards which were imported from Switzerland, Germany, and the United States. The Inawashiro Hydro Plant (37,500 kW) in 1914 was also equipped almost entirely with imports: water wheels from Germany, generators from England, and transformers, transmission towers, and insulators from the United States. Electric wire was the only domestically produced equipment used in this plant.

The introduction of electric technologies, which involved importation of entire plants, was much easier than the importation of manufacturing technologies. This was especially true in the case of electric utilities, which were considered to be so easy to manage that ex-samurai with no previous experience could handle the business, if enough capital were advanced. Consequently the time lag in introducing newly developed western electric technologies into Japan was very short. For example, TELC began to supply electricity to the public in 1887, only five years after the world's first public power station was established by the Edison Electric Company at Pearl St. in New York. Also, Japan was only nine years behind the United States in establishing a hydro-electric power plant for public use. The first such plant was erected in Appleton, Wisconsin in 1882, while the Keage Power Plant in Japan was completed in 1891. The high-voltage (115 kV) and long-distance (228 km) transmission between the Inawashiro facility of TELC and Tokyo is a further example of Japan's early introduction of up-to-date electric technologies. This transmission line, completed in 1914, was the third longest in the world at the time.

The Growth of the Electric Machine Industry

History before WWI

Pioneers. Like the electric light industry, pioneering engineers played decisive roles in establishing the electric machine industry.[19] Among them, Hisashige Tanaka, Ichisuke Fujioka, Shoichi Miyoshi and Hosui Shigemune were leading examples.

Tanaka, who was popular as the greatest *karakurishi* (traditional inventor and producer of machines) at the late Tokugawa and the early Meiji period, established the Tanaka Factory in 1875. This factory supplied telegraphic instruments to the government. This is the beginning of the electric machine industry in Japan. Later this factory shifted to the production of munitions. But in 1893 the factory was purchased by Mitsui Zaibatsu, and as the Shibaura Factory returned to the production of electric instruments.

[19] For the history of electric machine industry we have relied on Arisawa 1960c, part 4; Gendai Nippon Sangyō Hattatsushi Kenkyūkai 1964a, part 1.

Fujioka was one of the students at Kōbu University who, with the help of English professor named W. E. Ayrton, succeeded in lighting the first arc lamp in Japan by electricity generated by the battery for fifteen minutes. This was in 1878, 76 years after the discovery of the principle of arc light by Sir Humphry Davy and one year before the lighting of incandescent electric lamps by Thomas Alva Edison for two hours. Later Fujioka not only taught electric engineering at Kōbu University but also established electric industries. Besides initiating TELC, he made great contributions in establishing the electric machinery industry. At first, he and Miyoshi established the Hakunetsu Company to produce incandescent electric lamps in 1890. The Hakunetsu Company was not successful in business in the early years because of low level of production technology and the pressure of imports of electric blubs. It produced only 10-15 bulbs a day in 1891 and only about 240 bulbs in 1895. The price of bulbs was twice higher than that of imports and the quality was decisively inferior. This company, which changed its name to Tokyo Electric in 1896, decided to aquire capital and technological tie-ups with the General Electric of the United States in 1905. Since then the company showed a steady development. (Tokyo Electric and Shibaura Factory were united as Tokyo Shibaura Electric or Toshiba in 1939). Consequently imports of electric bulbs began to decrease and disappeared at the beginning of the 1910s. Secondly, Fujioka guided Miyoshi in producing heavy electric equipment.

Miyoshi, who had been a telegraphic engineer, established the Miyoshi Electric Factory in 1884. This was the first plant to produce heavy electric equipment in Japan. Miyoshi received strong engineering support from Fujioka, who was from the same province. Japan's first 15-kW direct-current dynamo, produced by this factory on the demand of the Yamaguchi Spinning Plant, lit incandescent lamps at the opening ceremony of the assembly hall of the Bank of Japan in 1885 for the purpose of trial use of the dynamo and of demonstration of electric lighting to the public. Since then its products were installed at various workshops of industries by TELC and at the generating plants of TELC. For instance the Nihonbashi Power Plant was equipped with a 25-kW dynamo of this factory in 1887. However the factory, suffering from the depression, closed its short lift in 1898.

Shigemune, one of seven apprentices of Miyoshi, established the Meiden Sha in 1897. It enjoyed increasing success in the production and sales of dynamos and electric motors. By introducing a monthly payment plan and a lease system, Shigemune stimulated the purchase of "Meiden Motors" by small and medium establishments in a wide range of industries including rice polishing, printing, and wood working.

Followers. Following these pioneering firms established by individual engineers, several factories to repair and produce heavy electric machinery appeared as annexes to the big companies since the 1890s and before WWI. They are the factories of the Ishikawajima Shipyard (1894), the Mitsubishi Shipyard (1906), and the Kuhara Mining (1911). Later the factories of Mitsubishi and Kuhara became independent as Mitsubishi Electric (1921) and the Hitachi Factory (1920) respectively.

The level of technology of both the pioneers and the followers was very low. Their products were merely imitations of imports with inferior quality with respect to imports. Let us take as an example the memorable products of the Ishikawajima Shipyard, four single-phase 200 kW alternators, which were installed in 1894 at the first large-scale generation plant of TELC, the Asakusa Thermal Generation Plant. But the user complained that the alternator was inefficient and easily led to accidents. Consequently TELC had to use imports in the expansion of the plant. That is, technological progress in the electric machine industry was too slow to keep up with the rapid developments in the electric utilities. Hence these Japanese producers made mainly small-capacity, low-voltage machinery.

History since WWI

Impact of the war. It is well-known that World War I (1914–15) had a positive impact on the development of various industries in Japn. The impact was decisive in the case of electric machinery production. Firstly, industrialization, which was accelerated by the expanding foreign market, increased the demand for machinery. An evidence for this is that both the share of export and that of fixed capital formation in GNE increased during and after WWI. In 1910 these shares were 15.1% and 17.5% respectively, while in 1920 they became 18.9% and 20.0% respectively.[20] Secondly, electrification proceeded with full-scale in manufacturing and railways during the 1910s and 1920s and stimulated electric machine production.

Thirdly, the import pressure by Western countries eventually disappeared; import from Germany stopped immediately because of the war and import from the United States became gradually difficult. This event stimulated the development of the Japanese electric machine production in two ways. First, it expanded the domestic and foreign market for the Japanese product. Second, it raised the technological level of the Japanese industry. That is, Japanese industry began to produce large-capacity machinery, which had been supplied exclusively from foreign countries. For instance, the Hitachi Factory succeeded in accepting an order of a 10,000 hp water turbine from the Tone Electric Generating Company in 1915. This was because a turbine, which had been ordered from the German Company, could not be brought to Japan. Its production was an epoch-making event for the Hitachi Factory, because the capacity of its previous products had not exceeded 1,000 hp.

Development since the war. As is shown in Table 7-11, domestic production of motors, dynamos, converters, transformers, and rectifiers increased conspicuously from 1906–10 to 1911–15 and still more to 1916–20. This occurred in spite of small increases in imports of motors and dynamos. Import substitution occurred sometime in the mid-1910s. Table 7-12 shows the percentage of domestic products among various categories of electric machinery installed in Japan. Unlike Table 7-11, this data is biased toward large-capacity and high-voltage machinery. For the period 1922–27, only 3% of steam turbines installed were domestic machines, while 54% of transformers installed were Japanese products. The proportion of all categories of domestic machines increased thereafter. The percentage of domestic steam turbines, for

[20] Figures are seven-year moving averages. Ohkawa *et al.* 1974, p. 178.

Table 7-11. Annual Imports and Domestic Output of Electric
Machinery: 1883–1940

(1,000 yen)

Year	Imports		Domestic Output		
	Motors and Dynamos	Other[a]	Motors and Dynamos	Converters, Transformers, and Rectifiers	Other[b]
1883– 85		3			
1886– 90		111			
1891– 95		204			
1896–1900	119	934			
1901– 05	1,151	737			
1906– 10	1,648	1,886	2,135[c]		902[c]
1911– 15	3,027	1,599	13,292[d]		8,042[d]
1916– 20	3,768	1,263	64,661[e]		55,269[e]
1921– 25	13,743	9,758	68,995		66,552
1926– 30	7,589	9,003	87,791		98,368
1931– 35	1,838	3,735	32,751	58,575	91,892
1936– 40	2,237	5,214	117,810	250,109	422,643

Sources: Imports: Figures for 1909–33 are taken from Tōyō Keizai Shinpōsha 1935, pp. 310–22. Figures for 1934–40 are taken from Nippon, Ōkurashō 1934, vol. 3, pp. 222–25 and 256–59; 1935, vol. 3, pp. 248–51 and 290–93; 1936, vol. 3, pp. 218–21 and 256–59; 1937, vol. 3, pp. 232–35 and 276–79; 1938, vol. 3, pp. 236–39 and 280–83; 1939, vol. 1, pp. 915–21; 1940, vol. 1, pp. 823–29. Domestic output: Figures for 1909–26 are taken from STF 1926, p. 513. Figures for 1927–35 are taken from STF 1935, pp. 839–41. Figures for 1936–40 are taken from STF 1940, vol. 1, pp. 328–32 (see Table A-2).
[a] Meters, batteries, wire and wireless apparatus, transformers, and other electric tools and machinery.
[b] Electric fans, electric heaters, insulated wire, cables, wire and wireless apparatus, batteries, and other electric tools and machinery.
[c] Figure for 1909.
[d] Figure for 1914.
[e] Figure for 1919 and 1920.

Table 7-12. Share of Domestic Products in Total Electric
Machinery Installed

(percent of kilowatts)

Electric Machinery	Year of Installation		
	1922 -1927	1928 -1932	1933 -1937
Water wheels	34.51	52.16	78.81
Hydro generators	41.27	58.28	85.65
Steam turbines	2.83	18.28	76.74
Turbine generators	12.17	20.17	79.49
Transformers	53.95	75.08	99.46

Sources: Hitachi Seisakujo 1960, table 1-2 on p. 6.

Table 7-13. Shares of Electric Machine Production in Total
Machine Production and in Total Manufacturing
Production

Year	Percentage of Electric Machine in	
	Machinery	Manufacturing
1909	2.7	0.2
1914	5.9	0.5
1919–20	3.7	0.4
1921–25	18.3	1.5
1926–30	21.0	1.8
1931–35	16.6	1.8
1936–40	16.2	3.1

Sources: Nippon, Tsūshō Sangyōshō 1961, pp. 5, 13, 131, 133.
Notes: Figures are for the private factories with five or more production workers.

instance, rose to 18 for 1928–32 and reached 77 for 1933–37. Thus, by
the early 1930s demand for large-scale electric machinery was almost
entirely met by domestic production. Also Table 7-13 demonstrates the

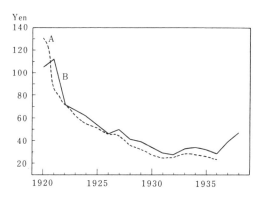

Fig. 7-1.   Price Trends for Standard One-Horsepower Electric
Motors

Sources: A: Hitachi Seisakujo 1960, fig. 5-5 on p. 118.
   B: Unpublished data from Hitachi.
Notes: 'A' indicates the unit price of induction motors and 'B' indicates the unit
price of single-phase repulsion motors.

increasing shares of electric machine production both in the total
machinery production and in the total manufacturing production for the
1920s and 1930s. That is, the relative importance of the electric machine
industry was elevated significantly after WWI.

Borrowed technology also predominated in the development of the
Japanese machinery industry. Almost all the major electric manufacturers had technological tie-ups with foreign manufacturers.[21] The first
affiliation was made between the Shibaura Factory and General Electric
in 1909. The steady growth of Shibaura since the affiliation lured
Mitsubishi Electric to have a foreign partner, since its products were
inferior to the products of Shibaura. Mitsubishi decided to have tie-ups
with Westinghouse of the United States in 1923. Furukawa Zaibatsu,
which had not had any experience in electric machine production,
established Fuji Electric in affiliation with Siemens of Germany in 1923.

Hitachi, the only major unaffiliated electric manufacturer at this time,

[21]   The introduction of Western technologies in electric machinery industry during the
inter-war period has been studied by Kozo Yamamura (1978).

finally introduced boiler technology from the Yarrow Shipyard of England in 1927, and turbine technology from AEG (Allgemeine Elektricitäts-Gesellschaft) of Germany in 1931. With imported production technologies, the capacity and voltage of Japanese products increased.

Another significant development within this industry in the late 1910s and early 1920s was the beginning of mass producction of standard small-capacity motors. Hitachi began to produce this type of motor at its Kameido Plant in 1918, and Tokyo Shibaura began production in 1919.[22] Figure 7-1 demonstrates that the price of Hitachi's one-hp electric motors declined sharply after 1920. This decline undoubtedly made electric power more accessible to smaller plants.[23]

In summary, the development of the domestic electric machine industry, though slower than that of the electric utilities, encouraged the electrification of manufacturing plants by providing electric machinery which was considerably less expensive than imports.

[22]   Tokyo Shibaura Denki K.K. 1963, p. 651.
[23]   Chūshō Kigyō Chōsakai 1960, p. 21.

PART III

THE IMPACT OF THE POWER REVOLUTION

In the preceding three chapters we have drawn a picture of the power revolution which occurred with the industrialization of the Japanese economy. We examined in detail three aspects of that revolution: the rapid increases, particularly during the first two decades of the twentieth century, in the proportion of powered factories and thus in the degree of mechanization of Japanese manufacturing; the expansion of total power capacity, which proceeded briskly throughout the period of industrialization; and the adaptation of manufacturing to more efficient, more modern sources of power through the transition from water to steam to electric engines. In examining these changes we implicitly viewed the power revolution as a natural outgrowth of the ongoing process of industrialization. We have often noted particular instances in which changes in power utilization were dependent on the level of industrial development or on the distinctive production characteristics of a given industry.

Thus, in terms of the central object of this book—to demonstrate the ways in which industrialization and power utilization mutually reinforce one another—up to this point we have foucused primarily on one side of this relationship, the changes in power utilization arising from industrial growth. Now, in the next seven chapters, we will take a different point of view and consider how changes in power utilization affected industrial growth. We will reveal the impact of the power revolution by examining the mechanization of non-powered factories and the transition of power capacity by engine type for selected industries. In addition, we will explore both the effects of these changes in power utilization on production technology and the consequences of such technological change on the growth of the industries involved.

Chapter 8

THE SILK-REELING INDUSTRY

This and the next two chapters treat the impact of the power revolution in three of Japan's textile industries—silk reeling, spinning, and weaving. It is widely known that textiles played a major role in Japan's economic growth before World War II. In quantitative terms, their contribution to the growth of manufacturing output was 34.9% for 1877–1900, 28.9% for 1900–20, and 21.6% for 1920–38 (Table 1-2). Furthermore, as was indicated in Table 4-2, this industry group had the largest number of factories among nine major industry categories. Textile factories comprised 45.9% of all manufacturing factories in 1909 and 25.2% in 1940. This proportion was undoubtedly over 50% during the years prior to 1909.

The growth of the textile industries motivated the take-off and stimulated the ensuing development of the modern Japanese economy primarily by giving rise to import substitution and by contributing significantly to export expansion.[1] According to panel A of Table 8-1, output of raw silk, cotton and other yarn, and finished fabric increased tremendously from 1874 to 1940. The proportion of these textile products in total manufacturing output increased markedly from 16.1% in 1874 to about 30% in 1900–20, although it then decreased to 12.0% in 1940. Panel B of the same table illustrates the important contribution of the textile industry to export expansion. The share of textile products in total merchandised exports was nearly 25% in 1890 and rose to more than 50% in 1910–30.

[1] Refer to Minami 1986, pp. 130–35 for a detailed discussion.

Table 8-1. Value of Output and Exports of Textile Products: 1868–1940

(million yen)

Year	Raw Silk	Cotton Yarn	Other[a] Yarn	Fabric	Total	Proportion[b] (%)
			A. Output			
1874	6	1	0	18	25	16.1
1880	20	1	1	40	62	18.7
1890	34	23	2	57	116	26.7
1900	90	70	5	178	343	29.0
1910	164	145	10	286	605	29.2
1920	570	706	132	1,440	2,848	29.7
1930	537	432	144	1,144	2,257	25.5
1940	986	622	498	1,898	4,004	12.0
			B. Exports			
1868	6	0	0	0	6	40.2
1880	9	0	0	0	9	30.3
1890	14	0	0	1	15	24.5
1900	45	21	0	25	91	44.6
1910	130	45	1	54	230	50.2
1920	382	152	9	501	1,044	53.6
1930	417	15	4	377	813	55.3
1940	453	63	80	593	1,117	30.6

Sources: Output: Shinohara 1972, pp. 141–43, 188–89, and 194–95. Exports: 1869–1930: Tōyō Keizai Shinpōsha 1935, pp. 2 and 50–79. 1940: Nippon, Ōkurashō 1940, vol. 1, pp. 2 and 152–284.

[a] Silk, hemp, wool, rayon, and spun rayon yarns.

[b] Proportion of all textile products in total manufacturing output (panel A) and in total merchandised exports (panel B).

In order to examine the impact of the power revolution on textile production we first take up the silk-reeling industry. This industry was one of the nation's leading exporters during the nineteenth century. (As Table 8-1 shows, raw silk accounted for almost all textile exports until

Table 8-2.   Proportion of Powered Factories (α) and Composition of Total Power Capacity (H) by Engine Type
in Silk Reeling: 1885–1915

(percent)

Year	Proportion of Powered Factories (α)	Composition of H			
		Electric Motors (β)	Steam Engines and Turbines	Internal Combustion Engines	Water Wheels and Turbines
1885			2.1		97.9
1890			69.4		30.6
1895			88.2		11.8
1900	49.6	0.1	82.4	0.0	17.5
1905	84.4	0.1	86.6	0.2	13.1
1910	82.3	0.9	78.6	0.5	20.0
1915	85.9	7.3	75.2	0.7	16.8

Sources: STAC. See Table A-1.

Notes: Figures are for the private factories with ten or more production workers. In
1885, 1890 and 1895 electric motors and internal combustion engines were not
included in STAC surveys. But they were negligible.

1900.) In the first section of this chapter we survey the quantitative facts
of power utilization in silk reeling. Then, in the second section we relate
developments in silk-reeling technology to changes in power utilization
and describe the impact of the power revolution on this industry.

Quantitative Survey of Power Utilization

Mechanization

Silk reeling was one of the industries in which mechanization started
earliest. According to Table 8-2 (which includes factories with 10 or
more workers), by 1900 the proportion of powered factories (α) in the
silk-reeling industry was almost 50%. In the same year α was only 32.3%

Table 8-3. Proportion of Powered Factories (α) by Factory
Scale in Silk Reeling

(percent)

Scale (persons)	1909	1914	1919	1930	1935	1940
All factories	67.4	76.5	84.1	94.1	94.4	96.6
5– 9	14.9	25.9	23.5	67.2	74.5	81.2
10– 29	57.9	61.2	79.2	95.2	94.8	98.2
30– 49	94.2	96.0	97.0	98.3	95.3	100.0
50– 99	96.2	98.3	99.1	98.8	98.7	99.6
100–499	99.3	99.4	99.5	98.8	99.7	100.0
500–999	100.0	100.0	100.0	100.0	100.0	100.0
1,000 or more	100.0	100.0	100.0	100.0	100.0	100.0

Sources: STF. See Table A-2.
Notes: Figures are for the private factories with five or more production workers.

in all manufacturing industries combined (Table 4-4). And, as is shown
in Table 8-3 (which includes factories with 5 or more workers), in 1909 α
was 67.4% in silk reeling, more than two times of that in manufacturing
sector as a whole (Table 4-5). As was mentioned in chapter 4, the early
mechanization of silk-reeling was due basically to the fact that this
industry was the first leading sector of industrialization.

Although silk-reeling as a whole was relatively highly mechanized by
1909, there did exist differentials in α by factory scale. According to
Table 8-3, α was only 14.9% in the smallest-scale category, while 100%
of factories in the two largest-scale categories were mechanized. In the
years after 1909, however, mechanization of the small factories proceeded rapidly. In the smallest-scale category, for example, α reached
67.2% in 1930 and 81.2% in 1940. As will be shown, the mechanization
of small silk-reeling factories occurred with the introduction of steam
engines and electric motors.

Transition of Power Capacity by Engine Type

As was mentioned in chapter 2, silk reeling had become a major manufacturing user of water power by the early Meiji period. Between 1884 and 1890 almost three-fourths of all water power employed in manufacturing was used for silk reeling (Table 2-3). In addition, water was the foremost source of power for this industry. Water power comprised 95.7% of total power capacity in silk reeling in 1884. This share rose to 97.9% in the following year, but then began to decline. Water power fell to 86.3% of total power capacity in silk reeling in 1886, to 61.1% in 1887, and in 1888 the share of water power fell bellow that of steam power.[2]

Among the industries in the textile group, silk reeling was unique in its heavy reliance on water power. The share of water power in spinning was surpassed by steam power in 1885, and water power was rarely used at all in weaving. In the textile industry as a whole, steam power exceeded water power by 1887. Moreover, in the total power capacity of all manufacturing industries excluding textiles, steam power already dominated water power by the mid-1880s.

According to Table 8-2, the share of steam power in silk reeling increased and reached a peak in the mid-1890s. As Tables 8-4 and 8-5 show, the decline in the share of steam power occurred as steam engines were replaced by electric motors. However, it was not until just before 1930 that the share of electric power exceeded that of steam power. The timing of this transition in the silk-reeling industry was very late when compared with that in other industries (Table 6-5). Moreover, this industry continued to rely more heavily on steam engines than did other industries. For example, in 1940 steam power comprised 34.1% of total horsepower in silk reeling (Table 8-4), while it contained only 16.4% in the manufacturing sector as a whole (Table 6-6).

Table 8-4 illustrates a significant development in power utilization by factory scale in the silk-reeling industry. In the early years of the twentieth century, small-scale reelers tended to depend on water power, while larger plants relied more heavily on steam power. In 1909, for example, 86.6% of the power capacity in the smallest-scale factories was

[2] Horsepower statistics for the silk reeling, spinning, and weaving industries are estimated from STAC. The estimation procedure is described in the Appendix.

Table 8-4. Composition of Total Power Capacity (*H*) by
Engine Type and by Factory Scale in Silk Reeling:
1909–1940

(percent)

Scale (persons)	Electric Motors (β)	Steam Engines and Turbines	Internal Combustion Engines	Water Wheels and Turbines
		1909		
All factories	0.4	79.2	0.3	20.1
5– 9	0.4	13.0	0.0	86.6
10– 29	0.2	59.1	0.5	40.2
30– 49	0.1	75.8	0.1	24.0
50– 99	0.2	82.1	0.2	17.5
100–499	0.8	84.8	0.2	14.2
500–999	0.4	97.0	0.2	2.4
1,000 or more	2.6	96.1	0.0	1.3
		1914		
All factories	5.5	77.9	0.2	16.4
5– 9	2.0	36.1	0.0	61.9
10– 29	1.7	66.3	1.2	30.8
30– 49	1.4	75.1	0.1	23.4
50– 99	2.3	80.4	0.2	17.1
100–499	7.9	82.8	0.0	9.3
500–999	16.1	79.4	0.7	3.8
1,000 or more	16.5	77.6	1.0	4.9
		1919		
All factories	8.6	84.9	0.5	6.4
5– 9	8.6	67.2	0.6	23.6
10– 29	8.8	65.5	0.2	25.5
30– 49	2.5	91.3	0.0	6.2
50– 99	8.7	74.5	0.8	16.0
100–499	8.6	88.5	0.4	2.5
500–999	26.2	67.2	3.0	3.6
1,000 or more	10.6	89.4	0.0	0.0

Table 8-4. (continued)

(percent)

Scale (persons)	Electric Motors (β)	Steam Engines and Turbines	Internal Combustion Engines	Water Wheels and Turbines
		1930		
All factories	50.2	47.1	0.9	1.8
5– 9	38.2	51.9	0.4	9.5
10– 29	52.0	37.1	0.4	10.5
30– 49	52.1	41.7	0.6	5.6
50– 99	40.3	53.3	0.8	5.6
100–499	50.3	48.1	0.5	1.1
500–999	57.6	40.5	1.8	0.1
1,000 or more	45.6	53.0	1.3	0.1
		1935		
All factories	52.6	42.6	2.8	2.0
5– 9	46.1	43.1	1.7	9.1
10– 29	37.9	49.5	1.6	11.0
30– 49	40.5	50.7	0.6	8.2
50– 99	44.9	49.5	2.4	3.2
100–499	57.8	38.3	3.1	0.8
500–999	53.2	44.0	2.4	0.4
1,000 or more	46.4	44.2	9.4	0.0
		1940		
All factories	60.3	34.1	4.6	1.0
5– 9	70.8	9.6	10.6	9.0
10– 29	58.7	26.6	7.6	7.1
30– 49	57.9	30.0	7.5	4.6
50– 99	53.0	37.0	7.2	2.8
100–499	60.5	34.4	5.0	0.1
500–999	60.3	36.2	2.8	0.7
1,000 or more	100.0	0.0	0.0	0.0

Sources: Same as Table 8-3.
Notes: See the note to Table 8-3.

Table 8-5. Composition of Primary Power Capacity (H') by Engine Type and by Factory Scale in Silk Reeling: 1909–1919

(percent)

Scale (persons)	Primary Electric Motors (β')	Steam Engines and Turbines	Internal Combustion Engines	Water Wheels and Turbines
		1909		
All factories	0.5	79.1	0.3	20.1
5– 9	0.4	13.0	0.0	86.6
10– 29	0.2	58.9	0.6	40.3
30– 49	0.1	75.7	0.1	24.1
50– 99	0.2	82.1	0.2	17.5
100–499	0.9	84.5	0.3	14.3
500–999	0.5	96.7	0.3	2.5
1,000 or more	2.6	97.4	0.0	0.0
		1914		
All factories	5.5	77.7	0.3	16.5
5– 9	2.0	36.1	0.0	61.9
10– 29	1.7	66.2	1.3	30.8
30– 49	1.4	75.0	0.2	23.4
50– 99	2.4	80.2	0.3	17.1
100–499	8.0	82.6	0.0	9.4
500–999	16.2	79.1	0.8	3.9
1,000 or more	16.5	77.4	1.1	5.0
		1919		
All factories	8.5	84.4	0.6	6.5
5– 9	8.4	67.2	0.7	23.7
10– 29	7.4	66.5	0.2	25.9
30– 49	2.5	91.3	0.0	6.2
50– 99	8.8	74.4	0.8	16.0
100–499	8.6	88.3	0.5	2.6
500–999	26.3	67.1	3.0	3.6
1,000 or more	10.6	89.4	0.0	0.0

Sources: Same as Table 8-3.

Notes: See the notes to Table 8-3.

supplied by water wheels and turbines, while steam engines supplied 96.1% of total power capacity for factories in the largest-scale category. This difference in power utilization by factory scale existed in 1914 as well. However after that year the share of steam power increased in the smaller factories. By 1919 it reached 67.2% in factories with 5-9 workers. This share of steam power was much higher than the average for this scale in the manufacturing sector as a whole (19.7% shown in Table 6-6). This diffusion of steam power to smaller plants during the 1910s was responsible for the silk-reeling industry's relatively longer dependence on steam engines and its slow electrification. Furthermore, the diffusion of steam power to small-scale plants was unique to this industry. The reasons for this are to be found in the particular advantages of new technology and new power sources to the silk-reeling industry which are examined in the next section.

The Power Revolution and Technological Progress

Development of the Machine Filature

Producing raw silk involves four processing stages: drying cocoons, boiling cocoons, finding the ends of threads, and reeling the threads.[3] Although all stages are important in obtaining a quality product, the mechanization of these processes in Japan centered on the last stage, reeling the threads. At the beginning of the Meiji period reeling was accomplished by the traditional *zakuri*, or sedentary reeling method, in which the operative picked up cocoon threads with her left hand and reeled them onto a bobbin with her right.

Because of the low productivity and low output quality of this method compared with the machine filature technique used in France and Italy, the Meiji government endeavored to transplant the European technique to Japan. As part of the *Shokusan Kōgyō Seisaku* (Policy to promote

---

[3] For the history of the silk-reeling industry before World War II we rely on Gendai Nippon Sangyō Hattatsushi Kenkyūkai 1964b; 1967b; Nippon Sen-i Kyōgikai 1958a; 1958b. See also Minami and Makino 1987.

industrialization), the government helped to establish two model reeling plants—the Tomioka Filature founded in 1870 and the Kankōryō Filature started in 1873. In addition, the Maebashi Clan established the Maebashi Filature in 1870, and a private company Ono Gumi set up the Tsukiji Filature in 1871. The Tomioka Filature stood out prominently among these plants as the one with the most modern equipment. It employed iron machine filatures which were operated by a steam engine. This equipment was imported from France. The other three plants were equipped with Italian-type wooden filatures which were operated by human or water power.[4]

Although these plants were commercial failures, they did stimulate the development of the silk-reeling industry in Japan by motivating other domestic improvements in reeling technology. The two most significant of these innovations were an improvement in the traditional reeling technique and the invention of a Japanese-type machine filature. The new reeling technique was the *kairyō zakuri* or improved sedentary method which was developed at plants in Jōshū (modern-day Gunma Prefecture) in about 1877. Although the improved technique still utilized only human power, it employed a part of the European-designed machine filature and involved twisting the threads in a manner similar to the modern machine method.[5] Because of the superiority of the improved method to the earlier method both in efficiency and in output quality, its use spread to many reeling plants in Gunma Prefecture.[6]

The Japanese-type machine filature, called the Suwa-type silk reeler or Nakayama-type silk reeler, was introduced by Nakayama Company in Suwa, Nagano Prefecture in 1875. This invention was prompted by the

[4] The Tomioka Filature was easily the largest of these plants. It employed 300 reeling operatives, compared with 48 (later 96) reelers in the Kankōryō Filature, 6 such workers (later 96) in the Maebashi Filature, and 60 (later 96) in the Tsukiji Filature. Gendai Nippon Sangyō Hattatsushi Kenkyūkai 1964, table II-25 on p. 96.

[5] Exactly which parts of the machine filature were introduced in the *kairyō zakuri* is unknown. Takahashi Keizai Kenkyūjo 1941, n. 4 on p. 389.

[6] Another improvement on the *zakuri* technique was the invention of a foot-powered machine around the year 1878. This new machine was superior to the *zakuri* in efficiency and output quality. Dai-Nippon Sanshikai 1935, p. 148; Takahashi Keizai Kenkyūjo 1941, p. 387.

fact that modern (European) machine filature technology was too expensive to be employed in the small-scale Japanese plants of the time. The filature introduced by the Nakayama Company blended two modern technologies, French and Italian, with the traditional Japanese technology to create a new reeling technique which required far less capital investment than the European technique. This invention involved the substitutions of water for steam in motive power, wood for iron in machinery, and ceramics for metal in cocoon-boiling basins and steam pipes. Because of these substitutions, total expenses for equipments of Nakayama Company with 100 basins were only ¥1,900, compared with ¥190,000 in the case of Tomioka Filature with 300 basins.[7] This technology differed significantly from both the traditional *zakuri* and the *kairyō zakuri* methods, because it used mechanical power and required a division of labor among the factory workers. This technology was widely used in Nagano Prefecture between 1877 and 1886. As a result of the spread of the Japanese-type machine filature, by 1894 the amount of raw silk produced exceeded the amount porduced by the *zakuri* method.

From the late nineteenth century to the early twentieth century continuing improvements in the silk-reeling industry caused several significant changes. First, these improvements brought about an increase in average factory size. Between 1896 and 1918, for example of all machine filature plants, the proportion of factories with less than 50 reeling operatives decreased from 65% to 37%. Such a change did not occur in plants employing the *zakuri* method. Among these plants, the proportion with fewer than 50 operatives rose from 77% in 1896 to 86% in 1918.[8]

Second, the introduction of the machine filature was an improvement in production efficiency. Under the renewed machine filature method water power was replaced by steam power and all-wooden machines gave way to wood-iron and iron machines. These changes in production technology raised output efficiency. The new machines were superior to

[7]   Nakamura 1980, p. 82.
[8]   Dai Nippon Sanshikai 1935, p. 428.

the all-wooden ones, because they were more accurate and did not become warped in the humid atmosphere of the silk-reeling plants.[9] As a result, the gap in labor productivity between the machine filature and the *zakuri* methods of production widened (Table 8-6), and early in the 1910s output of raw silk by the *zakuri* method regularly decreased.

Finally, an epochal innovation in the machine filature technology was an invention of the multi-ends reeling machine by Naosaburo Minorikawa in 1903. This multi-ends reeling machine could reel ten or more threads in one basin while the ordinary machine could do only a few threads. By this machine, which was run more slowly than the ordinary machine filature, the production efficiency increased and the product quality improved significantly. This technology was diffused rapidly after its first employment by the Katakura Silk Reeling and Spinning Company in 1928, and made a great contribution to an expansion of the Japanese exports of raw silk to the United States.[10] Products of Katakura which was named as "Minorikawa raw silk" gained a high reputation in the United States at that time.[11]

Characteristics of Machine Filature Technology

There was little possibility of employing mechanical power under the traditional hand-powered *zakuri*-reeling method.[12] The only recorded attempt to mechanize the *zakuri* reelers was, as mentioned in chapter 2, S. Numaga's attempt in the mid-1880s to run several sets of reelers with a water wheel.

On the other hand, machine filature techniques developed in France and Italy were originally designed to use mechanical power, either water or steam, and when this technology was introduced to Japan it was most often used in conjunction with mechanical power. Steam power was used in Tomioka Filature, and water power in Kankōryō Filature.

---

[9] Ono 1986, pp. 6–7.
[10] A proportion of the multi-ends filature in total number of machine filature increased from 0.1% in 1928 to 19.9% in 1934, and to 25.1% in 1937 (Kajinishi 1964, p. 583).
[11] Honda 1935, p. 397.
[12] Takahashi Keizai Kenkyūjo 1941, p. 505.

Although the Maebashi Filature and Tsukiji Filature machines were initially run by human power, in Maebashi human power was replaced by water power one year after operations began. Machine filatures in Nagano Prefecture relied largely on water wheels.

The choice of the kind of power utilized in these various operations was related to the type of machines employed. Iron machines were almost always run by steam power (Tomioka Filature), whereas wooden machines were usually operated by human and water power (in the case of the other model plants and the machine filatures in Nagano). This was not mere coincidence; wooden machinery could be used effectively with water wheels, but when this wooden equipment was run by steam engines, high speed and engine vibration tended to cause frequent breakdowns and rapid wearing out.

The particular way in which the modern reeling method was adopted at the three plants other than Tomioka Filature and at the machine filature plants in Nagano is worthy of special attention, because it demonstrates an important aspect of the borrowing of technology in Japan. These plants attempted to save on capital expenses by using human or water power instead of steam power and by using wooden machines instead of iron machines.[13] According to Gerschenkron, late comers have an advantage in being able to utilize production technologies developed by forerunners. Because such technologies are generally capital-using, they are, however, often difficult to introduce to later developing economies which have low wage-rental ratios. Therefore it is reasonable that late comers make capital-saving adjustments on these technologies before introducing them to their economies. This phenomenon sometimes occurred in Japanese industries (chapter 15). Typical examples are to be found in the ways in which many Japanese reeling plants adopted the European machine filature technology.[14] If these Japanese plants had not been able to make capital saving innovations, the introduction of modern silk-reeling technology would have

[13] Unlike Japan, in China iron machines imported from Europe were used without modifications. Mitani 1930, p. 326. This will be discussed more fully in chap. 15.

[14] This point was stressed by Ono (1986, pp. 5–9).

been delayed to a great extent, if not made altogether impossible.

The most important single feature of the machine filature, as differentiated from the *zakuri* method, was the utilization of mechanical power. According to the survey in 1893, among all silk-reeling factories with 10 or more basins 19.7% were steam powered, 44.2% were water powered, and 36.1% were human powered.[15] These percentages became 46.6%, 37.9%, and 15.5% in 1905, and, by the end of the Meiji period almost all machine filatures were equipped with mechanical power.

Even production with human-powered machine filatures, however, represented a significant improvement over the *zakuri* technique. The improvement lay in the division of labor instituted along with the machine filature production method. Under the new system one worker picked out the ends of the cocoon threads, while a different worker reeled the silk onto a set of bobbins which were connected together by a common shaft. Under the traditional *zakuri* method only a single worker selected the thread ends and reeled them at the same time.

Impact of Power Revolution

Mechanization. There are no statistical records which show directly the impact of the introduction of mechanical power on raw silk production. However, a comparison between the production efficiency under the *zakuri* and the machine filature techniques provides an indication of the significance of mechanical reeling. Table 8-6 shows that while labor productivity increased under the new method during the 1900s and 1910s, it did not increase under the traditional method. The increase in labor productivity in machine filature plants during this period was attributable both to the switch from human power to mechanical power and to the transition from water to steam power utilization. As a consequence of the greater efficiency of the mechanically powered method the ratio of labor productivity in machine filature plants to that in *zakuri* plants rose from 2.1 in 1896 to 7.6 by 1925. During the 1920s and 1930s productivity in plants retaining the *zakuri*

[15]   The survey is the *Zenkoku Seishi Kōjō Tōkei.* Takahashi Keizai Kenkyūjo 1941, p. 505.

Table 8-6.   Labor Productivity in *Zakuri* Reeling and Machine
Filature: 1896–1935

Year	Labor Productivity		Ratio of Machine Filature to *Zakuri*
	Zakuri	Machine Filature	
		(*kan*/person)	
1896	3.14	6.61	2.11
1900	2.94	8.45	2.87
1905	2.91	9.40	3.23
1908	2.96	10.61	3.58
1925	2.97	22.62	7.62
1930	5.65	25.75	4.56
1935	5.98	38.69	6.47

Sources: Fujino 1965, table 17-1 on p. 341.

method did increase. Furthermore, the greater efficiency of the machine filature method was clearly reflected in the wide gap in labor productivity between the two methods.

A relative advantage of respective production methods cannot be expressed strictly in terms of labor productivity, however, because a higher productivity is usually associated with larger inputs of capital and intermediate goods. The rate of net profit is the most appropriate index for indicating the advantage of technology. Table 8-7 presents the estimates, made by the present writer and Fumio Makino, of the rate of net profit (r) of the *zakuri* reelers and the machine filature.[16] In this estimation we suppose, for the *zakuri* production, the presence of an organization of one hundred farmers who were engaged in silk reeling separately at their individual homes (one hundred basins in total) and a reelers' association gathered their products at a workshop with seven laborers for final processing and shipping. As for the machine filature, we suppose a factory with one hundred basins-filature operated by one

[16]   See Makino forthcoming, for the estimating procedure and Minami and Makino 1987 for the analysis based on these estimates.

hundred reelers with twenty four workers for final processing and other works.[17]

The above mentioned estimates show no significant difference in the level of r between the two methods in 1888; it was 15.37% in the *zakuri* and 17.60% in the machine filature. In order to clarify this matter in more detail we can express r in the following relation:

$$r = (P_y Y - P_c C - W - O)/K \times 100$$
$$= \{y P_y (1 - C P_c / P_y) - w - o\}/K \times 100,$$

where we denote

Y:	volume of production of raw silk (*kan*/year)
C:	volume of cocoon input (*kan*/year)
W:	total wage cost (yen/year)
O:	other costs (material cost, interest payments, depreciations and others) (yen/year)
K:	total capital (fixed capital and working capital) (yen)
R:	net profit (yen/year)
L:	number of workers (persons)
D:	number of working days (days/year)
P_y:	price of raw silk (yen/*kan*)
P_c:	price of cocoon (yen/*kan*)
y:	labor productivity $[Y/(L \cdot D)]$ (*kan*/man day)
c:	ratio of cocoon input to output (C/Y)
w:	wage rate $[W/(L \cdot D)]$ (yen/man day)
o:	other costs per labor input $[O \cdot (L \cdot D)]$ (yen/man day)
r:	rate of net profit (R/K) (%)
k:	capital intensity $[K/(L \cdot D)]$ (yen/man day).

The above relation shows that r tends to increase by increases in labor productivity (y) and price of raw silk (P_y), and by decreases in relative price of cocoon to raw silk (P_c/P_y), a ratio of cocoon input to output (c), wage rate (w), other costs per labor input (o), and capital intensity (k).

[17] The estimates are not either for particular establishments or for all establishments in Japan. They are for 'fictious plants' which are supposed to have been typical at that time. We have obtained these estimates by using scattered statistics in various regions.

Table 8-8 indicates that the equality of r between the two systems came from the fact that in the *zakuri* production disadvantages of a lower productivity and a lower quality of products (a lower price of raw silk) were almost cancelled out by cost savings in materials (cocoons produced by farmers themselves), labor (opportunity cost of farmers was lower) and fixed capital (a dormitory for workers was not needed, a water wheel was cheaper than a steam engine, and the *zakuri* machine was cheaper than the filature).[18]

For the period of 1888–1908 the rate r decreased much more in the *zakuri* production relative to filature machine. It was 6.91% for the *zakuri* and 12.68% for the machine filature in 1908. Table 8-9 gives a decomposition of a change in r by changes in its seven components. This table reveals that a widening differential in labor productivity (16.16%) was the most important factor for the increasing differential in r;[19] r of the machine filature increased by 6.50 percentage point, whereas that of the *zakuri* decreased by 9.66 percentage point—a total differential of 16.16%. The next significant factor was attributed to a larger increase in the price of raw silk in the machine filature (7.81%). On the other hand, a larger increase in wage rate of the machine filature was the most important factor for reduction of differential in r (−16.29%). Conclusively, we can state that an appearance of a gap in r for this period was largely due to a rise in labor productivity and an improvement of output quality in the machine filature production. These changes in labor productivity and output quality in the machine filature were related to several factors such as an introduction of machines to dry cocoons,[20] an increase in the number of threads reeled by an operator,[21] a change of materials in the filature from wood to wood-iron

---

[18] Total fixed capital is estimated to be ¥3,391 for the *zakuri* and ¥12,833 for the machine filature in 1888 (Makino forthcoming).

[19] We have already argued on a change in the relative labor productivity between the two systems in Table 8-6.

[20] These machines were invented in the 1890s and 1900s (Honda 1935, pp. 294–98).

[21] The number of threads reeled by an operator was 1.53 in 1892 and 2.65 in 1908 (Fujino *et al.* 1979,p. 219).

Table 8-7.   Rate of Net Profit (r) in *Zakuri* Reeling and Machine
Filature: 1888–1934

(percent)

	Zakuri	Machine Filature	Multi-ends Machine Filature
1888	15.37 (6.27)	17.60 (6.75)	
1908	6.91 (2.52)	12.68 (4.70)	
1918		8.77/(4.21)	
1928		4.86 (3.37)	
1934		4.11 (4.31)	17.14 (17.97)

Notes: Figures are for the scale of production with one hundred reelers.
Rate of profit is a ratio of net profit to total capital (fixed capital + working capital).
Figures in the parentheses are the rate of profit at 1934–36 prices (r′).

and to iron,[22] and a change in motive power from water whcels to steam engines.[23]

The rate of profit at constant prices (r′) of the machine filature decreased from 6.75% to 4.31% during 1880–1934 (Table 8-7). Table 8-10 indicates that this reduction came mainly from an increase in the relative price of cocoons to raw silk (− 58.17%) and an increase in wage rate (− 33.16%). These effects were not cancelled out by an improvement in labor productivity (44.95%), a decrease in the ratio of cocoon input to output (44.47%), and a rise in the price of raw silk (22.79%). A rise in production efficiency and a saving in cocoon input were due to factors such as an improvement of the quality of cocoons (spread of the First Filial Hybrid)[24] and an improvement in the technology of boiling cocoons (division of work by an operator between boiling cocoons and

[22]   We have already referred to this fact.

[23]   This will be argued later.

[24]   The First Filial Hybrid, which appeared during the Taishō period (1912–26), required much less labor because the silk was easier to unravel and the individual threads were longer. See Kiyokawa 1980 for details.

Table 8-8. Determinants of Rate of Net Profit (r) in *Zakuri*
Reeling and Machine Filature: 1888

	Zakuri	Machine Filature	Ratio of Machine Filature to *Zakuri*
Labor productivity (y)	0.0192	0.0405	2.11
Price of raw silk (P_y)	37.16	39.54	1.06
Relative price of cocoon to raw silk (P_c/P_y)	0.056	0.066	1.18
Ratio of cocoon input to output (c)	10.27	9.95	0.97
Wage rate (w)	0.119	0.181	1.52
Other costs per labor input (o)	0.083	0.154	1.86
Capital intensity (k)	0.649	1.235	1.90

reeling).[25]

In Table 8-7 the rate of profit (r) for multi-ends filature is estimated only for 1934. This rate was 17.14% compared to 4.11% of the ordinary machine filature. According to Table 8-11, this was due to the higher price of the multi-ends machine filature products. The better quality of raw silk produced by new machines cancelled out the disadvantages created from the lower labor productivity and the higher capital intensity.[26]

Transition of Power Sources. The new sources of power which became available from the late nineteenth century had a significant impact on performance of the silk-reeling industry (machine filature). Power costs for reeling were, of course, greater in steam-powered factories than in water-powered ones which used natural streams.[27] In spite of this, total

[25] Hirano Mura Yakuba 1932, p. 354.
[26] Total fixed capital is estimated to be ¥90,602 for the multi-ends machine filature, compared to ¥73,227 for the ordinary machine filature in 1934 (Makino forthcoming).
[27] Ozaki 1954, p. 187.

Table 8-9. Changes in Rate of Net Profit (r) by Components in *Zakuri* Reeling and Machine Filature: 1888–1908

(percent)

	Change in r for 1888–1908	Components						
		Labor Productivity (y)	Price of Raw Silk (P_y)	Relative Price of Cocoon to Raw Silk (P_c/P_y)	Ratio of Cocoon Input to Output (c)	Wage Rate (w)	Other Costs per Labor Input (o)	Capital Intensity (k)
Machine filature (1)	4.92	6.50	24.94	2.87	1.59	−19.27	−10.30	−11.25
Zakuri reeling (2)	−8.46	−9.66	17.13	0.13	−0.69	−2.98	−7.10	−5.29
(1)–(2)	3.54	16.16	7.81	2.74	2.28	−16.29	−3.20	−5.96

192

Table 8-10. A Change in Real Rate of Net Profit (r') by
Components in Machine Filature: 1888–1934

(percent)

Change in r' for 1888–1934	Components			
	Labor Productivity (y)	Price of Raw Silk (P_y)	Relative Price of Cocoon to Raw Silk (P_c/P_y)	Ratio of Cocoon Input to Output (c)
−2.44	44.95	22.79	−58.17	44.47

	Components	
Wage Rate (w)	Other Costs per Labor Input (o)	Capital Intensity (k)
−33.16	−19.18	−4.14

operating costs were not necessarily smaller in factories which employed water to power reeling machines. These factories still had to generate steam to boil cocoons for the earlier stage of the silk production process. The use of steam to power reeling machines offered the advantage of eliminating this additional production cost. This particular advantage of steam power in silk reeling combined with other, more general merits of steam power—greater and more steady power, freedom from locational and climate considerations—stimulated the transition from water to steam power in the silk-reeling industry. Furthermore, the utilization of steam for boiling cocoons induced small-scale plants to convert from water to steam power during the 1910s and thereby contributed to the particularly lengthy age of steam power in the silk-reeling industry. According to Table 8-12, the rate of net profit (r) for machine filature

Table 8-11. Determinants of Rate of Net Profit (r) in Machine
Filature and Multi-ends Machine Filature: 1934

	Machine Filature	Multi-ends Machine Filature	Ratio of Multi-ends Machine Filature to Machine Filature
Labor productivity (y)	0.148	0.143	0.97
Price of raw silk (P_y)	42.70	48.08	1.13
Relative price of cocoon to raw silk (P_c/P_y)	0.090	0.080	0.89
Ratio of cocoon input to output (c)	7.94	7.81	0.98
Wage rate (w)	0.993	0.993	1.00
Other costs per labor input (o)	0.613	0.614	1.00
Capital intensity (k)	5.328	5.805	1.09

Table 8-12. Rate of Net Profit (r) in Machine Filature by Type
of Mechanical Power: 1888–1928

(percent)

	Water Wheel	Steam Engine	Electric Motor
1888	12.16	17.41	
1908	7.57	12.67	
1918		8.93	9.48
1928		4.86	5.35

with one hundred basins was larger when they used the steam engine
instead of water wheel both in 1888 and 1908.

Besides the principal advantage of electric power of a reduction of
capital costs and fuel costs, it offered other benefits to silk producers.
The smooth rotation of electric motors enabled this industry to reduce

thread breakage during the reeling process and to make threads of uniform thickness.[28] In other words, electrification contributed to increase production efficiency and to improve output quality. These factors were the most influential in stimulating the eventual electrification of the silk-reeling industry. Our estimation in Table 8-12 indicates that r was larger in the case of electric power than in case of steam power both in 1918 and 1928. A relatively small difference in the rate of profit clarifies a relatively slower electrification and a longer age of steam power compared with other industries.

[28] A similar phenomenon is reported by the spinning factory in England at the beginning of this century that output rose by 8% by means of a disappearance of thread breakage (Byatt 1979, p. 91).

Chapter 9

THE SPINNING INDUSTRY

The spinning industry, which began to develop somewhat later than the silk-reeling industry, was one of Japan's major industries prior to World War II. Output of yarns increased rapidly after the 1880s and exceeded output of raw silk some time in the 1910s (Table 8-1). This increase made import substitution possible and later stimulated export expansion. The first section of this chapter surveys the statistical dimensions of the power revolution in spinning and the second section explores its impact on the production of yarn in Japan.

This chapter concerns the spinning industry as a whole, but historical examples mainly refer to cotton spinning. Among the various spinning industries cotton spinning was by far the most important. In 1909, for example, there were 111 factories producing cotton yarn, compared with 19 producing hemp yarn, 9 producing silk yarn, and 4 producing woolen yarn.[1] Furthermore, the value of both output and export of cotton yarn was larger than that of all other types of yarn combined (Table 8-1). Thus, given the predominant position of cotton spinning, the impact of the power revolution in the spinning industry in general can be largely understood by examining the impact of power revolution on cotton spinning alone.

Quantitative Survey of Power Utilization

Mechanization

By the first decade of the twentieth century the spinning industry was

---

[1]   STF 1909. See Table A-2.

Table 9-1. Proportion of Powered Factories (α) and Composition of Total Power Capacity (H) by Engine Type in Spinning: 1885–1915

(percent)

| Year | Proportion of Powered Factories (α) | Composition of H | | | |
		Electric Motors (β)	Steam Engines and Turbines	Internal Combustion Engines	Water Wheels and Turbines
1885			69.9		30.1
1890			96.8		3.2
1895			94.5		5.5
1900	83.2	1.1	88.0	0.0	10.9
1905	82.4	1.7	87.4	0.1	10.8
1910	81.9	13.9	71.2	7.0	7.9
1915	98.6	25.6	71.2	1.1	2.1

Sources: Same as Table 8-2.
Notes: See the notes to Table 8-2.

already rather highly mechanized. As shown in Table 9-1, the proportion of powered factories (with 10 or more workers), α, in the spinning industry exceeded 80% in 1900. This α is more than double of that in manufacturing as a whole (32.3%, shown in Table 4-4) and also quite larger than α in silk reeling (49.6%, shown in Table 8-2) in the same year. By 1909 α had surpassed 90% in spinning plants with 5 or more workers (Table 9-2), while it was less than 30% in manufacturing plants as a whole (Table 4-5) and about 67% in silk-reeling plants (Table 8-3). These comparisons clearly indicate the leading position of spinning industry in mechanization during the early years of industrialization. Furthermore, at the turn of the century the degree of mechanization in spinning far exceeded even that in silk reeling (Tables 8-2, 9-1). This was the case even though silk reeling began to mechanize earlier than

Table 9-2. Proportion of Powered Factories (α) by Factory
Scale in Spinning

(percent)

Scale (person)	1909	1914	1919	1930	1935	1940
All factories	93.7	96.2	96.5	98.5	99.5	99.8
5– 9	68.4	100.0	90.6	95.5	99.1	99.8
10– 29	85.7	83.3	98.6	97.7	98.4	99.3
30– 49	100.0	25.0[a]	100.0	100.0	100.0	100.0
50– 99	100.0	100.0	100.0	100.0	100.0	100.0
100–499	100.0	100.0	100.0	100.0	100.0	100.0
500–999	100.0	100.0	100.0	100.0	100.0	100.0
1,000 or more	100.0	100.0	100.0	100.0	100.0	100.0

Sources: Same as Table 8-3.
Notes: Figures are for the private factories with five or more production workers.
[a] This abnormality is probably largely due to the very small sample for this scale (only
four factories).

spinning and most other industries.

The higher degree of mechanization in the spinning industry in the
earlier years resulted largely from the fact that mechanization in the
small-scale plants was more advanced in the spinning industry than
other industries. This fact is revealed in Table 9-2, which shows large
figures of α in these plants. In 1909, for example, α was 68.4% in the
smallest-scale category (5-9 workers) and 85.7% in the second smallest-
scale category (10-29 workers). Comparable figures for manufacturing
as a whole were 14.4% and 30.1% respectively. Moreover, in the same
year all spinning plants employing 30 workers or more were mechanized.
In the manufacturing sector as a whole, on the other hand, α ranged
from 63.7% to 100% in large-scale plants (Table 4-7).

Transition of Power Capacity by Engine Type

In 1884 water wheels were still the largest source of mechanical power
in the spinning industry, comprising 62.8% of total power capacity. But

199

Table 9-3. Composition of Total Power Capacity (*H*) by
Engine Type and by Factory Scale in Spinning:
1909–1940

(percent)

Scale (persons)	Electric Motors (β)	Steam Engines and Turbines	Internal Combustion Engines	Water Wheels and Turbines
1909				
All factories	7.3	86.1	1.1	5.5
5– 9	0.0	0.0	5.4	94.6
10– 29	16.3	4.6	11.8	67.3
30– 49	0.0	78.0	0.0	22.0
50– 99	0.0	84.2	0.0	15.8
100–499	3.7	74.0	0.1	22.2
500–999	0.5	93.9	1.9	3.7
1,000 or more	10.0	85.7	1.1	3.2
1914				
All factories	18.8	75.6	2.1	3.5
5– 9	8.3	19.4	11.1	61.2
10– 29	32.7	0.0	45.5	21.8
30– 49	0.0	0.0	0.0	100.0[a]
50– 99	42.3	0.0	0.0	57.7
100–499	22.7	42.4	2.0	32.9
500–999	6.2	91.5	2.3	0.0
1,000 or more	21.7	76.1	1.9	0.3
1919				
All factories	54.2	43.1	0.9	1.8
5– 9	21.9	0.0	38.0	40.1
10– 29	44.0	3.3	20.1	32.6
30– 49	58.1	13.9	11.8	16.2
50– 99	78.8	0.0	8.6	12.6
100–499	46.1	28.6	3.2	22.1
500–999	37.8	60.3	0.7	1.2
1,000 or more	56.8	42.0	0.6	0.6

Table 9-3. (continued)

(percent)

Scale (persons)	Electric Motors (β)	Steam Engines and Turbines	Internal Combustion Engines	Water Wheels and Turbines
		1930		
All factories	87.2	12.4	0.3	0.1
5– 9	61.2	7.8	0.0	31.0
10– 29	77.9	13.7	0.0	8.4
30– 49	90.7	4.4	0.0	4.9
50– 99	45.5	54.5	0.0	0.0
100–499	95.0	4.5	0.3	0.2
500–999	97.1	2.7	0.1	0.1
1,000 or more	74.9	24.7	0.4	0.0
		1935		
All factories	84.6	13.7	1.5	0.2
5– 9	66.7	0.0	0.0	33.3
10– 29	90.3	0.0	1.8	7.9
30– 49	89.2	2.2	0.0	8.6
50– 99	86.9	13.1	0.0	0.0
100–499	93.0	3.0	3.3	0.7
500–999	93.7	3.1	3.0	0.2
1,000 or more	79.3	20.1	0.6	0.0
		1940		
All factories	92.8	6.9	0.2	0.1
5– 9	69.0	0.0	1.2	29.8
10– 29	93.2	0.0	0.0	6.8
30– 49	98.6	0.0	0.0	1.4
50– 99	99.9	0.1	0.0	0.0
100–499	96.3	3.0	0.5	0.2
500–999	97.8	1.9	0.3	0.0
1,000 or more	86.2	13.8	0.0	0.0

Sources: Same as Table 8-3.
Notes: Figures are for the private factories with five or more production workers.
[a] See the notes to Table 9-2.

in the next year, due to rapid growth in the use of steam engines, steam power exceeded water power (Table 9-1). The share of steam power in total spinning power capacity peaked around 1890. The decline thereafter occurred because of the spreading application of electric motors. The share of electric power surpassed that of steam power between 1914 and 1919 (Table 9-3). By 1940 the share of steam had fallen to only 6.9%, compared with steam's 16.4% share of total power capacity in manufacturing as a whole (Table 6-6). Thus, one aspect of the power revolution, the replacement of steam by electricity, occurred particularly rapidly and intensely in the spinning industry.

There did, however, exist a clear difference in power utilization between spinning plants with less than 30 workers and plants of larger sizes.[2] As shown in Tables 9-3 and 9-4, in 1909 steam power was rarely used and water power was dominant in the smaller-scale plants, whereas steam was the primary source of power among large-scale plants. Among small-scale spinners the use of steam power decreased over the next decade, and by 1919 electric motors and internal combustion engines were widely used. Then, during the 1920s internal combustion engines were almost completely replaced by electric motors in these small plants. Large-scale spinning plants, on the other hand, rarely used internal combustion engines. Instead, these plants moved rather steadily to replace steam engines by electric motors. This substitution was largely completed by 1930.

The Power Revolution and Technological Progress

The Impact of Water Wheels and Steam Engines

Traditional sector. The spinning industry in Japan eventually developed along two lines. A large segment of the industry adopted modern western production methods, but there remained a significant

---

[2]   The number of factories with 5–29 workers increased rapidly from 40 in 1909 to 584 in 1940. Larger factories increased from 103 to 375 in the same period. STF 1909 and 1940. See Table A-2.

number of spinners who retained traditional domestic technology. Even in the traditional sector, however, the power revolution, particularly the introduction of water wheels, had a great impact on spinning technology and on yarn production.

During the early Meiji period cotton yarn was produced with the *gara*-spinning (cup-throstle spinning) technique. This method was invented in 1876 by Tatsuchi Gaun, a priest in Minami Azumi District of Nagano Prefecture, and was awarded the highest prize at the First Industrial Exhibition held in the following year.[3] The *gara* spinner, basically an improvement on the hand-spinning technique inherited from the Tokugawa period, used tubes made of tin plate, one inch in diameter and 5 to 7 inches long. Raw cotton was stuffed into revolving tubes. Twisted thread was formed by pulling the cotton through the tubes and winding it over bobbins.

The introduction of this technique raised labor productivity considerably. Daily output of a female worker, which had averaged 40–50 *monme* with the old spinner, increased to 650 *monme* with the *gara* spinner.[4] The rapid diffusion of the new spinner throughout the country was due both to its greater efficiency and its low equipment cost.

As the *gara* technique spread, water-powered versions of this equipment were developed. One document records that by introducing water wheels the number of spindles operated by one worker increased from 30 to 100.[5] The pairing of the water wheel and the *gara* spinner was responsible both for the high percentage of powered factories among small-scale spinners in the early years and for the heavy reliance of these plants on water power. In addition, water-powered *gara* spinning

[3] The readings of the characters for Gaun's given name offer several possible pronounciations (eg. Tatsuchi, Tokimune, Tatsumune, Shinchi), but it is now believed that Tatsuchi is the correct one..

For the history of *gara*-spinning technology, we referred to Gendai Nippon Sangyō Hattatsushi Kennkyūkai 1964b; 1967b; Nippon Sen-i Kyōgikai 1958b.

[4] Uchida 1960, p. 146.

[5] Kanbayashi 1948, p. 64. Uchida cites the fact that by introducing water power daily output per worker increased to 18 *kan* of fine thread and 7 *kan* of thick thread, but he does not give earlier output figures for comparison (1960, p. 146).

Table 9-4. Composition of Primary Power Capacity (H') by Engine Type and by Factory Scale in Spinning: 1909–1919 (percent)

Scale (persons)	Primary Electric Motors (β')	Steam Engines and Turbines	Internal Combustion Engines	Water Wheels and Turbines
		1909		
All factories	0.2	92.7	1.2	5.9
5– 9	0.0	0.0	9.1	90.9
10– 29	16.3	4.6	11.8	67.3
30– 49	0.0	78.0	0.0	22.0
50– 99	0.0	84.2	0.0	15.8
100–499	1.8	75.5	0.1	22.6
500–999	0.0	94.4	1.9	3.7
1,000 or more	0.0	95.2	1.2	3.6
		1914		
All factories	11.5	82.5	2.2	3.8
5– 9	8.3	19.5	11.1	61.1
10– 29	32.7	0.0	45.5	21.8
30– 49	0.0	0.0	0.0	100.0[a]
50– 99	42.3	0.0	0.0	57.7
100–499	21.5	42.9	2.1	33.5
500–999	3.1	94.5	2.4	0.0
1,000 or more	12.4	85.1	2.1	0.4
		1919		
All factories	33.5	62.7	1.2	2.6
5– 9	20.4	0.0	38.7	40.9
10– 29	44.0	3.3	20.1	32.6
30– 49	56.7	14.3	12.2	16.8
50– 99	78.8	0.0	8.6	12.6
100–499	31.0	36.6	4.1	28.3
500–999	33.2	64.7	0.8	1.3
1,000 or more	33.5	64.6	0.9	1.0

Sources: Same as Table 8-3.

Notes: Figures are for the private factories with five or more production workers.

[a] See the notes to Table 9-2.

became popular as a supplementary source of income for farmers. The spread of water-powered *gara* spinning made possible in large part the growth of domestic output of cotton yarn through the 1880s.

The water-powered *gara* spinner became the mainstay of the traditional spinning industry. The continued viability of this traditional sector was due largely to advances in the application of water power. To see the impact of water power on this technique we will take as an example the Mikawa region of Aichi Prefecture, where *gara*-spinning technique made the greatest progress. Here water wheels were utilized in two ways. They were boat spinning on the water and land-based water wheel spinning in the mountains.

The first method, boat spinning was introduced in 1878 by Rokusaburo Suzuki. In that year Suzuki learned of the high reputation which the *gara* spinner had earned at the industrial exhibition and visited Gaun to purchase some machines. Together, he and Gaun carried the spinners to Yokosuka Village in the Hazu District of Mikawa. After an unsuccessful attempt to operate the machines with a stationary water wheel, they installed the spinners in a boat floating on the Yahagi River and powered them with a water wheel set in the boat. As is shown in Table 9-5, the number of such spinning boats increased from only 3 in 1879 to 46 in 1882. Family members and employees of the owner often lived together on these boats. Boat spinning benefitted from several subsequent innovations. Around the year 1885 spinners with 30 to 90 spindles were driven by water wheels placed on one side of each boat, and around 1907 two water wheels, one on each side of every boat, turned machines with 240 to 320 spindles. The number of spinning boats began decreasing after reaching a peak in 1898. As boat spinning became less profitable than electric powered spinning, boat operators gradually switched to land-based factories. Finally in 1934 the last spinning boats disappeared, because of being less profitable and due to river conservation.

The second spinning method, land-based water wheel spinning, also developed in Mikawa in 1879. In that year Takisaburo Komura installed a *gara* spinner with 60 spindles in a communally owned water mill in

Table 9-5. Number of Spinning Boats at Nakahata in Mikawa

Year	Number of Boats
1879	3
1882	46
1898	59
1905	40
1917	27
1922	17
1926	13
1933	7
1934	0

Sources:. Nippon Sen-i Kyōgikai 1958b, table 1 of chap. 6 on p. 381.

Takaoka Village in the Aomi District. Later Komura moved to Tokiwa Village in the Nukata District and continued his experiment with water-powered spinners. His technique was quickly adopted in that village and in others in the Nukata District, a region with abundant streams. A number of water wheels which had previously been used only for processing rice and grinding rape seeds were converted to spinning. The number of spindles in establishments belonging to the association of *gara*-spinning in Mikawa tripled in the short span from 1884 to 1887 (Table 9-6).[6] The association's output quintupled over the same period.

According to Table 9-6, the number of spindles and output at the Mikawa establishments fell remarkably between 1887 and 1892. This setback in *gara* spinning was the result of the development of the modern cotton-spinning sector and of increased textile imports. Therefore, *gara* spinning could not compete with modern technology either inside or outside Japan.

Table 9-6 also shows, however, that after 1892 water-powered *gara* spinning experienced a recovery. Both output and the number of

[6] The association is the *Mikawa Garabō-Ito Kōgyō Kumiai* (Mikawa gara-spinning manufacturing association).

Table 9-6.   Number of Spindles and Quantity of Output of the
             Mikawa Gara-Spinning Manufacturing Association:
             1884–1937

	Number of Spindles	Quantity of Output
	(1,000)	(1,000 *kan*)
1884	44	62
1887	132	309
1892	75	187
1897	115	435
1902	123	666
1907	158	901
1912	173	1,236
1917	210	1,144
1922	365	1,964
1927	351	1,371
1932	399	1,956
1937	748	3,489

Sources: Nippon Sen-i Kyōgikai 1958b, table 3 of chap. 6 on p. 382.

spindles increased regularly over the twentieth century right up to World
War II.[7] This was due to the fact that, in order to survive in the face of
competition from modern technology, these traditional spinners spe-
cialized in producing low-quality, thick cotton yarns which were used in
weaving carpets, blankets, flannel, soles for *tabi* (Japanese socks), and so
forth. Futhermore, these spinners began to use rags, cotton discarded by
the modern spinning plants, and other waste thread in order to save on
production costs.

Modern sector. Modern cotton-spinning techniques were introduced
in the 1860s by the Satsuma Clan, which imported spinning machines

[7]   This fact seems to explain the aforementioned increase in the number of small
spinning plants between 1909 and 1940. See n. 2.

from England.[8] In 1867 this clan established Japan's first steam-powered factory, the Kagoshima Spinning Mill, and in 1870 erected a second steam-powered mill, the Sakai Spinning Mill. Although these two earliest modern spinning mills both employed steam engines, almost all other modern spinning plants established in the next few years were equipped with water wheels. Despite the initial simultaneous appearance of modern spinning technology and steam-powered spinning, water power was the main route by which the modern technology was introduced in Japan. The Kashima Spinning Mill, established in 1872, was powered by a 25-hp water wheel run by water supplied from the Senkawa Aquaduct, a branch of the Tamagawa Acquaduct.[9] In addition, those spinning mills which were erected between 1879 and 1885 either directly by the government or with the financial help of the government under the policy to promote industrialization were largely dependent on water power.[10] For example, the government-operated Aichi and Hiroshima Spinning Mills were powered by water wheels. And, among the fifteen privately owned mills established under this industrialization policy, eight were equipped with water wheels and one installed both a water wheel and a steam engine, and the rest of them was equipped with steam engines. These mills, seventeen in total, were all of approximately equivalent size. They are known as the *nisen-sui bōseki* (spinning mills with two thousand spindles).

The early dependence of spinning industry on water power was a reflection of the energy policy of the Meiji government to save coal consumption (chapter 2). Water-powered spinning should have been more profitable than steam-powered spinning in the power cost. Although no records are available to make this comparison in the Japanese spinning industry, the following two studies give indirect but

[8] For the history of the modern cotton-spinning industry before World War II, we referred to Gendai Nippon Sangyō Hattatsushi Kenkyūkai 1964b; 1967b; Kiyokawa 1973; Nippon Sen-i Kyōgikai 1958b.

[9] The Kagoshima, Sakai, and Kashima spinning mills are known as the *shiso san-bōseki* (three pioneer spinning mills).

[10] For the water power utilization in the modern cotton-spinning industry, refer to Harada 1973; Okamoto 1975; Sueo 1980, part 3.

suggestive informations. The first is a study by Peter Temin on cotton-spinning mills in the United States.[11] He compared the annual power costs per horsepower in the water-powered mills at Lowell, Massachusetts and the steam-powered mills at Newburyport, Massachusetts. He found that power costs were rather higher in the steam-powered mills, because of high operating costs, especially the high cost of coal. The second is a survey on the paper manufacturing industry in Japan for the late 1880s.[12] In 1890 the Fuji Paper Manufacturing Company established the Iriyamase Plant in Shizuoka Prefecture was equipped with three American made water turbines (total capacity of 1,222 hp). Before establishing this plant, the company estimated both capital costs and current costs expected in this plant and compared these costs with costs of a plant in Tokyo using steam power. These estimates show that although capital costs were almost equal in the two cases (¥33,684 in the former case and ¥32,912 in the latter case), annual current costs of the water-powered plant were much smaller (¥17,777 including costs to transport products to Tokyo,¥11,279) than in the steam-powered plant (¥66,455). The savings in current costs by using water wheels came largely from a saving in coal consumption (¥59,389).

However, these first modern spinning plants relying almost exclusively on water power were not successful and were shut down after sometime. There were several factors responsible for this failure. Among them we can point out a lack of good engineers, small-scale production without economies of scale, usage of low-quality domestic raw cotton, and unreliability of water power. The last factor requires more explanations. Although the cost of water power was less than that of steam power, water power was sometimes unreliable as it depended on seasonal fluctuations of water streams. Unlike the Kashima Spinning Mill, which was powered by an artificial water stream, almost all of the early modern spinning mills suffered from seasonal insufficiency in water because they relied on natural streams. Consequently some of those powered by water wheels installed steam engines as an additional source of

[11] Temin 1966, table 4 on p. 197.
[12] Sugiyama 1889, pp. 562–73.

power soon after their establishment. For instance the Mi-e Spinning Mill, established in 1883, found that water supply was insufficient.[13] Water supply decreased in summer owing to the irrigation of paddy field, and stopped completely in winter due to the dry season. The company estimated that the 30-hp water wheel generated only 10 hp on the average for all seasons. Consequently sometimes a part of the machines was stopped, and the speed of operation was very low. Thus, in 1885 the Mi-e Spinning added a 25-hp steam engine, which had been used at the Printing Bureau of the government.

The appearance of the Osaka Spinning Mill marked an epoch in the development of this industry.[14] Eiichi Shibusawa, the greatest enterpreneur in Meiji Japan, who was anxious about the large amount of import of cotton yarn, planned to erect a big cotton-spinning company in 1879. The company was established in 1882 by gathering capital from the aristocracy and cotton merchants and started production in 1883. Thus the company became the first commercially viable mill to use modern technology. Its success can be attributed to overcoming the aforementioned problems which afflicted the earlier mills. First, the company trained engineers in advance and did not suffer from a lack of skilled manpower. That is, Shibusawa persuaded Takeo Yamabe, who was a student of economics staying in London at that time, to participate in his plan. Thus Yamabe, after a study of cotton-spinning technology at Manchester, came back to Japan and, as a chief engineer and later a president of the company, greatly contributed to the development of the company. Furthermore Shibusawa trained four other engineers at the Japanese mills. Second, the Osaka Mill was much larger than the previous ones and its 10,000 spindle mules made it possible to reap the advantages of economies of scale. Third, the Osaka Mill used high-quality imported raw cotton in place of the inferior domestic raw cotton used by the previous plants.

Fourth, the mill was equipped from the outset with a steam engine,

[13] Tōyō Bōseki K.K. 1953, pp. 52–53.
[14] The Osaka Spinning Mill, merging the Mi-e Spinning Mill, became Toyo Spinning Company in 1914.

and therefore it was free from unreliability of water power. It is interesting to point out, however, that Shibusawa's original plan was to use water power. He and Yamabe together, with the assistance of an engineer who had installed the water wheel in the previous spinning mills and a Dutch engineer on public works, made a survey on water resources in various regions. The survey revealed that the 140–150 hp of water power, which would be required to run 10,000 spindle machines was not available. Thus Shibusawa changed the original plan and decided to use steam power.[15] In addition to these four factors, a double-shift labor force system introduced at Osaka Spinning significantly reduced production costs and contributed to the plant's success as a commercial venture.

The success of Osaka Spinning motivated the fusciculation of other modern, large spinning mills. In 1887 plants with more than 10,000 spindles were built by a number of companies including Tenman Spinning, Tokyo Spinning, Kanegafuchi Spinning, and Hirano Spinning. Over the next few years production of cotton yarn increased considerably and exceeded domestic demand in 1891. In 1897 exports of cotton yarn surpassed imports.[16] The substantial development of the spinning industry, to the point of achieving import substitution and subsequently expanding yarn exports, was made possible by the introduction of steam power in the modern spinning sector.

Electrification

Electric lighting. In spinning mills, as well as in other kinds of factories, electric lighting was introduced much earlier than electric motive power. A pioneer in this field was the Sangenya Plant of Osaka Spinning. In 1886 Tokyo Electric Light Company lit electric lamps in this plant by electricity generated by an American-made 25-kW direct-current dynamo.[17] This innovation contributed to the reduction of

---

[15] Harada 1973, pp. 175, 177.

[16] Gendai Nippon Sangyō Hattatsushi Kenkyūkai 1964b, appendix table III-6.

[17] Arisawa 1960d, p. 39; Gendai Nippon Sangyō Hattatsushi Kenkyūkai 1964a, chronological table.

production costs by extending production time. Although Osaka Spinning had begun operating with a night shift before the introduction of electric lights, there had been a movement for the abolition of night shifts because of the danger of fire from kerosene lamps.[18] Electrification eliminated this danger and permitted the widespread use of the efficient night-shift system.

Introduction of motors. Where in Japan electric motors were first used in spinning is unknown. One document suggests that a mill in Kyoto may have been the first in the spinning industry to employ electricity for motive power.[19] Keage Power Plant began generating electricity for this mill in 1892, but it is not certain whether the electricity was used for driving motors or simply for lighting. According to the same document, however, it is certain that the Suruga Koyama Plant of Fuji Gas Spinning employed electricity for motive power in 1903. The records clearly state that this plant ran a 150-hp direct-current motor from a 120-kW dynamo.

Substantial progress in the electrification of spinning mills was realized with the development of electric utilities which supplied cheap electric power. The Shikanjima Plant of Osaka Spinning was one of the first spinning plants electrified by purchased power. This occurred in 1907.[20] Electrification spread throughout the spinning industry during the 1910s and 1920s. By eliminating the power plant through the use of purchased power, spinning mills saved greatly on capital and operating costs. Thus, purchased electricity proved cheaper than either direct drive or indirect drive by steam power.

It was the shift from group drive to unit drive, however, which gave electrification a decisive advantage. In a group-drive system, power was transmitted by long shafts and a group of belts from one or two engines to individual machines, whereas with unit drive an individual machine was run directly by its own small motor. From the end of World War I until the middle of the 1920s, unit drive was employed with the spinning

[18] Arisawa 1959, p. 67.
[19] Meiji Kōgyōshi Hensan Iinkai 1928, pp. 455–56.
[20] Nippon Sen-i Kyōgikai 1958a, p. 788.

machinery which required shifts in speed, while group drive was still widely used with other machinery. An increase in the domestic production of small induction motors facilitated the diffusion of the unit-drive system beginning in the 1920s.[21] Between 1930 and 1931 the Inami Plant of Kureha Spinning and the Sasazu Plant of Tenman Weaving introduced this system to all production stages up to and including the actual spinning operation. Then, in 1932, the Sekigahara Plant of Dai-Nippon Spinning became the first to employ this system for all processes from mixing raw cotton to twisting and reeling.[22]

The advantage of the unit-drive system. The shift from group drive to unit drive was one of the major technological advances in the spinning industry before World War II.[23] The advantages of unit drive were several. First, long shafts and groups of belts no longer restricted the location of machinery within plants. As a result, factory layout could be organized with regard to production efficiency. Second, because of the reduction in required space and lack of need for sturdy structures to support the shafts and belts, the unit-drive system led to savings in capital costs. Third, abolishing the drive belts reduced the scattering of cotton dust and improved sanitary conditions for the workers. Fourth, the elimination of shafts and belts kept the running speed of machinery constant, which in turn resulted in improvement of output quality.[24] Fifth, with unit-drive system some machines could stand idle without wasting energy. This advantage was particularly significant to the spinning industry, which was characterized by frequent reductions in operations.[25]

Although it is undeniable that the introduction of the unit-drive

[21]   These motors, which were of 6–8 hp, were called "ring motors". Tsunekawa 1916, p. 93.

[22]   Moriya 1948, p. 81.

[23]   The advantages of unit drive in spinning have been pointed out by many authors: Arisawa 1960d, p. 59; Iijima 1949, pp. 201–02; Kajinishi 1948, pp. 90–91; Moriya 1948, pp. 80–81; Nippon Sen-i Kyōgikai 1958a, p. 788; 1958b, pp. 33–34. We have relied heavily on these studies.

[24]   Matsumura emphasized this advantage (1923, p. 159).

[25]   Kiyokawa 1973, p. 133.

system raised productivity and decreased production costs, there are practically limited quantitative studies which examine these effects of the unit-drive system. A 1937 study by an engineer Sakio Imamura, which was made public by Fumio Moriya, is one of the rare examples. This study shows that daily output of 40-count cotton yarn increased from 39.25 *monme* to 51.30 *monme* per spindle with the shift from group to unit drive. At the same time electric power consumption increased from 692 kWH to 825 kWH. Moriya, who was skeptical of Imamura's estimates of electric power consumption, presented alternative estimates which show that in production of 20-count yarn, power consumption fell from 283 kWH with group drive to 263 kWH with unit drive.[26] In contrast to Imamura's study, Moriya's figures indicate that the shift to unit drive both raised output per spindle and reduced electric power consumption.

Although unit drive may have reduced operating costs by reducing electric consumption, a third study by Shigetaro Matsumura indicates that the cost of equipment excluding electric power generators (electric wire, motors, shafts, and so forth) was probably greater for the unit-drive than for the group-drive system. Matsumura studied spinning mills which used steam-generated electric power and found that equipment costs ranged between ¥83 and ¥95 per kWH for the unit-drive system while they were only ¥75 for the group-drive system.[27] From these few studies we cannot reach a precise conclusion about the net effect of the introduction of the unit-drive system on total production costs. Nevertheless, the increase in output and production efficiency coupled with the numerous advantages of the elimination of the shafts and belts most certainly made unit-drive production in the spinning industry far superior to the group-drive system.[28]

[26] Moriya 1948, p. 80.
[27] Matsumura 1923, p. 154.
[28] The advantages of the unit-drive system will be studied generally in chap. 14.

Chapter 10

THE WEAVING INDUSTRY

Weaving was another important part of Japan's textile industry. The value of weaving output was much larger than that of silk reeling or spinning for all the years from 1874 to 1940 (panel A, Table 8-1). Also, export of woven goods was larger than that of spun yarn in every year from 1890 to 1940 (panel B, Table 8-1). The important place of weaving in the textile industry is also evident from statistics on the number of factories. There were 8,436 weaving plants with 5 or more workers in 1909 and 16,288 in 1940. By comparison, there were 3,720 silk-reeling plants in 1909 and 1,854 in 1940, and there were only 143 spinning mills in 1909 and 959 in 1940.[1]

One of the conspicuous features of this industry was the predominance of small-scale factories. About 90% of all weaving factories in 1909 were those employing 5 to 29 workers, and the proportion of these small plants remained close to 90% even in 1940. In other textile industries comparable figures are 52.0% and 40.0% for silk reeling and 28.0% and 60.9% for spinning in 1909 and 1940 respectively.[2]

By examining the weaving industry, then, some conclusions can be reached about the impact of the power revolution in the small-scale factories which predominated in the Japanese economy as a whole.

The first section of this chapter surveys the history of the power

---

[1] STF 1909 and 1940. See Table A-2.

Out of all 8,436 weaving plants in 1909, 3,568 were engaged in cotton weaving, 4,723 in silk weaving and silk and cotton weaving, and 145 in hemp and wool weaving. STF 1909. See Table A-2.

[2] See n. 1.

revolution in quantitative terms. The second section examines the motives for introduction of power looms. The third section treats the impact of power looms on small-scale weaving plants, and the last section discusses the impact of electrification on large-scale weaving plants.

Quantitative Survey of Power Utilization

Mechanization

In the early twentieth century, the proportion of factories which were mechanically powered in the weaving industry was quite low compared with other industries. In weaving factories with 10 or more workers the proportion of powered factories, α, was merely 5.1% in 1900 and 9.3% in 1905 (Table 10-1). By contrast, in manufacturing as a whole, α was 32.3% in 1900 and 43.8% in 1905 (Table 4-4).[3] For weaving factories with 5 or more workers estimates are given in Table 10-2. In 1909 14.0% of these factories were mechanized, a proportion only half of that in manufacturing as a whole (Table 4-5). Mechanization was least advanced in the smaller weaving plants. In 1909 α was only 5.2% in the smallest scale, 5-9 workers, and 16.4% in the second smallest scale, 10–29 workers (Table 10-2). Comparable figures for manufacturing as a whole were 14.4% and 30.1% (Table 4-7). Because of the predominance of small plants in the weaving industry, the very low degree of mechanization in these plants explains, for the most part, the reason why the weaving industry as a whole was less dependent on mechanical power than other industries.

An increasing tendency in α can be seen after 1909. This increase was especially noticeable between 1919 and 1930, when α increased from 53.5% to 90.5%. During this period drastic changes were attributed first to the smallest-scale weaving plants and second to the next smallest-scale weaving plants, 53.8% point and 34.6% point respectively. Because of the progress of mechanization in small weaving plants, α in the weaving

[3]   STAC 1900 and 1905. See Table A-1.

Table 10-1. Proportion of Powered Factories (α) and Composition of Total Power Capacity (H) by Engine Type in Weaving: 1890–1915

(percent)

Year	Proportion of Powered Factories (α)	Composition of H			
		Electric Motors (β)	Steam Engines and Turbines	Internal Combustion Engines	Water Wheels and Turbines
1890			100.0		0.0
1895			96.2		3.8
1900	5.1	0.1	92.1	2.2	5.6
1905	9.3	2.7	91.7	2.9	2.7
1910	30.8	11.6	71.5	15.2	1.7
1915	56.1	29.0	52.6	17.2	1.2

Sources: Same as Table 8-2.
Notes: See the notes to Table 8-2.

Table 10-2. Proportion of Powered Factories (α) by Factory Scale in Weaving

(percent)

Scale (persons)	1909	1914	1919	1930	1935	1940
All factories	14.0	37.5	53.5	90.5	93.8	94.4
5– 9	5.2	17.3	33.4	87.2	92.0	92.9
10– 29	16.4	43.2	58.5	93.1	94.3	95.3
30– 49	39.1	72.0	85.7	96.5	97.3	96.6
50– 99	54.9	81.8	92.7	98.9	98.4	98.4
100–499	74.7	90.9	97.2	99.6	99.7	99.7
500–999	100.0	100.0	100.0	100.0	100.0	100.0
1,000 or more	100.0	100.0	100.0	100.0	100.0	100.0

Sources: Same as Table 8-3.
Notes: Figures are for the private factories with five or more production workers.

Table 10-3. Composition of Total Power Capacity (H) by
Engine Type and by Factory Scale in Weaving:
1909–1940

(percent)

Scale (persons)	Electric Motors (β)	Steam Engines and Turbines	Internal Combustion Engines	Water Wheels and Turbines
		1909		
All factories	13.6	68.7	13.1	4.6
5– 9	13.6	8.7	44.4	33.3
10– 29	11.1	17.0	63.5	8.4
30– 49	13.4	42.7	42.0	1.9
50– 99	21.7	56.1	21.0	1.2
100–499	17.6	70.3	1.9	10.2
500–999	3.4	87.1	2.7	6.8
1,000 or more	15.1	84.7	0.2	0.0
		1914		
All factories	29.4	45.8	22.9	1.9
5– 9	49.7	5.2	33.8	11.3
10– 29	27.7	10.4	57.8	4.1
30– 49	24.9	18.8	53.8	2.5
50– 99	24.1	33.9	39.9	2.1
100–499	28.0	50.3	19.9	1.8
500–999	32.5	64.6	0.1	2.8
1,000 or more	31.3	62.8	5.9	0.0
		1919		
All factories	64.8	19.3	14.7	1.2
5– 9	64.6	0.7	29.8	4.9
10– 29	51.7	1.5	44.6	2.2
30– 49	57.0	10.0	32.0	1.0
50– 99	54.6	18.4	26.1	0.9
100–499	51.2	31.2	16.5	1.1
500–999	66.0	27.7	0.0	6.3
1,000 or more	78.7	21.3	0.0	0.0

Table 10-3. (continued)

(percent)

Scale (persons)	Electric Motors (β)	Steam Engines and Turbines	Internal Combustion Engines	Water Wheels and Turbines
		1930		
All factories	81.9	9.1	6.2	2.8
5– 9	93.5	0.2	5.9	0.4
10– 29	94.5	0.5	4.7	0.3
30– 49	93.6	1.4	4.5	0.5
50– 99	94.9	2.7	2.3	0.1
100–499	82.2	2.5	14.9	0.4
500–999	91.9	7.5	0.6	0.0
1,000 or more	66.1	24.9	0.3	8.7
		1935		
All factories	82.8	12.2	4.9	0.1
5– 9	92.9	0.2	6.8	0.1
10– 29	90.1	0.2	9.6	0.1
30– 49	87.6	0.8	11.4	0.2
50– 99	86.7	1.6	11.5	0.2
100–499	87.4	5.1	7.4	0.1
500–999	86.2	13.8	0.0	0.0
1,000 or more	73.1	26.9	0.0	0.0
		1940		
All factories	91.2	6.3	2.4	0.1
5– 9	96.7	0.1	2.9	0.3
10– 29	96.0	0.0	4.0	0 0
30– 49	95.0	0.0	4.9	0.1
50– 99	95.2	0.4	4.2	0.2
100–499	94.5	2.6	2.9	0.0
500–999	86.8	13.1	0.1	0.0
1,000 or more	80.7	19.3	0.0	0.0

Sources: Same as Table 8-3.
Notes: Figures are for the private factories with five or more production workers.

Table 10-4. Composition of Primary Power Capacity (H') by
Engine Type and by Factory Scale in Weaving:
1909–1919   (percent)

Scale (persons)	Primary Electric Motors (β')	Steam Engines and Turbines	Internal Combustion Engines	Water Wheels and Turbines
1909				
All factories	7.6	73.5	14.0	4.9
5– 9	13.6	8.7	44.4	33.3
10– 29	11.1	17.0	63.5	8.4
30– 49	13.3	42.7	42.1	1.9
50– 99	21.5	56.3	21.0	1.2
100–499	16.1	71.6	1.9	10.4
500–999	1.0	89.3	2.8	6.9
1,000 or more	0.0	99.8	0.2	0.0
1914				
All factories	20.4	51.7	25.8	2.1
5– 9	49.8	5.2	33.7	11.3
10– 29	27.5	10.5	57.9	4.1
30– 49	24.9	18.8	53.8	2.5
50– 99	24.0	33.9	40.0	2.1
100–499	14.7	59.7	23.5	2.1
500–999	11.8	84.5	0.1	3.6
1,000 or more	19.4	73.6	7.0	0.0
1919				
All factories	62.9	20.4	15.5	1.2
5– 9	64.4	0.7	30.0	4.9
10– 29	51.2	1.5	45.1	2.2
30– 49	56.2	10.2	32.6	1.0
50– 99	52.9	19.1	27.1	0.9
100–499	49.3	32.4	17.1	1.2
500–999	59.2	33.3	0.0	7.5
1,000 or more	77.1	22.9	0.0	0.0

Sources: Same as Table 8-3.
Notes: Figures are for the private factories with five or more production workers.

industry as a whole reached 90.5% in 1930, exceeding the 82.5% average in the manufacturing sector (Table 4-7). As will be shown later, this rapid diffusion of mechanical power contributed greatly to increase in production efficiency, especially in small weaving plants.

Transition of Power Capacity by Engine Type

A distinctive feature of power utilization in Japan's weaving industry during the early years of industrialization was the predominance of steam power over water power. According to Table 10-1, the share of steam power in total power capacity was 100.0% in 1890, and this share remained above 90% until 1905. As Tables 10-3 and 10-4 show, steam was by far the most important source of power for large-scale weaving plants between 1909 and 1914. Though, figures on power utilization by scale for these early years are not available, these large plants were undoubtedly even more dependent on steam power before the turn of the century. The predominance of steam power in large weaving plants and the low degree of mechanization in small weaving plants together account for the high percentage of steam power in total power capacity for the weaving industry as a whole during the early twentieth century.

From 1919 onward, power utilization in the weaving industry was characterized by wide-scale electrification. As Tables 10-3 and 10-4 show, electric motors became the most important source of power in weaving plants of all sizes. The diffusion of electric power in the weaving industry was particularly significant in small factories. These plants, which had remained largely without mechanical power up to the 1910s, were mechanized through the introduction of electric motors.

Power utilization in the weaving industry was also characterized by relatively wide diffusion of internal combustion engines during the 1900s and 1910s. The share of internal combustion engines in total power capacity (H) was 13.1% in 1909, 22.9% in 1914 and 14.7% in 1919 (Table 10-3). In the manufacturing sector as a whole, on the other hand, internal combustion engines comprised 6.2%, 7.0%, and 4.8% of H in the same three years (Table 6-6).[4] The share of these engines in H' was also higher in the weaving industry (Table 10-4) than in manufacturing as a whole (Table 6-7). The relatively greater use of internal combustion engines in weaving was primarily concentrated in small- and medium-scale weaving plants. In fact, for a short time internal combustion engines were the largest source of power for these plants. In 1914, internal combustion engines comprised 34 to 58% of H in weaving plants with 5-99 workers (Table 10-3), while their share of power capacity in small manufacturing plants as a whole was only 9 to 20% (Table 6-6). Internal combustion engines thus played a more important role in the weaving industry before the age of electric power than they did in other industries.

The Introduction of Modern Technology

The Introduction of Batten and Jacquard

There were two groups of modern weaving technologies introduced to Meiji Japan.[5] They were the batten and jacquard apparatus, and the power loom.

In the traditional hand loom, a weaver depressed treadles with his foot in a sequence suited to the pattern and the scheme of drawing the warp through healds. The warp thread ascended or descended with healds to form a shed for a shuttle to be passed through ('shedding'). The shuttle was thrown between the divided warp by one hand and caught at the opposite side selvage by another hand ('picking'). With the batten (flying shuttle) invented by John Kay in England in 1733, an operator could set the shuttle in motion by giving a sharp jerk to the cord attached to the picker instead of throwing the shuttle. The batten increased the speed of weaving, because it freed one hand of the weaver and made it possible to devote the hand exclusively to the manipulation of the 'beating up'

---

[4] Among internal combustion engines, oil engines were more prevalent than gas engines in 1909, but in the next several years after 1909 gas engines became decisively predominant over oil engines. STF 1909, 1914, and 1919. See Table A-2.

[5] For the history of weaving technologies, we rely on Gendai Nippon Sangyō Hattatsushi Kenkyūkai 1964b.

motion.[6] The batten and the jacquard (the attachment to form figured patterns invented by Joseph-Marie Jacquard in 1801) were brought first from Lyon, France to Nishijin in Kyoto City, one of the representative districts for silk-weaving in Japan. Three weavers in Nishijin (Tsunehichi Sakura and others), went to Lyon to study the modern weaving technology in Lyon responding to the order of the Kyoto Prefecture in 1872, and returned to Japan in the next year with the batten and jacquard apparatus. In 1874 the Kyoto Prefecture demonstrated this apparatus at the exhibition and established a model plant to teach the imported technology in Kyoto. Besides this route, modern weaving technology was introduced from Austria to Tokyo in 1873, and also from the United States to Kiryū, Gunma Prefecture in 1886.

The batten and jacquard apparatus was soon copied by local carpenters in Nishijin, Kiryū, Ashikaga (Tochigi Prefecture) and other districts. For instance a carpenter (Kohei Araki) in Nishijin succeeded in making a copy after a two-year trial in 1877, only three years after its introduction to Nishijin. The copy made by these carpenters was made of wood and was much simpler in mechanism than the original. Because of easiness in production and cheapness in price, the batten and jacquard apparatus was soon adopted by weaving plants in various regions and was widely used until the end of the nineteenth century. These attachments, which raised productivity of the hand loom to a considerable extent, greatly contributed to the development of the weaving industry.

An interesting question to be asked is why the three students from Nishijin brought with them the old technology (hand loom with batten and jacquard), but not the new and more efficient technology (power loom), which had been already available in France. According to the study by Tadashi Ishii, they seemed to decide to bring what could easily be copied in Japan, and thought that the power loom could not be produced by the under-developed machine industry in Japan at that

---

[6] Weaving consists of three major motions; shedding, picking and beating up (Encyclopaedia Britannica 1958, p. 461).

time.[7] Thus it seems to me that their inclination to the hand loom rather than the power loom can be taken as an example of an appropriate choice of technology (chapter 15).

The Diffusion of Power Looms

History. The power loom, which was invented by Edmund Cartwright in England in 1785, was a mechanism in which the three motions for weaving (shedding, picking and beating up) were made simultaneously by mechanical power. Owing to this mechanism one weaver could attend several looms at the same time.[8] This merit of the power loom was responsible for a greater impact on the weaving industry than the batten and jacquard apparatus.

The power loom was first imported to Japan by the Satsuma Clan and used in the water-powered factory to weave cotton cloth between 1856 and 1858. Also in 1867 one hundred English-made looms powered by water wheels were imported to Satsuma Clan's spinning mill (Kagoshima Spinning Mill). However the substantial diffusion of power looms was seen not until the late 1880s. The first private cotton weaving factory to introduce power looms was the Shibuya Cotton Fabric Mill (later, Onagigawa Cotton Fabric Mill), which installed these looms in 1885. In the next ten years after 1885 many large, export-oriented factories producing cotton fabric were set up. In 1887, for instance, Kyoto Cotton Weaving and Osaka Weaving were established.

The broad power looms (power loom for broad fabrics) installed in these factories and other large weaving plants established at that time were all imported. Sakichi Toyoda invented a wooden narrow power loom (power loom for narrow fabrics) in 1897 and a wooden-iron narrow power loom in 1907. Toyoda also invented three types of all-iron

---

[7] Ishii 1979, p. 39.

[8] The treadle loom was similar to the power loom in that three motions were made simultaneously. A difference was that the former was operated by pressing down the treadle by foot of an operator. The origin of the treadle loom in Japan is unknown; it is considered that it was developed by imitating the imported treadle loom or by modifying the imported power loom in the late Meiji period (Sanpei 1961, p. 70).

narrow machines in 1908, 1909 and 1914.[9] After these developments imported power looms were gradually replaced by domestic ones.

In contrast to large weaving plants, which were equipped with modern technology from the time of their establishment in the 1880s, small cotton weaving plants continued to employ traditional hand looms until the 1910s. Although these machines had been improved by the batten and jacquard apparatus, they were still operatted by human power. The appearance of domestically produced narrow power looms finally made mechanization of small weaving plants possible, because the cost of these machines were brought within reach. The narrow power loom invented by Toyoda in 1897, for example, cost only ¥93, compared with ¥872 for a German machine and ¥389 for a French one. Small-scale cotton weaving plants rapidly switched from hand looms to power looms once the new technology became affordable.

The first application of power looms to silk weaving occurred in 1872 in Kiryū. In 1882 Nishijin Kyōshin Weaving Company wove satin by steam power. Just as in the cotton-weaving industry, the substantial diffusion of power looms in the silk-weaving industry was made possible by the domestic production of small, inexpensive machines. A Japanese, Yonejiro Tsuda, completed a power loom designed for silk weaving in 1900.

A number of large-scale plants producing worsted fabric were established during the 1880s. These plants, like large-scale cotton weaving plants, were all equipped with modern power looms. Small- and medium-scale worsted weaving plants however, did not begin to introduce power looms until well into the first decade of the twentieth century. The Tokyo Kurihara Plant was the first small-scale worsted factory to use these machines. In 1907 this company also installed 10 English and 10 Japanese power looms to produce muslin.

The automatic loom, which was invented by John H. Northrop in the United States in 1894, was an improvement of the power loom. The former was equipped with devices for stoppage of motions in case of

[9] For the history of developing the power loom in Japan, see Ishii 1979 and 1987; Minami, Ishii and Makino 1982, pp. 347–56.

225

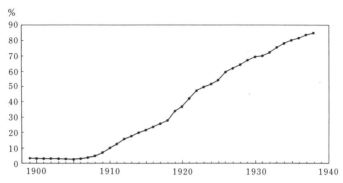

Fig. 10-1. Proportion of Power Looms (γ) in Weaving

Sources: 1899–1923: STAC. 1924–38: STMCI.
Notes: γ is the proportion of power looms in total looms (hand, treadle and power looms).

Table 10-5. Proportion of Power Looms (γ) by Type of Products in Weaving: 1922–1938

(percent)

	Silk	Cotton	Worsted	Hemp
1922	35.60	56.95	64.00	13.34
1925	41.97	65.41	73.79	14.71
1930	58.91	78.35	96.77	19.58
1935	75.25	86.16	97.77	29.77
1938	80.67	90.61	94.41	41.07

Sources: Same as Fig. 10-1.

warp breakage and for providing new weft thread automatically (replenishing the shuttle by replacing the exhausted bobbin with a full one). This new machine raised a number of looms which could be operated by one weaver. This machine was imported to the large-scale weaving plants operated by cotton-spinning companies such as Mie Spinning, Osaka Spinning and Kanakin Seishoku Companies at the turn of the century. In 1925 Sakichi Toyoda invented the automatic loom with a different mechanism to supply new weft (shuttle-changing loom) from the Northrop Loom. A substantial diffusion of the automatic loom was seen, however, only alfter WWII.

In the weaving industry (cotton, silk, worsted and others) as a whole, the proportion of power looms (including automatic looms) in the total number of looms (expressed as γ) increased from a negligible figure in the late 1900s to 85% in 1938 (Fig. 10-1). Diffusion of power looms was not uniform among industries; γ was higher in worsted, cotton, silk and hemp in that order (Table 10-5). In 1922, for instance, there was a 28 percentage points difference between worsted and silk.

Conditions for the diffusion: hypotheses. The speed of diffusion of power looms differed widely among regions even in the same industry group; in 1922, for instance, there was an 89 percentage points difference between Fukui and Isezaki (Gunma Prefecture) for silk weaving, and an 85 percentage points difference between Sennan (Osaka Prefecture) and Ōme (Tokyo Prefecture) for cotton weaving, and a 70 percentage points difference between Hyōgo and Bisai (Aichi Prefecture) for worsted weaving. This fact reveals clearly the importance of a study of the regional differences in the speed of the diffusion of power loom technology. These considerations may be essential to reveal the conditions for the diffusion of this technology.

The present writer and Fumio Makino have studied a difference in the utilization of power looms among different regions in the cotton weaving industry and its change over time.[10] In this study we have put forth three factors to explain the regional difference; (1) the diffusion of the factory system, (2) the technological ease to adopt power looms depending on products by kind, and (3) the availability of electric power.

(1) Power looms tend to be adopted more easily in the factory system than in the domestic production system dominated, largely, by the putting-out system (pieceworkers worked on looms and yarns given from clothiers and received wages for weaving from them) mainly because of three reasons.

a) Incentives for mechanization are decisively larger in the factory system

[10]   Minami and Makino 1983a.

Table 10-6.   Proportion of Power Looms (γ) by Type of Plants
and by Scale of Plants in Weaving: 1905–1938

(percent)

| | Putting-out System | | Independent Weavers | | |
	Weavers	Master Weavers	Domestic Weavers	Factories[a]	Average
1905	0.58	0.15	0.98	19.46	2.59
1910	0.62	2.87	1.57	49.19	9.56
1915	1.78	11.35	3.34	73.58	22.08
1920	9.95	26.49	10.60	83.80	36.77

Scale (Number of Looms)

	1–9	10–49	50 or More	Factories (10 or More)	Average
1922	9.21	75.68	95.07	86.20	47.72
1925	12.30	85.00	97.72	92.48	54.63
1930	21.05	93.62	98.63	96.71	69.90
1935	31.35	94.42	98.81	97.10	80.54
1938	34.48	94.77	98.94	97.39	84.97

Sources: Same as Fig. 10-1.
[a]   Plants with ten or more employees.

than in the traditional system. In the latter, weaving is a side job of the peasants in their slack season, therefore labor costs (measured by their opportunity cost) are so small that benefits of labor-saving innovation are negligible.[11] Also peasants are not interested in profitability of weaving, because this activity is inseparably connected with farming and household economy.[12] On the other hand factory owners, who have strong interests in their business, are keen on cost-down through

[11]   Sakai 1962, p. 137.
[12]   Tamaki 1957, p. 76.

mechanization.

b) Because of small-scale of production, with a few power looms in the traditional system, the power costs per loom tend to be so high that mechanization is not lucrative. Even one-horsepower electric motor can operate Several power looms. Consequently, in a factory with a large number of power looms, average power cost of operation can be maintained at a low level.

c) Factory owners have much larger financing ability than peasants to buy and run modern equipments.[13]

Advanced mechanization in the factory system as compared with that in the traditional system is confirmed by Table 10-6. For 1905–20 γ is much higher in the former than in the latter. The factory here is defined as a plant with ten or more employees. For 1922–38 γ was decisively higher in the factory or the plant with ten or more looms than the smaller scales. Factories, especially those equipped with power looms, have economic advantages over traditional production units. This brought about a change-over from the traditional to the modern production system. A ratio of the number of looms of factories to the total number (x), which is an index for the diffusion of factory system, showed a steady increase for the entire period from 1905 to 1938 (Fig. 10-2).

(2) Introduction of power looms is easier in weaving fabrics of simpler structure.[14] For cotton weaving, mechanization is the easiest in plain fabrics such as *shiro momen* (gray cloth), shirtings and sheeting. It is the most difficult in figured texture, *kasuri* (cottons woven with mottled thread) and stuff for an *obi*. Cotton crape, striped cloth and cotton carpet lie somewhere between the two. For silk weaving, mechanization is easier in *habutae* (plain silk) than in silk crape, striped cloth, figured texture, *obi* and *tsumugi* (pongee). This assertion (technical ease and difficulty to mechanize weaving is defferent among products) may be

[13]   Kajinishi 1964, p. 482; Kosho 1980, pp. 11–12.

[14]   This is evident in the fact that the revolution of a power loom with 36 inches reed are only 130–140 per minute in weaving figured cloth, while they are 180 in weaving plain cloth (Tsuda 1925, p. 212).

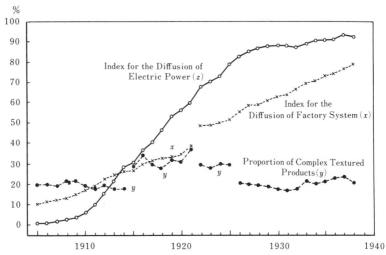

Fig. 10-2.   Variables Explaining Diffusion of Power Looms in
Cotton Weaving

Sources: See Minami and Makino 1983a, fig. 3 on p. 8.

Notes: x = proportion of looms in plants with ten or more employees in total
looms in all plants for 1905–21 and that of looms in plants with ten or more looms
in total looms in all plants for 1922–38.

y = proportion of complex textured products such as striped cloth, figured cloth,
crape, cotton carpets, *kasuri, tsumugi* and *obi* in total products.

z = proportion of households with electric light in total households.

endorsed by the episode of a cotton weaving company in Higashi
Mikawa (Aichi Prefecture), which wove simple cloth in its own factory
with power looms and made peasants weave more complex textured
cloth by treadle looms, which had been used before in the company.[15]

A ratio of the output of complex texture such as figured cloth, striped
cloth, crape, cotton carpet, *kasuri, tsumugi* and *obi* to that all weaving
products, y, is calculated and drawn in Fig. 10-2. Because of changes in
classification of products in 1915, 1922 and 1926, y is discontinuous in
these years. During respective sub-periods (1905–14, 1915–21, 1922–25
and 1926–38) the ratio did not show any distinct trends.

[15]   Aida 1974, p. 86.

(3) Power looms tend to be easily employed when and where electric power is available. Of course, electric power is not the only source of power: large-scale factories run by cotton-spinning companies operated power looms by steam engines, and some small- and medium-scale weaving plants utilized internal combustion engines.[16] However the internal combustion engine did not complete mechanization of small weavers: in 1909 95% of weaving plants with 5-9 employees were not mechanized and in 1919, 67% were still in the same condition (Table 10-2). Full mechanization of small plants was first realized when local electric power companies began to supply electric power. The internal combustion engine was more suitable for small-scale production than the steam engine in the divisibility of power and the ease in use, but much less suitable than the electric motor.[17] As an index of the availability of electricity we calculate a ratio of the number of house-holds which used electric light to the total households. Changes in the ratio, denoted as δ, indicate that availability of electricity was very limited until about 1910, increased very rapidly thereafter until it reached a saturation level in the latter half of the 1920s.[18]

Conditions for the diffusion: analysis. By estimating simple regressions of the proportion of power looms (γ) with three independent variables (x, y, z) using prefectural statistics for seven years (1905, 1910, 1915, 1920, 1930, 1935 and 1938), we have proved that our three hypotheses were all significant.[19] Furthermore, we have analyzed the significance of our conclusions:

(1) Significance of the Diffusion of Factory System

The diffusion of factory system had the largest contribution in the diffusion of power looms with respect to both the changes overtime and to the regional differences. Furthermore, its contribution increased relatively to those of other variables.

---

[16] Wide utilization of gas engine and petroleum engines was seen in plants with 5–49 employees during the 1910s (Table 10-3).

[17] Refer to chap. 7.

[18] Kurihara 1964, pp. 180–81.

[19] Minami and Makino 1983a, table 6 on p. 11.

The effect of the diffusion of factory system is substantiated by the following historical examples:

a) Traditional silk weaving regions such as Kiryū, Ashikaga and Nishijin, which faced with an increased demand, could increase production simply by expanding the putting-out system. On the other hand the newly developed regions such as Ishikawa and Fukui, which did not have the foundation of this system, were forced to introduce power looms based on the factory system. In this way there appeared a considerable difference in the diffusion of power looms between the two groups of silk weaving regions.[20]

b) Bisai, a region of cotton and worsted cloth production, was characterized by a fairly well developed putting-out system. It is said that this caused a delay in introducing power looms, because of small incentives for mechanization in the domestic production. An important fact is that within this region there was a local difference in the diffusion of power looms, which can be attributed to a difference in the development of the putting-out system. In Kaifu Gun (province) where the putting-out system was most developed, power looms were rarely employed, while in Nakajima Gun without the well-developed putting-out system power looms were widely introduced.[21]

Finally we must put a reservation to the conclusion that the development of the factory system (or an underdevelopment of the putting-out system) facilitated the diffusion of power looms. That is, there are some authors who emphasize the relation that the former was a result of the latter.

1) Small weavers, who employed power looms, succeeded in output expansion and capital accumulation, and finally became independent of the putting-out system. In many regions including Mikawa and Enshū (Shizuoka Prefecture) the putting-out system declined and the factory system developed during the WWI prosperity owing to this reason.[22]

2) Introduction of power looms was underdeveloped in Kiryū and

[20] Kajinishi 1964, pp. 478–79; Kobayashi 1960, pp. 245–48, 251.
[21] Tamaki 1957, pp. 72–76, 113–14.
[22] Suzuki 1951, pp. 120–23; Yamazaki 1969, p. 98.

Nishijin, because hand looms were rather suitable to the small-scale production of wide-variety of products. As a result of this the putting-out system remained unchanged for a long time.[23]

Nobody can deny these possibilities; strictly speaking the relationships between the diffusion of factory system and the mechanization were mutually reinforcing to some extent.

(2) Significance of the Technical Ease to Adopt Power Looms Depending on Products by Kind

Although a change in the composition of products by kind did not contribute significantly to the diffusion of power looms through time, a regional difference in the composition caused a regional difference in the diffusion of power looms.

Introduction of power looms started in regions producing plain cloth, in cotton weaving for instance Sennan, Chita (Aichi Prefecture), Mikawa and Enshū. Owing to an improvement in power looms and a rise in wages, the power loom utilization diffused to regions which produced more complex textured cloth. Ōme, which produced striped cotton cloth, was one of these regions. Mechanization was delayed the most in regions producing *kasuri* such as Kurume (Kumamoto Prefecture), Satsuma (Kagoshima Prefecture) and Iyo (Ehime Prefecture).

It is appropriate here to put two comments to this conclusion:

a) Some authors argue that power looms tended to be introduced earlier in the regions with larger concerns with foreign markets rather than domestic market. A reason for this is that export activities are based on mass-production of few kinds of products, while production for domestic demand is characterized with small-quantity production of various kinds of products.[24] In our view, however, the distinction between export-oriented production and that for domestic use in explaining a difference in the timing of the power loom utilization seems to come eventually from the distinction among kinds of products which we have emphasized. That is, the export products were largely plain cloth such as shirtings, sheeting, and *habutae*, while production for domestic demand

[23] Horie 1976, p. 103; Kobayashi 1960, p. 246; Sanpei 1961, p. 417.
[24] Kajinishi 1964, pp. 210–12, 478; Kiyokawa 1973, p. 134.

was mainly of more complex textured cloth such as striped and figured cloth, *kasuri* and *tsumugi*.

b) Influence of the difference in products is not necessarily independent of an influence of the differences in the types of management. It is said, for instance, that striped cotton weavers in Bisai, organized in the putting-out system, inclined towards diversification of products based on manual labor, because small-scale unmechanized production was appropriate to side-jobs of peasants.[25]

(3) Significance of the Diffusion of Electric Power

The diffusion of electric power facilitated substantially the power loom utilization, even though it did not cause the regional difference in the utilization. This is attributable to the fact that electric power became available during the 1910s and 1920s rather uniformly among the prefectures.

The relation between the timing of the establishment of electric utilities and that of the introduction of power looms is confirmed by the following examples.[26]

a) The introduction of power looms in silk weaving enterprises in Kiryū and Ashikaga occurred after the Watarase Electric Company began supplying electric power in 1908.

b) Silk, cotton, and worsted weaving plants in Ichinomiya (Aichi Prefecture) introduced power looms after cheap electric power became available from the Ichinomiya Electric Company founded in 1923.

c) Power looms gained widespread application among silk weaving plants in Yonezawa (Yamagata Prefecture) after the establishment of the Yonezawa Hydro-Electric Company in 1897.

d) In the silk weaving district of Kawamata (Fukushima Prefecture) power looms were introduced after the establishment of the Kawamata Electric Company in 1907.

e) Mechanization of silk weaving in Fukui was attributable to the foundation of an electric utility there during WWI.

f) The introduction of power looms among silk weaving plants in

[25] Kajinishi 1964, p. 248.
[26] The following examples (from 1 to 6) are cited from Sanpei 1961, p. 408.

Ishikawa Prefecture followed the development of electric companies such as Komatsu Electric and Daishōji Electric.

g) The number of power looms increased rapidly after electric power became available in 1921 in Chichibu (Saitama Prefecture).[27]

h) In Higashi Mikawa electric power became available by the establishment of Okazaki Electric Light Company in 1914 and in the next year they started to run power looms by electric power.[28]

Two comments are needed to close this section:

1) Electric power was not a unique power source; for instance, in a part of Sennan without electric distribution line, gas engines were widely used, and in mountainous regions of Enshū, gas engines and petroleum engines were employed.[29] But small-scale weaving plants were not fully mechanized in the stage of internal combustion engines, because the production of small-capacity engines appropriate to these plants was technically impossible and because unsmooth rotation of these engines caused uneven weaving.

2) There were big differences among regions within individual prefectures with regard to availability of electric power, because public utilities in the early years were very small in scale and their service areas were very limited. Therefore weaving plants located in remoted places, sometimes, could not utilize this power. It is assumed in our study that both the network of electric power distribution and weaving plants were distributed uniformly within respective prefectures.

Impact of the Introduction of Power Looms

In this section we examine the impact of mechanization in the weaving industry, first through statistical accounts for the consequences of introducing power looms on production efficiency and cost performance, and then by estimating production functions including the pro-

---

[27] Katsura 1925, p. 54.
[28] Tanihara 1958, p. 85; Aida 1974, p. 82.
[29] Nōshōmushō Kōmukyoku 1925, pp. 65, 108–9.

portion of power looms as another independent variable.

Study of Production Efficiency and Cost Performance

Framework. Here we are making a comparison of production efficiency and cost performance between the hand loom and the power loom. This study is based on our previous studies on the choice of technology in the cotton-weaving industry among five alternative technologies;[30]

1. Batten
2. Treadle loom
3. Narrow power loom
4. Broad power loom
5. Automatic loom

Among them batten and treadle looms were driven by human power and the other three by mechanical power. Therefore the impact of introduction of mechanical power in weaving can be revealed by studying a difference in efficiency between batten and treadle looms on the one hand, and power and automatic looms on the other hand.

We assume that fifteen batten looms and the same number of treadle looms were installed in the putting-out system and in 'manufacture' (small-scale factory without mechanical power), respectively. On the other hand, power looms were almost always used in factories; we assume that fifteen narrow power looms or the same number of broad power looms were used in small-scale independent factories equipped with mechanical power (cotton weavers independent hereafter), and one hundred broad power looms or the same number of automatic looms were used in large-scale factories operated by cotton-spinning companies (cotton spinning-weaving firms thereafter).[31]

---

[30] Minami and Makino 1986a. This is a revison of the estimation in Minami and Makino 1983c. See Minami and Makino 1983b for analyses based on this estimation.

[31] In the cotton weaver independent we assume that a 5 hp-petroleum engine was used in 1902, and a 5 hp-electric motor in 1915, 1926 and 1938. In the cotton spinning-weaving firm we assume a 20 hp-steam engine in 1902 and 1915, and a 20 hp-electric motor in 1926 and 1938.

Table 10-7. Productivity of Looms by Type in Cotton Weaving:
1902 and 1938

		1902			
		Batten Loom	Treadle Loom	Narrow Power Loom	Broad Power Loom[a]
Output (*tan*/day)	O	39	48	65	842[b]
Number of looms	K	15	15	15	100
Number of weaving workers	L	15.00	15.00	5.13	34.25
Labor productivity (*tan*/man day)	O/L	2.62	3.20	12.66	24.59[b]
Number of looms per worker	K/L	1.00	1.00	2.92	2.92
Output of one loom (*tan*/day)	O/K	2.62	3.20	4.33	8.42[b]

		1938				
		Batten Loom	Treadle Loom	Narrow Power Loom	Broad Power Loom[a]	Auto-matic Loom[a]
Output (*tan*/day)	O	39	48	93	133[b]	959[b]
Number of looms	K	15	15	15	15	100
Number of weaving workers	L	15.00	15.00	2.84	2.84	2.50
Labor productivity (*tan*/man day)	O/L	2.62	3.20	32.64	46.96[b]	383.60[b]
Number of looms per worker	K/L	1.00	1.00	5.29	5.29	40.00
Output of one loom (*tan*/day)	O/K	2.62	3.20	6.18	8.89[b]	9.59[b]

Sources: Minami and Makino 1983c for estimating procedures.
[a] One shift.
[b] Narrow fabrics equivalent.

Labor productivity. The most direct impact of the substitution of power looms and automatic looms for batten looms and treadle looms was a rise in labor productivity.

According to Table 10-7, in 1902; daily production[32] of plain cotton cloth per worker (O/L) was 2.6, 3.2, 12.7, and 24.6 *tan*[33] by batten loom, treadle loom, narrow power loom and broad power loom respectively. This demonstrates a big impact of the substitution of power looms on production efficiency; for instance, an employment of narrow power loom and broad power loom in place of batten loom should have raised labor productivity by 5 times and 9 times, respectively.

The rise in labor productivity could occur in two ways: from an increase in the number of looms operated by each worker (K/L) and from an increase in output per loom (O/K). First, with regard to K/L, although one operator could operate only 1 hand loom and 1 treadle loom, she could run 3 narrow power looms and 3 broad power looms in 1902. Next, there was a wide differential also in O/K among four kinds of looms; it was 2.6, 3.2, 4.3 and 8.4 for batten loom, treadle loom, narrow power loom and broad power loom respectively.

In 1938 differentials in O/L, K/L and O/K were all larger than respective figures in 1902. Comparing the figures of 1938 with that of 1902 we see that O/L, K/L and O/K increased in the power looms but not in the batten and the treadle looms. This means an increase in the relative advantage of the power looms over the traditional looms. By 1938 automatic loom was already available. This new loom had a larger efficiency than the power looms; O/L of the automatic loom was 12 times as large as the narrow power loom and 8 times as large as the broad power loom.

Rate of net profit. As was mentioned in chapter 8, production

---

[32] Daily production (O) depends on various variables; the most important are revolutions per minute of loom (V) and coefficient of operation of loom (ratio of working days in which a loom is actually operating). See Minami and Makino 1983b, p. 220; 1986a, p. 17.

[33] The length of one *tan* varied among various kinds of fabrics and changed over time. It was roughly equivalent to eight meters.

Table 10-8. Rate of Net Profit (r) by Type of Looms in Cotton Weaving: 1902–1938

(percent)

Year	Batten Loom (Putting-out System)	Treadle Loom (Weaver Independent)	Narrow Power Loom (Weaver Independent)	Broad Power Loom (Weaver Independent)	Broad Power Loom (Spinning Weaving Firm)	Automatic Loom (Spinning Weaving Firm)	Broad Power Loom (Spinning Weaving Firm)	Automatic Loom (Spinning Weaving Firm)
	1 Shift						2 Shifts	
1902	1.2 (−0.3)	−45.1 (−49.2)	15.0 (17.3)	7.9 (10.6)	8.6 (11.5)		27.9 (36.4)	
1915	−13.3 (−9.3)	−46.6 (−52.1)	9.5 (11.8)	9.5 (13.1)	7.0 (10.1)		22.8 (31.7)	
1926	−97.0 (−93.3)	−103.6 (−114.1)	5.3 (5.5)	17.6 (18.1)	11.8 (12.1)	13.1 (12.9)	27.2 (27.8)	32.7 (32.2)
1938	−118.2 (−134.9)	−79.3 (−99.0)	2.6 (3.2)	18.6 (23.0)	17.5 (21.6)	19.6 (24.4)	28.1 (33.7)	37.6 (45.2)

Notes: Figures in parentheses are the rate of net profit at 1934-36 prices (r').

efficiency and cost performance can be measured more strictly in terms of the rate of profit than in terms of labor productivity.

(1) Batten Loom and Treadle Loom

According to Table 10-8 the rate of net profit (r) of batten looms used in the putting-out system exceeded the rate earned by treadle looms in 'manufacture' in each year. But it should be noted that some advantages of the cooperative 'manufacture' sytem over the putting-out system are neglected in this calculation. First, because in the 'manufacture' system different production processes for the same product were combined in a single workshop the interval between processes would be shortened[34] and consequently the turnover of capital would be more rapid in the 'manufacture' system than in the putting-out system. Second, transportation costs would be less in the 'manufacture' system because distribution of raw materials and collection of finished goods from pieceworkers was unnecessary.[35] Third, in a single workshop it was possible to check embezzlement of raw materials while this would have been difficult in a system where materials were given out to individual pieceworkers by clothiers.[36] Considering these advantages, it will be evident that the rate r on batten looms used in the putting-out system was overestimated and that on treadle looms employed in 'manufacture' was underestimated. The productivity of the treadle loom, however, was such that it could not recover the fixed capital cost arising from establishment of a factory. The development of the 'manufacture' system was discouraged by the low productivity of hand and treadle looms.[37]

---

[34] Hattori 1955, pp. 116–17.

[35] Hattori 1955, p. 120. The commission paid to intermediaries employed by clothiers to distribute materials to pieceworkers and collect goods from them amounted to 10–15% of total weaving cost in Iyo region from the early 1910s to the middle of the 1920s (Kawasaki 1943, pp. 8, 59, 63).

[36] Hattori 1955, p. 120. This was the main incentive to bring together weavers into a single workshop in the English woolen industry (Ashton 1970, p. 88).

[37] Sanpei 1961, p. 386. There was an upper limit in the scale of the 'manufacture' system employing throw-shuttle looms and those that exceeded the limit were hired out to pieceworkers in Bisai region in the middle of the 19th century, because costs incurred by enlargement of workshops employing throw-shuttle looms exceeded benefits of cooperative system (Shiozawa and Kawaura 1957, p. 162). Even after 1892 when batten

The ratio of hand and treadle looms owned by 'manufacture' (here defined as factories with 10 and more workers without mechanical power) to total looms was only about 10% from 1905 and to 1921.[38]

(2) Narrow Power Loom

The rare r for the narrow power loom (15.0%) already exceeded that of the batten looms (1.2%) in 1902. But the supply of power looms was limited and they tended to break down easily during the early years of the 1900s.[39] Therefore, the ratio of power looms to total looms, illustrated in Fig. 10-1, was low during this period. The difference in r between the narrow power loom and the batten loom expanded between 1902 and 1915 so that choosing narrow power looms became more profitable than before. As a result, in regions where; 1) the factory system had developed, 2) products could be easily produced by power looms, and 3) electric power, as a cheap power source, was available, the ratio of power looms increased rapidly after 1910 (e.g. Chita, Sennan and Enshū).

Two factors, productivity of loom and wage cost per loom, chiefly accounted for the difference in r of the narrow power loom and that of hand looms. Table 10-9 presents gross profit (gross value added minus wage cost) per loom when the values of productivity per loom and the number of workers per loom for narrow power loom are replaced with those for the batten loom and treadle loom. The relative contribution of each factor to the profitability of the narrow power loom is also shown in the same table. The difference in profitability between the narrow power loom and the batten loom was caused largely by the 'labor saving effect'; it was 65–67% for 1902–26 and 76% for 1938. Almost the same conclusion can be obtained for a comparison between treadle loom and narrow power loom. Relative comparison between batten and power

apparatus was introduced there, 'manufacture' entrepreneurs hired out more batten looms than those used in their own workshops (Ishikawa 1977, pp. 31–33). This implies that enlargement of workshops employing hand looms had an upper limit whether they were equipped with batten apparatus or not.

[38] STAC.
[39] Tamura and Asai 1901, p. 41.

Table 10-9. Relative Contributions of Factors for Technological Progress in Cotton Weaving: 1902–1938

	Change from Batten Loom to Narrow Power Loom					
Year	Gross Profit[a] for Narrow Power Loom (yen per year)				Relative Contributions (%)	
	Actual Value	Case 1[b]	Case 2[c]	Case 3[d]	Productivity Effect	Labor Saving Effect
	(1)	(2)	(3)	(4)	$\dfrac{(1)-(3)}{(1)-(2)} \times 100$	$\dfrac{(1)-(4)}{(1)-(2)} \times 100$
1902	718	−1,110	74	−466	35.2	64.8
1915	1,088	−1,475	185	−572	35.2	64.8
1926	1,514	−6,723	−696	−4,513	26.8	73.2
1938	1,294	−4,535	−116	−3,125	24.2	75.8

	Change from Treadle Loom to Narrow Power Loom					
1902	718	−867	316	−466	25.3	74.7
1915	1,088	−1,196	464	−572	27.3	72.7
1926	1,514	−6,268	−241	−4,513	22.6	77.5
1938	1,294	−4,248	172	−3,125	20.3	79.7

[a] Gross value added – wage payments.

[b] Calculated by replacing values of the number of revolutions per minute (V), coefficient of operation (F) and the number of workers per loom on narrow power loom with those on the batten loom and treadle loom, respectively. See n. 31 of this chapter.

[c] Calculated replacing V and F on the narrow power loom with those on the batten and treadle loom, respectively.

[d] Calculated by replacing the value of number of workers per narrow power loom with that per batten and treadle loom, respectively.

loom, the 'productivity effect' is smaller in this comparison, because of a higher productivity of treadle loom over batten loom. In both of the two comparisons the labor-saving effect increased in 1938 from 1926. This was due to a larger increase in the real wage rate deflated by the price of cotton fabrics.

The quality of cotton fabrics was improved by mechanical weaving.[40] Although this advantage for power looms over hand looms could not be measured quantitatively, it certainly provided an incentive for entrepreneurs to introduce power looms for cotton weaving. Due to these advantages for power looms, cotton weaving entrepreneurs could increase their net profit rate by replacing hand looms with power looms.

(3) Broad Power Loom and Automatic Loom

In both 1902 and 1915 the rate r of the broad power loom was higher, regardless of its management organization (independent weavers vs. cotton spinning-weaving firms), than that of the narrow power loom only when the two shifts system was employed (Table 10-8). Since only cotton spinning-weaving firms used the two shifts system, choosing the broad power loom was only profitable for them, on that period. Or rather, they might have employed the two shifts system so as to compete with small-scale cotton weavers using the narrow power loom. The rate r of the broad power loom in both of the two management organizations exceeded that of the narrow power loom in 1926 even if the one shift system was used. Hence, it became profitable even for small-scale cotton weavers to introduce broad power looms. This resulted in high rates of diffusion of broad power looms. The ratio of broad power looms to total looms increased rapidly from the late 1910s and exceeded 50% in representative cotton weaving regions (Sennan, Banshū and Aichi prefecture) in the middle of the 1920s.[41]

The first reason why profitability on the broad power loom went up rapidly from the late 1910s was due to a change in the demand structure for cotton fabrics. English cotton fabrics were driven away from Asian market during WWI and Japanese costume became more westernized

[40] Fujii 1960, p. 135; Tsukada 1937, p. 33.
[41] Minami and Makino 1986a, fig. 2 on p. 124.

causing demand for wide fabrics to increase in both foreign and domestic market.[42] This was reflected by price changes for both wide and narrow fabrics; the per unit price of wide fabrics (triple-width shirting) had been 8 to 9 times that of narrow fabrics (gray cloth) before 1920. In the early 1920s the relative price of wide fabrics increased to 13 or 14 times that of narrow fabrics. This relative advantage of wide fabrics over narrow fabrics persisted until 1938.[43]

A second reason for the increased profitability of broad power looms was that technological progress in the production of looms made it possible to easily remodel narrow power looms into broad power looms,[44] and narrow fabrics could be produced simply by cutting off wide fabrics due to advancement in printing techniques.[45] Adopting broad power looms or replacing narrow power looms with broad power looms was facilitated by these technological changes.

Automatic looms had not been widely used prior to WWII. The ratio of automatic looms in the cotton weaving industry was only 15% even in 1938 and cotton spinning-weaving firms accounted for about 70% of total automatic looms in the late 1930s. This fact can be explained by the relative profitability of automatic looms. The rate r for automatic looms was larger than that of broad power looms (spinning-weaving firms), only in the case of two shifts. Hence, the only firms for which it was profitable to introduce automatic looms in prewar Japan were cotton spinning-weaving firms that employed the two shifts system.

Production Function Approach

Because we have more statistical data for weaving than for other industries we can analyze the impact of power looms in a more rigorous statistical fashion. Here we employ two types of econometric analysis in order to find the effect of mechanization on production efficiency in the weaving industry.

---

[42] Sanpei 1961, pp. 301, 303.
[43] Ohkawa *et al.* 1967, pp. 155–56.
[44] Tanaka 1950, p. 22; Fujii 1960, p. 145; Kobayashi 1981, pp. 209–10.
[45] Sanpei 1961, pp. 300–1.

Time-series study. The first analysis is a time-series study of the cotton-weaving industry from 1922 to 1938. In this analysis the conventional production-function approach is followed, in that we consider labor productivity, p_t, as a function of the level of technology and the capital-labor ratio, k_t. However, while the level of technology is usually expressed as a simple time trend, here we make a different and important assumption, simply considering that the level of technology is expressed by the proportion, γ_t, of power looms in total looms. The following model is set forth:

$$\ln p_t = a_0 + a_1 \gamma_t + a_2 \ln k_t + u_t,$$

where ln signifies the natural log and u_t is an error term. We are most interested in the second term, $a_1 \gamma_t$, which measures the increase in labor productivity stemming from technological progress (defined as a shift in the production function). The parameter a_2 is the output elasticity of capital.

The volume of cotton production (thousand yards, in wide-width equivalent) per worker is used as a measure of p_t, and the number of looms (in power loom equivalent) per worker is assigned to k_t. All of the series p_t, k_t, and γ_t show steadily increasing trends for the entire 1922–38 period, with the single exception that p_t dipped slightly in 1938.

The results of estimating this equation are given in panel A of Table 10-10. Because of the abnormal drop in p_t in 1938, due perhaps to wartime industrial dislocation, estimates of the equation excluding this year have also been given in panel A. The high coefficient of determination in both cases suggests that our model is an appropriate one to describe the weaving industry. Although there is some serial correlation, parameter a_1 is almost the same in both time spans, and it is statistically significant at the 95% significance level. This indicates that labor productivity was sensitive to the diffusion of power looms. Parameter a_2 is also significant for 1922–37 but not for 1922–38.[46]

[46] Our estimates for the output elasticity of capital (0.272 and 0.471) are rather close to the estimates provided by Kiyokawa (0.391) for the weaving sector of cotton-spinning companies from 1903 to 37 (1973, p. 129).

Table 10-10. Time-Series Estimates of Production Function and
Annual Rate of Growth of Productivity by Component in Cotton Weaving: 1922–1938

A. Estimates of a Production Function

Period	Parameters			$\bar{R}^2$	d
	a_0	a_1	a_2		
1922–38	−0.912 (0.88)	0.0427 (2.85)	0.272 (0.44)	0.946	0.75
1922–37	−0.909 (2.06)	0.0426 (6.64)	0.471 (1.79)	0.990	1.07

B. Annual Rate of Growth of Labor Productivity and Its
Components (%)

Period	$\Delta \ln p$	$u_1 \Delta \gamma$	$a_2 \Delta \ln k$	Error
1922–37	1.49 (100)	1.28 (86)	0.30 (20)	−0.09 (−6)

Sources: p_t: Physical quantity of output of narrow-width cloth is converted to units of
wide-width cloth by multiplying by 0.316, the price ratio of the former to the latter for
the period 1926–28. Prices are obtained by dividing nominal value of output by the
physical quantity of output, both of which are taken from STMCI 1929, pp. 5–11. See
Table A-3.

k_t: The number of hand looms is multiplied by 0.267 in order to convert that into units
of power looms (0.267 is a ratio of the price of hand loom to that of power loom). The
prices used, ¥3,000 for hand looms and ¥11,250 for power looms, are taken from
Uchida 1960, p. 185.

Figures for narrow-width output, wide-width output, the number of power looms, the
number of hand looms, and the number of production workers are all taken from
STMCI 1924, pp. 8–12; 1929, pp. 2–11; 1938, pp. 2–11. See Table A-3.

Notes: Numbers in parenthesis in panel A are student *t*-values.

Therefore we employ the estimates for the former period.

From the above equation we obtain

$$\Delta \ln p_t = a_1 \Delta \gamma_t + a_2 \Delta \ln k_t + \Delta u_t,$$

where Δ signifies the changes in variables. Because each variable is expressed in terms of natural logs, the increase expresses the exponential rate of growth of that variable. This relation is calculated for 1922–37 in panel B. From these figures we learn that the rate of growth of labor productivity was 1.49% per year and that this increase came largely from an increase in the level of technology (i.e., the diffusion of power looms). $a_1 \Delta \gamma_t$ is calculated at 1.28%, which explains 86% of $\Delta \ln p_t$. The relative contribution of the increase in the number of looms per worker, on the other hand, was only 20%.

Cross-sectional study. The second econometric study is a cross-sectional analysis of prefectural statistics for five selected years. To begin with, the correlation coefficient of the relationship between the value of production (in thousands of yen) per worker p_i and the proportion of power looms γ_i in each prefecture (where i stands for prefecture) are calculated. These figures are shown in Table 10-11. Correlation coefficients for the weaving industry as a whole have been estimated for all five years, but, because of the lack of data, we are limited to examining only the last three of these five years for individual weaving industries (cotton, silk, worsted and hemp). With the exception of worsted weaving in 1924, the correlation coefficients are all statistically significant. On a prefecture-by-prefecture basis, there was a very close relation between the diffusion of power looms and labor productivity.

One problem with this study is that p_i is affected by the number of looms (power loom equivalent) per worker k_i, an index of the capital-labor ratio. The pure effect of γ_i on productivity can be identified by estimating the following production function:

$$\ln p_i = a_0 + a_1 \gamma_i + a_2 \ln k_i + u_i.$$

The results of estimation of this relation are given in Table 10–12 (1). With the single exception of the silk-weaving industry in 1924, param-

Table 10-11. Coefficients of Correlation between Labor Productivity (p) and Proportion of Power Looms (γ)
in Weaving: 1914–1934

Industry	Year	Correlation Coefficient
Total	1914	0.829*
	1919	0.818*
	1924	0.602*
	1929	0.611*
	1934	0.755*
Cotton	1924	0.547*
	1929	0.616*
	1934	0.698*
Silk and mixed	1924	0.622*
	1929	0.616*
	1934	0.800*
Worsted and mixed	1924	0.235
	1929	0.585*
	1934	0.767*
Hemp and mixed	1924	0.620*
	1929	0.648*
	1934	0.645*

Sources: 1914 and 1919: STAC 1914, pp. 232–249; 1919, pp. 164–173. See Table A-1.
1924, 1929 and 1934: STMCI 1924, pp. 8–31; 1929, pp. 2–34; 1934, pp. 2–34. See
Table A-3.

* signifies that the correlation coefficient is statistically significant at the 99%
significance level.

eter a_1 is always significant at the 95% significance level. Therefore,
prefectural differentials in the diffusion of power looms can be identified,
as one factor explaining the differential in a labor productivity. On the

other hand, with the exception of the worsted-weaving industry in 1929 and 1934, parameter a_2 is not significant. In other words, a differential in the capital-labor ratio can not be presumed to cause a differential in labor productivity. The estimates of parameter a_1 under the assumption that $a_2 = 0$ (shown in (2) of Table 10-12) are not considerably different from the original estimates (shown in (1) of the same table).

Both the time series study and the cross-prefectural study reveal that the diffusion of power looms shifted the production function for weaving. To put this in another way, technological progress in small-scale weaving was attributable largely to mechanization, which this in turn was largely related to electrification. The above results show the inportance of electrification to Japan's small-scale weaving plants.

Impact of Electrification

Table 10-13 gives our estimates on the rate of net profit (r) in cotton-weaving factories by large and small scale for 1910 and 1926 under the assumption that power looms were run by three types of engines respectively; steam engine, petroleum engine and electric motor. According to this table, electric motor had the highest r for small- and large-scale factories in both years. A major reason for the relatively greater advantage of the electric motor was, as is shown in Table 10-14, saving in the costs of capital (depreciation of capital assets and interest payments) and that in wage payments. The former saving came from a low price of electric motor relative to the steam engine and petroleum engine, and the latter was due to a non-existence of special workers to operate those engines (such as boiler men in the case of steam engines).

The huge profitability of factories with electric motors gave rise to the rapid electrification in this industry, which was seen in Tables 10-1 and 10-3. The diffusion of electric motors was not yet evident in about 1910. This was because the transmission network of electric power was eventually limited to large cities; consequently, a proportion of households with electric light in total households (z) was only 5% in 1910

Table 10-12. Cross-Prefectural Estimates of Production Function in Weaving: 1924–1934

Industry	Year		Parameters			$\bar{R}^2$
			a_0	a_1	a_2	
Cotton	1924	(1)	−0.100 (0.53)	0.0059 (2.30)	0.510 (1.52)	0.454
		(2)	−0.345 (3.49)	0.0091 (6.00)		0.438
	1929	(1)	−0.394 (2.70)	0.0086 (4.49)	0.164 (0.78)	0.564
		(2)	−0.475 (4.72)	0.0097 (7.67)		0.568
	1934	(1)	−0.739 (3.93)	0.013 (5.03)	0.140 (0.48)	0.714
		(2)	−0.811 (7.32)	0.014 (10.66)		0.719

Industry	Year		Parameters			$\bar{R}^2$
			a_0	a_1	a_2	
Worsted and mixed	1924	(1)	−0.0089 (0.29)	0.0080 (2.83)	0.243 (0.69)	0.466
		(2)	−0.248 (1.22)	0.0091 (4.01)		0.485
	1929	(1)	−0.177 (0.61)	0.011 (4.03)	0.676 (2.28)	0.780
		(2)	−0.753 (4.71)	0.015 (6.97)		0.725
	1934	(1)	−0.177 (0.61)	0.011 (4.03)	0.676 (2.28)	0.780
		(2)	−0.753 (4.71)	0.015 (6.96)		0.725

Industry	Year		Parameters			$\bar{R}^2$
			a_0	a_1	a_2	
Silk and mixed	1924	(1)	0.493 (1.33)	0.0012 (0.24)	0.552 (0.93)	0.193
		(2)	0.157 (2.14)	0.0057 (3.49)		0.196
	1929	(1)	−0.586 (1.75)	0.011 (2.59)	−0.357 (0.63)	0.396
		(2)	−0.382 (4.50)	0.0085 (5.68)		0.404
	1934	(1)	−0.585 (2.36)	0.011 (3.55)	−0.192 (0.46)	0.645
		(2)	−0.475 (7.34)	0.0099 (9.23)		0.652

Industry	Year		Parameters			$\bar{R}^2$
			a_0	a_1	a_2	
Hemp and mixed	1924	(1)	−0.939 (3.02)	0.016 (4.70)	0.146 (0.30)	0.555
		(2)	−1.021 (6.89)	0.017 (6.56)		0.568
	1929	(1)	−0.862 (2.19)	0.015 (2.69)	0.692 (1.11)	0.619
		(2)	−1.256 (7.28)	0.020 (6.90)		0.616
	1934	(1)	−1.359 (2.40)	0.020 (3.03)	−0.177 (0.20)	0.594
		(2)	−1.256 (5.44)	0.019 (5.86)		0.613

Sources: Same as Table 10-11.

Table 10-13. Rate of Net Profit (r) in Cotton-Weaving Factories by Factory Scale and by Type of Engines: 1910 and 1926

(percent)

Year	Large-scale Factory[a]			Small-scale Factory[b]		
	Steam Engine[c]	Petroleum Engine[c]	Electric Motor[c]	Steam Engine[d]	Petroleum Engine[e]	Electric Motor[e]
1910	16.7 (17.3)	12.0 (12.5)	21.0 (21.5)	6.7 (7.1)	11.3 (11.8)	20.2 (20.7)
1926	14.1 (14.0)	10.2 (10.4)	17.9 (18.4)	6.7 (6.7)	10.3 (10.6)	17.6 (18.1)

Notes: Estimates under the assumption of one shift.
[a] Factory with 100 power looms (narrow looms in 1910 and broad looms in 1926).
[b] Factory with 15 power looms (narrow looms in 1910 and broad looms in 1926).
[c] 20 hp.
[d] 12 hp.
[e] 5 hp.

(Figure 10-2). In areas without the electric power network they were using steam engines and petroleum engines.

An interesting finding in Table 10-13 is that r was almost the same between the large and small scales in the case of electric motors and petroleum engines, whereas it was very low in the small-scale factory compared to the large-scale factory in the case of steam engines in both years. In the large-scale factory r was the lowest in case of the petroleum engine, whereas in the small-scale factory r was the lowest in case of steam engine. Variation in r was mainly due to changes in overhead cost (capital cost and wage payments to workers to run engines). In the case of electric motors and petroleum engines with low overhead cost, r did not differ among scales of production (Fig. 10-3). In the case of steam engines with high overhead cost, on the other hand, r tended to increase with an increase in production scale.

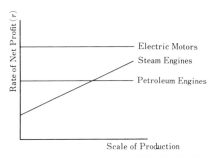

Fig. 10-3.   Relation between Rate of Net Profit (r) and Scale of
Production by Type of Engines in Weaving

Merits of the electrification in weaving was not limited to savings in
cost or increase in profit. The most important among other merits was
an improvement of output quality. In Kawamata, *habutae* produced by
hand looms was not of uniform quality even in a single day. This
problem sometimes brought complains from customers in France, the
United States and other foreign countries. This dissatisfaction, when
reported by trading companies to the weavers in various districts,
encouraged the introduction of power looms. It was reported that the
introduction of electrically driven power looms in Kawamata, completely solved the problem of uniformity because these motors ran at
constant speed.[47] Furthermore in 1910 Sukeo Hayashi, an electric
engineer, emphasized the same impact of the electrification in weaving.[48]
According to him, due to the constant speed of rotation of electric
motors, threads were rarely broken, therefore, an operator could run
five or six electrically driven machines of four power looms in case of
non-electric engines.

[47]   Tsunekawa 1916, p. 94.
[48]   Hayashi 1910, pp. 755–56.
  The same phenomenon was reported in weaving plants in other countries; for example in
the United States, threads were easily broken when machines were run by steam engines or
gas engines, but this problem was completely solved by replacing these engines with electric
motors (*Electrical World* 1918, p. 989). In England, output increased by 4% owing to this
innovation (Byatt 1979, p. 91).

Table 10-14. Production Costs Occurring Directly from Operation of Engines by Factory Scale and by Type of Engines   (yen)

| | 1910 | | | | | |
| | Large-scale Factory | | | Small-scale Factory | | |
	Steam Engine	Petro-leum Engine	Electric Motor	Steam Engine	Petro-leum Engine	Electric Motor
Depreciation for engine	373 (607)	194 (317)	100 (163)	224 (364)	54 (87)	25 (41)
Depreciation for transmission	203 (330)	203 (330)	203 (330)	45 (73)	45 (73)	45 (73)
Depreciation for engine room	43 (70)	12 (20)	6 (10)	21 (35)	6 (10)	3 (5)
Interest payments	104 (188)	52 (103)	37 (79)	52 (89)	13 (?6)	9 (18)
Sub-total (A)	723 (1,195)	461 (770)	346 (582)	342 (561)	118 (196)	82 (137)
Wage payments to workers who operate engine	554 (902)	185 (301)	0 (0)	185 (301)	0 (0)	0 (0)
Maintenance cost for engine	108 (176)	41 (66)	26 (43)	27 (44)	10 (17)	7 (11)
Fuel cost	646 (1,052)	3,106 (5,056)	1,128 (1,836)	97 (158)	466 (758)	169 (275)
Sub-total (B)	1,308 (2,130)	3,332 (5,423)	1,154 (1,879)	309 (503)	476 (775)	176 (286)
Total (A+B)	2,031 (3,325)	3,793 (6,193)	1,500 (2,461)	651 (1,064)	594 (971)	258 (423)

Table 10-14. (continued)   (yen)

	1926					
	Large-scale Factory			Small-scale Factory		
	Steam Engine	Petro-leum Engine	Electric Motor	Steam Engine	Petro-leum Engine	Electric Motor
Depreciation for engine	604 (544)	455 (408)	85 (77)	364 (328)	99 (90)	22 (20)
Depreciation for transmission	307 (277)	307 (277)	307 (277)	68 (61)	68 (61)	68 (61)
Depreciation for engine room	111 (100)	32 (29)	16 (14)	56 (50)	16 (14)	8 (7)
Interest payments	184 (165)	113 (102)	57 (51)	92 (83)	26 (23)	13 (12)
Sub-total (A)	1,206 (1,086)	907 (816)	465 (419)	580 (522)	209 (188)	111 (100)
Wage payments to workers who operate engine	2,076 (1,869)	692 (623)	0 (0)	692 (623)	0 (0)	0 (0)
Maintenance cost for engine	228 (205)	86 (78)	58 (52)	57 (51)	22 (19)	14 (13)
Fuel cost	2,068 (1,861)	7,621 (6,860)	2,732 (2,459)	310 (279)	1,143 (1,029)	410 (369)
Sub-total (B)	4,372 (3,935)	8,399 (7,561)	2,790 (2,511)	1,059 (953)	1,165 (1,048)	424 (382)
Total (A+B)	5,578 (5,021)	9,306 (8,377)	3,255 (2,930)	1,639 (1,475)	1,374 (1,236)	535 (482)

Notes: See the notes to Table 10-13.

From this study we have learned that electrification gave great advantage to the weaving industry. In small plants, the introduction of electric motors made mechanization possible; it promoted the transition from hand looms to power looms, which raised production efficiency and improved cost performance. In large plants, the transition from non-electric engines to electric motors decreased production costs and improved output quality.

Chapter 11

THE LUMBERING INDUSTRY

with Fumio Makino

The lumbering industry is taken up as an object of the study in this chapter because of the threee major reasons. One reason is the importance of lumber products and woods in the early stage of economic development of Japan. First, buildings were generally made of lumber rather than iron and concrete. Second, lumber was used as materials for machines such as looms and reeling machines. Third, woods were major energy source before the introduction of coal or petroleum. B. Hindle emphasized on the importance of woods and lumbers in the early phase of economic development in the United States and called pertinently that era as "wooden age".[1] In Japan, the period until the end of the nineteenth century could be taken as the wooden age, and even in the twentieth century before World War II woods and lumbers seemed to play an important role as natural resources.[2]

Another reason for the selection of this industry is the unique pattern of power revolution in this industry; that is, wide spread of mechanical power (water wheels) in the early years, longer dependence on steam power, and rapid decline on the usage of steam power in the 1930s. Due to these facts, the impact of mechanization and the advantage of using steam engines can be examined clearly.

Here an attention should be paid to the dualistic structure of this

---

[1] Hindle 1975, p. 3.
[2] Studies on this aspect of Japanese economic development are few; a study by Kumazaki (Umemura *et al.* 1966, chaps. 2 and 8) is an exception.

Table 11-1. Number and Composition of Factories by Factory
Scale in Total Manufacturing and Lumbering:
1909–1940

Year	Number of Factories		Composition (%)	
	5–9 (persons)	Total	5–9 (persons)	Total
Total manufacturing industry				
1909	16,780	32,124	52.2	100.0
1919	20,034	43,723	45.8	100.0
1930	35,614	61,768	57.7	100.0
1940	76,433	137,142	55.7	100.0
Lumbering industry				
1909	777	1,201	64.7	100.0
1919	1,340	2,305	58.1	100.0
1930	1,600	2,386	67.1	100.0
1940	3,653	6,113	59.8	100.0

Sources: Total manufacturing industry: Minami 1965, pp. 228–31 (original source is
STF). Lumbering industry: STF.
Notes: Figures are for the private factories only. Factory scale is measured by the
number of production workers employed.

industry; the coexistence of small-scale rural sawmills and large-scale
urban mills.[3] The former type of sawmills, which is the object of this
study, have been located near the forest, whereas the latter have been
established on the lower part of rivers or near ports, where logs were
carried in floats from the upriver or shipped from other ports.

In the first section, the structure of this industry is overlooked, and the
process of power revolution in this industry is reviewed quantitatively.
In the second section, factors for promoting the power revolution in the

[3] Rural sawmills were not always competitive with urban ones, because square
lumbers were chiefly sawn in the former and boards were produced in the latter (Miyahara
1956, p. 88).

lumbering industry are examined, under the assumption that entrepreneurs choose the most profitable technology among alternatives.

Structure of Industry and the Process of Power Revolution

Structure of the Industry

Japanese lumbering industry posessed two conspicuous characteristics
before WWII. The first was the dominance of small-scale plants;
sawmills with 5–9 operatives occuping 58–67% of total sawmills,
compared to 46–58% in the manufacturing industry as a whole (Table
11-1).

Comparable figures on the number of sawmills and that of other
manufacturing plants with four or less workers are not available.
However, the two surveys conducted by the Nōshōmushō (Ministry of
Agriculture and Commerce) in 1919 and Nōrinshō (Ministry of
Agriculture and Forestry) in 1933 demonstrate the existence of a large
number of sawmills with four or less workers. According to these
surveys, mechanically powered sawmills with 4 or less workers amounted to 2,599 and 7,436 in 1919 and 1933, respectively, exceeding that
with 5–9 workers (Table 11-2).[4]

STF for 1919 reveals a positive relation between the ratio of powered
factories to total factories (α) and factory size in the lumbering industry
(Table 11-2). Considering this relation, it is assumed that α was 60% for
sawmills with 4 or less workers. Thus, the total number of sawmills of
this scale, both mechanized and non-mechanized, is estimted to be 4,322
($=2,599 \div 0.60$). For the scale of 5–9, 10–29, and 30 and more workers

---

[4]   There is a gap in the number of sawmills between the two sets of statistics; STF in
1919 and 1930 and the data compiled by the Ministry of Agriculture and Commerce (the
Ministry of Agriculture and Forestry) in 1919 and 1933. The number of powered sawmills
with 9 or more production workers of the latter is larger than that of the former in the two
years (1919 and 1930–33), respectively. A gap is larger than in 1930–33 than 1919; this
results from an increase in the number of sawmills during 1930–33. The number of
sawmills with null production workers in the latter statistics is 23 and 68 in 1919 and 1933
respectively, where lumbers were probably sawn by the clerical worker.

Table 11-2. Number of Factories by Factory Scale in Lumbering: 1919–1933

Year	Type of Factories	Scale (persons)				Total	
		0~4	5~9	10~29	30 or more	5 or more	0 or more
(A)	**Statistical Table for Factory**						
1919	Total factories		1,340	737	228	2,305	
	Powered factories		979	638	219	1,836	
	Proportion of powered factories (α, %)		73.06	86.57	96.05	79.65	
1930	Total factories		1,600	614	172	2,386	
	Powered factories		1,571	605	171	2,347	
	Proportion of powered factories (α, %)		98.19	98.53	99.42	98.37	
(B)	**Surveys by the Ministry of Agriculture and Commerce, and the Ministry of Agriculture and Forestry**						
1919	Total factories[a]	(4,332)	(1,705)	(717)	(194)	(2,616)	(6,948)
	Powered factories	2,599	1,245	621	186	2,053	4,652
	Proportion of powered factories (α, %)[b]	(60.00)	(73.06)	(86.57)	(96.05)		
1933	Total factories[a]	(8,262)	(2,144)	(841)	(215)	(3,200)	(11,462)
	Powered factories	7,436	2,144	841	215	3,200	10,636
	Proportion of powered factories (α, %)[b]	(90.0)	(100.0)	(100.0)	(100.0)		

Sources: (A) STF, 1919 and 1930.
(B) Nōshōmushō Sanrinkyoku 1921 and Nōrinshō Sanrinkyoku 1935.
[a] Estimated as the number of powered factories divided by the proportion of powered factories (α) × 100.
[b] Estimated value. Refer to text for estimating procedure.

Table 11.3. Location of Factories of Total Manufacturing and
Lumbering

(percent)

	Total Manufacturing Industry[a] 1932	Lumbering Industry[b]	
		1919	1919
City	51.7	15.9 (23.2)	15.7 (29.0)
County	48.3	84.1 (76.8)	84.3 (71.0)
(Town)		27.5 (28.8)	29.8 (29.6)
(Village)		56.6 (48.0)	54.5 (41.4)
Total	100.0	100.0 (100.0)	100.0 (100.0)

Sources: Total manufacturing industry: Shōkōshō Kōmukyoku 1934. Lumbering industry: Same as Table 11-2.
Notes: Figures are the composition of the number of factories and those in parentheses are the composition of power capacity of prime movers. All city and all county are defined in accordance with the boundaries at that time of each survey.
[a] Private factories with 5 and more production workers.
[b] Factories operated by mechanical power.

respectively, α calculated from STF is respectively applied to the number of mechanized sawmills to estimate the total number of sawmills. Summing up these figures of respective scales, the total number of sawmills in 1919 (6,948) has been obtained. As for 1933, through a similar procedure, the number of sawmills with 4 or less workers and the total number of all scales have been estimated to be 8,262 and 11,462, respectively. This set of estimation demonstrates the importance of small-scale factories in the lumbering industry. That is, the number of sawmills with 9 or less workers increased by 70% between 1919 and 1933, compared to a 30% increase in that with 10 or more workers. Furthermore the share of sawmills with 9 or less workers in total sawmills was very large; 87% and 91% in respective years.

The second feature of the Japanese lumbering industry was its concentration in rural areas. The share of sawmills located in rural areas (towns and villages) was 77% in 1919 and 71% in 1933 (Table 11-3),[5] compared to the 48% share of rural plants in all manufacturing plants in 1932. These rural sawmills were supposed to be of small scale. In these plants, logs were cut down in the near forest, and were processed into lumber, which was delivered to middlemen in the lower part of the river. Rural sawing had some advantages over urban sawing; that is, it was easier to get logs because of their location and they could save transportation cost because of smaller bulk of lumber than that of unprocessed logs. On the other hand, large-scale sawmills were almost located in the lower part of the rivers or ports, where logs, which were carried in floats from upriver or "imported" from Hokkaidō,[6] Sakhalin and the United States of America, were sawn. Location near consumer cities was an advantage of these plants over rural plants.[7]

Lumbering areas in Shizuoka prefecture, a representative lumbering region in Japan, were divided into two districts; Tenryū and Shimizu. The number of sawmills in Tenryū district, in which both small-scale rural sawmills and large-scale downriver sawmills existed, exceeded the number in Shimizu district (Table 11-4). Rural sawmills in Tenryū district were located near the forest of Japanese ceder and cypress spread along the Tenryū River and its tributary streams.[8] They sawed logs and hauled lumber products through the Tenryū River to the mouth of the River. This is why the proportion of domestic logs in all logs consumed was so high in Tenryū district (Table 11-4). Shimizu was a typical large-scale urban lumbering area. Average number of workers per sawmill was

[5]   Coverage of plant size in total manufacturing industry is not the same as that in the lumbering industry; mechanical sawmills with 4 or less production workers are included in the latter and not in the former. This partly explains why the composition of rural factories is higher in the lumbering industry.

[6]   Hokkaidō was conventionally taken as a foreign country in the lumbering industry before World War II.

[7]   Minato 1927, pp. 7–10.

[8]   According to another survey in 1935, 78% of sawmills in the Tenryū district was located along the upper Tenryū River and the rest of the sawmills was along the lower part of the river. Whereas a mean of the number of production workers in the former was 7.5, that in the latter was 50.9 (Zenkoku Sanrinkai Rengōkai 1938, pp. 118–19).

THE LUMBERING INDUSTRY

Table 11-4. Sawmills in Shizuoka Prefecture

Tenryū District

Year	Number of Plants	Horsepower Capacity of Prime Movers	Number of Workers	Share of Domestic Logs Consumed (%)
1919	63	1,725		
1923	99	2,920	1,739	86.0
1927	102	3,067	1,535	83.8
1930	108	2,686	1,450	94.3
1934	119	2,840	1,810	93.5
1937	200	4,209	2,221	97.7

Shimizu District

Year	Number of Plants	Horsepower Capacity of Prime Movers	Number of Workers	Share of Domestic Logs Consumed (%)
1919	30	414		100.0
1923	30	1,400	645	100.0
1927	60	2,429	1,463	98.5
1930	61	3,412	1,415	95.5
1934	43	2,243	1,243	87.9
1937	41	1,978	1,175	67.2

Sources: Shizuokaken 1968, pp. 355, 357–61, 366, 374.
a   Including prime movers for producing wooden boxes.
b   Including timbers for pulpwood.

22–29, three or four times as many as that in Tenryū. Sawmills in Shimizu consumed the northern timbers shipped from Hokkaidō and Sakhalin; their share in total logs consumed was almost as high as 100% until 1930. However, this share decreased and the share of domestic logs

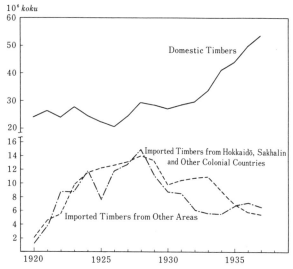

Fig. 11-1.   Supply of Timbers by Source

Sources: Hagino 1957, p. 341.
Notes: Timbers include both rough timbers and products timbers.

increased during the 1930s. This tendency was seen in all other regions in Japan as will be refered to later.

A sharp contrast can be seen in the changing pattern of sawmills between Tenryū and Shimizu in Table 11-4. In Tenryū, the number of plants, horsepower capacity of prime movers and the number of workers were stagnant between 1923 and 1930, and increased after 1930. On the other hand, in Shimizu, these figures grew remarkably for 1919–30 but decreased rapidly in the 1930s. These changes in the two districts resulted from the availability of logs, especially imported ones.

Because profitability of sawmills depended largely on the availability of logs and their prices, the relative advantage between rural and urban sawmills varied with the changes in the availability and the price of both domestic and imported logs. Imported timbers increased during 1920–28 and decreased after 1928, while from that time on domestic timbers increased again (Fig. 11-1). The decrease in imported timbers was caused by two factors; firstly, the change in the forestry policy of the Sakhalin government (export of timbers to Inland Japan was prohibited and their exclusive sale to pulp plants in Sakhalin was encouraged), secondly, the rising tariff rate during the 1920s[9] and the devaluation of yen's exchange rate.

Quantitative Survey of Power Revolution
Industry as a Whole. Lumbering was one of the earliest industry in which mechanization was proceeded. The proportion of powered factories (α) with 10 or more workers in 1900 was 46% (Table 11-5), compared to 32% of all manufacturing industry as a whole (Table 4-4). The proportion α for factories with 5 or more workers in the lumbering far exceeded a mean for all manufacturing for 1909–19; in the former α was 54% and 80% in 1909 and 1919 respectively (Table 11-6), while in the latter it was 28% and 61% respectively (Table 4-5).

Regarding the transition of power sources by kind, the lumbering showed three characteristics mentioned before. 1) Proportion of water wheels and turbines in total horsepower capacity of all engines was 61% in the wood and wood products industry (including the lumbering industry) in 1889. This proportion was very high compared to other industries; a mean of all manufacturing industries was merely 19% in 1887 (Table 6-3). 2) Proportion of steam power in the lumbering industry decreased from early 20th century, but its decrease was moderate relative to other industries (Tables 11-5, 11-7). The proportion was still 53% and 39% in 1919 and 1930 respectively, compared to 28% and 11% respectively in all manufacturing as a whole (Table 6-6). This signifies a delay in electrification in the lumbering industry. To show this more clearly, the year in which electric power exceeded steam power first was 1921 in the wood and wood products industry (Table 6-5) and 1925 in the lumbering industry. This periodization was the most

[9]   The tariff rate (value of tariff collected/value of imports × 100) of lumbers was 0.17% in 1924 and 15.52% in 1933. These values are compared with the rate for total imports; 4.65% and 6.03%, respectively (Yamazawa and Yamamoto 1979, pp. 249, 251).

Table 11-5. Proportion of Powered Factories (α) and Composition of Total Power Capacity (H) by Engine Type in Lumbering: 1900–1915

(percent)

Year	Proportion of Powered Factories (α)	Composition of H			
		Electric Motors (β)	Steam Engines and Turbines	Internal Combustion Engines	Water Wheels and Turbines
1900[a]	45.5	—	89.4	—	10.6
1905[b]	54.3	1.5	93.4	0.6	4.5
1910[c]	74.7	5.6	87.4	2.9	4.1
1915[c]	78.0	13.1	78.5	3.5	4.9

Sources: Same as Table 8-2.
Notes: See the notes to Table 8-2.
[a] Including factories of barrels and pails.
[b] Including factories of barrel, pails, match wood, materials of match boxes, wood bobbins, and equipments for *sake* brewing.
[c] Including factories of barrels, pails, wooden bent-work goods, and wooden clogs and others.

delayed among nine industry groups and delayed five to eight years after the manufacturing industry as a whole (1917). 3) The proportion of steam power decreased rapidly in the 1930; it decreased from 39% to 11% between 1930 and 1940. This transition of power sources was notable among various industry groups, and in the manufacturing industries as a whole the composition of power capacity did not change any more for the 1930s.

Small-scale Sawmills. Characteristics of the lumbering industry as a whole in the pattern of the power revolution, which have been revealed in the above, are also applicable to small-scale sawmills, which occupied large share of the Japanese lumbering industry. Having supposed the plants with 5-9 workers as a representative of the small-scale sawmills, the following four conclusions can be made (Tables 4-7, 6-6, 11-6, 11-7).

Table 11-6.   Proportion of Powered Factories (α) by Factory
Scale in Lumbering

(percent)

Scale (persons)	1909[a]	1914[a]	1919[a]	1930	1935	1940[b]
All factories	54.2	64.7	79.7	98.4	98.4	99.2
5– 9	48.1	54.6	73.1	98.2	98.3	99.2
10– 29	63.0	74.9	86.6	98.5	98.5	99.2
30– 49	69.2	96.4	95.4	99.1	100.0	98.9
50– 99	80.0	94.4	95.7	100.0	98.8	100.0
100–499	100.0	100.0	100.0	100.0	100.0	100.0

Sources: Same as Table 8-3.
Notes: Figures are for the private factories with five or more production workers.
[a]   Including factories of barrels, pails, wooden bent-work goods, and wooden clogs and
others.
[b]   Including factories of plywood.

1) Early mechanization: the proportion α was 48% and 73% in 1909 and
1919 respectively in the lumbering industry, compared to 14% and 46%
in all manufacturing industry as a whole. 2) Large reliance on water
power in early years. The proportion of water power in 1909 was slightly
larger in the lumbering industry (23%) than all manufacturing industry
(21%). But in earlier years, when statistics by factory scale are not
available, the proportion in the lumbering industry should have been
very large compared to all manufacturing industry. This supposition is
verified by our previous study on the industry as a whole. 3) Longer
reliance on steam power: the proportion of steam power was still 16% in
1930 in the lumbering industry, compared to 6% of all manufacturing
industry. 4) Rapid decline in steam power in the 1930s: the proportion of
steam power decreased from 16% to 3% between 1930 and 1940 in the
lumbering industry, while comparable figures were 6% and 1% in the
manufacturing as a whole in the same respective years. Factors re-

Table 11-7. Composition of Total Power Capacity (H) by Engine Type and by Factory Scale in Lumbering: 1909–1940

(percent)

Scale (persons)	Electric Motors (β)	Steam Engines and Turbines	Internal Combustion Engines	Water Wheels and Turbines
		1909[a]		
All factories	5.6	80.5	4.2	9.7
5– 9	7.4	61.8	7.6	23.2
10– 29	5.4	85.7	3.7	5.2
30– 49	0.6	96.0	2.5	0.9
50– 99	6.0	91.3	0.5	2.2
100–499	4.2	95.8	—	—
		1914[a]		
All factories	14.7	73.5	4.5	7.3
5– 9	19.1	56.5	8.2	16.2
10– 29	14.4	79.5	2.5	3.6
30– 49	11.2	79.6	1.6	7.6
50– 99	5.7	85.3	6.2	2.8
100–499	13.3	82.2	4.5	—
		1919[a]		
All factories	32.2	53.0	4.7	10.1
5– 9	38.4	34.5	6.0	21.1
10– 29	35.9	53.5	3.4	7.2
30– 49	22.4	70.9	1.8	4.9
50– 99	22.6	72.1	2.0	3.3
100–499	21.7	63.7	12.7	1.9

Table 11-7. (continued)

(percent)

Scale (persons)	Electric Motors (β)	Steam Engines and Turbines	Internal Combustion Engines	Water Wheels and Turbines
		1930		
All factories	56.8	38.6	1.9	2.7
5– 9	71.7	15.8	5.7	6.8
10– 29	69.4	26.9	0.7	3.0
30– 49	53.8	45.9	0.3	—
50– 99	56.1	43.4	—	0.5
100–499	16.7	82.5	0.8	—
		1935		
All factories	72.5	19.3	5.7	2.5
5– 9	69.4	13.5	10.9	6.4
10– 29	70.9	22.6	4.6	1.9
30– 49	72.7	22.6	4.7	—
50– 99	76.6	20.6	2.3	0.5
100–499	80.0	18.9	1.1	—
		1940[b]		
All factories	78.4	10.7	7.8	3.1
5– 9	78.1	3.0	13.0	5.9
10– 29	80.7	10.1	6.7	2.5
30– 49	78.2	18.4	2.6	0.8
50– 99	75.2	20.5	3.3	1.0
100–499	68.8	29.4	1.8	—

Sources: Same as Table 8-3.
Notes: See the notes to Table 11-6.

Table 11-8.   Composition of Primary Power Capacity (H') by Engine Type and by Factory Scale in Lumbering: 1909–1919

(percent)

	Primary Electric Motor (β')	Steam Engines and Turbines	Internal Combustion Engines	Water Wheels and Turbines
		1909		
All factories	5.1	81.0	4.2	9.7
5– 9	7.4	61.8	7.6	23.2
10– 29	5.4	85.8	3.7	5.1
30– 49	0.6	96.0	2.5	0.9
50– 99	0.6	96.5	0.6	2.3
100–499	4.2	95.8	—	—
		1914		
All factories	13.9	74.3	4.5	7.3
5– 9	19.1	56.5	8.2	16.2
10– 29	14.4	79.6	2.5	3.5
30– 49	11.1	79.7	1.6	7.6
50– 99	4.6	86.3	6.3	2.8
100–499	5.9	89.3	4.8	—
		1919		
All factories	30.9	54.0	4.8	10.3
5– 9	38.2	34.6	6.0	21.2
10– 29	34.6	54.5	3.5	7.4
30– 49	21.7	71.6	1.8	4.9
50– 99	21.2	73.3	2.1	3.4
100–499	16.1	68.3	13.6	2.0

Sources: Same as Table 8-3.

Notes: Figures are for the private factories with five or more production workers.

sponsible for these characteristics will be revealed in the next section.[10]

Factors Responsible for the Power Revolution

Analytical Framework and Summary of Estimation of Rate of Net Profit

The purpose of this section is to analyse factors responsible for the power revolution in small-scale rural sawmills; that is, earlier mechanization, longer reliance on steam engines, and rapid diffusion of electric motors in the 1930s. The analysis is based on the hypothesis that entrepreneurs choose a technology among alternatives that brings them the highest rate of profit. Rate of net profit is estimated on four types of sawmills; those operated by human power, water wheel, steam engine and electric motor, respectively.[11] Those sawmills are assumed to be located along the upper Tenryū River, because of three reasons: Firstly, it is a representative rural lumbering district. Secondly, in Japan, private mechanical sawing was first started in that location. Thirdly, data for estimating the rate of net profit in this district is more available.[12]

The rate of net profit (r) is a ratio of net profit (NP) to total capital (K), where, net profit $(NP) =$ value of lumber products $(V_1) +$ value of by-products $(V_2) -$ cost of logs consumed $(V_L) -$ fuel cost $(FC) -$ wage cost $(WC) -$ maintenance cost of prime mover $(MC) -$ transportation cost of products $(TC) -$ interest paid $(IC) -$ depreciation cost (DC), that is to say

$$(1) \quad r = (V_1 + V_2 - V_L - FC - WC - MC - TC - IC - DC)/K \times 100,$$

where total capital (K) is a sum of fixed capital (KF) and working capital (KZ).

The value of lumber products (V_1), that of by-products (V_2) and cost

---

[10]   Statistics relating with the power revolution in the Tenryū district is given in Minami and Makino 1986, table 9.

[11]   For the detail, see Minami and Makino 1986b, statistical appendix.

[12]   Of the four types of sawmill, hand sawmills had already disappeared in Tenryū at that time. But we assumed a hypothetical hand sawmill and calculated its rate of net profit to show that hand sawing was not economically viable.

of logs consumed (V_L) is obtained by multiplying respective amount of product (Y_1, Y_2, L) by their respective prices (P_1, P_2, P_L). The amount of logs consumed (L) is a product of three variables; labor productivity (daily consumption of logs per production worker; $l = L/(N_1 + N_2)/D$), annual working days (D) and the number of production workers ($N_1 + N_2$). The amount of lumber product (Y_1; composed of boards, square flitch and so on) is estimated as a product of the amount of logs consumed (L) and the yield rate (a ratio of the amount of lumber produced (Y_1) to that of logs consumed (L); $y = Y_1/L$). Therefore, $Y_1 = L \times y = l \times D \times (N_1 + N_2) \times y$. By-products are sawmill wastes such as sawdust, wood flour, and wooden wastes produced in sawing process. Their common disposal was either to be sold to residential consumers or to be burned in steam-powered sawmills. In the former case, the amount of by-products for sale (Y_2) is equal to the total amount of by-products produced which is assumed to be a difference between the amount of logs consumed and that of lumber products ($Y_2 = L - Y_1$). In the latter case, however, the amount of by-products used as fuel is deducted from the total amount. Let the ratio of the value of by-products (V_2) to the value of total products ($V_1 + V_2$) be coefficient of by-products (b), then the value of by-products (V_2) can be expressed as the following equation $V_2 = V_1 \times b/(1 - b)$.

Fuel cost (FC) is calculated only for sawmills operated with coal-fired steam engine and electric motor. It can be calculated by multiplying annual fuel consumption (F) by fuel price (P_F). Wage cost (WC) is a product of the number of workers (N_j), wage rate (w_j) and the number of annual working days (D); $WC = D \times \sum(N_j \times w_j)$. It is assumed that there are seven workers in mechanical sawmill ($\sum N_j = 7$); four sawyers (N_1), two bearers (N_2) engaged in rolling logs from log storage and taking away lumbers to yard piles, and one clerical worker (N_3).[13] In the case of hand sawmills, six sawyers (the same number as that of production workers = sawyers and bearers in mechanical sawing; $N_4 = N_1 + N_2$) are assumed. As for the wage rate of the respective worker, relative wage differential such as $w_3 > w_1 > w_2 = w_4$ is assumed. Maintenance cost of prime

[13]   The number of bearer for steam engine is three including a boiler man.

mover (MC) is calculated by multiplying maintenance charge per horse-power per month (P_M) by power capacity of the prime mover (hp) and 12 months. Transportation cost (TC) accrues from hauling lumber products to wholesalers. It is a product of unit transportation charge (P_T) and the amount of lumber product (Y_1). Interest paid (IC) is estimated by multiplying the rate of interest (i) by the amount of borrowing capital, which is assumed to be equivalent to working capital (KZ). Depreciation cost (DC) is obtained by applying the annuity method to fixed capital (KF). Therefore, depreciation cost is a function of fixed capital and interest rate; $DC = f(KF, i)$. Fixed capital (KF) in mechanical sawmill is composed of two circular saws,[14] a 15-hp prime mover (water wheel, steam engine, or electric motor), other equipments and buildings. The composition of fixed capital for hand sawmills are assumed to be six handsaws and factory buildings with the same space for mechanical sawmills. Working capital (KZ) is the cost logs consumed for two months both for mechanical and hand sawmill $(KZ = V_L/6)$.[15] Substituting these relations into the equation (1), we have the following relation:[16]

[14]   Three types of mechanical saws; circular saws, frame saws and band saws, were available at that time. Usually small-scale rural sawmills used circular saws. See Minami and Makino 1986b, section III.1 for the history of sawing technology in Japan.

[15]   Average capacity of prime mover (hp) was 15.3, the number of saws was 3.4 (in which 1.7 was circular saw) and the number of workers was 7.5 in rural sawmills in the upper Tenryū River (Zenkoku Sanrinkai Rengōkai 1938, pp. 116–19).

[16]

$$
\begin{aligned}
(2) \quad r &= (V_1 + V_2 - V_L - FC - WC - MC - TC - IC - DC)/K \times 100 \\
&= [(P_1 \times Y_1 + P_2 \times Y_2 - P_L \times L - P_F \times F - D \times \sum(N_j \times w_j) - P_M \times \mathrm{hp} \times 12 \\
&\quad - P_T \times Y_1 - P_L \times L/6 \times i - f(KF, i)]/(KF + KZ) \times 100 \\
&= \{P_1 \times Y_1 + P_1 \times Y_1 \times b/(1-b) - P_L \times L - P_F \times F - D \times \sum(N_j \times w_j) \\
&\quad - P_M \times \mathrm{hp} \times 12 - P_T \times Y_1 - P_L \times L/6 \times i - f(KF, i)\}/(KF + P_L \times L/6) \times 100 \\
&= [Y_1 \times \{P_1/(1-b) - P_T\} - P_L \times L \times (1 - i/6) - P_F \times F \\
&\quad - D \times \sum(N_j \times w_j) - P_M \times \mathrm{hp} \times 12 - f(KF, i)]/(KF + P_L \times L/6) \times 100 \\
&= [D \times l \times (N_1 + N_2) \times \{y \times (P_1/(1-b) - P_T) - P_L \times (1 - i/6)\} \\
&\quad - P_F \times F - D \times \sum(N_j \times w_j) - P_M \times \mathrm{hp} \times 12 - f(KF, i)]/\{KF + D \times l \\
&\quad \times (N_1 + N_2) \times P_L/6\} \times 100
\end{aligned}
$$

273

Table 11-9. Rate of Net Profit (r) in Lumbering by Type of
Power: 1900–1935

(percent)

Year	Human Power	Water Wheel	Steam Engine (1)	Steam Engine(2)	Electric Motor
1900	− 17.4	10.3			
1914	− 27.1	10.7	10.6	9.0	13.5
		(5.1)	(4.7)		(5.9)
1935		2.5	1.2	− 8.0	12.5
		(2.2)	(1.0)		(11.4)

Sources: For estimating procedures and data source, see Minami and Makino 1986b.
Notes: Steam engine (1) stands for the engines fired by self-supplied wood fuel, and
steam engine (2) does the engines fired by coal purchased.
Figures in parentheses are the rate of profit at 1934–36 prices (r').

$$(2) \quad r = [D \times l \times (\bar{N}_1 + \bar{N}_2) \times \{y \times (\bar{P}_1/(1 - \bar{b}) - \bar{P}_T)$$
$$- \bar{P}_L \times (1 - \bar{i}/6)\} - P_F \times F - D \times \sum(N_j \times \bar{w}_j)$$
$$- P_M \times \text{hp} \times 12 - f(KF, \bar{i})]/$$
$$\{KF + D \times l \times (\bar{N}_1 + \bar{N}_2) \times \bar{P}_L/6\} \times 100$$

The results of estimation of r are shown in Table 11-9.

Comparison of Profitability between Hand and Mechanical Sawing

Profitability of hand sawing is compared here with that of mechanical
sawing with water wheels, because most of early mechanical sawmills in
rural area used water wheels. In 1900 the rate r was 10.3% in mechanical sawing, whereas it was − 17.4% in hand sawing.[17] Furthermore the
gap between hand and mechanical sawing widened in 1914.

In the equation (2) notation $\bar{x}$ represents that same figure was used to
estimate r for both mechanical sawmill with water wheel and hand

[17] The minus rate of profit of hand sawing was consistent with the fact that hand
sawing had already disappeared in Tenryū at that time (see n. 12).

Table 11-10. Factors for Difference of Rate of Net Profit (r) between Hand and Mechanical Sawing

	1900			1914		
	Hand (1)	Mechanical (Water Wheel) (2)	Difference of r (2)−(1)	Hand (1)	Mechanical (Water Wheel) (2)	Difference of r (2)−(1)
Rate of net profit (r) (%)	−17.4	10.3	27.7	−27.1	10.7	37.8
Factors for difference of r						
Annual working days (D) (day/year)	253 (122)	208 (100)	−6.0%	253 (122)	208 (100)	−5.3%
Labor productivity (l) (koku/man/day)	0.46 (21)	2.20 (100)	67.4%	0.46 (17)	2.78 (100)	74.2%
Wage rate (w) (yen/man/day)	0.28 (74)	0.38 (100)	−6.0%	0.45 (74)	0.61 (100)	−7.2%
Maintenance cost (MC) (yen/year)	0 (0)	163 (100)	−6.2%	0 (0)	243 (100)	−7.1%
Fixed capital (KF) (yen)	1,675 (52)	3,241 (100)	−21.5%	1,849 (52)	3,573 (100)	−16.8%

Notes: Figures in parentheses are the index with 100 for mechanical sawing.

275

sawmill. Since fuel cost is not necessary for both mechanical sawmill with water wheel and hand sawmill, difference of r is dependent on remaining five variables. The estimation of these five variables and their contribution to the difference of rate of profit between mechanical sawmill and hand sawmill are listed in Table 11-10.[18]

The first variable, annual working days (D) was 45 days shorter in mechanical sawing by water wheel than in hand sawing because the operation by water power was often disturbed by natural accidents. Due to the shorter period of operation, r for mechanical sawing was 6.0% point and 5.3% point lower than that for hand sawing in 1900 and 1914 respectively. The second variable, labor productivity (l) was about five times higher in mechanical sawing than in hand sawing. Because of higher labor productivity, r for mechanical sawing was 67.4% point and 74.2% point higher than that for hand sawing in 1900 and 1914 respectively. The third variable is composition of workers (N_j). As hand sawmills were generally managed by lumber dealer, there was not any clerical worker in hand sawmill itself, and the wage rate of hand sawyer is assumed to be equal to that of the bearer in mechanical sawmill ($w_4 = w_2$) whose wage rate is the lowest among other workers. Weighted average wage rate (w'), therefore, was 26% higher in mechanical sawing. This caused lower r for mechanical sawing by 6.0% point and 7.2% point in 1900 and 1914 respectively. The fourth variable, maintenance cost of water wheel (MC) is included only in mechanical sawing. The rate of profit in mechanical sawing was 6.2% point and 7.1% point lower than that for hand sawing in 1900 and 1914 respectively due to the mainte-

---

[18]   Let the rate of net profit equation be $g(f_{ij})$, where f_{ij} is the jth factor of the rate of net profit in the ith power source. Difference of rate of net profit between power sources (Δ) can be defined as

$$\Delta = g(f_{11}, f_{12}, \cdots, f_{1n}) - g(f_{21}, f_{22}, \cdots, f_{2n})$$
$$= g(f_{11}, f_{12}, \cdots, f_{1n}) - g(f_{21}, f_{12}, \cdots, f_{1n})$$
$$+ g(f_{21}, f_{12}, \cdots, f_{1n}) - g(f_{21}, f_{22}, \cdots, f_{1n})$$
$$\cdot$$
$$+ g(f_{21}, f_{22}, \cdots, f_{1n}) - g(f_{21}, f_{22}, \cdots, f_{2n}) .$$

nance cost. Fixed capital (KF), the fifth variable, was almost two times larger in mechanical sawing than in hand sawing. Rate of profit in the former was 21.5% point and 16.8% point lower than that in the latter in 1900 and 1914 respectively because of larger fixed capital in the former. Putting all the factors together, the rate of net profit for mechanical sawing exceeded by 27.7% point and 37.8% point that for hand sawing in 1900 and 1914 respectively. Among five factors mentioned above, only one factor, labor productivity, favored mechanical sawing. This advantage cancelled out disadvantages of shorter working days, higher wage cost, maintenance cost of water wheel and larger fixed capital in mechanical sawing.

There were two advantages of mechanical sawing over hand sawing which due to their unquantitative nature are not taken into consideration in the estimation of r. The first was the higher quality of lumber produced by mechnical sawing; the tail of a log were left not sawn in hand sawing and surface of lumber was uneven or rough, whereas mechanical sawing were free from these problems.[19] The second was the labor management problems. In the hand sawing, which was usually made as side business of peasants, operation was confined to sluck season of agricultural activity and they were not settled down in one place. Furthermore they often demanded higher wage in case of strike and did not keep the standard requirements of lumber products.[20] These problems were less serious in the mechanical sawing, because mechanical sawing was less labor intensive and mechanical sawyers were not members of the craft union of hand sawyers.

Even with a development of mechanical sawing, hand sawyers were not completely driven out and hand sawing could coexisted with it to some extent, because large logs could not be sawn by circular saws. There are only few informations on hand sawyers and hand sawmills. In Akita prefecture there were 34 hand sawmills and 568 hand sawyers in 1904, and, only 8 sawmills in 1909. In Japan as a whole (excluding Hokkaidō)

[19]   Miyahara 1950, p. 31.
[20]   Miyahara 1956, pp. 11–13; Noshiro 1979, pp. 551–52; Shizuokaken 1968, p. 168.

there were 132 hand sawmills,[21] compared to 964 mechanical sawmills.[22] Because of the diffusion of band saws which could saw large logs,[23] the substitution of mechanical sawing for hand sawing was completed.

Comparison of Profitability of Mechanical Sawing among Power Sources

In 1914 the rate r of steam engine (10.6%) was almost equal to water wheel (10.7%) and slightly lower than electric motor (13.5%) (Table 11-9). This fact as well as the underdevelopment of electricity network in rural areas were responsible to the longer reliance on steam power in the lumbering industry.

After 1914 r decreased remarkably in steam engine from 10.6% to 1.2% between 1914 and 1935. The decrease was also confirmed in terms of the real rate of profit (r')[24] which decreased from 4.7% to 1.0% for 1914–35. In the case of electric motor, however, r was almost unchanged and r' increased remarkably. Such a difference in the changes in the rate of profit between steam power and electric power accounted for both the rapid decrease in the proportion of steam power in total power capacity and the rapid increase in the proportion of electric power, in the 1930s.

Differential in r was 2.8% and 10.0% in 1914 and 1935 respectively between electric motor and water wheel, and 2.9% and 11.3% in 1914 and 1935 between electric motor and steam engine. Of the fifteen variables in the equation (2), seven variables are different among water wheel, steam engine and electric motor (Table 11-11).

The first variable is the number of working days (D): It is smaller in water wheel than in other engines because water-powered sawmills could not be operated in the water shortage and were sometimes destructed by flood. Difference of r caused by the difference of the number of working days was 3.5% point and 3.1% point between electric motor and water wheel in 1914 and 1935 respectively and −0.2% point between electric

[21] Hagino 1972, p. 82.
[22] Strictly, it is the number of sawmills established before 1909 and existed in 1916.
[23] Miyahara 1950, p. 32.
[24] Real rate of profit stands for a ratio of "net profit" to "capital stock," both of which are expressed at 1934–36 prices.

motor and steam engine in both 1914 and 1935.

The second variable is labor productivity (l): This tended to vary among the types of prime movers due to a difference in the efficiency of adjustment of revolutionary speed to cope with load variation. In the case of electric motors with the highest productivity, it was possible to start with heavy load and to adjust the speed freely.[25] In the case of steam engines the speed was adjusted by the governor apparatus. However, its efficiency was reduced considerably when load varied. Difference of r caused by the difference in labor productivity was 1.1% point and 2.0% point between electric motor and steam engine in 1914 and 1935 respectively. In the case of water wheels with the lowest productivity, gearing was used for the adjustment. Energy loss was considerable; in case of wooden water wheels it amounted to 20–30% of total energy. Furthermore the maximum capacity of water wheel sometimes could not be utilized due to water shortage.[26] As a result, r for electric motor exceeded by 16.0% point and 10.3% point of that for water wheel in 1914 and 1935, respectively.

The third and fourth variables relate to disposal of sawdusts and wooden wastes (by-products coefficient, b), and to fuel cost ($P_F \times F$): As for the disposal, there were two alternative ways; one was to sell sawdusts and wooden wastes to household (this was the case of electric motors and water wheels) and another was to use them as fuel for running steam engines.[27] This is a reason why in the case of steam engines fuel cost was null and the by-products coefficient was lower in Table 11-9. Difference of fuel cost resulted in the difference of r by -21.9% point and -10.1% point between electric motor and water wheel in 1914 and 1935 respectively because fuel cost was not necessary for the latter. Difference of by-products coefficient and fuel cost combined together contributed to the difference of r by -1.3 ($= 19.0 - 20.3$)% point and 3.8 ($= 13.3 - 9.5$)% point between electric motor and steam engine in 1914 and 1935 respectively.

[25] Sonomura 1937, p. 29.
[26] Minato 1927, pp. 36, 43, 44.
[27] As is discussed later, it was possible to buy coal and sell by-products.

Table 11-11.   Factors for Difference of Rate of Net Profit (r) in
Lumbering between Types of Engines

	1914				
	Water Wheel (1)	Steam Engine (2)	Electric Motor (3)	Difference of r EM − WW (3)−(1)	EM − SE (3)−(2)
Rate of net profit (r) (%)	10.7	10.6	13.5	2.8	2.9
Factors for difference of r					
Annual working days (D)	208	253	251	3.5%	−0.2%
(day/year)	(83)	(101)	(100)		
Labor productivity (l)	2.78	3.71	3.98	16.0%	1.1%
(*koku*/man/day)	(70)	(93)	(100)		
By-products coefficient (b)	0.10	0.034	0.10	0%	19.0%
	(100)	(34)	(100)		
Fuel cost (FC)	0	0	1,434	−21.9%	−20.3%
(yen/year)	(0)	(0)	(100)		
Wage rate (w')	3.66	4.16	3.66	0%	0.7%
(yen/day)	(100)	(114)	(100)		
Maintenance cost (MC)	243	88	22	4.1%	0.2%
(yen/year)	(1100)	(400)	(100)		
Fixed capital (KF)	3,573	4,995	3,332	1.1%	2.4%
(yen)	(107)	(150)	(100)		

The fifth variable is wage cost ($\sum(N_j \times w_j)$): As boiler man had to be employed to operate steam engine, wage cost for steam engine was 12 and 14% higher than that for other prime movers. The rate r for steam engine was reduced by 0.7% point and 1.2% point in 1914 and 1935 respectively due to the employment of a boiler man. The sixth variable is maintenance cost ($P_M \times hp \times 12$): This was extremely high for water wheel, because water wheels, made of wood and powered by natural energy, were more fragile and apt to suffer from natural disasters. As electric motors were small and easy to operate, their maintenance cost

Table 11-11. (countinued)

	Water Wheel (1)	Steam Engine (2)	Electric Motor (3)	Difference of r EM − WW (3) − (1)	EM − SE (3) − (2)
			1935		
Rate of net profit (r) (%)	2.5	1.2	12.5	10.0	11.3
Factors for difference of r					
Annual working days (D)	208	253	251	3.1%	−0.2%
(day/year)	(83)	(101)	(100)		
Labor productivity (l)	3.33	3.90	4.42	10.3%	2.0%
($koku$/man/day)	(75)	(88)	(100)		
By-products coefficient (b)	0.076	0.021	0.076	0%	13.3%
	(100)	(21)	(100)		
Fuel cost (FC)	0	0	1,107	−10.1%	−9.5%
(yen/year)	(0)	(0)	(100)		
Wage rate (w')	6.45	7.21	6.45	0%	1.2%
(yen/day)	(100)	(112)	(100)		
Maintence cost (MC)	386	144	36	4.0%	0.7%
(yen/year)	(1,100)	(400)	(100)		
Fixed capital (KF)	6,102	7,541	5,156	2.7%	3.8%
(yen)	(118)	(146)	(100)		

Notes: Figures in parentheses are the index with 100 for electric motor.
WW, SE and *EM* stand for water wheel, steam power, and electric motor respectively.

was the lowest among three. As a result, r for electric motor exceeded by 4.1% point and 4.0% point over that for water wheel in 1914 and 1935 respectively. The seventh variable is the amount of fixed capital (KF): This was the highest for steam engine and the lowest for electric motor. Difference of fixed capital contributed to the difference of r by 2.4% point and 3.8% point between electric motor and steam engine, and by 1.1% point and 2.7% point between electric motor and water wheel, in 1914 and 1935 respectively.

Table 11-12.   Changes in Factors for Rate of Net Profit (r) in
Lumbering between 1914 and 1935

Factors	Year	Water Wheel	Steam Engine	Electric Motor
Labor productivity (l)	1914	2.78	3.71	3.97
($koku$/man/day)	1935	3.33	3.90	4.42
Yield rate (y)	1914	62	62	62
(percent)	1935	65	65	65
Price of lumber products (P_1)	1914	6.79	6.79	6.79
(yen/$koku$)	1935	6.46	6.46	6.46
Price of by-products (P_2)	1914	1.24	1.24	1.24
(yen/$koku$)	1935	0.98	0.98	0.98
Price of logs (P_L)	1914	3.45	3.45	3.45
(yen/$koku$)	1935	3.36	3.36	3.36
Electricity charge (P_F)	1914			58.2
(yen/10^3 kWH)	1935			30.7
Wage rate (w')	1914	0.82	0.82	0.82
(yen/man/day)	1935	1.02	1.02	1.02
Transportation charge (P_T)	1914	0.32	0.32	0.32
(yen/$koku$)	1935	0.58	0.58	0.58
Fixed capital (KF)	1914	5,740	7,620	5,260
(yen)	1935	6,110	7,600	5,180

Notes: All figures are expressed at 1934–36 prices.

Factors responsible for the changes in the real rate of net profit (r') for 1914–35 are revealed in the two tables; Table 11-12 which gives determinant factors for r' and Table 11-13 which presents their contributions to over-time increments of r'. It is evident that there were six factors causing widening differential of r' among three engines. The first factor is the real electric charge (fuel price), which increased r' for electric motor by 4.6% point. The second factor is an increase in labor productivity. Its effect for steam engine was about 3–4% point lower than that for other prime movers, because of changes in the conditions of supply of logs, especially of imports. Imported timbers tended to

Table 11-13. Changes in Real Rate of Profit (r') in Lumbering
between 1914 and 1935 and Their Factors

(percent)

	Water Wheel	Steam Engine	Electric Motor
Rate of profit (r')			
1914	5.1	4.7	5.9
1935	2.2	1.0	11.4
Increment	-2.9	-3.7	$+5.5$
Factors			
Labor productivity (l)	$+4.6$	$+1.0$	$+3.8$
Yield rate (y)	$+5.2$	$+6.0$	$+7.3$
Relative price	$+7.0$	$+8.0$	$+10.1$
of products to logs (P_1/P_L)			
Price of by-products (P_2)	$+1.0$	$+0.3$	$+1.4$
Electricity charge (P_F)			$+4.6$
Wage rate (w')	-6.0	-5.7	-6.4
Transportation charge (P_T)	-10.5	-12.2	-14.9
Fixed capital (KF)	-4.3	-2.6	-2.2
Miscellaneous	$+0.2$	$+1.5$	$+1.9$

Notes: Sum of respective factors is equal to the increment of the rate of profit.

decrease after 1928 which were mentioned in the first section, and as a result the relative price of imported logs to domestic ones went up rapidly. This change discouraged urban sawmills depending on imported logs.[28] Because steam engine was chiefly employed in urban areas, increase in labor productivity was lower than that of other engines, especially with respect to water wheel used in rural sawmill consuming domestic logs. The fact that water wheels increased again and steam engines decreased considerably during the 1930s (Table 11-7) can be taken as a reflection of the decline in the urban sawmills which depended

[28] For example, sawmills in Shimizu, a representative urban lumbering district, were forced to stop operation or remove to rural areas to obtain domestic logs (Shimizu 1962, p. 119).

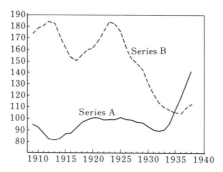

Fig. 11-2.　Relative Price of Fuel by Kind

Sources:　Wood fuel and coal: Ohkawa *et al.* 1967, pp. 184, 192–93.
Electricity charge: Minami 1965, p. 222.
Notes:　Series A: Wood fuel price index ÷ electricity charge index × 100.
Series B: Wood fuel price index ÷ coal price index × 100.
Seven-year moving averages.

on steam engines.

The third factor is the lower by-products coefficient of steam engine (Table 11-11). The coefficient was low because a large part of sawdust and wooden wastes were not sold and used as fuel. Even if productivity increased, its effect on increasing profit was cancelled out by the increase of the consumption of sawdust and wooden wastes as fuel. A disadvantage of steam engine consuming sawdusts and wooden wastes as fuel is observed in Fig. 11-2, where the wood fuel price index is a proxy of the by-products price (by-products sawdusts and wooden wastes were supposed to be used as residential fuel). Series A, which indicates relative price of wood fuel to electric power, went up rapidly from the early 1930s. The rapid increase signifies that consuming electricity and selling sawdusts and wooden wastes became profitable from that time on. This was largely responsible for the substitution of electric motors for steam engines.

The fourth is a contribution of an increasing yield rate. Its contribution was smaller in water wheel by 2 and 1% point than in electric motor and steam engine, respectively. This came from the fact that annual amount of lumber products was the smallest in water wheel, because of its shortest annual working days and lowest labor productivity (Table 11-11). The fifth is an increasing relative price of product to raw materials. This effect was also smaller in water wheel by 3 and 1% point than in electric motor and steam engine respectively due to the same reason just mentioned above.

The sixth is a negative effect upon profitability of increasing fixed capital. This was the smallest for electric motor, because of a decrease in price of electrical machinery equipments due to the development of electrical machinery industry. For instance, price of 3 hp-electric motor declined from 95 yen in 1926 to 76 yen in 1935.[29]

Choice of Fuel for Steam Engines

Steam engines in the lumbering industry had two alternative fuel sources; one was sawdusts and wooden wastes produced in sawing process, and the other was coal purchased.[30] The rate r for steam engine (1) in Table 11-9 relates to the former case (self-supplied wood fuel), while steam engine (2) does the latter case (purchased coal). It is obvious that the former case was more profitable than the latter both in 1914 and 1935. The relative advantage depended on the two variables; the value of fuel cost saved by using sawdusts and wooden wastes, and the income obtained from selling sawdusts and wooden wastes to residential consumers (Table 11-14). In 1914, by-product income was 640 yen and 2,014 yen, and fuel cost was null and 1,501 yen for two fuel sources, respectively. Consequently, net gain (a difference of by-products income and fuel cost) was 640 yen and 523 yen, respectively. In 1935 relative advantage of the steam engine to use wood fuel increased drastically; the net gain was 585 yen and −453 yen, respectively. The increasing disadvantage to use coal-fired steam engines was due to a rise in the relative increase in coal price compared to wood fuel price, which is

[29] Hibi 1956, p. 165.
[30] A special type of boiler must be installed for wood fuel; it is not possible to consume wood fuel in the boiler designed for coal consumption (Doi 1953, p. 35). For the simplicity, however, price of boiler is assumed equal among various types of boilers.

shown as a decline in Series B in Fig. 11-2.

In this chapter the power revolution (mechanization and transition of power sources) in the lumbering industry has been examined. It was indicated that the power revolution gave significant impacts on production efficiency of lumbering. Three conspicuous characteristics in the power revolution in this industry could be given in the following: Firstly, mechanization in the lumbering industry proceeded far more rapidly than in other industries, because of higher labor productivity in mechanical sawing. At early stage of mechanization, water wheel was widely utilized as the power source, especially in rural sawmills. Secondly, the ratio of steam engines in total power capacities was higher in the lumbering industry than in other industries. This was due to the fact that sawdusts and wooden wastes were used as fuel of steam engines to save energy cost. Thirdly, steam engines were replaced gradually by electric motors from the end of 1920s. This change was chiefly dependent on the supply of cheaper electric motors and rapid decrease of electricity charge. These processes in the power revolution was the result of the rational behavior of entrepreneurs to seek the most profitable technologies at respective point in time.

Table 11-4. Comparison of Fuel Cost for Steam Engine in Lumbering by Kind of Fuel

(yen)

	1914		1935	
	Saw Dusts and Wooden Wastes	Coal	Saw Dusts and Wooden Wastes	Coal
By-product income	640	2,024	585	2,274
Fuel cost	0	1,501	0	2,727
Difference	640	523	585	−453

Chapter 12

THE MATCH INDUSTRY

The subject of this chapter is power utilization in the Japanese match industry. This industry has been selected for study for three reasons. First, match making was typical of one segment of Japanese manufacturing—the labor-intensive, export-oriented sector.[1] The fact that match making and other labor-intensive industries became export leaders and thus helped to shape the nation's economic development was unique to Japan among the advanced countries at that time. Total power capacity per worker, H/L, is an index of the capital-labor ratio and thus provides an indication of labor intensity. In 1909 this ratio was merely 0.008 hp/person in the match industry, compared to 0.35 of the manufacturing sector as a whole. Although H/L in the match industry increased to 0.18 in 1935, it was still smaller than that in manufacturing (1.99), and it was somewhat below the ratios in printing and binding (0.51) and in miscellaneous (0.96), the two groups which showed the smallest figures among the nine major industry categories (Table 5-11).[2] Export of matches increased steadily after about 1877. During the first two decades of the twentieth century matches became one of the nation's major exports, following raw silk, silk fabric, cotton yarn, coal, and tea. Matches comprised 1.3% of total merchandized export in 1880, 2.6% in 1890, and 2.8% in 1900. This percentage gradually decreased in this

---

[1] Gendai Nippon Sangyō Hattatsushi Kenkyūkai 1967b, p. 541.
[2] Horsepower statistics are from STF. See Table A-2. The number of production workers is from STF 1909, p. 42; 1935, p. 23. All figures are for factories with five or more production workers.

century, but it was still 1.5% in 1920.[3]

The second reason for selecting the match industry is that mechanization came very late in this industry. Therefore we expect that the impact of introducing mechanical power should be very easy to discern. The third reason lies in the fact that match-making technology was very simple compared with other manufacturing technology and the technology itself is thus more easily understood. Before examining the impact of mechanization and the changes in technology, we survey the utilization of power in the match industry.

Quantitative Survey of Power Utilization

Mechanization

One notable characteristic of power utilization in the match industry was the delay in mechanization. Among match factories with 10 or more production workers the proportion of powered factories was only 2.6% in 1900 and 3.6% in 1915 (Table 12-1). Comparable figures for the manufacturing sector as a whole were 32.3% and 63.4% (Table 4-4). By comparison, in the weaving industry, one of the slowest of the major industry groups to mechanize, α was 5.1% in 1900 and 56.1% in 1915 (Table 10-1). Among match-producing factories with 5 or more workers, α was 8.9% in 1909 (Table 12-2). This figure was much smaller than the manufacturing average (28.2%, Table 4-5) and even smaller than the weaving industry average (14.0%, Table 10-2).

The low degree of mechanization in the match industry was attributable to the low utilization of mechanical power in small- and medium-scale factories. In 1909 no factories with 10-49 workers reported using any mechanical power, and less than one-fourth of the plants with 100-499 workers were mechanized. After 1909 the degree of mechanization in the match industry grew significantly, and by 1930 α had reached 86.1%. This increase was caused by a remarkable rise in the proportion of small- and medium-scale factories which employed mechanical

[3] Tōyō Keizai Shinpōsha 1935, pp. 40 and 46.

Table 12-1. Proportion of Powered Factories (α) and Composition of Total Power Capacity (H) by Engine Type in Match Making: 1890–1915

(percent)

Year	Proportion of Powered Factories (α)	Composition of H			
		Electric Motors (β)	Steam Engines and Turbines	Internal Combustion Engines	Water Wheels and Turbines
1890			100.0		0.0
1900	2.6				
1905	4.9	0.0	35.0	65.0	0.0
1910	9.0	4.8	36.8	58.4	0.0
1915	3.6	40.3	35.0	24.7	0.0

Sources: Same as Table 8-2.
Notes: See the notes to Table 8-2.

Table 12-2. Proportion of Powered Factories (α) by Factory Scale in Match Making

(percent)

Scale (persons)	1909	1914	1919	1930	1935	1940
All factories	8.9	26.3	49.2	86.1	92.5	93.2
5– 9	14.3	0.0	0.0	80.0	83.8	50.0
10– 29	0.0	5.6	23.1	78.9	93.0	86.4
30– 49	0.0	17.2	30.4	100.0	88.2	100.0
50– 99	4.3	19.4	48.6	100.0	100.0	100.0
100–499	23.6	50.8	83.3	100.0	100.0	100.0
500–999	100.0	100.0	100.0	100.0	100.0	100.0

Sources: Same as Table 8-3.
Notes: Figures are for the private factories with five or more production workers.

Table 12-3. Composition of Total Power Capacity (H) by Engine Type and by Factory Scale in Match Making: 1909–1940

(percent)

Scale (persons)	Electric Motors (β)	Steam Engines and Turbines	Internal Combustion Engines	Water Wheels and Turbines
		1909		
All factories	0.0	57.8	42.2	0.0
5– 9	0.0	100.0	0.0	0.0
10– 29	—	—	—	—
30– 49	—	—	—	—
50– 99	0.0	100.0	0.0	0.0
100–499	0.0	57.7	42.3	0.0
500–999	0.0	0.0	100.0	0.0
		1914		
All factories	34.7	31.6	33.7	0.0
5– 9	—	—	—	—
10– 29	16.7	83.3	0.0	0.0
30– 49	100.0	0.0	0.0	0.0
50– 99	69.2	0.0	30.8	0.0
100–499	25.8	37.3	36.9	0.0
500–999	62.5	0.0	37.5	0.0
		1919		
All factories	67.3	23.1	8.5	1.1
5– 9	—	—	—	—
10– 29	57.1	42.9	0.0	0.0
30– 49	100.0	0.0	0.0	0.0
50– 99	100.0	0.0	0.0	0.0
100–499	67.7	23.4	7.3	1.6
500–999	47.7	33.6	18.7	0.0

Table 12-3. (continued)

(percent)

Scale (persons)	Electric Motors (β)	Steam Engines and Turbines	Internal Combustion Engines	Water Wheels and Turbines
		1930		
All factories	81.1	15.4	3.2	0.3
5– 9	81.1	14.3	10.7	4.3
10– 29	81.2	4.9	13.9	0.0
30– 49	95.8	4.2	0.0	0.0
50– 99	63.7	35.3	1.0	0.0
100–499	98.5	1.5	0.0	0.0
500–999	100.0	0.0	0.0	0.0
		1935		
All factories	76.9	17.7	4.0	1.4
5– 9	80.0	0.0	0.0	20.0
10– 29	75.1	18.3	6.6	0.0
30– 49	59.8	0.0	40.2	0.0
50– 99	100.0	0.0	0.0	0.0
100–499	96.6	1.7	1.7	0.0
500–999	58.6	41.4	0.0	0.0
		1940		
All factories	79.2	19.5	1.3	0.0
5– 9	100.0	0.0	0.0	0.0
10– 29	100.0	0.0	0.0	0.0
30– 49	90.5	0.0	9.5	0.0
50– 99	95.8	0.0	4.2	0.0
100–499	69.5	30.5	0.0	0.0
500–999	100.0	0.0	0.0	0.0

Sources: Same as Table 8-3.
Notes: Figures are for the private factories with five or more production workers.

Table 12-4. Composition of Primary Power Capacity (H') by Engine Type and by Factory Scale in Match Making: 1909–1919

(percent)

Scale (persons)	Primary Electric Motors (β')	Steam Engines and Turbines	Internal Combustion Engines	Water Wheels and Turbines
1909				
All factories	5.6	54.5	39.9	0.0
5– 9	0.0	100.0	0.0	0.0
10– 29	—	—	—	—
30– 49	—	—	—	—
50– 99	0.0	100.0	0.0	0.0
100–499	7.1	53.6	39.3	0.0
500–999	0.0	0.0	100.0	0.0
1914				
All factories	34.7	31.6	33.7	0.0
5– 9	—	—	—	—
10– 29	16.7	83.3	0.0	0.0
30– 49	100.0	0.0	0.0	0.0
50– 99	69.2	0.0	30.8	0.0
100–499	25.8	37.3	36.9	0.0
500–999	62.5	0.0	37.5	0.0
1919				
All factories	67.4	23.1	8.4	1.1
5– 9	—	—	—	—
10– 29	57.1	42.9	0.0	0.0
30– 49	100.0	0.0	0.0	0.0
50– 99	100.0	0.0	0.0	0.0
100–499	67.7	23.4	7.3	1.6
500–999	47.7	33.6	18.7	0.0

Sources: Same as Table 8-3.
Notes: Figures are for the private factories with five or more production workers.

power. In that year α was 100% in all plants with 30 or more workers and about 80% among smaller factories with 5–29 workers.

Transition of Power Capacity by Engine Type

The transition of mechanical power by engine type in the match industry followed a pattern similar to that in the weaving industry, which was previously studied. The first stage, the 19th century phase, was marked by the predominance of steam power over water power. Location of plants in urban areas was probably a major reason why no water wheels were reported to have been employed in the match industry (Table 12-1).

The second stage, which ran from roughly 1900 to 1920, was marked by the relatively wide diffusion of internal combustion engines.[4] In 1909 these engines accounted for 42.2% of total power capacity (Table 12-3) and 39.9% of primary power capacity (Table 12-4). Comparable figures for manufacturing as a whole were 6.2% (Table 6-6) and 6.7% (Table 6-7), while those for the weaving industry were 13.1% (Table 10-3) and 14.0% (Table 10-4). Thus, the match industry was unique among those studied here because prior to electrification it relied heavily on internal combustion engines.

One significant difference between power utilization in match production and power utilization in weaving was the size of plants in which internal combustion engines were used. In the match industry big plants relied heavily on this engine while in weaving use of the internal combustion engine was mostly confined to smaller plants. In 1909 and 1919 there were no internal combustion engines at all in match-making plants with fewer than 100 workers, and in 1914 none of these engines were employed in plants with fewer than 50 workers. This was responsible for the aforementioned low degree of mechanization among

[4] The utilization of steam power in smaller plants in 1909 and 1914 should be noticed. In 1909, for instance, all of the engines used in the scales with 5–9 workers and 50–99 workers were steam engines. However there was in fact only one factory with 5–9 workers in that year, and there were only two plants in the 50–99 scale category. Thus, the high dependence on steam power in these scales came from an exceptionally small number of factories.

these plants. Generally speaking, these smaller plants first introduced mechanical power with electric motors, and thus, the impact of electrification on small match-making factories was especially large.

The Power Revolution and Technological Progress

History of Technology

Match making in Japan dates back to 1872, when a foreigner erected a plant at Nokeyama in Yokohama. This first venture ended in bankruptcy, but three years later the Shinsui Company became the first successful producer of matches in Japan. The company started production in a temporary building in 1875 and in a new plant at Yanagihara in the Honjo section of Tokyo in the next year. After about 1880 a number of plants appeared in various regions of the country and repeated Shinsui's success.[5]

Match making involves producing matchsticks and boxes, affixing chemicals to the sticks, and putting the sticks into boxes.[6] Large manufacturers performed all three steps within their plants, but most small match making firms in Japan generally engaged in only the second and third steps, after purchasing sticks and boxes from special producers. The arraying of matchsticks for spreading chemicals was the most important process, and the introduction of machinery and motive power was regulated by the requirements of this production step.

There were three stages in the development of the procedure for affixing the chemicals to matchsticks. At first boys and girls arrayed matchsticks by hand. Then, after about 1895 female workers performed the function with treadle machines. These machines were invented by Makoto Shimizu (a founder of the Shinsui Company) and other and were based on German made equipment. Finally, German-type machinery which usually run by electric motors and made of iron was

---

[5]   Meiji Kōgyōshi Hensan Iinkai 1925, p. 943.

[6]   For the history of match-making technology, we rely on Komiyama 1941, pp. 166–69; Meiji Kōgyōshi Hensan Iinkai 1925, pp. 966–68.

introduced. This machinery, called *doitsu* (the Japanese word for "German"), had been known in the early Meiji period but came into wide use only in late Meiji when Japan began to export matches.[7] Usually adult male workers operated this machinery. The productivity of workers on the *doitsu* was several times greater than that of workers using treadle machines.

Mechanization and Electrification

The shift from treadle to German-typen machinery was exclusively dependent on the introduction of engines, particularly electric motors. This was especially true in small factories where electric motors eventually became the only source of mechanical power. If these factories had attempted to run one or two German-type machines (about 2 hp) with steam engines, they probably could not have survived in face of the heavy burden of capital and operating costs.

The Japanese match industry suffered severe setbacks with the establishment of the Sweden Match Trust in 1921. The Trust drove Japanese matches out of foreign markets and then attempted to dominate the market in Japan by founding two large match-making companies, Daidō Match and Asahi Match. However, this plan was not completely successful, in part because of the persistence of a number of small-scale factories. These small Japanese-run plants survived partly by virtue of the decline in nominal wages for unskilled workers during the depression years of the 1920s and partly by mechanizing production during and after World War I.[8]

It is said that the match-making industry in Japan was a "modern industry" producing modern products; matches had been invented in the West and were only introduced to Japan during the Meiji period. However, until World War I match-making technology in Japan was not

[7] The German-type machine was used first at the Shinsui Company in 1876 and later such machines were installed at a prison in Hyōgo Prefecture in 1882–83.

[8] Whereas wages of skilled workers remained almost constant during the depression years of the 1920s, the wages of unskilled workers decreased (Minami and Ono 1979). The match industry relied heavily on the cheap labor force. The abnormally low ratio of power capacity to the number of workers in this industry should be kept in mind.

modern; it depended mainly on human power, with mechanical power limited to a small number of large-scale factories. The low wage-rental ratio in Japan encouraged Japanese entrepreneurs to adjust imported technology to less capital-intensive power sources. The match-making industry was a typical example of "modern industry" depending on premodern technology, one phenomenon of Japanese industrialization.

Severe competition with foreign makers in domestic and foreign markets eventually compelled Japanese match producers to modernize technology. This modernization was accomplished by introducing the German-type machines run by electric motors. In other words, electrification modernized this "modern industry".

Chapter 13

THE PRINTING INDUSTRY

The printing industry has been selected for study in this chapter because of the unique pattern it followed in utilizing mechanical power. This pattern was characterized, first, by a direct transition from human to steam power with no intervening use of water wheels and, second, by a subsequent rapid transition from steam to electric power. Because of these characteristics, the impact on production technology by the introduction of steam power and by the electrification can be seen much more clearly in printing than in other industries. The first section of this chapter describes the course of the power revolution in printing by examining statistics on power utilization and power capacity.[1] The second section analyzes the effects of steam power utilization and electrification on printing technology.

Quantitative Survey of Power Utilization

Mechanization

From the Meiji period until World War II the proportion of powered factories, α, in printing and binding was quite large compared to other industries, and the rate of growth of α was consistently higher than in

---

[1] In this study printing and binding are treated as a single industry because early printing data and binding data were not tabulated separately. This substitution is of minor significance, because the relative number of binding plants was quite small. In 1930, for instance, there were only 340 binding plants with 5 or more production workers, compared with 2,419 printing plants. STF 1930, p. 20.

other industries. As in shown in Table 13-1, in 1900 the proportion α in printing and binding factories with 10 or more workers was 44.3%, compared with only 32.3% in manufacturing as a whole (Table 4-4). Owing to steady increases thereafter, by the mid-1910s, printing and binding was the most mechanized among all industry groups (chapter 4). In 1930 the proportion α in printing and binding (here for factories with 5 or more workers) reached 96.3%, indicating that almost all printing plants were mechanized by that time (Table 13-2).

As was stated in chapter 4, even among factories belonging to the same industry the introduction of mechanical power in Japan proceeded at quite different rates in factories of different scale. This was also the case in printing. For instance, according to Table 13-2, in 1909 α was positively correlated with plant scale. Although only 18.3% of the smallest-scale plants (5–9 workers) were mechanized, mechanization was complete in plants with 100 or more workers. After 1909 the differential by factory scale tended to decrease, and by 1930 almost all smaller-scale plants were also mechanized.

Transition of Power Capacity by Engine Type

Table 13-1, 13-3, and 13-4 show the composition of power capacity by type of engine in printing and binding. They reveal several characteristics of the transition in mechanized power within this industry group. They show first that water wheels were not utilized in printing and binding even in the early stages of mechanization. In the whole manufacturing sector, on the other hand, water wheels contributed more than 10% of total power capacity in the 1900s (Table 6-3). Water wheels were for the most part found only in rural areas and had an uneven speed of rotation, so they were not suitable for printing, a predominantly urban industry which needed a steady and controllable power source.

Tables 13-1, 13-3 and 13-4 show, secondly, that steam engines remained the dominant source of mechanical power in printing and binding for only a brief time. In other words, early mechanization by steam power was followed shortly by a rapid decrease in the proportion of total printing capacity supplied by steam engines. From 1900 to 1910

Table 13-1. Proportion of Powered Factories (α) and Composition of Total Power Capacity (*H*) by Engine Type in Printing and Binding: 1890–1915

(percent)

| Year | Proportion of Powered Factories (α) | Composition of H | | | |
		Electric Motors (β)	Steam Engines and Turbines	Internal Combustion Engines	Water Wheels and Turbines
1890			100.0		0.0
1895			100.0		0.0
1900	44.3	2.2	72.0	25.5	0.3
1905	52.6	14.0	24.7	61.1	0.2
1910	68.6	38.5	14.2	47.3	0.0
1915	82.0	62.7	9.3	28.0	0.0

Sources: Same as Table 8-2.
Notes: See the notes to Table 8-2.

Table 13-2. Proportion of Powered Factories (α) by Factory Scale in Printing and Binding

(percent)

Scale (persons)	1909	1914	1919	1930	1935	1940
All factories	42.4	65.3	81.5	96.3	97.0	97.0
5– 9	18.3	47.1	66.8	94.4	96.0	95.8
10– 29	48.3	72.3	89.7	98.7	97.9	98.5
30– 49	86.5	92.2	100.0	99.4	99.5	99.5
50– 99	92.3	100.0	98.8	100.0	100.0	100.0
100–499	100.0	100.0	100.0	100.0	100.0	100.0
500–999	100.0	100.0	100.0	100.0	100.0	100.0
1,000 or more	—	100.0	100.0	100.0	100.0	100.0

Sources: Same as Table 8-3.
Notes: Figures are for the private factories with five or more production workers.

THE IMPACT OF THE POWER REVOLUTION

Table 13-3. Composition of Total Power Capacity (*H*) by Engine Type and by Factory Scale in Printing and Binding: 1909–1940

(percent)

Scale (persons)	Electric Motors (β)	Steam Engines and Turbines	Internal Combustion Engines	Water Wheels and Turbines
		1909		
All factories	39.3	16.9	43.8	0.0
5– 9	39.8	0.0	60.2	0.0
10– 29	66.0	0.7	33.3	0.0
30– 49	32.6	11.2	56.2	0.0
50– 99	49.4	0.4	50.2	0.0
100–499	19.8	40.3	39.9	0.0
500–999	5.5	55.0	39.5	0.0
		1914		
All factories	54.0	10.9	35.1	0.0
5– 9	77.1	0.8	22.1	0.0
10– 29	70.5	0.0	29.2	0.3
30– 49	52.8	0.4	46.8	0.0
50– 99	65.2	1.3	33.5	0.0
100–499	40.2	28.1	31.7	0.0
500–999	15.5	32.1	52.4	0.0
1,000 or more	45.0	3.7	51.3	0.0
		1919		
All factories	83.0	5.9	11.1	0.0
5– 9	95.8	0.0	4.2	0.0
10– 29	89.5	0.0	10.3	0.2
30– 49	76.0	0.6	23.4	0.0
50– 99	84.5	1.5	14.0	0.0
100–499	73.4	16.1	10.5	0.0
500–999	100.0	0.0	0.0	0.0
1,000 or more	100.0	0.0	0.0	0.0

300

Table 13-3. (continued)

(percent)

Scale (persons)	Electric Motors (β)	Steam Engines and Turbines	Internal Combustion Engines	Water Wheels and Turbines
		1930		
All factories	99.5	0.1	0.4	0.0
5– 9	99.7	0.0	0.2	0.1
10– 29	99.0	0.1	0.9	0.0
30– 49	97.5	0.0	2.5	0.0
50– 99	99.5	0.0	0.5	0.0
100–499	99.7	0.1	0.2	0.0
500–999	100.0	0.0	0.0	0.0
1,000 or more	100.0	0.0	0.0	0.0
		1935		
All factories	97.4	0.1	2.5	0.0
5– 9	99.8	0.0	0.2	0.0
10– 29	99.3	0.2	0.5	0.0
30– 49	97.0	0.0	3.0	0.0
50– 99	93.8	0.0	6.2	0.0
100–499	99.6	0.2	0.2	0.0
500–999	92.9	0.0	7.1	0.0
1,000 or more	100.0	0.0	0.0	0.0
		1940		
All factories	97.4	0.0	2.6	0.0
5– 9	99.4	0.0	0.6	0.0
10– 29	99.4	0.0	0.6	0.0
30– 49	98.8	0.0	1.2	0.0
50– 99	99.7	0.0	0.3	0.0
100–499	98.6	0.0	1.4	0.0
500–999	90.5	0.0	9.5	0.0
1,000 or more	100.0	0.0	0.0	0.0

Sources: Same as Table 8-3.
Notes: Figures are for the private factories with five or more production workers.

301

Table 13-4. Composition of Primary Power Capacity (H') by Engine Type and by Factory Scale in Printing and Binding: 1909–1919

(percent)

Scale (persons)	Primary Electric Motors (β')	Steam Engines and Turbines	Internal Combustion Engines	Water Wheels and Turbines
1909				
All factories	39.2	17.0	43.8	0.0
5– 9	39.8	0.0	60.2	0.0
10– 29	66.0	0.7	33.3	0.0
30– 49	32.6	11.2	56.2	0.0
50– 99	49.3	0.4	50.3	0.0
100–499	19.3	40.6	40.1	0.0
500–999	5.5	55.0	39.5	0.0
1914				
All factories	52.3	11.3	36.4	0.0
5– 9	77.1	0.8	22.1	0.0
10– 29	70.5	0.0	29.2	0.3
30– 49	52.7	0.4	46.9	0.0
50– 99	65.3	1.3	33.4	0.0
100–499	38.2	29.1	32.7	0.0
500–999	15.5	32.1	52.4	0.0
1,000 or more	21.9	5.2	72.9	0.0
1919				
All factories	83.0	5.9	11.1	0.0
5– 9	95.8	0.0	4.2	0.0
10– 29	89.5	0.0	10.3	0.2
30– 49	76.0	0.6	23.4	0.0
50– 99	84.4	1.5	14.1	0.0
100–499	73.0	16.3	10.7	0.0
500–999	100.0	0.0	0.0	0.0
1,000 or more	100.0	0.0	0.0	0.0

Sources: Same as Table 8-3.

Notes: Figures are for the private factories with five or more production workers.

the share of steam engines in printing and binding establishments with 10 or more workers decreased by 57.8 percentage points (Table 13-1). This was the largest decrease in the nine sub-groups of manufacturing and was much larger than the decrease in manufacturing as a whole. By 1930 steam engines supplied only 0.1% of total power capacity in printing and binding (Table 13-3). This was the lowest percentage among all nine industry groups and was far smaller than that of the manufacturing average (11.4%, Table 6-6). This decrease in the share of steam power was caused not only by an increase in the utilization of other engines (internal combustion engines and electric motors) but also by a big decline in the use of steam engines.

The third characteristic of the power revolution in printing and binding was a relatively heavy reliance on internal combustion engines in earlier years. In 1909, for instance, these engines contributed 43.8% to total power capacity, compared with 6.2% for all industry groups as a whole (Table 6-6). However, use of internal combustion engines decreased rapidly after 1909.

The fourth characteristic of power utilization in this industry was the early application of electric motors. In 1909 electric power already exceeded the percentage of steam power in printing and binding, although steam was by far the greatest source of power for manufacturing as a whole. By 1930 99.5% of printing and binding power capacity, the greatest proportion among all industries, was derived from electric engines. Electrification proceeded at the highest speed in printing and binding and eventually became dominant within this industry.

Tables 13-3 and 13-4 show how sources of mechanical power differed by plant scale. In 1909, steam engines were rarely utilized in plants with less than 99 workers, while internal combustion engines and electric motors were widely used. On the other hand, in large-scale plants with 100 or more workers steam engines remained the main source of power. After 1909 small-scale plants shifted from internal combustion engines to electric motors, while large-scale factories replaced steam power with electric power.

The Power Revolution and Technological Progress

The Introduction of Steam Engines to Newspaper Plants

Newspaper plants are in many respects typical of large printing establishments in Japan, and the transition of mechanical power in the newspaper industry illustrates well the role of steam engines in the development of printing technology.

History in England. Before examining the impact of steam power on Japanese newspaper production it is helpful to take a comparative look at the history of technology in newspaper printing in England, where most modern printing technology was developed. For this purpose a history of the *Times* (London), a world leader in the newspaper business, is most informative.[2]

In England no significant improvements were made in the basic printing machine, the wooden hand-press from the time of its invention in the 15th century until the beginning of the 19th century. The long stagnant period in printing technology ended with Earl Stanhope's invention of the iron hand-press in 1800. The Stanhope press was quickly adopted in newspaper plants because it was much faster than the old wooden press. *The Times* plant employed a number of Stanhope presses between 1800 and 1814, and their utilization enabled the paper to increase its circulation.

It is generally acknowledged, however, that the first truly practical modern press was the one invented by Friedrich Koenig. Koenig's innovation was to drive yet another type of press, the cylinder press, by steam power. Although the hand-powered cylinder press had been patented by William Nicholson in 1790, this invention had not been widely used. In 1814 John Walter, an operator for *The Times*, installed two sets of Koenig's cylinder presses along with two 2-hp steam engines, and the first newspaper in the world printed by steam power was issued on November 29 of that year.

[2]   This history is summarized from Times Publishing Company 1935, chaps. 16 and 17; Steinberg 1959, pp. 198–206.

The physical effort required to operate the old Stanhope press had been considerable. Pressmen worked at a frantic pace for long hours. Great endurance was required. This fact accounted for the generous supply of malt liquor in printing plants. Koenig's steam-driven cylinder press spared the human frame laborious effort and raised production efficiency. Printing speed increased from 300 sheets per hour with the Stanhope press to 1,100 sheets, and printing costs declined by 25%. As might well be expected, the introduction of mechanical power was enthusiastically received by both management and labor. As Walter himself wrote in the commemorative first issue, this was "the greatest improvement connected with printing since the discovery of the art itself."[3] *A Newspaper History* by *the Times* says "modern newspaper production was born" with Koenig's invention.[4]

After that development in 1814 incessant efforts were made to improve the printing press. A 4-cylinder press invented for *The Times* by Augustus Applegarth and Edward Cowper in 1828 printed 4,000 sheets per hour. The rotary press, invented and build for *The Times* in 1866, printed 12,000 perfected copies an hour. By 1939 improvements in the rotary press had increased printing speed at *the Times* to 40,000 copies an hour for a 32-page paper.

Thus it was by steam power, and not by water power, that mechanization of printing was realized in England. Even though water power was widely used there during the early stage of the Industrial Revolution, there are no records to show that water wheels were utilized for printing newspapers. Water wheels were, however, used in several general printing offices in England during the 19th century.[5]

History in Japan. Newspaper companies in Japan depended on human physical effort for a considerable period of time. This was true not only with Japanese application of the hand press, but also with Japanese application of cylinder presses which had been designed to be operated by steam power. In 1874 and 1879, the *Tokyo Nichinichi* and the *Osaka*

[3] Steinberg 1959, p. 201.
[4] Times Publishing Company 1935, p. 138.
[5] Times Publishing Company 1935, p. 158.

Asahi, both pioneers in the Japanese newspaper business, imported cylinder presses, but without steam engines. These presses were driven by human power, and the work was so laborious that a team of two persons operated the press alternately at a lower speed than that attained by steam power.[6] Reminiscent of malt liquor in British printing offices, sake and sweets were provided to encourage workers.[7] Importation of the press without steam engines shows a characteristic of borrowed technology in Japan: foreign technology was often adopted with capital-saving modifications (chapter 15).

The first and epochal application of steam power to printing in Japan occurred in April, 1876 at the *Tokyo Nichinichi*. The *Yomiuri* (Tokyo) applied steam power in November of the same year.[8] Little is known about the engine installed at the *Nichinichi* plant, but the *Yomiuri* used a steam boat engine. Koun Hirayama, an engineer at the plant, had been in charge of casting guns for the Ōgaki Clan during the Tokugawa period. He bought the engine in Yokohama and reconditioned it before its installion at the newspaper plant.[9] At the *Osaka Asahi* a 10-hp steam engine was installed in 1886 and two sets of 16-hp engines were purchased in 1891.[10] The *Osaka Mainichi*, irritated by the signs of steam power puffing from the tall chimney of the *Osaka Asahi*, finally installed its own steam engine in 1891.[11] Thus, the big newspaper plants in Japan had begun to mechanize printing by the early 1890s.

Compared with these plants the *Tokyo Asahi* has a unique history,

[6] Mainichi Shinbunsha 1972, p. 436; Asahi Shinbunsha 1972, p. 146. Also see the painting of the *Osaka Mainichi* workshop which is reprinted as the frontispiece of Minami 1976b.

[7] Asahi Shinbunsha 1949, pp. 14–15; 1961, pp. 14–15.

[8] The Government Printing Bureau introduced several 6-hp steam engines in the same year. Before this the cylinder press had been run by human power. Nippon, Ōkurashō, Insatsu Kyoku 1972, p. 115.

[9] Yomiuri Shinbunsha 1976, pp. 140–41.

[10] Asahi Shinbunsha 1969, appendix table of chronology; 1970, pp. 548–51. The first history of this company states that a 16-hp steam engine was installed in 1885. Asahi Shinbunsha 1949, p. 15. Other, unpublished documents of this company state, however, that this is erroneous. Asahi Shinbunsha 1970, pp. 551–53.

[11] Mainichi Shinbunsha 1972, p. 451.

because the introduction of mechanical power occurred by electrification. The *70-Year History of the Asahi Newspaper* records that a cylinder press was purchased and driven by an electric motor in 1888.[12] The *Annual Record of the Asahi Newspaper* states that the electric motor was introduced when the plant moved to Takiyama Chō in that year. Additional evidence to this effect has been supplied by Umesaburo Moriyasu, an employee of the *Asahi*, who recalled in 1940 that his paper was the first among Japanese newspaper plants to replace oil lamps with electric lights and to substitute electric motors for human power.[13] However, the *50-Year History of the Tokyo Electric Light Company*, without any reference to this fact, states that it sold a 7.5-hp electric motor to the *Tokyo Asahi* and 3-hp motors to two other newspaper companies, the *Miyako* and the *Tokyo Shinpō*, and started to transmit electric power to these plants in 1892.[14] We can infer from these scanty records that the electric motor installed in 1888 at the *Tokyo Asahi* was probably driven by electricity generated within the plant.

Increasing demand for newspapers revealed the limitations of the cylinder press. The *Tokyo Asahi* which planned to print the minutes of the Diet as an extra edition of the newspaper, needed much more efficient machinery. The Official Gazette Bureau, which later merged with the Printing Bureau, felt the same need because it regularly had to print the minutes as an extra edition of the official gazette. In 1890 the director of the Bureau together with Torajiro Tsuda, and engineer of the *Osaka Asahi*, went to France and bought rotary presses invented by Hippolyte Marinoni. This press had the capacity to print 30,000 sheets an hour (20 times the capacity of the cylinder press). It could also cut the sheets automatically, and it could be operated rather easily with a few workers. After strenuous effort Tsuda succeeded in installing and maintaining normal operation of the rotary press. Because of the extremely high performance of this press, the *Tokyo Asahi* added another in 1891, and the *Osaka Asahi* installed similar presses in 1892,

[12] Asahi Shinbunsha 1949, p. 40.
[13] Asahi Shinbunsha 1972, p. 147.
[14] Tokyo Dentō K.K. 1936, p. 32.

1894, and 1897.[15] The good results from the Marinoni Press prompted its introduction by other companies, for example, the *Osaka Mainichi* in 1894, the *Hōchi* and the *Jiji* in 1896, the *Yorozu Chōhō* in 1897, and the *Yomiuri* in 1900.[16] It is worthy of attention that Tsuda, who repeatedly dismantled and repaired the Marinoni Press, succeeded in building an imitation of the press at an experimental station annexed to the *Osaka Asahi* printing plant. This homemade press, called the Asahi Rotary press, was installed at the *Tokyo Asahi* and the *Osaka Asahi* in 1904.[17]

Almost all rotary presses in use at that time were driven by steam engines. This was the case at the Printing Bureau, the *Osaka Asahi*, and the *Osaka Mainichi*.[18] Apparently only the *Tokyo Asahi* ran the rotary press by electric power.[19]

In summary, in most of the big newspaper plants, steam power replaced human power in cylinder presses and also made it possible to introduce the more efficient rotary press. These technological developments in turn made possible a marked increase in newspaper circulation. The total annual circulation of the five biggest newspapers in Tokyo and Osaka increased from 11,891,000 in 1881 to 50,961,000 in 1891 and to 119,368,000 in 1901.[20] The annual rate of growth was 32.9% from 1881

[15]   Asahi Shinbunsha 1949, pp. 57–59, 64–65.

[16]   Yomiuri Shinbunsha 1976, p. 213.

[17]   Asahi Shinbunsha 1949, p. 65. The Tokyo Machinery Company also built its own Marinoni-type rotary press in 1906. Insatsu Seihon Kikai 100-Nen-Shi Jikkō Iinkai 1975, p. 34.

[18]   I am indebted to Mr. Toshio Kato of the Printing Bureau for this information about its printing plant. Reference to steam-driven presses at the *Osaka Asahi* is found in Mainichi Shinbunsha 1972, p. 451. Mr. Tsunehiko Mimuro, a director of the Office of Editing History at the Mainichi Newspaper Company kindly supplied the information about this company

[19]   Asahi Shinbunsha 1966, pp. 94, 101.

[20]   The five companies were the *Tokyo Asahi*, the *Tokyo Nichinichi*, the *Yomiuri*, the *Osaka Asahi*, and the *Osaka Mainichi*. We have prepared an annual series on newspaper circulation for the years 1881 to 1901. For some years figures were taken from the following sources: Tokyo Fu 1881–1889; Osaka Fu 1881–1898; Asahi Shinbunsha 1969, appendix table of chronology; Mainichi Shinbunsha 1972, p. 355; Shinohara 1972, p. 111; Yomiuri Shinbunsha 1976, p. 221. For other years circulation figures were estimated by linear interpolation.

to 1891 and 13.4% from 1891 to 1901. Although we cannot estimate labor productivity in the printing industry for the 19th century, it is safe to say that it increased rapidly.[21] In other industries where water power preceded steam power notable increases in labor productivity regularly occurred. Therefore, it can be concluded that labor productivity increased in printing, an industry which moved not from water power but from hand power to steam power. Thus, there is no doubt that the introduction of steam power revolutionized the printing industry, because it replaced human power.

The Introduction of Electric Motors

Electrification was of great significance to the development of printing technology throughout the world, but the transition from steam to electric power occurred much more rapidly among big printing plants in Japan than in other countries. Moreover, mechanization of small printing plants in Japan was first accomplished with electric power, unlike in other industries where steam power intervened. In order to highlight the significance of electrification for printing in Japan it is helpful to look again at the history of this process in an early developed country.

History in England. The *Times* found printing by steam power cumbersome.[22] Power had to be transmitted through a system of shafts, pulleys, and belts placed underneath the presses. "Inching" (slow movement) of the presses could only be done by slipping the belt, which was very dangerous work. Because of the inability to control the output of steam power, *The Times* installed its first electrically driven press in 1905, and its steam engines were entirely removed in 1908. Before that time,

[21] There is little specific documentation of the effect of mechanization on labor productivity. According to one *Asahi* printshop employee, the output of the cylinder press increased from 800–900 sheets an hour by human power to 1,500 sheets when mechanical power was introduced in 1888. Asahi Shinbunsha 1972, pp. 146–47. Also, when the Marinoni Press was installed at the *Tokyo Asahi*, the company discharged several printers. Asahi Shinbunsha 1966, p. 82.

[22] The history of electrification in British printing offices comes from Times Publishing Company 1935, pp. 159–60.

electrification had been attempted in several other printing plants. The first attempt in England, at the *Somerset County Gazette* in 1884, was not successful, and after a short time the plant reverted to steam power. At the *Birmingham Daily Gazette* a 24-hp electric motor was installed in 1891 to drive rotary presses. This was the first attempt in England to use electric power on the rotary machines. All these machines were, however, belt-driven and were thus not much of an improvement over steam-powered printing. The first utilization of the electric motor with a direct-drive system was attempted by the *Liverpool Daily Post* in 1898. At this plant each press was connected directly to a 40-hp electric motor. As a result of this innovation, more than fifty British newspapers were electrified by 1901. In 1898 the *Liverpool Courier* adopted an even more advanced two-motor drive system in which a main motor was used to drive the machine at full running speed, while an auxiliary motor was used for starting, inching and slow-running. Today various versions of these direct-drive electric systems are universally employed to power printing presses.

History in Japan. Electrification in Japanese printing plants was, as stated previously, initiated by the *Tokyo Asahi* in 1888. Furthermore this company, which was the first Japanese printer to use the rotary press, began running this press by electric power in 1890. In two ways these events illustrate the nature of the mechanization of printing in Japan. First, both electrification itself and the application of electric power to drive the rotary press occurred very early in the Japanese printing industry compared with its Western counterparts. This timing is quite significant considering differences in the overall level of economic development in Japan and the West. (In England, for example, the rotary press was first attached to an electric motor in 1891, one year later than in Japan, and electrification in 1884 occurred only 4 years ealier than in Japan). The electrification of Japanese printing at a very early stage of economic development can be explained by the early introduction of electric technology to Japan, following only a short time after its introduction in the more developed nations (chapter 7). Second, it was unique in the world-wide newspaper business at that time because the *Tokyo Asahi* directly substituted electric power for human power, and also its first rotary press was driven by electric power. There was no prolonged age of steam power in Japan. The short time-lag between the diffusion of steam power and that of electric power resulted in a much shorter age of steam power in Japan than in the developed countries (chapter 15).

It was in the 1910s, however, that full-scale electrification occurred in the big printing plants in Japan. The Government Printing Bureau's plants began generating their own electric power in 1906 and 1915.[23] The Toppan Printing Company replaced gas engines with electric motors in 1910. The immediate motivation for this changeover was an interrupted gas supply which occurred when the Tokyo Gas Plant flooded. But the basic incentive was the cheap electric power made available in 1907 through long-distance transmission from the Tokyo Electric Light Company's Komabashi Power Plant.[24] The *Osaka Asahi* electrified its new building in 1916.[25] In 1909 the contribution of electric power to total power capacity was merely 19.8% in printing plants with 100–499 workers and only 5.5% in plants with 500 or more workers, but by the end of the 1910s these figures had reached 73.4% and 100.0% respectively. And by 1930 almost all printing plants were electrified (Table 13-3).

The advantages of electric drive. The merits of electrification, especially the advantages of the direct-drive or unit-drive system, were much more obvious in printing than in other industries. There are numerous historical documents, mainly concerning American printing plants, which illustrate the advantages of electric power. The first of these advantages was an economy in current costs of production. In the model establishment of the W. B. Conkey Company of Hammond, Indiana, coal consumption decreased by two-thirds with electrification of the plant in 1898.[26] In the U.S. Government Printing Office in Washington D.C. the

[23]   Nippon, Ōkurashō, Insatsu Kyoku 1972, pp. 117–18.
[24]   Toppan Insatsu K.K. 1961, pp. 52–53.
[25]   Haruhara 1969, p. 72.
[26]   Damon 1898, p. 504.

total cost of coal and gas decreased from $27,812 per year in 1894 to $5,615 per year following electrification in 1899.[27] The savings in fuel consumption were partly attributable to the higher efficiency of electric motors compared to steam engines and partly to a decline in the power rate brought about by technological progress in generating and transmitting electricity. The decisive factor was, however, the ability to avoid wasting power when presses were in "stand-by". With steam power boiler pressure had to be maintained constantly, even when the presses were idle, because it took a long time to make steam from cold water. The fuel savings of electric powered printing became substantial with the transition from the belt-drive to the unit-drive system. The United Brethren Publishing Company of Dayton, Ohio, realized more than a 60% savings in power by means of electrification and transition to the unit-drive system.[28]

The second advantage of electrification was the space savings realized by the abolition of bulky steam engines and their cumbersome system of shafting and belts. Such space saving advantages were reported by the (Birmingham) *Daily Gazette*, which installed two motors in 1891 and by the (Lowell, Mass.) *Daily News*, which replaced a 4-hp steam engine and a 5-hp boiler with a 3-hp electric motor in 1887.[29] The Boston Bank Note and Lithograph Company stated that their 10-hp electric motor occupied a space of less than 18 cubic feet, while a comparable steam engine would occupy from 10 to 15 times more room.[30]

The third advantage was that electric motors could be started and stopped quickly. Such control was particularly important in printing because the flow of work was not constant and presses frequently had to be stopped. This advantage of electrification was emphasized in records of the (Birmingham) *Daily Gazette* and of other printers.[31]

A fourth and related advantage was the control over the speed of the

[27] *Electrical World and Engineer* 1901, p. 521.
[28] *Electrical World* 1897, p. 335.
[29] *American Machinist* 1892, p. 10; *Electrical World* 1888, p. 279.
[30] *Electrical World* 1890, p. 432.
[31] *American Machinist* 1892, p. 10; Bel'kind 1960, p. 295; Dellenbaugh 1915, p. 193.

electric motor.[32] This feature is significant because printing requires steady power and a wide range of speeds. In the U.S. Government Printing Office the constant speed provided by direct-drive electric motors completely eliminated slurring and poor registration. With belting there had always been some degree of slippage.[33] The fifth advantage, which was claimed by Conkey and others, was that the abolition of the belt and its associated mass of shafting made possible unobstructed lighting and hence improved workmanship.[34] Sixth, the Conkey firm and others documented that electric installations were clean.[35] In particular, they were free from oil dripping from overhead bearings and from dirt being thrown about by flying belts. Finally, a report by the U.S. Government Printing Office states that its sick list shrank by 20 to 40% after electric motors were introduced. This is direct evidence that sanitary conditions at printing plants improved with electrification.[36]

It is reasonable to assume that these advantages all obtained in Japanese plants as well, because printing technology did not differ basically among countries.[37] It can be concluded, therefore, that electrification of the big printing plants in Japan made considerable contributions toward expanding output, reducing production costs, and improving the quality of products.

Electrification in small printing plants. The next problem is to examine the significance of electrification in small-scale printing plants. In 1909, the proportion of powered factories was 18.3% for establishments employing only 5–9 workers and 48.3% for those employing 10–29 workers. As mechanization proceeded over the next decade, these proportions increased to 66.8% and 89.7% (Table 13-2). Within powered factories in 1909, electric motors supplied 39.8% of total power

[32] Dellenbaugh 1915, p. 193; Bishop 1897, p. 419.
[33] *Electrical World* 1898, p. 117.
[34] Bishop 1897, p. 419; Damon 1898, p. 503; Dellenbaugh 1915, p. 193.
[35] Bishop 1897, p. 419; Damon 1898, p. 504.
[36] *Journal of the Franklin Institute* 1901, p. 4.
[37] Despite considerable efforts, I was unable to find any historical documents which specifically evaluated the impact of electrification on printing in Japan.

capacity for plants with 5–9 employees and 66.0% for plants with 10–29 employees. By 1919, 95.8% of the power in the smallest-scale plants and 89.5% of total power capacity in the next larger scale came from electric motors (Table 13-3). These figures explain that mechanization of small-scale printing plants first occurred with the introduction of electric motors.

These motors were run by electricity from central public power plants. Electrification brought mechanical power within reach of small establishments which could not afford to install big steam engines. Thus, the electrification of these plants was comparable in importance to the introduction of steam power to the large printing offices. The introduction of mechanical power to smaller plants by electrification was not unique to this industry, but was a phenomenon which occurred throughout Japanese manufacturing at the time (chapter 14).

Overall evaluation of the effects of electrification. It may be argued that electrification raised the level of technology in both large and small plants much faster in printing than in other industries. R. Du Boff claims that printing and publishing was a leader both in electrification and in productivity growth among American industries.[38] J. W. Kendrick's estimates of total factor productivity in the United States show that printing and publishing had the fifth highest rate of growth for the period 1909–19 among twenty industry groups in manufacturing.[39] In Japan, as Table 13-5 shows, printing and binding had the highest rate of growth of labor productivity among nine industry groups during the decade of extensive electrification.[40] It seems clear, then, that the high rate of technological progress in printing was closely associated with its rapid electrification.

Electrification of printing plants had one further impact on production technology. The increased efficiency in printing due to mechanization motivated the mechanization of typesetting. Typesetting was first

[38] Du Boff 1967, p. 516.
[39] Kendrick 1961, table D-III.
[40] Total factor productivity cannot be calculated because of a lack of capital stock data by sub-industry group.

Table 13-5. Rate of Growth of Labor Productivity by Industry
Group: 1909–1919

Industries	Ratio of Labor Productivity 1919/1909
All manufacturing	1.60
Textiles	1.51
Metals and metal products	1.26
Machinery	1.71
Ceramics	1.46
Chemicals	0.97
Wood and wood products	1.49
Printing and binding	2.00
Food	1.74
Miscellaneous	1.30

Sources: Real output is obtained by deflating nominal output by the price indexes by
industry group estimated by Shinohara 1972, p. 149.
Figures for nominal output and labor force are from the STF. Nippon, Tsūshō
Sangyōshō 1961, pp. 180–99.
Notes: Figures are for the establishments with 5 or more production workers.

mechanized in the middle 1880s with the inventions of the linotype by
Ottmar Mergenthaler and the monotype by Tolbert Lanston.[41]
Importation of these machines to Japan, which started in the late 1910s,
was limited to special plants which printed materials in foreign languages, because imported linotype and monotype machines could not
be used to set Japanese characters. The first monotype for Japanese
characters was developed by Kyota Sugimoto, an inventor of the
Japanese typewriter, and manufactured by the Nippon Typewriter
Company in 1920.[42] These machines were installed at the *Osaka
Mainichi* in 1920 and at the *Tokyo Nichinichi* in the year after. The
linotype was not produced and was rarely used in Japan before World

[41] Steinberg 1959, p. 205.
[42] Insatsu Seihon Kikai 100-Nen-Shi Jikkō Iinkai 1975, pp. 91–94.

War II.[43] Thus, in Japan mechanization of the step before printing did not occur as early or as rapidly as the mechanization of printing itself. This was partly because the imported linotype and monotype could not be used in setting Japanese characters: a clear case of cultural inhibitions to the diffusion of technology. Nevertheless it can be argued that widescale electrification of printing plants in the 1910s stimulated the development of typesetting technology for Japanese characters.

[43] Mainichi Shinbunsha 1972, p. 486.

Chapter 14

THE IMPACT OF ELECTRIFICATION
ON THE MANUFACTURING SECTOR

In the preceding six chapters we analyzed the effect of the power revolution on production efficiency in six industries. The introduction of steam power brought about great changes in silk reeling, cotton spinning, lumbering, and newspaper printing, but electrification was found to be the most significant aspect of the power revolution for the cotton-spinning, weaving, lumbering, match-making, and printing industries. This chapter aims at drawing some general conclusions about the impact of electrification in the manufacturing sector. One of the major conclusions derived from the preceding industry studies is that in the history of power utilization electrification played a different role in large-scale plants than it did in small-scale plants. Generally speaking, electrification amounted to the substitution of electric power for steam power in large plants, while it coincided with the transition from human to mechanical power, or mechanization itself, in small manufacturing plants. For this reason, the impact of electrification is examined separately for these two cases.

The Case of Large-Scale Factories

The electrification of large manufacturing plants can be divided into two phases. In the early phase electric power was mostly generated within the factories themselves, but in the later phase cheap electric power became available from public utilities. Purchased electric power exceeded electric power generated within the plants around the year 1909 in factories with 100–499 workers and between 1914 and 1919 in factories with 500 or more workers (Table 5-2). Thus, the late 1910s marks the critical point between the two phases of electrification in large-scale factories.

Cost Savings in the Two Phases of Electrification

The introduction of electric motors had somewhat different consequences for large-scale plants in these two phases. In the first phase, the substitution of electric motors for steam engines did not necessarily produce savings in capital costs, because factories still needed large plants for electric power generation. Savings generally occurred only in fuel consumption, because of the greater efficiency of electric motors compared with steam engines. This advantage of electrification is documented in the results of a 1923 experiment by Shigetaro Matsumura. He found that slightly more power was transferred to spinning machinery when a steam engine was used to generate electro-motive power than when the same engine was employed to operate the spinning machinery directly.[1] In addition, Du Boff reports that engineers in the United States in the mid-1890s found a 20 to 70% increase in efficiency under various configurations employing electro-motive power versus direct steam-powered production.[2] The greater power efficiency of production with electric motors resulted, of course, in savings in total fuel consumption and fuel costs.

In the second phase, when electric power could be purchased from public utilities, electrification brought much greater monetary benefits for large-scale manufacturing plants.[3] Capital costs were saved by

[1] Matsumura 1923, p. 39. Matsumura found the ratio of the horsepower of spinning machines to the horsepower of a steam engine (a measure of efficiency) was 0.698 when the spinning machines were driven by electric motors and 0.670 when the machines were driven directly by the steam engine.

[2] Du Boff 1967, p. 510.

[3] The merits of electric motors in this phase of electrification were pointed out by Chas. F. Scott (1915, p. 7).

abolishing the generation plants, and labor costs were saved by eliminating maintenance workers in the power generation plants. Finally, by eliminating coal consumption entirely, electrification through public utilities reduced fuel costs to a much greater extent than in the early phase. Savings in fuel costs occurred also because of a decline in the price of electric power relative to coal accompanied the development of public utilities.

A number of reports documented the monetary benefits of electrification in large manufacturing plants. First, a 1910 record of a Japanese weaving plant indicates that the total wage bill for production workers was halved by replacing oil engines with electric motors (chapter 10). Second, a superintendent of the Baldwin Locomotive Works in Philadelphia reported at a meeting in 1900 that electrification reduced labor costs by 20 to 25%.[4] Third, the Siemens factory in Germany repoted in 1895 that 3,000 tons of coal per year were saved by substituting 72 electric motors for 18 steam engines.[5] Fourth, according to a paper published in 1913, a large pen factory in England equipped with 250-hp electric motors estimated production costs (including fuel, wages and repairs, interest, depreciation, and all other charges) to be $18.43 per hp per year, while the cost of steam-driven production was estimated at $47.50 per hp per year.[6] Fifth, an American engineer estimated in 1896 that by dismantling steam engines and purchasing electric power a firm might cut power costs by 70 to 83%, taking into account expenses for fuel, labor, and above all capital.[7] Finally, reports at the turn of the century indicate that considerable amounts of coal and gas were saved with the electrification of the W. B. Conkey printing plant in Hammond, Indiana and the Government Printing Office in Washington D.C. (chapter 13).

---

[4]   *Journal of the Franklin Institute 1901*, p. 8.
[5]   *Electrical World* 1895b, p. 400.
[6]   *Electrical World* 1913, p. 842.
[7]   Emery 1896, p. 174, cited in Du Boff 1967, p. 512.

The Advantages of the Unit-Drive System

The greatest significance of electrification for large-scale plants was the fact that it made possible the shift from the group-drive to the unit-drive production system. This shift occurred during the second phase of electrification. The introduction of this new production system eliminated the shafts and belts which had been a symbol of the factory in the age of steam power and which remained necessary even in the early phase of electrification.[8]

The elimination of the shafts and belts had numerous consequences for the overall production efficiency and organization of large manufacturing plants.[9] First, under the new system the loss of power in transmission decreased considerably. With group drive much power was lost even when the shafts and belts were in good condition, and misalignment further reduced the power transmitted to production machinery. Several reports in England in the 1890s gave the estimation of average power loss in shafting and belting varing from 20% to 60%.[10] Also three studies in the United States in the same decade documented the inefficiency of the shaft and belt transmission system. One study, for example, reported that with the group-drive system the power lost from friction amounted to 1.66 times the useful load, while with the unit-drive system the power loss was not more than half the useful load.[11]

Japanese engineers held a similar view of the inefficiency of the shaft and belt system, although they have not left any quantitative studies to

[8] These two systems, group drive and unit drive, are illustrated by Devine (1983, chart 2 on p. 351).

[9] Advantage of the unit drive is discussed by many authors; e.g., Devine 1983.

[10] Byatt 1979, pp. 87–88.

[11] *Electrical World* 1895a, p. 207. According to a second report even under conditions of fairly good alignment, from 30 to 50% of the power generated in mills and factories was unremunerative because of the power wasted by belt friction. With the unit-drive system, however, it was estimated that fully 85% of the power generated could be used in production. Hussey 1891, pp. 343–44. A third study reported that if the average useful work were 100, the average waste in pulleys and shafting was 75, and in engine friction it was 60. Thus, the ratio of power loss to average load was 1.35. *Electrical World* 1896, p. 106.

document their opinions. Takeshiro Maeda claimed that in spinning plants the loss of power coming from shaft friction, slipping belts, pressure on bearings, and so forth was so great as to be immeasurable.[12] Sukeo Hayashi reported that in weaving plants the loss of power caused by incomplete transmission was considerable (chapter 10). Both of these men emphasized the decisive superiority of the unit-drive system.

Not only was the system of shafts and belts relatively less efficient in transmitting power, but moreover the belts were hazardous and inconvenient. Because of the danger to workers the use of exposed belts in garment factories was forbidden by law in several states in the United States.[13] In addition, the belts had to be kept at the proper tension, and the need to adjust the belts resulted in production delays. For instance, a 1916 report by an American metallurgical engineer stated that the time lost in usage of flotation machines due to belt trouble was always considerable.[14] Furthermore the shafts and belts sometimes spoiled the products by dripping oil, and they affected the health of workers by scattering dust in the air. These problems were completely solved by introducing the unit-drive system in the spinning, weaving, and printing industries (chapters 9, 10 and 13). Finally, in the printing industry at least, elimination of the belt and its associated mass of shafting ended the obstruction of plant lighting and resulted in higher quality workmanship (chapter 13).

The unit-drive system brought savings in capital costs because the new system did not require either the vast floor space or the sturdy structures which had been necessary to house the shafts and belts. This fact has been pointed out with reference to the spinning, weaving, and printing industries (chapters 9, 10 and 13), but such advantages likely occurred in all large manufacturing plants which switched to the unit-drive system. For example, a Japanese engineer in 1916 showed that an electric motor needed a fraction of the floor space required by a steam engine with a

[12] Maeda 1903, p. 6.
[13] Easton 1918, p. 74.
[14] Shores 1916, p. 567.

boiler.[15] In addition, the Baldwin Locomotive Works estimated in 1900 that steam-driven equipment required 40% more floor space than electric-driven equipment for the same level of production.[16]

Not only could floor space be reduced with the elimination of the shafts and belts, but also more efficient overall factory layout and design became possible. In chapter 9 we described the remodeling of spinning plants in Japan, but manufacturing plants in other industries also benefited from the reorganization of the physical plant provided by the unit-drive system. The Asano Cement Company and the wood working industry in the United States have left records describing this consequence of the switch to unit drive.[17] This merit of electrification has been emphasized by Lewis Mumford and I. C. R. Byatt. They stated as follows.

> "The electric motor created flexibility in the design of the factory: not merely could individual units be placed where they were wanted, and not merely could they be designed for the particular work needed: but the direct drive, which increased the efficiency of the motor, also made it possible to alter the layout of the plant itself as needed."[18]

> "When shafting was used, the layout of the factory was often dominated by the power plant. With electric driving, more attention could be given to arranging the position of the machinery so as to achieve better handling of materials and give simpler access to machinery.—Many contemporary workshops and factories were inconveniently arranged; machinery was— often badly laid out and difficult to manage. There is some justice in the comment that it was the state of buildings and layout rather than the age of the machine tools that contributed to the allegedly high costs of British industry."[19]

In addition to eliminating all the problems and restrictions associated with the shaft and belt system, the introduction of individual electric motors directly increased production efficiency. First, the operation of the machines at uniform speed improved the output quality in the

[15] Tanaka 1916, p. 88. The same view appears in Asano Semento K.K. 1940, p. 673.
[16] *Journal of the Franklin Institute* 1901, p. 8.
[17] Asano Semento K.K. 1940, p. 673; Black 1918, p. 821.
[18] Mumford 1934, p. 224.
[19] Byatt 1979, pp. 85–86.

spinning, weaving, and printing industries, and it raised productivity in the silk-reeling industry (chapters 8, 9, 10 and 13). In addition, as a 1916 document shows, uniform speed was of vital importance for edge trimmers and similar machines in the shoe manufacturing industry in the United States, since varying conditions of speed resulted in imperfect work.[20] Furthermore at Sir Thomas Richardson's engine works at West Hartlepool in England, output rose by 20% by electrification.[21] Second, under the unit-drive system machines could be partly idle without wasting energy. This advantage of unit drive was especially important in spinning, where frequent reduction of operation occurred, and in newspaper printing companies, where work was necessarily intermittent (chapters 9 and 13). According to Mumford, in the unit-drive system

"each unit could work at its own rate of speed, and start and stop to suit its own needs, without power losses through the operation of the plant as a whole."[22]

As evidence of the advantage of this system he referred to the calculations of a German engineer which showed that the unit-drive system raised performance efficiency by fifty percent.

Finally, factory expansion, which had been awkward and expensive with the group-drive system, became a relatively simple matter with the unit-drive system. Under the old system, when the plant was expanded, an additional engine had to be installed in order to drive the increased load or the old engines had to be replaced with a new one with sufficient capacity to carry the entire load. In some cases it practice to install initially a larger engine than immediately necessary in order to allow for easy expansion in the future. Under the unit-drive system, on the other hand, additional motors could be installed at low cost and with little or no inconvenience. This feature of unit drive was acclaimed by American engineers in 1914–15.[23]

In summary, in the early phase of electrification, when electric power

[20] Meade 1916, p. 709.
[21] Byatt 1979, p. 89.
[22] Mumford 1934, p. 224.
[23] Rickards 1914, p. 218; Smith and Kyle 1915, p. 405.

was generated within manufacturing plants, the advantages of electrification were limited. The only major benefit was a saving in fuel costs provided by the greater efficiency of electric motors over steam engines. In the later phase, when electric power was supplied largely by public utilities, electrification produced savings in capital costs and labor costs in addition to savings in fuel costs. An epochal innovation during this phase was the unit-drive system. It raised production efficiency, improved output quality and labor conditions of workers, and increased flexibility in layout and factory organization. Largely because of the advantages of the unit-drive system, electrification was major factor for technological progress in large-scale manufacturing before World War II.

The Case of Small-Scale Factories

Mechanization by Electrification

The fundamental significance of electrification in small-scale factories lies in the fact that electric motors made mechanization of these plants practical.[24] Although gas and oil engines were used to a limited extent in small factories before electrification, generally they were not well suited to the production requirements of small factories.

The relation between electrification and mechanization was strong in case of small-scale factories. In factories with 5–9 persons, the share of electric power in total power capacity, β, increased from 10.6% in 1909 to 89.3% in 1940 (Table 6-6), while the proportion of powered factories, α, increased from 14.4% in 1909 to 78.5% in 1940 (Table 4-7). The correlation coefficient between β and α for 1909–40 is 0.993.[25] By contrast, in the largest scale factories, those with 1,000 or more workers,

---

[24]   The first example of the electrification in small factories was the installation of a 1-hp motor in a watch-making plant in Kyoto City. This motor was run by direct-current electricity supplied by the Keage Power Plant. Meiji Kōgyōshi Hensan Iinkai 1928, p. 453.

[25]   Sample years are 1909, 1914, 1919, 1930, 1935, and 1940. These are the same years as used in the estimates for the largest scale.

β increased from 18.3% in 1909 to 74.8% in 1940, while α was almost constant at 100% during these years. The correlation between electrification and mechanization in these large plants is only 0.415. The high cost of steam engines and the availability of cheap labor discouraged early mechanization in small-scale plants. However, the decline in the electric power rate in the 1920s, the availability of small and inexpensive motors, and the rise in nominal wages after World War I motivated these plants to electrify. A small capacity motor, say a one-horsepower engine, could be installed very easily and did not require reconstruction of the building.[26] By installing electric wire and this type of motor in ordinary houses, family-operated establishments were also mechanized. Consequently mechanization of small establishments through electrification changed the production organization from family-centered to factory-type organization.[27]

Impact of Mechanization

The shift from human power to mechanical power (electric power) benefited the small enterprises in a number of ways. This has been noted in reference to such industries as weaving, match making, and printing. Among these studies, that of the weaving industry provided the most detailed illustration of the impact of electrification. It revealed that the diffusion of power looms with electrification raised both labor productivity and total factor productivity (chapter 10). This same phenomenon seems to have occurred in the small plants of a variety of industries at that time.

In the depression years of the 1920s, large factories made great efforts to keep profits from declining by introducing new technologies and discharging unskilled workers. Smaller plants, on the other hand, raised profitability by introducing motive power.[28] A number of scholars of

[26]   Hoshino 1956, p. 181.

[27]   Sanpei 1961, p. 396.

[28]   Our view that technological progress was accelerated during the 1920s is consistent with the fact that the rate of growth in total factor productivity in manufacturing and mining was during this decade highest among the prewar subperiods indicated in Table 1-1.

Japanese economic history have viewed the agricultural sector and smaller enterprises as a pool of disguised unemployment. They have noted that workers discharged from large enterprises during this decade were absorbed by both agricultural and small-scale non-agricultural enterprises. It appears that this absorption would not have been possible without improvements in technology in the smaller enterprises. Therefore, it may be said that electrification helped to mitigate the unemployment problem.

International Comparison

The fact that electrification mechanized smaller plants and raised productivity was not unique to Japan. There are many documents which demonstrate similar results in Western countrries. Among them we can cite four examples. First, according to Mumford

> "the efficiency of small units worked by electric motors . . . . has given small-scale industry a new lease on life: on a purely technical basis it can, for the first time since the introduction of the steam engine, compete on even terms with the larger unit."[29]

He states also that

> "with electricity, the advantages of size . . . . become questionable" and that "bigger no longer automatically means better."[30]

A second example comes from Friedrich Klemm, who cited two engineers who expressed the same view. Franz Reuleaux claimed in 1875 that engineers could support the artisan by providing cheap, small engines to this class, who had been left without mechanical power.[31] Werner Siemens wrote in the 1880s that the invention of electric motors resolved the problem of providing small units of power to small workshops and thereby made small shops competitive with large factories.[32] Third, J. H. Clapham claimed that in France the electric motor and the internal combustion engine delayed the demise of many

[29] Mumford 1934, p. 225.
[30] Mumford 1934, p. 226.
[31] Klemm 1959, pp. 340–41.
[32] Klemm 1959, p. 354.

small factories and gave many others permanent vitality.[33] Finally, Du Boff claimed in 1967 that by electrification smaller plants earned a new lease on life in the United States.[34]

The major difference between Japan and the West lies in Japan's shorter age of steam power and in her faster electrification. As was mentioned in chapter 6, the share of steam power in total power capacity reached a peak at almost the same time in Japan and as in the United States. This occurred during the first half of the 1890s (Fig. 6-2) in Japan and at the turn of the century in the United States (Table 6-8). But the share of electric power exceeded that of steam power much earlier in Japan than in the United States. This critical point occurred in the latter part of the 1910s in Japan (Table 6-5), but not until the second half of the 1920s in the United States (Table 6-9).

The shorter age of steam power in Japan had a noticeable effect on the structure of the Japanese manufacturing sector. In the West during the age of steam power the productivity differential between large and small factories widened because small plants could not take advantage of the greater efficiency of steam power. Consequently the number of these plants declined drastically. If the era of steam engines had continued in Japan for as long as it did in the West, smaller establishments would likely have lost out to large enterprises equipped with steam engines. Thus, the survival of smaller establishments in Japan was in part due to the timing of the age of electric power in Japan's industrial development.[35] The existence of surplus labor has usually been pointed out as the basic reason for the dual structure of the Japanese economy, but the very rapid transformation of motive power from steam to electricity was clearly an additional factor in the coexistence of small and large enterprises in the Japanese manufacturing sector.

[33] Clapham 1928, p. 260.

[34] Du Boff 1967, p. 518.

[35] The role of electrification in the survival of smaller establishments in Japan has not been properly appreciated. Some reference has been made in the following literature: Kanbayashi 1948, p. 177; Nakamura 1971, pp. 161–62; Suzuki 1936, p. 92; Teikoku Tsūshinsha 1928, p. 414.

PART IV

SUMMARY REMARKS

Chapter 15

NOTES ON TECHNOLOGICAL PROGRESS
IN JAPAN

To conclude our study of Japan's power revolution we set forth in this chapter some of the more general features of and factors for technological progress in Japan. First, we summarize our major findings concerning the history of the power revolution and identify what we believe to be the three most distinguishing characteristics of Japanese technological progress. Second, we clarify how these threee aspects of technological progress affected industrialization. Third, we compare the Japanese history of technological progress with the Western experience summarized by Gerschenkron. Fourth, we discuss Japan's social capacity to adopt modern technologies. Finally we discuss the implications of this study for contemporary developing countries.

Characteristics of Technological Progress in Japan

Major Findings on the Power Revolution

At around 1885, Japan's starting point of industrialization, slightly more than half of total power capacity in Japanese manufacturing was provided by water wheels. The utilization of this traditional source of power was in effect limited to the textile industry. For the years 1884–90 textiles consumed on the average about 90% of all water power. The machine filature and *gara*-spinning industries were the centers of this water power utilization (chapter 2).

The proportion of steam power in total mechanical power increased rapidly since 1885. It reached a peak in the mid-1890s in the manufacturing sector as a whole. At first glance, this seems to indicate that the "classical" European transition from water power to steam power occurred in Japan as well. But this would be a rather superficial view. Apart from the textile industry and a few small industries like lumbering, an age of water power never really existed in Japan (chapter 6).

Steam power utilization was initiated in Japan later than in earlier developed countries, but it proceeded with a more rapid pace. The introduction of steam power to Japan in the 1860's lagged behind Watt's invention by 70 to 80 years, but steam power exceeded 70% of total manufacturing power as early as 1887 and reached 90% in 1889 (Table 2-4). By comparison, the rate of steam power utilization in the United States manufacturing in 1889 was only 78.4% (Table 6-8).

The internal combustion engines was introduced after the steam engine, but it did not become a dominant source of power in Japan. At its highest point of utilization in about 1910 the internal combustion engine provided only 7% of total power capacity. That was even less than the 12% utilization rate of the water wheel at the same time (Table 6-3).

Electric power utilization, which started in the 1880s, increased considerably in the early twentieth century. This new source of power exceeded steam power in the late 1910s and reached 80% of total manufacturing power capacity in the 1930s. The Japanese experience with electrification was characterized by a later start and faster progress than in the West. Japan's first application of electric power lagged behind Gramme's invention of the direct-current dynamo by more than 10 years. Yet it was not until the years between 1919 and 1925, later than in Japan, that the use of electric power exceeded that of steam power in the United States manufacturing (Table 6-9).

Characteristics of the Japanese Power Revolution

The essential characteristics of the Japanese power revolution may be summarized as follows: First, unlike in earlier developed countries,

332

water power utilization in Japan was rather limited. Second, the transitions from water to steam and from steam to electricity both started later but proceeded faster in Japan than in earlier developed countries.

The first characteristic, the limited usage of water power, may be accounted for in the following way. Before the introduction of modern technology, traditional manufacturing industries had not sufficiently developed to require mechanical power. The existence of cheap labor and of the water concession of farmers had even inhibited the use of water wheels. By contrast, in the West water power was widely used in traditional production activities. In Japan even after the introduction of modern technology water power utilization was of limited significance. On the advice of the Japanese government Western-type water wheels were used by some modern factories during the early Meiji period, but this utilization never reached substantial proportions because by that time steam power technology was already available.

The second distinguishing characteristic of Japan's power revolution, its later start and its faster progress, may be explained in the following manner. In the process of transition from water power to steam power, steam power became dominant very quickly because of the limited utilization of water power. Thus, introduction of modern technologies was made largely in conjunction with steam engines. In other words, early industrialization was coincident with the age of steam power in Japan, whereas in England it was coincident with the age of water power. A roughly parallel situation occurred with electrification. Before the mechanization of manufacturing plants was completed, electric power had been introduced. The remaining non-mechanized factories, which were almost small-scale factories, mechanized through electrification.

Time Lag in the Application of Modern Technologies

Our discussion of the progress of the power revolution in Japan has revealed that the time lag between Western invention and Japanese utilization was shorter for electric power utilization than for steam power utilization. This also suggests the hypothesis that in developing

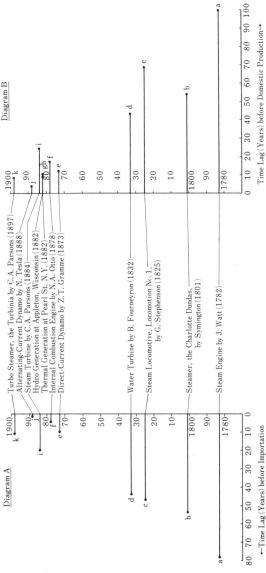

Fig. 15-1. Comparison of the Date of Application of Modern Power Technologies in Japan
with Date of Invention in the West

Sources: Chronology of application of modern power technologies is based on chaps. 3, 6 and 14, and
Gendai Nippon Sangyō Hattatsushi Kenkyūkai 1964, chronological table and Watto Tanjō 200-Nen
Kinenkai 1938, chronological table.

Notes: The figures in parentheses following the year indicates the number of years between invention or
production in the West and application in Japan.
Diagram A:
a The Nagasaki Ironworks owned by the Tokugawa Shogunate imported three steam engines of 6, 8
and 15 horsepower from the Netherlands in 1861 (79).

334

b A steam-powered warship, the Kankō Maru, was donated by the Netherlands to the Shogunate in 1855 (54).

c The Shinbashi-Yokohama Line of the Japanese National Railways (JNR) was opened in 1872 (47). The steam locomotives were imported from England.

d The Umezu Paper Plant installed a 75-hp German-made water turbine in 1876 (44).

e The Tokyo Electric Light Company (TELC) installed a dynamo to light arc-lamps in the Yokosuka Shipyard in 1883 (10). Evidently the dynamo was imported.

f The Kōbu University imported a gas engine in 1882–83 (4–5).

i The Fukagawa Power Plant of Tokyo City Railways installed two 500-kw steam-turbine dynamos imported from the United States in 1904 (20).

j The Nishi Dōtonbori Power Plant of Osaka Electric Light Company began to supply alternating current electricity by using a 30-kw American-made alternator in 1889 (1).

k Two English-made turbo steamers, the Hirafu Maru and the Tamura Maru, appeared on the Aomori-Hakodate Line of JNR in 1908 (11).

Diagram B:

a Japanese production of the stationary steam engine is believed to have started during the second decade (1877–86) of Meji. In this chart the year is assumed to be 1882 (100).

b The Satsuma Clan produced a steam engine in 1855 (54) under the guidance of a Dutch engineer. It was installed in a ship, the Unkō Maru.

c The Kobe Factory of JNR produced a locomotive with the assistance of an English engineer in 1893 (68).

d Domestic production of the water turbine started sometime in the 1870s mainly in the shipyards. In this diagram the year is assumed to be 1875 (43).

e Direct-current dynamos, first produced by the Miyoshi Electric Factory, were used to light arc-lamps in 1885 (12).

f The Tokyo Artisan School made a copy of the English-made oil engine in 1895 (17).

g The Nihonbashi Station of TELC began in 1887 (5) to supply electricity to the public by using a 25-kw direct-current dynamo.

h The Keage Power Plant of Kyoto City began its operation by using two Pelton wheels and nineteen small dynamos in 1892 (10).

i The Mitsubishi Nagasaki Shipyard produced a 500-kw Parsons turbine dynamo in 1908 (24).

j The Miyoshi Electric Factory provided a 30-kw single-phase alternator to Nikkō Electric Power Company in 1892 (4).

k The Mitsubishi Nagasaki Shipyard began producing the Parsons marine turbine in 1904 (7).

economies there will be a shorter time lag for newer power technologies than for older ones.

To test this hypothesis in a more comprehensive way, let us examine Fig. 15-1. This figure shows, the relationship between the years of application of representative modern power technologies in the West and the time lag before their application for the eighteenth and nineteenth centuries in Japan. The date of initial application in the West is approximated by the year of invention, while the date of initial application in Japan is estimated both by the year of importation (Diagram A) and by the year of the first domestic production (Diagram B). For example, in Diagram A, the line connecting point a to the vertical axis indicates that the stationary steam engine was imported to Japan 79 years after it was invented by James Watt in 1782. The corresponding line in Diagram B indicates that this engine was first produced in Japan 100 years after it was invented in the West.

Both Diagram A and Diagram B reveal a negative relation between the date of application in the West and the time lag. In other words, the later a technology was invented the more quickly it was adopted in Japan. In Diagram A the time lag decreased from 79 years in the case of the steam engine (point a) to 44–54 years for technologies developed in the early nineteenth century (b, c, d). For technologies appearing in the late nineteenth century (e, f, i, j, and k) this time lag was shortened to 1 to 20 years. In Diagram B the lag between Western invention and domestic Japanese production decreased from 100 years in the case of the steam engine (a) to 43–68 years for technologies invented in the early nineteenth century (b, c, and d). For technologies developed in the late nineteenth century (e, f, g, h, i, j, and k) the lag was only 4 to 24 years.

This analysis has been limited to power technologies, but it is probably safe to generalize to other technologies. Clearly, we can conclude that:

(1) The time lag between the development of modern technologies and their application in Japan did tend to be increasingly shorter with newer technologies than with older ones.

Furthermore, this conclusion leads to the following two corollary statements:

(2) In Japan the length of time for which one technology was dominant was shorter with newer technologies than with older ones.

(3) The length of time for which one technology was dominant tended to be shorter in Japan than in the West. In other words, technological transition was much faster in Japan than in the West.

These three statements summarize the main distinguishing characteristics of Japan's technological development.

Significance of the Introduction of New Technology in Japan

Impact on the Rate of Manufacturing Growth

The third characteristic of Japan's technological progress, her comparatively rapid transition from older to newer technologies, may largely account for the higher rate of technological progress in Japanese manufacturing than in earlier developed countries. In Japan the annual rate of growth of total factor productivity in manufacturing and mining combined, 2.9% for 1908–38 (Table 1-3), was higher than the 2.5% rate in American manufacturing for 1909–37 (chapter 1). This higher rate of technological progress was partly responsible for the higher rate of growth in manufacturing output in Japan than in more industrialized countries. Japan's annual rate of manufacturing growth (5.6% for 1881–1938) was the highest among the United States, Sweden, Germany, Italy, and the United Kingdom (chapter 1). Furthermore, this higher rate of manufacturing growth was a significant factor in Japan's overall higher rate of economic growth. The annual rate of economic growth for Japan for 1889–1938 was 3.2%.[1] This was considerably above the rate of most other advanced economies for 1881–1940. For example, these figures were 1.5% for the United Kingdom, 1.6% for Italy, 2.2% for Australia

---

[1]   The annual rate of economic growth is an average of $(Y_t - Y_{t-1})/Y_{t-1} \times 100$, where Y stands for real GNE (seven-year moving average). Y is from Ohkawa *et al.* 1974, p. 213.

(1881–1939), 2.8% for Sweden, 2.9% for Germany (1881–1935), and 3.3% for the United States (1893–1940).[2] Japan's remarkable economic progress and her rapid introduction of imported modern technologies provide convincing evidence for the well-known Gerschenkron thesis that industrialization is more promising in proportion to the backlog of technological innovation which a country can borrow. We share with other economists the opinion that this thesis is supported by the Japanese experience.[3]

To test this hypothesis in an international perspective, we have estimated the relationship between the annual rate of economic growth $G(Y)$ for the long period since the beginning of modern economic growth until the 1960s and the per capita income at the beginning of modern economic growth (y), as well as the relationship between the rate of growth of per capita income $G(Y/N)$ and y, in both cases using the data for 14 countries including Japan. The beginning of modern economic growth differs among countries, that is, from 1765 in England to 1886 in Japan. The relationships are as follows:

$$G(Y) = 2.54 - 0.0007y \qquad \bar{r}^2 = -0.038 \quad F = 2.14$$
$$G(Y/N) = 2.35 - 0.0018y \qquad \bar{r}^2 = 0.324^4 \quad F = 7.22$$

The second relationship is significant at the 95% significance level, while the first is not. One of the major reasons for the non-existence of a relationship between $G(Y)$ and y is that the rate of population growth depends on various factors other than economic factors. The relationship between $G(Y/N)$ and y, which signifies that economic growth tends to be more promising in countries with lower per capita income, may be taken as an evidence of the Gerschenkron hypothesis, because the initial level of per capita income expresses the state of technology.

Next, let us examine the significance of the second characteristic of Japan's technological progress, the shortening time lag in the introduction of more modern technologies. In our view, this phenomenon

[2] Minami 1986, table 3-4 on p. 54.
[3] Ohkawa and Rosovsky 1973; Rosovsky 1961.
[4] Minami 1986, chart 3–2 on p. 40.

should have caused an increasing trend in the rate of technological progress. In chapter 1 we have argued that the rate of technological progress showed an increasing trend for 1908–30. This was responsible for an increase in the growth rate of manufacturing output, which was responsible in turn for the increase in the rate of economic growth, or the "trend acceleration" phenomenon, identified by Ohkawa and Rosovsky.[5] Thus, it is our conclusion that this trend acceleration was a consequence of the fact that modern technologies were applied in Japan with shorter and shorter time lags.

Impact on the Structure of Manufacturing

Japan's more rapid transition from older to newer technologies compared with the West affected not only her rate of economic growth but also the structure of her manufacturing sector. The shorter age of steam power and the earlier arrival of the age of electric power in Japan relating to the West supported the survival of small-scale establishments and the dual structure of Japan's manufacturing sector (chapter 14).

As in the West, during the age of steam power small Japanese establishments had been left without mechanical power because of the non-divisibility of the power capacity of steam engines. Internal combustion engines had been installed in some small plants, but they did not succeed in mechanizing all small-scale factories. A substantial portion of these plants were mechanized by electrification. The decline in the price of electric power and the production of inexpensive small-capacity motors by Japanese companies in the 1920s were basic factors behind the mechanization of the remaining small-scale plants through electrification.

[5]   Ohkawa and Rosovsky 1973, especially chap. 8.
Fitting the annual growth rate in real GNE (Y) and that in real GNE per capita (Y/N) to a linear function of time (t) for 1889–1938, we get

$$G(Y) = -67.33 + 0.0368t \qquad \bar{r}^2 = 0.129$$
$$G(Y/N) = -54.21 + 0.0294t \qquad \bar{r}^2 = 0.070 \ .$$

The correlation is statistically significant at 99% and 95% significance levels respectively. This is the most strict test for the existence of trend acceleration. Minami 1986, chart 3-3 on p. 44.

Electrification became practical for small Japanese plants at a very critical time. During the depression of the 1920s, large enterprises attempted to prevent profit declines by introducing new technologies, discharging unskilled workers, and so forth. Small-scale plants, on the other hand, survived because of the benefits of mechanization (electrification). If the era of steam engines had continued in Japan as long as it had continued in the earlier developed countries of the West, it was likely that the smaller establishments which were unable to compete with the larger steam-powered enterprises would have been swept away. However, only a short time after steam power was introduced to large establishments in Japan, electric power became available to the smaller enterprises and enabled them to mechanize and remain viable. Thus, the comparatively rapid transition from steam to electric power in Japan contributed to the maintenance of the dual structure which still characterises the Japanese economy today.

Applicability of the Gerschenkron Model to Japan

Western Model of Gerschenkron

What we identified as the three characteristics of Japanese technological progress undoubtedly all stem from the fact that technologies adopted in Japan were basically "borrowed technologies" in the sense defined by Alexander Gerschenkron. Furthermore, as was stated above, Gerschenkron's hypothesis on the relation between the backlog of technologies and the promise of industrialization appears to be applicable to Japan. Despite these facts, however, Japan's experience did *not* strictly follow the model proposed by Gerschenkron to describe the industrialization of France, Germany, and Russia, which all began to develop later than England.

The four main points of the Gerschenkron model have been summarized by Henry Rosovsky as follows:[6]

1. Prior to industrialization, there is a period of tension between the

[6] Rosovsky 1961, p. 57.

actual state of economic activities and the great promise inherent in development.

2. Industrialization is more promising in proportion to the backlog of technologies. The traditional view that in backward countries labor is cheap and capital is expensive is not true: industrial labor, in the sense of a stable and disciplined work force, may be extremely expensive.

3. In the face of competition from more advanced countries, backward countries adopt the most modern and most labor-saving technologies. As a result, they tend to concentrate development in a sector where technological progress has been particularly rapid. Backward countries in nineteenth century Europe concentrated on "newer" industries like iron and steel and not on cotton textiles which had been the foundation of England's industrialization.

4. Industrialization implies two kinds of bigness: large units of production and a "revolutionary" industrial eruption.

Here we will examine the applicability of this model to Japan. This examination will reveal the features of Japan's experience which is distinguished from Western experience. First, the point that tension is a pre-condition for industrialization, is clearly applicable to Japan, where great political and social turmoil preceded and followed the Meiji Restoration. The military and economic threat of the advanced countries stimulated nationalism which encouraged the rapid modernization of Japan. Second, the relative advantage of backward countries to exploit the backlog of technologies has already been shown to apply to Japan. Third, referring to Gerschenkron's assertion of "bigness", we have seen that Japan's industrialization coincided with the growth of large-scale enterprises (chapter 5). Furthermore, her industrialization was revolutionary in the sense that it was accomplished though borrowed technologies.

Choice of Industry in Japan

On the remaining points, however, the Gerschenkron model is not applicable to Japan. Japan's industrialization was not founded on modern industries which depended on the most up-to-date technology.

Rather, Japan concentrated on the traditional textile industry—and there employed basically labor-using technology—to provide the moving force behind her economic development.[7] In the later phases of development Japan shifted gradually to heavy industries with relatively capital-using technologies (chapter 1).[8] The fundamental pattern of development in Japan, then, was the traditional course of industrialization followed by England, and not the course followed by the later developing European economies.

The difference between Japan's pattern of industrialization and the Western model of backward countries resulted from the fact that labor *was* abundant and comparatively cheap in Japan. The choice of the textile industry in the early years was the means by which the Japanese economy as a whole accommodated the development of a modern manufacturing sector (and borrowed technology) to domestic factor prices. In concentrating on the textile industry Japan used her most abundant resource, labor. With the development of this industry the foreign exchange saved by import substitution and earned through export expansion of textile products was spent to purchase the modern production equipment and modern technology which sustained her early industrialization.

Another reason for the relative advantage of the textile industry over other industries lies in the fact that the traditional technologies of silk reeling, spinning, and weaving had already been developed before industrialization. The presence of these traditional technologies seems to have been an important reason for the later successful introduction of modern technologies. For instance, the first successful application of the machine filature in Nagano Prefecture, was achieved by blending new technology with a traditional one (chapter 8).

The choice of the textile industry is not the only example of the way in

[7] This difference between Japan and the West has been discussed by Rosovsky (1961, pp. 98–102).

[8] The Japanese textile industry enjoyed comparative advantage over other Japanese industries with higher capital-labor ratio than textiles and over the textiles industry in advanced countries with higher wage-rental ratio.

which the need to acquire modern, expensive, borrowed technolgoy was accommodated to the reality of domestic factor prices. The evolution of the dual economic structure (1), the organization of production (2), and the modification of machinery (3) all reflect a similar adjustment to the relative costs of labor and capital in Japan.

Through the persistent growth of small establishments and the creation of the dual economic structure the Japanese manufacturing sector as a whole was able to realize the benefits of both modern technologies and domestic factor prices (1). Small establishments concentrated on more labor-using technologies and thereby took advantage of the country's low wages and excess supply of labor. Large establishments, on the other hand, took full advantage of modern technology.[9]

Our study in part 3 provided four examples in which the persistence of small establishments complemented the growth of large establishments. First, in the cotton spinning industry, small plants equipped with *gara* spinners produced low quality cotton yarn exclusively for the domestic market, while large-scale plants equipped with modern spinning machinery produced high quality yarn both for domestic and foreign markets (chapter 9). Second, in the weaving industry, small plants used hand looms and later narrow-width power looms to produce cloth for domestic sale, and large-scale plants produced cloth for export on wide-width power looms (chapter 10). Third, in the lumbering industry, there was a coexistence of small-scale plants disposing of lumbers cut down in the neighboring forestry and large-scale plants being located in the horbors and disposing imported materials. With a decrease in imports the former plants increased conspicuously in the prewar period (chapter 11). Fourth, the match industry in Japan consisted of a large number of small plants which relied on boys and girls to array matchsticks by hand for spreading chemicals, the most important step of production. By contrast, the Western match industry at that time relied on mass-production techniques utilizing mechanical power. It was in the 1920s that small Japanese match factories introduced the German-type machine run by

---

[9] The significance of the sub-contracting system can be understood in this framework.

mechanical power, but for a decade or more before this period the match industry, relying only on human power and traditional techniques, was a major export industry which earned a part of needed foreign exchange with which Japan could purchase modern technology (chapter 12).

The persistence of these small establishments contributed in yet another way to Japan's industrialization: it mitigated the unemployment problem. Together with agriculture, small manufacturing and service enterprises formed a large pool of what has been called "disguised unemployment."[10] Without this outlet, growing unemployment resulting from the efforts of large enterprises to cope with the depression of the 1920s would likely have created serious social instability during those tumultuous years.

In summary, Gerschenkron's argument that industrialization implies large-scale production is basically applicable to Japan. However, in spite of the growth of large-scale enterprises in Japan, there was also the continued growth of small-scale enterprises. The contribution of traditional technologies to Japan's industrialization, although much smaller than that of the modern technologies, should be properly appreciated.

The organization of production in Japanese factories also illustrates accommodations to modern technology (2). The multiple workshift system, which was initiated at the Osaka Spinning Mill and which later spread throughout the cotton-spinning industry, was a device which mitigated the incongruity between domestic factor prices and the factor proportions dictated by borrowed technologies.

Choice of Technology

The fact that Western machinery was modified prior to its application in Japanese plants as a means of adjustment to the domestic price structure would also demand a modification of the Gerschenkron model (3).

Theoretical Framework. Before we present this argument it is worthwhile to set forth a general framework for discussion of the patterns of borrowing modern technologies. According to Akira Ono borrowed

[10] See Minami 1973 for a detailed discussion.

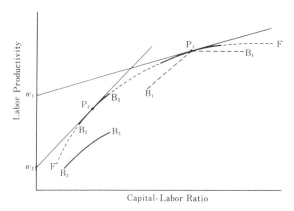

Fig. 15-2. Patterns of Borrowed Technologies

technologies are classified into three categories.[11] The first is the introduction of the most modern technology prevalent in earlier developed countries without any prior modification. In Fig. 15-2 this technology is expressed by a portion, of the production function (F) indicated by a solid line. With the prevalent wage rate in the developed country (w_1), point P_1 is selected because the rate of profit is at its maximum. However, this technology is taken as a limitational production function (curve $B_1 B_1$ kinked at point P_1) by a late-comer who intends to introduce this technology, because there are no possibilities for modification. To the late comer with a wage rate (w_2) the modern technology ($B_1 B_1$) is not profitable, because it is too capital-intensive for an economy characterized by labor abundance and capital scarcity. However, this type of borrowed technology has often been adopted by certain late comers, because modification is substantially impossible in some kinds of technologies, or even if modification were possible, the late comer lacks the social ability for modification, or nationalistic sentiments or both may sometimes demand the introduction of the most modern technology.

The second type is the modern technology introduced with capital-

[11] We owe this part to the discussion by Akira Ono (1986).

saving modification prior to its application. That is, the late comer develops a portion of the production function (B_2B_2) by reconstructing imported capital equipments. This technology is the most profitable for this country with a lower wage rate (w_2). (Note that technology B_2B_2 is more profitable than the first type of technology B_1B_1 even with the latter's higher labor productivity, because more labor force with low wages can be exploited in B_2B_2.) In developing this technology the traditional technology inherited from the pre-modern society (B_3) sometimes plays a role by providing the basic condition that allows the late comer to develop B_2B_2 by combining B_1 and B_3.

The third type is the traditional and less efficient technology (B_2) which is still available in the traditional sector of the earlier developed country. Its introduction has a significance similar to the application of modern technology after modification (the second type). Both the second and the third types of borrowed technologies, which are located between the modern technology (B_1) and the traditional technology (B_3) in terms of level of efficiency (labor productivity) and which are the most profitable to the late comer with an abundant labor force, correspond to the concept of "intermediate" and "appropriate" technology.[12]

The Japanese experience. The first type of borrowed technology was the most common among the three types of technologies borrowed by Japan. Typical examples are found in the public utilities sector. Railroad technology in Meiji Japan was a complete introduction from England.[13]

Construction of the first railway between Shinbashi (Tokyo) and Yokohama, which started in 1870 and was completed in 1872, was made under the direction of an English engineer, Edmund Morel. Aside from him many other foreign engineers were employed in this project; their number was 19 in 1870 and 62 in 1871. Furthermore, almost all equipments for this project were imported; for instance the locomotives were entirely made in England (some of which were imports of used ones in India). Surprisingly even sleepers and tickets were also imported.

Electric generating and transmitting technology was introduced from

[12] For the concept of this technology, refer to Robinson 1979b.
[13] Gendai Nippon Sangyō Hattatsushi Kenkyūkai 1965, p. 43.

346

the United States and Germany (chapter 7). For instance, the five power plants of the Tokyo Electric Light Company (TELC) installed direct-current dynamos made in the United States (1887–90) while the Asakusa Thermal Generation Plant of TELC employed six German-made alternators as well as four alternators made by the Ishikawajima Shipyard (1895). Also the Osaka Electric Light Company began to supply alternating-current electricity based on technology from the United States (1889). Even the construction of the Inawashiro Power Plant and the long-distance transmission line from this plant to Tokyo by TELC, which was taken as an epochal event in the Japanese history of electric utilities, was dependent basically on imported equipment from the United States, Germany, and England.

This type of borrowed technology was also seen among manufacturing industries. Cotton spinning is taken as an example. Out of seventeen spinning mills erected for 1879–85—*nisensui bōseki* (spinning mills with two thousand spindles)—ten mills were powered by water wheels and one mill was equipped with a water wheel and a steam engine (chapter 9). The heavy reliance on water power was a reflection of the energy policy of the government to minimize coal consumption. However, these mills were commercially a failure. The first successful modern spinning mill was the Osaka Spinning Mill (founded in 1882). This was equipped with the most modern technology of large-scale production (10,000-spindle machines) depending on steam power. The success of this enterprise, however, relied on the lessons learned from the unsuccessful experience of earlier mills (small-scale production with unreliable water power, lack of skilled workers, use of inferior domestic raw cotton and so forth) and on the fact that the domestic market for its products had expanded widely enough to absorb the large-scale production. This signifies that the first type of borrowed technology was applied successfully only after a process of trials and error and with the expansion of demand for products.

A good example of the second type is the machine filature technology (chapter 8). The Tomioka Filature (founded in 1870) was equipped with the most modern technology introduced from France (B_1). Because this capital-intensive technology was too expensive for the small-scale Japanese plants, it did not diffuse widely. In 1875 the Nakayama Company in Nagano Prefecture blended this technology with the traditional Japanese technology (B_3) and created a new reeling technology (B_2). This new technology was capital-saving in that water wheels were substituted for steam engines, wood was substituted for iron in machinery, ceramics was substituted for metal in cocoon-boiling basins and steam pipes. Without this modification the quick diffusion of the machine filature technology or the substantial development of the silk reeling industry could not have taken place at that time.

A similar modification can be found in the weaving industry. The imported power looms were expensive because they were made of iron and were big in size (for broad fabrics). Therefore, they were inappropriate for small-scale weavers. At the turn of the century, Sakichi Toyoda invented smaller-size power looms suitable to weave narrow-width fabrics for domestic demand. These power looms were much cheaper because they were made of wood; the first Toyada loom invented in 1897 was made of wood and the second one in 1907 was made of wood and iron. The substitution, which significantly saved production cost of looms, was possible because there was no need of strong frames in weaving narrow-width fabrics (chapter 10).

The printing industry provides another example of such modification (chapter 13). Japanese newspaper companies imported cylinder presses (B_1) in the 1870s, but found that they could not afford to import expensive steam engines used in the West to power these presses. Instead, they took advantage of the low wage-rental ratio in Japan and ran the presses by human power (B_2).

In the modern paper manufacturing of the early Meiji period, rags were used as the main raw material (chapter 6). Faced with the increasing difficulty to collect a large volume of rags, however, Heizaburo Okawa, a chief engineer of Shōshi Company (the present Ōji Paper), proposed the use of rice straws as a substitute for rags in a written memorial submitted to the president, Eiichi Shibusawa in 1879.[14] Rice

[14] Gendai Nippon Sangyō Hattatsushi Kenkyūkai 1967a, pp. 71–77.

straws were available in large quantity and at cheap prices in Japan. Okawa went to the United States and studied the paper manufacturing technique using wheat straws at a factory in New England. From this technique he developed the process of using rice straws (B_2). The company, which employed this new process in 1882, succeeded in increasing output and established a dominant position in this industry.

The third type of borrowed technology can be identified in the introduction of weaving technology (chapter 10). Three students from Nishijin, Kyoto, brought with them the hand loom with batten apparatus from Lyon, France to Nishijin in 1873. They did not bring the most modern weaving technology, namely the power loom (B_1), probably because they thought the production of the power loom was impossible at the contemporary level of engineering in Japan. The batten apparatus (B_2), which could be easily made by local carpenters, was fitted into the traditional hand loom (B_3) and raised the production efficiency of the hand loom. In the process of improvement of this B_2 technology the treadle loom appeared. The wide development of the treadle loom opened the way for the diffusion of the most modern technology (B_1).

Concluding Remarks

In summary, we can state that the Western model of industrialization has not been strictly applicable to Japan, because in the developing manufacturing sector more labor-intensive technologies were employed in Japan than in the West. Moreover, while a skilled, modern industrial work force may indeed be expensive to train, the fact remains that labor was relatively cheap and capital relatively expensive in Japan. This fact was essential in presenting the course of industrialization in Japan.

It is appropriate to make two comments here. First, in spite of the different pattern of industrialization, the historical sequence of various technologies in Japan was in principle similar to that in the countries which exported these technologies. The transition to more modern and more capital-intensive technologies occurred at a rapid pace in Japan. In many industrial sectors the traditional transformation of power technology from water to steam and from steam to electric power took place faster in Japan than in the West. The transition to more modern and more capital-intensive technologies is confirmed by the rising capital-labor ratio in manufacturing. In the light of the Japanese experience, then, we cannot accept the assertion of Fei and Ranis that "capital shallowing" accompanies industrialization in a labor surplus economy.[15]

Second, it should be mentioned that the choice of concentration in the textile industry, which employed the multiple workshift system, and applied capital-saving modifications to imported technologies were not unique to Japan. Similar phenomena occurred in other countries. For instance, in England the multiple workshift was common in the textile industry during the Industrial Revolution. And in the United States the New England textile industry was a leading sector in the early phase of industrialization. This industry adapted to the limited supply of coal in New England by depending largely on water power instead of steam power. Moreover, as Nathan Rosenberg has pointed out, American manufacturers often made other modifications when they introduced technologies from England.[16]

Japan's Social Capacity to Absorb Modern Technologies

Importance of Social Capacity

The above discussion demonstrates the relative advantage of late-comers in exploiting the backlog of modern technologies. However, simply having a backlog of technology available is not a sufficient basis for the successful emergence of a modern economy. As Simon Kuznets has pointed out, it is necessary also to pay due attention to the capacity of a society to absorb new technologies.[17] According to Kuznets' thesis,

[15] A summary and a critique of their argument can be found in Minami (1973, pp. 255–62).

[16] Rosenberg 1972, chap. 3.

[17] Kuznets 1968, pp. 391–92.

the successful introduction of Western technologies in Japan can be perceived for only by referring to this capacity. Its presence or absence within a society is best revealed by the society's choice of appropriate technologies.[18]

In the above section we have argued that Japanese history has demonstrated many examples of choice and creation of appropriate technologies. That is, the social capacity of late comers to make these kinds of adjustments is a basic condition for the successful transfer of technologies. We agree with Rosenberg, who claims that

> "new techniques frequently require considerable modification before they can function successfully in a new environment. This process of modification often involves a high order of skill and ability, which is typically under-estimated or ignored. Yet the capacity to achieve these modifications and adaptations is critical to the successful transfer of a technology."[19]

Thus Japan's position as a late comer and her social capacity enabled her to exploit the modern technologies available from the West.

The capacity of Japan to exploit the backlog of modern Western technologies depended on a wide-range of factors, which lies beyond the scope of this study. Nonetheless, some of the more significant conditions at the outset of the modern period deserve specific mention.

Human Resources

A most important factor to create this social capacity is the existence of individuals who committed themselves wholeheartedly to applying the newly available production techniques. With regard to human resources we will refer to three groups of people: ordinary workers, engineers, and leaders of the country and industry.

Ordinary workers. Availability of eligible labor force at the beginning of industrialization in Japan was one of the most prominent inheritances from the premodern society. Eligibility seems to have been a consequence of the *terakoya* education during the premodern period.[20]

[18] Appropriate technologies in light of the Japanese experience have been studied by Shigeru Ishikawa (1979).

[19] Rosenberg 1972, pp. 61–62.

[20] We owe to Dore 1965, chap. 8 for the discussion of the *terakoya* education.

*Terakoya*s were small-scale private schools with 20–50 pupils, in which samurai, masterless samurai, priests and others taught reading, writing and *soroban* (abacus). It is estimated that the number of *terakoya* was more than 10,000, and at the time of the Meiji Restoration (1868) 43% of boys and 10% of girls had been educated in this system.[21] Thus R. P. Dore, who made a study of this education system, claims that the literacy rate in Japan in 1870 was considerably higher than in most of the developing countries today and even in some contemporary European countries. Also he refers to the facts that the rate of school attendance was only 20–25% in the major industrial towns of England in 1837 and that a Frenchman wrote in 1877 that "primary education in Japan has reached a level which should make us blush."[22]

Contributions of traditional educational system to modern economic growth seem to have been significant. Without the ability of citizens to read and write, government proclamation and execution of the new land-tax system, the new registration system and other organizational changes would have been difficult. According to Dore, the impact of the *terakoya* education, at the very least, is that it gave "a training in being trained".[23] Because of this impact unskilled workers became an excellent work force in the modern factory after short-time training. It is a necessary condition for modern economic growth that the ordinary people adapt themselves to the new environment of the modern society and the modern production system.

The *terakoya* education was gradually replaced by the modern compulsory education which started in 1872.[24] The percentage of attendance at primary schools reached 28 in 1873 and exceeded 80 at the turn of the century.[25] Here attention should be paid to the timing of the start of this type of education. Compulsory education started relatively

[21] Dore 1965, p. 321.
[22] Dore 1965, p. 291.
[23] Dore 1965, p. 292.
[24] We owe this discussion on the history of modern education to Nippon, Monbushō 1962.
[25] Nippon, Monbushō 1962, p. 180.

early in Japan compared with earlier developed countries other than Germany, if we take into consideration the difference in the timing of the start of modern economic growth. The compulsory education started in the 1760s in Germany (Proicen), in the 1850s in the United States (Massachusetts), in the 1870s in England and in the 1880s in France. This means that, while the start of modern education preceded modern economic growth in Germany (1850s), it came later than the start of economic growth in the United States (1830s), England (1760s), and France (1830s).[26] Undoubtedly the modern educational system contributed to industrialization by supplying high quality human resources.

In the 1890s middle schools (including high schools in the present educational system) and various schools providing vocational training to the graduates of compulsory education were established. The rate of attendance at these schools increased in this century reflecting an increasing demand for receiving higher education by the populace and for better quality work-force by industry. It was 8.3% in 1900, 47.2% in 1920 and 83.4% in 1940.[27]

It is generally agreed, however, that the skill of workers was fostered largely at factories themselves rather than at schools.[28] Some big firms established training centers for the employees and their families. For instance, the Mitsubishi Nagasaki Shipyard established a school in 1899, which gave five years training (four years since 1906) to the graduates of compulsory education. According to Konosuke Odaka, however, the importance of this education was not so large.[29] A survey in 1932 for manufacturing and mining shows that, only 12% of factories had such kind of facilities.[30] Furthermore, half of the attendance in these training centers was made up of family members of employees. Therefore, we can state that skill formation of employees was dependent largely on on-the-

---

[26]   We owe to Kuznets 1971, table 2 on p 24 for the demarcation of modern economic growth of Western countries.
[27]   Nippon, Monbushō 1962, p. 181.
[28]   We owe to Odaka 1972 for the history of after-school trainings.
[29]   Odaka 1972, p. 223.
[30]   Odaka 1972, p. 223. Factories surveyed numbered only 2,400 and were limited to medium and large-scale factories.

job training. Excellent workers, even if they were graduates of compulsory education, were sometimes promoted to the rank of foremen. This stimulated ordinary workers to learn seriously from the training at factories.

Engineers. At the beginning of industrialization, Japanese industry relied heavily on the guidance of foreign engineers.[31] Railway construction was an example which we have already referfed to. Foreign engineers were gradually replaced by Japanese engineers who were trained at factories and at various educational institutions both in Japan and in foreign countries.[32] As for Japanese institutions, the Kōbu University (University of Engineering, established in 1877, otherwise known as the Department of Engineering of the University of Tokyo since 1886), the Tokyo Artisan School (established in 1881; the Tokyo University of Engineering since 1929) and several Higher Industrial Schools established by local governments may be pointed out. The number of students of natural sciences and engineering at these schools increased from 962 in 1880 to 9,844 in 1920 and to 41,429 in 1940.[33] Among these institutions the Kōbu University was the main source of leading engineers. For instance, pioneering electric engineers including Ichisuke Fujioka were almost all graduates from this school (chapter 7).

These engineers made a direct contribution to the introduction of modern technologies. They studied foreign technical documents, examined imported machinery, and copied what they saw, often adding original modifications to tne Western models. Furthermore we must refer to the contribution of engineers as business executives, some of whom established new companies and inaugurated new industries. For instance Fujioka, who lighted the first electric light in Japan, was a founder of TELC and an inaugurator of the electric power industry. Namihei Odaira, an engineer graduated from the Department of Engineering of the University of Tokyo, founded the Hitachi Factory in 1920 and employed new graduates from the university as engineers.

---

[31] See Yoshida *et al.* 1978- for details.
[32] See Iwauchi 1973; Yuasa 1972 for the emergence of engineers.
[33] Nippon Monbushō 1962, p. 187.

Later those engineers occupied a central position of management and became the driving force of the company. This was the case as well in the Nippon Nitrogen Fertilizer (established in 1908), the Nippon Soda (established in 1920), and not a few newer companies which appeared during the inter-war period.[34]

In reference to the role of engineers, a similar role of local carpenters should be pointed out. They studied imported wooden machinery, copied, and sometimes modified them. For instance carpenters in various weaving districts produced the batten and jacquard apparatus soon after their introduction to Japan and developed the treadle loom (chapter 10). Also the wooden machine filature was made by carpenters (chapter 8). Without these artisans the quick and wide diffusion of the improved hand loom and the machine filature would not have been possible in the Meiji period. This fact might be true for the later period, although to a lesser extent.

Leading class. As for leaders of the country and industry we refer to politicians, bureaucrats and entrepreneurs. Almost all politicians and bureaucrats in the Meiji period were of samurai origin. However the origin of entrepreneurs in this period is a controversial issue. Takao Tsuchiya and recently Kenjiro Ishikawa argued that the samurai class was a main source of entrepreneurs.[35] On the other hand Johannes Hirschmeier and Kozo Yamamura criticized this common view and claimed that entrepreneurs had been supplied from various classes.[36]

Later on graduates from universities and colleges were substituted for these people. The rate of attendance at universities and colleges, which was only 0.3–0.5% for the 1880s and the 1890s, became 1% in the 1910s and 3–4% in the 1930.[37] Among these schools national universities including the University of Tokyo and the Tokyo Higher Commercial School (later the Hitotsubashi University), and big private universities such as Keio and Waseda were a main source of the leading class.

[34] Uchida 1977, p. 143.
[35] Tsuchiya 1954, p. 171; Ishikawa 1974, p. 107.
[36] Hirschmeier 1964, pp. 253–57; Yamamura 1974, p. 143.
[37] Nippon, Monbushō 1962, p. 181.

Level of Engineering Technology

The rise in the level of engineering technology in Japan seems to have increased the social capacity, because the higher the social capacity, the easier will be the understanding and introduction of new technologies.

Traditional technology. The diffusion of traditional technologies facilitated the application of modern technologies in two ways. First, rural manufacturing industry, generally taking the form of putting-out family enterprise, gave the farmer opportunities to be prepared for work in modern factories in urban areas. According to Thomas C. Smith, "rural industry had given him a certain quickness of hand and eye, a respect for tools and materials, an adaptability to the cadences and confusion of moving parts."[38] Smith claimed conclusively that "few countries have embarked on industry with a superior labor force at hand."[39]

Second, the traditional technology served in some cases as a basis to absorb modern technologies. As was already mentioned, for instance, the substantial diffusion of machine filature was attained by blending the traditional reeling technology with foreign technology. Also the nation-wide distribution of artisans such as carpenters and blacksmiths seems to have eased the development of the modern machinery industry. Local carpenters were producers of production equipments made of wood (e.g., filature, spinners and looms). Furthermore, some artisans worked at modern factories such as ship carpenters who were employed at shipyards.[40]

The contribution of traditional technologies in absorbing modern technologies seems to have decreased in the process of industrialization. This is due to technical and economic reasons. One technical reason is that the increasing gap between the level of traditional and modern technologies made "blending" more difficult. An economic reason is that capital accumulation and increase in wages reduced the necessity for the economy to rely on capital-saving and labor-intensive technologies. In other words, the tendency towards capital-saving, labor-

[38]   Smith 1959, p. 212.
[39]   Smith 1959, p. 212.
[40]   Nakagawa 1977a, p. 36.

intensive technology as well as capital-saving modification of the imported technology was gradually weakened.

Research and development. Importation of foreign technologies sometimes necessitates research and development (R & D) before the actual application.[41] R & D in Japan originated in the machinery, metals and chemicals industries after the Russo-Japanese War (1904–05).[42] For instance planning departments were established at the Mitsubishi Nagasaki Shipyard in 1908 and the Kawasaki Shipyard in 1911. It was only since WWI, however, that R & D was conducted in a substantial scale. The war-time interruption of machinery imports and acquisition of technical information from abroad forced the Japanese industry to expand R & D activities. The government together with a group of enterprises founded the Physical and Chemical Research Institute in 1917, while large companies such as the Mitsui Mining, the Mitsubishi Shipyard, the Tokyo Electric, and the Nisshin Flouring established their own institutes. These activities were much more animated in the non-*Zaibatsu* companies than in the *Zaibatsu* concerns.[43] Among the former group of companies the Hitachi Factory was a notable example. The development of new technologies and import substitution were taken as targets of the company, which was directed by a group of engineers.

Research and development in small-scale enterprises should not be overlooked. These enterprises were often members of trade associations. For instance a weaving association in a particular region included all

[41]   Relationship between importation of foreign technologies and domestic R & D activities can be quantitatively tested for the post WWII period. For 1956–80 a correlation coefficient adjusted by a degree of freedom ($\bar{r}$) is estimated at 0.801 between the two time-series variables; a growth rate of the number of imported technologies and a growth rate of real R & D expenditure, both in mining and manufacturing industries. (Both the number of technologies and the R & D expenditure are seven-year moving averages.) A similar relationship is revealed by using cross-sectional data by industry group in manufacturing. Coefficient $\bar{r}$ between the ratio of payments of imported technologies to net value added and the ratio of R & D expenditure to net value added for 1971–80 is estimated at 0.948. See Minami 1986, pp. 144–48. The same argument is found in Blumenthal 1976, p. 252.

[42]   We owe to Uchida 1977 for the discussion on the history of R & D.

[43]   One reason is that the *Zaibatsu* included trading companies which imported foreign machinery (Uchida 1977, p. 139).

occupations which were related to weaving in this region. Some of these associations had research institutes. The Weaving Association of Mikawa, Aichi Prefecture, established an institute in 1927. This institute aimed at the study of dyeing and weaving technologies, examination of raw materials and products, lending of machinery to members, vocational training to members and so forth.[44] These institutes made a great contribution in developing technologies appropriate to small-scale enterprise.

In this way the level of technology rose in Japanese industries. However the capability to develop new technologies still remained smaller in Japan than in the Western countries. Hoshimi Uchida argued that the development of new technologies in the Japanese chemical industry relying on basic information from the Western countries, was substantially a repeat of the original development done in these countries.[45] Probably, besides chemical industry this was true in the machinery as well as metal industries.

Development of the capital goods producing sector. The development of the capital goods producing industries, facilitating the production of machines embodying new technologies and the capital-saving modifications of foreign technologies, promoted technological progress. A proportion of capital goods in total manufacturing output, which was 11–12% for 1874–1910, increased to 17% in 1911–40 with the exception of 1921–30 including depression years.[46] This figure shows that the capital goods producing sector started a substantial growth after WWI. The growth in this period was caused directly by an interruption of imports from developed countries and a steadily growing domestic demand for machines and equipments. The increasing demand was a consequence of the industrialization since the mid-1880s.

Social Overhead Capital and Institutional Factors

Social overhead capital. Social capacity involves the existence of social

---

[44] Kobayashi 1981, pp. 197–212.

[45] Uchida 1972, p. 83.

[46] Minami 1987, table 1-3 on p. 10.

overhead capital. Road network, although in poor condition, was well developed during the Tokugawa period because of the *sankin-kōtai* travels of the *daimyō*s (feudalistic lords) between their clans and Edo.[47] Water transportation was more developed than land transportation, because geographically Japan is surrounded by water.

During the Meiji period the government made considerable effort to develop modern transportation facilities.[48] Since the start of the railway business with the opening of the Shinbashi-Yokohama line of the National Railways in 1872, the railway network expanded quickly. Operation-kilometers of national and private railways combined increased from 29 in 1872 to 5,999 in 1900 and to 27,289 in 1940.[49] The railway service contributed conspicuously to industrialization by transporting freight and passengers in large volume, at high speed, and at low cost. Transportation of *habutae* (silk) from Fukui to Tokyo is a good example of the role of such social overhead capital. With the opening of the Tōkaidō line in 1889 the cost of transporting silk fabric from Fukui to Tokyo decreased from 1.32 yen per 10 *kan* to 0.62 yen. Also, transportation time decreased from 10 to 4 days. Generally the decline in transportation costs reduced production cost and the decrease in transportation time speeded up the rotation of capital. In addition, the railways improved passenger transportation and thus encouraged internal migration and contributed to the establishment of a national labor market.[50] In this way cheap labor from rural areas became available to the burgeoning modern industrial sector.

Railway has been taken as an example of modern social overhead capital. The other component of social overhead capital, accumulated by the government as well as by the private sector, include roads, harbors, riparian works, communication facilities, banking, and electric,

[47] Ohkawa and Rosovsky 1973, pp. 7–8.
[48] As for the history of land transportation, see Gendai Nippon Sangyō Hattatsushi Kenkyūkai 1965.
[49] Minami 1965, pp. 204–205.
[50] Minami 1965, table 1-3 on p. 8.

gas and water-supply utilities.[51] As an index of social overhead capital, total gross capital stock of public works, railroads and electric utilities increased from 804 million yen in 1880 to 2,348 million yen in 1900 and to 14,097 million yen in 1940 (all in 1934–36 prices).[52]

Institutional factors. Social capacity depends on some institutional factors as well. Among them the existence of a well-established government organization, the capability to acquire and diffuse information on new products and new technologies as well as stable industrial relations may be pointed out.

The positive role of the Japanese government is sometimes highly appreciated.[53] There is no doubt that institutional changes in the early Meiji period, such as the establishment of a centralized modern state, the abolition of restriction of travel and communication, the start of compulsory education, the settlement of public finance by the new land-tax, the construction of social overhead capital, and the establishment of model factories, constituted the prerequisite condition for industrialization.[54]

In this connection two comments are in order. Firstly, these changes were merely necessary conditions for industrialization, while the sufficient condition was the emergence of animated private activities characterized by a rise in the private investment and saving ratio in national income, the introduction of Western sciences, technologies, and production equipment, and so forth. Secondly, the role of the government became moderate in later years. As was argued by W. W. Lockwood, government activities "only accelerated a process of in-

[51] As for the history of the banking system, see Patrick 1967. Development of this system was very rapid in Japan compared with Western countries. Cameron 1967, p. 303.

[52] Ohkawa *et al.* 1966, pp. 160, 162.

[53] An appraisal of the efficiency of the bureaucratic organization of the Tokugawa regime is not settled. Those including Ohkawa and Rosovsky (1973, p. 7) and Yui (1977, p. 196) gave a favorable appraisal, while Yamamura criticized this view (1974, p. 85).

[54] The impact of government enterprises on the Japanese industrialization has been emphasized by many authors (for instance, Smith 1965, p. 103). Recently it is generally agreed, however, that the impact was moderate (Landes 1965, pp. 100–06). Rather they tend to emphasize the role of government as a founder of various institutions and social overhead capital (Rosovsky 1966, p. 113).

dustrialization which was latent in the whole conjuncture of forces at work."[55] However the well-organized bureaucratic organization continued to sustain economic growth by stimulating (or at least never retarding) private activities, and by providing considerable conveniences to the private sector.

As for the capability of Japan to acquire information on new products and new technologies developed in the Western countries, we must note her geographical handicap in being located so far away from the industrialized countries. In spite of this obstacle, however, Japan was rather quickly informed of what was happening in the world owing to the world-wide information network of the *Zaibatsu* and the general trading company, which had a lot of branches all over the world.[56] The Suzuki company, which developed rapidly since WWI as a large trading company second only to the Mitsui Bussan, made inroads into manufacturing activities based on its advantage of ready access to international information. For instance, the impetus to hardened fat production in Japan came about when Naokichi Kaneko, a prominent clerk of the Suzuki Company, which had exported fish oil to a German company, found that Europe, faced with a shortage of solid fat, developed a process to produce soap and margarine by hardening fish oil. The Suzuki Company erected plants in 1916–17, which became the Standard Fat in 1921 and further developed into the Gōdō Fat Glycerin in 1923.[57]

On the other hand, Japan had a big advantage in diffusing information within the country, for being geographically, narrow with a high population density, and a homogeneous people and language eased internal communication. The existence of local trade associations also proved to be another factor facilitating internal communication. These associations acquired new information from both foreign countries and big Japanese companies, delivered these information to

[55]   Lockwood 1968, p. 574.

[56]   The *Zaibatsu* and the general trading company developed in close association with each other. As for the history of the *Zaibatsu* and the general trading company, see Hirschmeier and Yui 1975; Yamamura 1976; and Yasuoka 1976.

[57]   Katsura 1976, p. 206.

their members, and guided them to respond to such information.[58]

"Japanese-type" industrial relations characterized by a familistic ideology in business management and the permanent employment system, seem to have eased the introduction of modern technologies. That is, the resistance against labor-saving innovations, which was often seen in England during the Industrial Revolution, did not occur in Japan.[59] Familistic ideology was strongly advocated by the management in this century, of which Shinpei Goto, a president of the Japanese National Railways (JNR), was a notable example. When JNR was faced with a big problem to merge seventeen private railways with various wage and employment systems in 1906–07, Goto preached that JNR was a family, in which mutual reliance and devotion among workers were needed.[60] The permanent employment system appeared in large enterprises during the 1920s as a device to preserve skilled workers to keep high production efficiency during this difficult period.[61]

Concluding remarks. Conclusively it can be said that Japan have had a large capacity to absorb modern technologies. This is the basic reason for the successful application of modern technologies, which in turn led to the success of industrialization. It should be noted, however, that there is no reason to believe that the capacity was constant over time; indeed the capacity seems to have increased during industrialization owing to a number of factors. Among these are the diffusion of higher education, the training of skilled workers, the rise in the level of technologies, the development of research and development activities, the accumulation of social overhead capital, and the expansion of network to acquire technical information from abroad. This increasing absorptive capacity may have been responsible for the rise in the rate of technological progress during the prewar period (Table 1-3).[62]

[58] Kobayashi 1981, pp. 197–212.
[59] Ohkawa and Rosovsky 1973, p. 220.
[60] Hirschmeier and Yui 1975, p. 207.
[61] Hyodo 1971, pp. 453–65.
[62] Ohkawa and Rosovsky assume that the increasing capacity to absorb modern technologies is explained by a rise in the capital-labor ratio. Under this supposition an increase in the rate of technological progress is attributed to a rise in the growth rate in the

Role of demand. In exploring the factors for Japan's success in industrialization, attention should be paid to the role of demand in addition to the role of social capacity. A market big enough to absorb the modern sector's products as well as its considerable expansion thereafter was another condition that eased the application of modern technologies.

As it has been mentioned, one of the factors for the success of the Osaka Spinning Mill was the emergence of domestic demand for cotton yarn (chapter 9). Also the development of the cotton spinning industry thereafter, much faster than in any other country, became possible only with an expansion of the market. From a macro-view point, it may be stated that the Japanese economy had been characterized by excess demand for goods and services, which caused a steady increase in price. The GNP deflator increased for the entire period of industrialization with the only exception of some years in the 1920s. The annual rate of growth recorded was 3.8% for 1889–1938.[63] This is much higher than the rate of growth for 1863–1935 in earlier developed countries: Sweden (2.1%), Germany (1.4%), England (0.9%), and the United States (0.3%), although lower than the rate in France (5.2%).[64]

The main source of the steady increse in total demand was due to domestic rather than foreign demand. For the period 1888–1938 the ratio of increase in domestic demand (personal and government consumption, gross capital formation and import) to the increase in total demand (a total of domestic demand and foreign demand or export) is estimated at 84.0%. That is, only 16% of the increase in total demand was attributable to the demand from the foreign market.[65] Among the

capital-labor ratio (1973, chap. 8). However this supposition seems to be too simple and rather groudless. Minami 1986, n. 15 of chap. 3 on pp. 438–39.

[63] Minami 1986, table 11-1 on p. 370.

[64] Minami 1986, p. 370.

[65] Relative importance of the domestic market compared with that of the foreign market in Japanese economic growth has been emphasized by W. W. Lockwood (1954, pp. 309, 369, 576), Ryoshin Minami (1986, pp. 173–80, 223–24), and Kazushi Ohkawa and Henry Rosovsky (1973, p. 174). This view is contrasted with the "export-led growth" hypothesis which was applied to the Japanese economy by Miyohei Shinohara (1962, p. 74).

components of domestic demand, personal consumption made the largest contribution to total demand (37.0%), followed by capital formation (19.7%), import (17.9%) and government consumption (9.4 %).[66] Conclusively the rapid expansion in domestic market for consumption and investment, which was largely responsible for the inflationary growth, was one of the features of the Japanese economy, which eased the application of modern technologies.[67]

Implications for Developing Countries

The main similarity between Japan after the Meiji Restoration and countries initiating development today is the common existence of a backlog of unexploited technologies. Japan succeeded in her industrialization by aptly importing and utilizing this storehouse of technological developments. How can developing countries today do the same? Let us explore five implications of the Japanese experience in coping with this problem.

First, among various industries Meiji Japan selected textiles as a leading sector. This selection was appropriate to the contemporary economy characterized by a low level of science and technology and by a low wage-rental ratio, due to an abundant labor supply and poor capital accumulation. Industrialization based on heavy industry (machinery, metals and chemicals) may be difficult to achieve because of these reasons. Firstly, understanding and introduction of the sophisticated technology of the heavy industry will not be easy for a country with an underdeveloped science and technology. Secondly, capital-using and labor-saving heavy industry provides less of an economic advantage than the light industry (textiles) for a country with abundant labor and scarce capital. Thirdly, the development of the capital-using industry

---

[66] Minami 1986, table 6-7 on p. 177. GNE and its components are expressed in 1934–36 prices.

[67] The factors and significance of the Japanese inflation have been argued by Minami (1986, chap. 11).

will necessarily increase import of capital equipments from earlier developed countries and may lead to a deterioration of the balance of payments.

Second, the contribution of small-scale enterprises to Japanese industrialization should not be neglected. The development of these enterprises was one of the devices of labor-intensive modifications of modern technology, and absorbed a part of the labor surplus which characterized the Japanese economy before 1960. This type of industrialization seems to be particularly appropriate for those developing countries which have abundant labor and scarce capital. In this respect deliberate policies to promote the growth of small-scale enterprises are needed. Moreover the Japanese experience demonstrates the significant role of trade associations in respective industries and districts.

Third, with respect to the above argument, the role of electrification-based mechanization in supporting small-scale factories in Japan should be adequately noted. The Japanese experience implies that electrification would support the growth of such small factories in developing countries. However, the construction of electric utilities and a nation-wide transmission system requires huge amounts of capital. Consequently the cost of electricity at the end of a grid extension becomes very high.[68] Thus, an alternative and more promising strategy for developing countries today would be to mechanize small factories by powering them with internal combustion engines.[69] These engines offer advantages

[68] For this reason the World Bank's policy on rural electrification is cautious (Baron 1980, p. 544). A detailed discussion on rural electrification in developing countries is found in Turvey and Anderson 1977, chap. 7. A study on the impact of rural electrification in the Philippines has been made by Alejandro N. Herrin (1979).

[69] Although a rise in oil prices for these years has decreased the relative advantage of internal combustion engines over electric motors, the former are still more economical than the latter, if we take into consideration the construction costs of electric utilities and transmission lines.

similar to electric motors to the needs of rural establishments.[70] The use of internal combustion engines would contribute especially to the development of small factories, which use such engines, and to the development of machinery factories which produce and repair them. These developments may be expected to initiate industrialization.

Fourth, modern technology was introduced to Japan sometime after labor-using modifications. In these modifications the traditional technology played an important role; the modern and the traditional technologies were blended together to create new technology appropriate to the contemporary economy. Such type of borrowing technology is advisable to developing countries with abundant labor and scarce capital. That is, in the research and development activities of developing countries exploring this type of technology should be emphasized.

Finally, according to Japanese experience, the success of industrialization and application of modern technologies in Japan depended on a wide-range of factors, economic and non-economic, which were summed up under the concept of social capacity. Policies to develop such capacity are of decisive importance. That is, the development of human resources through school education and factory training, the accumulation of social overhead capital, the development of research and development activities, the enhancement of administration efficiency, and the establishment of an efficient network to acquire information on technologies from foreign countries and distribute them among domestic industries must be kept in mind.

[70] Frank C. Child and Hiromitsu Kaneda state that approximately half of all private tube wells in the Punjab of Pakistan are diesel powered. One of the reasons for this is the inavailability of electricity. They also cite a study by other authors who claim that in Pakistan while the private cost of delivering of an acre foot of water by diesel tube well is 50% above that for an electric tube well, the utilization of diesel turns out to be more economical in the economy as a whole, if the government's heavy subsidies of the electric power industry are considered (1975, pp. 259–60).

APPENDIX

ESTIMATION OF POWER CAPACITY FOR MANUFACTURING AND MINING

Private Manufacturing

We have estimated the power capacity of engines in private manufacturing factories.[1] These estimates are based on two sets of official statistics: *Nōshōmu Tōkei Hyō* (Statistical Tables for Agriculture and Commerce; henceforth STAC) and *Kōjō Tōkei Hyō* (Statistical Tables for factories; henceforth STF).

Power Capacity Estimates Based on STAC

STAC gives horsepower statistics for factories with ten or more production workers for the years 1884 to 1919 (see Table A-1).[2] There are two problems with the STAC data. First, information is sometimes available only for the number of engines, not for horsepower. This problem is often encountered in the data for water wheels in the earlier years. The following example will illustrate how we estimated power capacity in these cases.

| | Water Wheels | |
	Number	Power Capacity
Silk reeling, 1885	6	12 hp
	336	unknown

In this example, the power capacity is given for six water wheels in the silk-

---

[1] Electric motors are included in these engines. The reasons for including electric motors are discussed in chap. 5.

[2] Horsepower statistics are available from 1886 for wood and wood products and for printing and binding, and from 1889 for miscellaneous. The power capacity of gas engines, oil engines, and electric motors has been included in the surveys since 1898.

reeling industry in 1885. The combined power capacity of these 6 wheels is 12 hp. But STAC does not record the power capacity for the other 336 water wheels. We obtain a power capacity estimate for these water wheels by multiplying the average power capacity (2 hp) for the cases in which full information is available by the number of water wheels in the incomplete category. Assuming that the average power capacity of 336 water wheels is equal to that of the 6 water wheels, this procedure produces an estimate of 672 total power capacity in the missing category. In a worse case no information at all is available for power capacity. In such cases we are forced to substitute an average power capacity figure calculated from statistics for other years.

The second problem is that STAC horsepower statistics frequently appear inconsistent from year to year. When we encountered such abnormal fluctuations we estimated power capacity by linear interpolation.

Power Capacity Estimates Based on STF

STF gives horsepower data for factories with five or more workers for the years 1909 and 1914, and annually for the period 1919 to 1940 (see Table A-2). Unlike STAC this data is tabulated by factory scale as well as by industry group. Therefore we have estimated the power capacity of various engines by industry group and by factory scale for some selected years (1909, 1914, 1919, 1930, 1935, and 1940). For the intermediate years (1920–29, 1931–34, and 1936–39) we estimated power capacity by industry group only.

One big problem with the STF data is that separate figures for the power capacity of primary and secondary electric motors are given only for the four years 1909, 1914, 1919, and 1920. In the other years the total power capacity of both types of electric motors is reported by a single figure. We have therefore estimated the power capacity of the two types of electric motors by both industry group and factory scale for 1909, 1914, and 1919 and by industry group alone for 1920.

We used the following procedures to arrive at our annual estimates of primary and secondary electric power capacity by industry for the period 1921 to 1940. From 1929 to 1940 STF gives electric power consumption by source—electric power supplied from electric utilities and that generated within factories. We assumed that the ratio of power capacity of primary electric motors to total electric power was equal to the ratio of purchased power consumed to total electric power consumption. This assumption seems to be appropriate. We then multiplied total electric power by the proportion of purchased power consumed in order to obtain the power capacity of primary electric motors. For the years 1921 to 1928, when power consumption by source is not reported, we estimated the ratio by linear interpolation for 9 industry groups. We then multiplied this ratio by total electric power capacity to obtain the estimate of primary electric power.[3]

The two problems encountered in using the STAC data are present in the STF data as well. The first, inavailability of horsepower statistics, is resolved in the same way as described above for the STAC estimates. However, because the problem of inconsistent data is less serious in STF than in STAC, we did not make any adjustment when we encountered abnormal changes.

Our estimates of power capacity by engine type, by 9 industry groups and by 7 (9 in later years) factory scales for 1909, 1914, 1919, 1930, 1935 and 1940 can be found in table 29 of *Tetsudō to Denryoku* (Railroads and electric utilities) published in 1965. However, in this table electric motors are not broken down by primary and secondary types. Primary electric power by industry group and by factory scale for 1909, 1914, and 1919 is given in appendix table 4 of *Dōryoku Kakumei to Gijutsu Shinpo* (Power revolution and technological progress) in 1976b. Secondary electric power can be easily calculated from these two tables.

Linkage of the Two Estimates

In order to obtain a long-run series of power capacity for 1884–1940 by industry group, we had to link estimates from STF with those from STAC. We employed the STF estimates for 1909, 1914, and 1919–40 as benchmarks. For the other years the STAC estimates were used after slight adjustments to make them consistent with the STF estimates. (Small factories, those with 5–9 workers are excluded in the STAC estimates but are included in the STF figures.) The adjustments were made in the following way. For 1884–1908 the ratio of the STF figures to the STAC figures in 1909 was multiplied by the annual STAC series for 1884–1908 to calculate the adjusted series. For 1910–13 the ratio was estimated by linear interpolation based on the benchmarks in 1909 and 1914, and for 1915–18 the ratio was estimated by interpolating between the benchmark figures for 1914 and 1919.

Thus we have the power capacity of various engines in private manufacturing factories with five or more workers by nine industry groups for 1884–1940. This series is a revision of our previous estimates, which were included as table 27 of

---

[3] This trend over time has been examined in chap. 5.

APPENDIX

Table A-1. Data Sources for the Number of Factories and Power Capacity of Engines in Manufacturing and Mining and Their Respective Number: 1884–1923

Statistical Tables for Agriculture and Commerce

Title	Publica-tion Year	Page Number Manufacturing	Mining
Dai-1-Ji Nōshōmu Tōkei Hyō (STAC 1884)	1886	272–294	
Dai-2-Ji Nōshōmu Tōkei Hyō (STAC 1885)	1887	317–323, 329–362 378–389	
Dai-3-Ji Nōshōmu Tōkei Hyō (STAC 1886)	1888	4–47	
Dai-4-Ji Nōshōmu Tōkei Hyō (STAC 1887)	1889	not available	
Dai-5-Ji Nōshōmu Tōkei Hyō (STAC 1888)	1890	370–401	
Dai-6-Ji Nōshōmu Tōkei Hyō (STAC 1889)	1891	274–304	
Dai-7-Ji Nōshōmu Tōkei Hyō (STAC 1890)	1892	274–305	
Dai-8-Ji Nōshōmu Tōkei Hyō (STAC 1891)	1893	152–191	
Dai-9-Ji Nōshōmu Tōkei Hyō (STAC 1892)	1894	141[a]	
Dai-10-Ji Nōshōmu Tōkei Hyō (STAC 1893)	1895	219[a]	
Dai-11-Ji Nōshōmu Tōkei Hyō (STAC 1894)	1896	247[a]	
Dai-12-Ji Nōshōmu Tōkei Hyō (STAC 1895)	1897	310[a]	
Dai-13-Ji Nōshōmu Tōkei Hyō (STAC 1896)	1898	443	
Dai-14-Ji Nōshōmu Tōkei Hyō (STAC 1897)	1899	393	
Dai-15-Ji Nōshōmu Tōkei Hyō (STAC 1898)	1900	406–414	
Dai-16-Ji Nōshōmu Tōkei Hyō (STAC 1899)	1901	496–502	
Dai-17-Ji Nōshōmu Tōkei Hyō (STAC 1900)	1902	615–622	
Dai-18-Ji Nōshōmu Tōkei Hyō (STAC 1901)	1903	520–528	
Dai-19-Ji Nōshōmu Tōkei Hyō (STAC 1902)	1904	510–523	
Dai-20-Ji Nōshōmu Tōkei Hyō (STAC 1903)	1905	278–285	
Dai-21-Ji Nōshōmu Tōkei Hyō (STAC 1904)	1906	284–291	
Dai-22-Ji Nōshōmu Tōkei Hyō (STAC 1905)	1907	284–291	
Dai-23-Ji Nōshōmu Tōkei Hyō (STAC 1906)	1908	298–305	
Dai-24-Ji Nōshōmu Tōkei Hyō (STAC 1907)	1909	304–311	459–475
Dai-25-Ji Nōshōmu Tōkei Hyō (STAC 1908)	1910	296–305	453–471
Dai-26-Ji Nōshōmu Tōkei Hyō (STAC 1909)	1911	312–319	485–503
Dai-27-Ji Nōshōmu Tōkei Hyō (STAC 1910)	1912	320–327	503–521
Dai-28-Ji Nōshōmu Tōkei Hyō (STAC 1911)	1913	320–327	505–523
Dai-29-Ji Nōshōmu Tōkei Hyō (STAC 1912)	1914	344–353	
Dai-30-Ji Nōshōmu Tōkei Hyō (STAC 1913)	1915	348–357	
Dai-31-Ji Nōshōmu Tōkei Hyō (STAC 1914)	1916	344–353	
Dai-32-Ji Nōshōmu Tōkei Hyō (STAC 1915)	1917	342–351	

Table A-1. (continued)

Statistical Tables for Agriculture and Commerce

Title	Publica- tion Year	Page Number Manufacturing	Mining
Dai-33-Ji Nōshōmu Tōkei Hyō (STAC 1916)	1918	352–361	
Dai-34-Ji Nōshōmu Tōkei Hyō (STAC 1917)	1919	364–373	551
Dai-35-Ji Nōshōmu Tōkei Hyō (STAC 1918)	1920	260–268	434–435
Dai-36-Ji Nōshōmu Tōkei Hyō (STAC 1919)	1921	251–257	388–389
Dai-37-Ji Nōshōmu Tōkei Hyō (STAC 1920)	1922		324–325
Dai-38-Ji Nōshōmu Tōkei Hyō (STAC 1921)	1923		168–169
Dai-39-Ji Nōshōmu Tōkei Hyō (STAC 1922)	1924		54–57
Dai-40-Ji Nōshōmu Tōkei Hyō (STAC 1923)	1925		62–65

Notes: The editor is Nippon, Nōshōmushō (Japan, Ministry of Agriculture and Commerce).

ᵃ The last part of three.

Tetsudō to Denryoku and as appendix tables 3 and 6 of *Dōryoku Kakumei to Gijutsu Shinpo*. The major difference between the present estimates and the previous ones is in the method of calculating power capacity of water wheels from STAC.

In addition to estimates of power capacity we have also tabulated estimates of the number of powered factories and total factories based on STAC (see Table A-1) and STF (see Table A-2). In table 28 of *Tetsudō to Denryoku* these figures are shown by industry group and by factory scale for the years 1909, 1914, 1919, 1930, 1935 and 1940. The annual long-run series for 1896-1940 by nine industry groups is given in appendix table 2 of *Dōryoku Kakumei to Gijutsu Shinpo*.

Mining

Total power capacity (H) and primary power capacity (H′) in the mining industry were calculated from three official sources: STAC for 1907–11 and 1917–23 (see Table A-1), the *Shōkōshō Tōkei Hyō* (Statistical tables of the Ministry of Commerce and Industry) for 1924–36 (see Table A-3), and *Honpō*

Table A-2. Data Sources for the Number of Factories and Power Capacity of Engines in Manufacturing and Their Respective Number: 1909–1940

Statistical Tables for Factories

Title		Publication Year	Page Number
Meiji 42-Nen Kōjō Tōkei Hyō	(STF 1909)	1911	1–8
Taishō 3-Nen Kōjō Tōkei Hyō	(STF 1914)	1916	1–8
Taishō 8-Nen Kōjō Tōkei Hyō	(STF 1919)	1921	52–61
Taishō 9-Nen Kōjō Tōkei Hyō	(STF 1920)	1922	34–39
Taishō 10-Nen Kōjō Tōkei Hyō	(STF 1921)	1923	338–339
Taishō 11-Nen Kōjō Tōkei Hyō	(STF 1922)	1924	76–77
Taishō 12-Nen Kōjō Tōkei Hyō	(STF 1923)	1925	76–81
Taishō 13-Nen Kōjō Tōkei Hyō	(STF 1924)	1926	76–81
Taishō 14-Nen Kōjō Tōkei Hyō	(STF 1925)	1927	76–81
Shōwa Gan-Nen Kōjō Tōkei Hyō	(STF 1926)	1928	76–81
Shōwa 2-Nen Kōjō Tōkei Hyō	(STF 1927)	1929	76–81
Shōwa 3-Nen Kōjō Tōkei Hyō	(STF 1928)	1930	76–81
Shōwa 4-Nen Kōjō Tōkei Hyō	(STF 1929)	1931	298–317
Shōwa 5-Nen Kōjō Tōkei Hyō	(STF 1930)	1932	286–303
Shōwa 6-Nen Kōjō Tōkei Hyō	(STF 1931)	1933	286–303
Shōwa 7-Nen Kōjō Tōkei Hyō	(STF 1932)	1934	286–303
Shōwa 8-Nen Kōjō Tōkei Hyō	(STF 1933)	1935	286–303
Shōwa 9-Nen Kōjō Tōkei Hyō	(STF 1934)	1936	286–303
Shōwa 10-Nen Kōjō Tōkei Hyō	(STF 1935)	1937	200–217
Shōwa 11-Nen Kōjō Tōkei Hyō	(STF 1936)	1938	200–217
Shōwa 12-Nen Kōjō Tōkei Hyō	(STF 1937)	1939	190–207
Shōwa 13-Nen Kōjō Tōkei Hyō	(STF 1938)	1940	190–207
Shōwa 14-Nen Kōgyō Tōkei Hyō	(STF 1939)	1941	226–245[a]
Shōwa 15-Nen Kōgyō Tōkei Hyō	(STF 1940)	1942	226–245[a]

Notes: The editor is Nippon, Nōshōmushō (Japan, Ministry of Agriculture and Commerce) for 1909–23, and Nippon, Shōkōshō (Japan, Ministry of Commerce and Industry) for 1924–40.
[a] The second volume of three.

Kōgyō no Sūsei (Trends in Japanese mining) for 1938–40 (see Table A-4). For the years not covered by these sources, 1912–16 and 1937, H and H′ were estimated by linear interpolation.

APPENDIX

Table A-3. Data Sources for Power Capacity of Engines in Mining: 1924–1936

Statistical Tables of the Ministry of Commerce and Industry

Title		Publication Year	Page Number
Dai-1-*Ji Shōkōshō Tōkei Hyō*	(STMCI 1924)	1926	234–235
Dai-2-*Ji Shōkōshō Tōkei Hyō*	(STMCI 1925)	1927	202–203
Dai-3-*Ji Shōkōshō Tōkei Hyō*	(STMCI 1926)	1927	148–149
Dai-4-*Ji Shōkōshō Tōkei Hyō*	(STMCI 1927)	1928	148–149
Dai-5-*Ji Shōkōshō Tōkei Hyō*	(STMCI 1928)	1929	148–149
Dai-6-*Ji Shōkōshō Tōkei Hyō*	(STMCI 1929)	1930	148–149
Shōwa 5-*Nen Shōkōshō Tōkei Hyō*	(STMCI 1930)	1931	148–149
Shōwa 6-*Nen Shōkōshō Tōkei Hyō*	(STMCI 1931)	1932	148–149
Shōwa 7-*Nen Shōkōshō Tōkei Hyō*	(STMCI 1932)	1933	152–153
Shōwa 8-*Nen Shōkōshō Tōkei Hyō*	(STMCI 1933)	1934	156–157
Shōwa 9-*Nen Shōkōshō Tōkei Hyō*	(STMCI 1934)	1935	156–157
*Shōwa*10-*Nen Shōkōshō Tōkei Hyō*	(STMCI 1935)	1936	158–159
*Shōwa*11-*Nen Shōkōshō Tōkei Hyō*	(STMCI 1936)	1937	158–159
*Shōwa*12-*Nen Shōkōshō Tōkei Hyō*	(STMCI 1937)	1938	
*Shōwa*13-*Nen Shōkōshō Tōkei Hyō*	(STMCI 1938)	1939	

Notes: The editor is Nippon, Shōkōshō (Japan, Ministry of Commerce and Industry).

Table A-4. Data Sources for Power Capacity of Engines in Mining: 1938–1940

Trend in the Japanese Mining

Year of Survey	Title	Year of Publication	Page Number
1938	*Shōwa* 13-*Nen Honpō Kōgyō no Sūsei*	1940	305
1939	*Shōwa* 14-*Nen Honpō Kōgyō no Sūsei*	1948	291
1940	*Shōwa* 15-*Nen Honpō Kōgyō no Sūsei*	1948	299

Notes: The editor is Nippon, Shōkōshō, Kōzan Kyoku (Japan, Ministry of Commerce and Industry, Bureau of Mining).

BIBLIOGRAPHY

Aida, Shoji. 1974. "Higashi Mikawa Men Orimonogyō ni okeru Kōjōsei Seisan no Seiritsu—Hoi Gun Mitani Chō H-Ke no Keiei o Chūshin toshite." *Shakai Keizai Shigaku*, 39: January, pp. 74–102.

American Machinist. 1892. "Newspaper Printing by Electricity." 15: 29 September, p. 10.

Arisawa, Hiromi, ed. 1959. *Kindai Sangyō no Hatten. Gendai Nippon Sangyō Kōza*, vol. 1. Tokyo: Iwanami Shoten.

──────. 1960a. *Enerugī Sangyō. Gendai Nippon Sangyō Kōza*, vol. 3. Tokyo: Iwanami Shoten.

──────. 1960b. *Kikai-Kōgyō, I. Gendai Nippon Sangyō Kōza*, vol. 5. Tokyo: Iwanami Shoten.

──────. 1960c. *Kikai-Kōgyō, II. Gendai Nippon Sangyō Kōza*, vol. 6. Tokyo: Iwanami Shoten.

──────. 1960d. *Sen-i Sangyō. Gendai Nippon Sangyō Kōza*, vol. 7. Tokyo: Iwanami Shoten.

Asahi Sinbunsha. 1949. *Asahi Shinbun 70 Nen Shōshi.* Tokyo.

──────. 1961. *Asahi Shinbun Shōshi.* Tokyo.

──────. 1966. *Tokyo Asahi Shinbun Hennenshi: Meiji 23-Nen.* Tokyo.

──────. 1969. *Asahi Shinbun no 90-Nen.* Tokyo.

──────. 1970. *Asahi Shinbun Hennenshi: Meiji 18-Nen.* Tokyo.

──────. 1972. *Asahijin Kaisōroku*, vol. 1. Tokyo.

BIBLIOGRAPHY

Asano Semento K.K. 1940. *Asano Semento Enkakushi.* Tokyo.

Ashton, T. S. 1970. *The Industrial Revolution 1760–1830.* London: Oxford University Press.

Baron, C. 1980. "Energy Policy and Social Progress in Developing Countries." *International Labour Review* 119: September–October, pp. 531–46.

Bel'kind, L. D. *et al. 1960. Ningen to Gijutsu no Rekishi,* vol. 1, translated by Nonaka, Akio. Tokyo: Shōkō Shuppansha.

———. 1966. *Ningen to Gijutsu no Rekishi,* vol. 2. Tokyo Tosho K.K.

Bishop, Reed R. 1897. "Electric Power for Operating Printing and Binding Machinery, I." *Electrical World* 30: 9 October, pp. 419–20.

Black, W. A. 1918. "Solving Woodworking Drive Problems: Method by Which One Company Has Practically Eliminated Repairs and Reduced Power Bills by the Proper Selection of Drives and Correct Mounting of Motors." *Electrical World* 71: 20 April, pp. 821–23.

Blumenthal, Tuvia. 1976. "Japan's Technological Strategy." *Journal of Development Economics* 3: September, pp. 245–55.

Byatt, I. C. R. 1979. *The British Electrical Industry 1875–1914.* Oxford: Oxford University Press.

Cameron, Rondo, ed. 1967a. *Banking in the Early Stages of Industrialization: A Study in Comparative Economic History.* London, New York and Toronto: Oxford University Press.

———. 1967b. "Conclusion." In Cameron 1967a, pp. 290–321.

Child, Frank C. and Kaneda, Hiromitsu. 1975. "Links to the Green Revolution: A Study of Small-Scale, Agriculturally Related Industry in the Pakistan Punjab." *Economic Development and Cultural Change* 23: January, pp. 249–75.

Chōki Keizai Tōkei Iinkai. 1968. *Chōki Keizai Tōkei no Seibi Kaizen ni Kansuru Kenkyū,* vol. 2. (*Keizai Kenkyū Chōsa Shiryō,* no. 11). Tokyo: Keizai Kikakuchō, Keizai Kenkyūjo.

BIBLIOGRAPHY

Chūshō Kigyō Chōsakai, ed. 1960. *Chūshō Kigyō no Tōkeiteki Bunseki*. Tokyo: Tōyō Keizai Shinpōsha.

Clapham, J. H. 1928. *The Economic Development of France and Germany, 1815–1914*. 3rd ed. Cambridge: Cambridge University Press.

Dai-Nippon Sanshikai, ed. 1935. *Nippon Sanshigyōshi*. vol. 2. Tokyo.

Damon, George A. 1898. "The Electrical Equipment of a Model Printing Establishment." *Electrical World* 32: November, pp. 499–504.

Deane, Phyllis. 1979. *The First Industrial Revolution*. 2nd ed. Cambridge: Cambridge University Press.

Dellenbaugh, F. S., Jr. 1915. "Electric Drive for Small Printing Plants." *Electric Journal* 12: May, pp. 192–94.

Derry, T. K. and Williams, T. I. 1960. *A Short History of Technology: From the Earliest Times to A.D. 1900*. Oxford: Clarendon Press.

Devine, Warren D. Jr. 1983. "From Shafts to Wires: Historical Perspective on Electrifiction." *Journal of Economic History* 43: June, pp. 347–72.

Doi, Sadao. 1953. *Jitsuyō Seizai Gijutsu*. Tokyo: Morikita Shuppan.

Dore, R. P. 1965. *Education in Tokugawa Japan*. London: Routledge and Kegan Paul.

Du Boff, Richard B. 1966. "Electrification and Capital Productivity: A Suggested Approach." *Review of Economics and Statistics* 48: 426–31.

——————— 1967. "The Introduction of Electric Power in American Manufacturing." *Economic History Review* Second Series 20: December, pp. 509–18.

Easton, William H. 1918. "Electricity in Garment-Making Factories." *Electric Journal* 15: February, pp. 74–76.

Economic Commission for Europe, Research and Planning Division. 1951. "Motive Power in European Industry." United Nations, *Economic Bulletin for Europe* 3: pp. 24–40.

377

Electrical World. 1888. "The Electric Motor in Newspaper Offices" 11: 2 June, p. 279.

—————. 1890. "Fine Printing Done by Electric Power." 15: 28 June, p. 432.

—————. 1895a. "Electric Power for Isolated Factories." 25: 16 February, p. 207.

—————. 1895b. "Electric Power in Factories." 25: 30 March, pp. 400–01.

—————. 1896. "Electrically-Operated Factories." 27: 25 January, p. 106.

—————. 1897. "Direct Connected Motors." 29: 6 March, p. 335.

—————. 1898. "The Electric Plant of the Government Printing Office II." 31: 22 January, pp. 115–18.

—————. 1913. "Economies in the Use of Electric Power." 61: 19 April, p. 842.

—————. 1918. "Electricity in the Silk Industry." 71: 11 May, p. 989.

Electrical World and Engineer. 1901. "Electric Power in the Government Printing Office." 37: 30 March, p. 521.

Emery, Charles E. 1896. "The Relations of Electricity to Steam and Water Power." *Journal of the Franklin Institute* 142: September, pp. 165–86.

Encyclopaedia Britannica, Inc. 1958. *Encyclopaedia Britannica*, vol. 23. Chicago.

Fenichel, Allen H. 1966. "Growth and Diffusion of Power in Manufacturing, 1838–1919." In N.B.E.R., *Output, Employment, and Productivity in the United States After 1800* (*Studies in Income and Wealth*, vol. 30), pp. 443–78. New York: Columbia University Press.

Forbes, R. J. 1956. "Power." In Singer *et al.* 1956, pp. 589–622.

Fujii, Shigeru. 1960. "Men-orimono Kōgyō no Hattatsu: Banshūori no Seisei to Hatten." In Oshikawa *et al.* 1960, pp. 95–172.

Fujino, Shozaburo 1965. *Nippon no Keiki Junkan: Junkanteki Hatten Katei no Rironteki, Tōkeiteki, Rekishiteki Bunseki.* Tokyo: Keisō Shobō.

—————— *et al.* 1979. *Sen-i Kōgyō. Chōki Keizai Tōkei: Suikei to Bunseki,* vol. 11. Tokyo: Tōyō Keizai Shinpōsha.

Gendai Nippon Sangyō Hattatsushi Kenkyūkai. 1964a. *Denryoku. Gendai Nippon Sangyō Hattatsushi,* vol. 3. Tokyo: Kōjunsha.

——————. 1964b. *Sen-i, Jō. Gendai Nippon Sangyō Hattatsushi,* vol. 11. Tokyo: Kōjunsha.

——————. 1965. *Riku-un, Tsūshin. Gendai Nippon Sangyō Hattatsushi,* vol. 22. Tokyo: Kōjunsha.

——————. 1967a. *Kami, Parupu. Gendai Nippon Sangyō Hattatsushi,* vol. 12. Tokyo: Kōjunsha.

——————. 1967b. *Sōron, Jō. Gendai Nippon Sangyō Hattatsushi,* vol. 29. Tokyo: Kōjunsha.

Gerschenkron, Alexander. 1962. *Economic Backwardness in Historical Perspective: A Book of Essays.* Cambridge, Mass.: Harvard University Press, Belknap Press.

Hagino, Toshio. 1957. *Hokuyōzai Keizaishiron.* Tokyo: Rinya Kyōsaikai.

——————. 1972. *Hattenki ni okeru Akitazai Keizaishi.* Tokyo: Ringyō Keizai Kenkyūjo.

Harada, Toshimaru. 1973. "Wagakuni Shoki Kikaibōseki ni okeru Jōkiryoku no Riyō ni tsuite." *Osaka Daigaku Keizaigaku* 23: pp. 171–80.

Haruhara, Akihiko. 1969. *Nippon Shinbun Tsūshi: Shimen Kuronikuru.* Tokyo: Gendai Jānarizumu Shuppankai.

Hashimoto, Yasuto, 1937. *Komugi Seifun to Seimen.* Tokyo: Nishigahara Kankōkai.

Hattori, Yukifusa. 1955. "*Manyufakuchā Shi Ron.*" Tokyo: Rironsha.

Hayashi, Sukeo. 1910. "Shokki oyobi Seimaiki e Dendōki-Ōyo ni tsuite

BIBLIOGRAPHY

Torishirabetaru Jikō." *Denki No Tomo* 268: December, pp. 753–59.

Herrin, Alejandro N. 1979. "Rural Electrification and Fertility Change in the Southern Philippines." *Population and Development Review* 5: March, pp. 61–86.

Hibi, Tanekichi, ed. 1956. *Nihon Denki Kōgyōshi*. Tokyo: Nihon Denki Kōgyōkai.

Hills, Richard L. 1970. *Power in the Industrial Revolution*. Manchester: Manchester University Press.

Hindle, Brook. 1975. *America's Wooden Age: Aspects of Its Early Technology*. New York: Sleepy Hollow Restorations.

Hirano Mura Yakuba, ed. 1932. *Hirano Sonshi Ge-Kan*. Hirano, Nagano Ken.

Hirschmeier, Johannes. 1964. *The Origins of Entrepreneurship in Meiji Japan*. Cambridge: Harvard University Press.

————— and Yui, Tsunehiko. 1975. *The Development of Japanese Business, 1600–1973*. London: George Allen and Unwin.

Hitachi Seisakujo. 1960. *Hitachi Seisakujo Shi*, vol,1. rev. ed. Tokyo.

Honda, Iwataro, ed. 1935. *Nippon Sanshigyō Shi, Dai 2-Kan*. Tokyo: Dai Nippon Sanshikai.

Horie, Hideichi. 1976. *Bakumatsu Ishinki no Keizai Kōzō*. Tokyo: Aoki Shoten.

Hoshino, Yoshiro. 1956. *Gendai Nippon Gijutsushi Gaisetsu*. Tokyo: Dai-Nippon Tosho.

Hunter, Louis C. 1975. "Waterpower in the Century of the Steam Engine." In *America's Wooden Age: Aspects of Its Early Technology*, ed. by Brooke Hindle. New York: Sleepy Hollow Restorations, pp. 160–92.

—————. 1979. *A History of Industrial Power in the United States, 1780– 1930*, vol. 1, *Waterpower in the Century of the Steam Engine*, Charlottesville: University Press of Virginia.

Hussey, C. S. 1891. "Electricity in Mill Work." *Electrical World* 17: 9 May, pp.

343–44.

Hyodo, Takashi. 1956. *Nippon ni okeru Rōshikankei no Tenkai.* Tokyo: University of Tokyo Press.

Iijima, Hanji. 1949. *Nippon Bōsekishi.* Tokyo: Sōgensha.

Imazu, Kenji. 1964. *Kindai Gijutsu no Senkusha: Tōshiba Sōritsusha Tanaka Hisashige no Shōgai.* Tokyo: Kadokawa Shoten.

Insatsu Seihon Kikai 100-Nenshi Jikkō Iinkai, ed. 1975. *Insatsu Seihon Kikai 100-Nenshi.* Tokyo: Zen-Nippon Insatsu Seihon Kikai Kōgyōkai.

Ishii, Tadashi. 1979. "Tokkyo kara Mita Sangyō Gijutsushi: Toyoda Sakichi to Shokki Gijutsu no Hatten, 2" *Hatsumei* 76: February, pp. 35–42.

——————. 1987. "Rikishokki Seizō Gijutsu no Tenkai." In Minami and Kiyokawa 1987, pp. 131–49.

Ishikawa, Kenjiro. 1974. "Meijiki ni okeru Kigyōsha Katsudō no Tōkeiteki Kansatsu." *Osaka Daigaku Keizaigaku* 23: March, pp. 85–118.

Ishikawa, Kiyoshi. 1977. "Bisai Chihō ni okeru Bōseki Gaisha no Setsuritsu." *Meijyō Shōgaku* 27: July, pp. 26–46.

Ishikawa, Shigeru. 1979. "Appropriate Technologies: Some Aspects of Japanese Experience." In Robinson 1979a, pp. 75–139.

Ishiwata, Shigeru. 1975. "Minkan Kotei Shihon Tōshi." In Ohkawa and Minami 1975, pp. 15–33.

Journal of the Franklin Institute. 1901. "The Electric Distribution of Power in Workshops." 151: January, pp. 1–28.

Kajinishi, Mitsuhaya. 1948. *Gijutsu Hattatsushi: Keikōgyō. Nippon Shihonshugi Kenkyū Kōza*, vol. 46. Tokyo: Kawade Shobō.

——————. ed. 1964. *Sen-i: Jō-Kan–Gendai Nippon Sangyō Hattatsushi 11-Kan.* Tokyo: Gendai Nippon Sangyō Hattatsushi Kenkyūkai.

Kanbayashi, Teijiro. 1948. *Nippon Kōgyō Hattatsushi Ron.* Tokyo: Gakusei

Shobō.

Katsura, Ko. 1925. "Saitama Ken Chichibu Chihō ni okeru Syokki Syurui no Hensen to koreni Tomonau Sangyō Soshiki no Henka." *Shakai Seisaku Jihō* 46: July, pp. 42–61.

Katsura, Yoshio. 1976. "Zaibatsu no Zasetsu: Suzuki Shōten." In Yasuoka 1976, pp. 177–223.

Kawamura, Seiichi. 1952. "Shuzō Manyufakuchā to Suisha." *Kobe Gaidai Ronsō* 2: pp. 23–36.

Kawasaki, Saburo. 1943. "Iyo Kasuri no Kenkyū." In *Nippon Tokushu Sangyō no Tensō: Iyo Keizai no Kenkyū*, ed. by Hideo Kagawa. Tokyo: Daiyamondosha, pp. 3–82.

Kendrick, John W. 1961. *Productivity Trends in the United States*. N.B.E.R., General Series, no. 71. Princeton: Princeton University Press.

Kiyokawa, Yukihiko. 1973. "Menkōgyō Gijutsu no Teichaku to Kokusanka ni tsuite." *Keizai Kenkyū* 24: April, pp. 117–37.

——————. 1980. "Sanhinshu no Kairyō to Fukyū Denpa: Ichidai Kōzatsushu no Baai, Jō and Ge." *Keizai Kenkyū* 31: January, pp. 27–39 and April, pp. 135–46.

Klein, L. and Ohkawa, Kazushi, eds. 1968. *Economic Growth: The Japanese Experience since the Meiji Era*. Homewood: Richard D. Irwin.

Klemm, Friedrich. 1959. *A History of Western Technology*, translated by Dorothea Waley Singer. New York: Charles Scribner's Sons.

Kobayashi, Yoshio. 1960. "Kinu Jinken Orimonokōgyō no Hattatsu." In Oshikawa *et al.* 1960, pp. 231–77.

Kobayashi, Tatsuya. 1981. *Gijutsu-Iten: Rekishi kara no Kōsatsu. Amerika to Nippon*. Tokyo: Bunshindō.

Komiyama, Takuji. 1941. *Nippon Chūshō Kōgyō Kenkyū*. Tokyo: Chūo Kōronsha.

Kosho, Tadashi. 1980. "Ashikaga Orimonogyō no Tenkai to Nōson Kōzō."

BIBLIOGRAPHY

Tochi Seido Shigaku 86: January, pp. 1–17.

Kurihara, Toyo. ed. 1964. *Denryoku–Gendai Nippon Sangyō Hattatsushi 3-Kan.* Tokyo: Gendai Nippon Sangyō Hattatsushi Kenkyūkai.

Kuroda, Toshiro, Tamaoki, Masami, and Maeda, Kiyoshi. eds. 1980. *Nippon no Suisha*: Tokyo, Daiyamondosha.

Kuroiwa, Toshiro and Tamaoki, Masami. 1978. *Sangyō Kōkogaku Nyūmon.* Tokyo: Tōyō Keizai Shinpōsha.

Kuznets, Simon. 1968. "Notes on Japan's Economic Growth." In Klein and Ohkawa 1968, pp. 385–422.

—————. 1971. *Economic Growth of Nations: Total Output and Production Structure.* Cambridge: Harvard University Press.

Landes, David S. 1965. "Japan and Europe: Contrasts in Industrialization." In *The State and Economic Enterprise in Japan: Essays in the Political Economy of Growth*, ed. by W. W. Lockwood. Princeton: Princeton University Press, pp. 93–182.

—————. 1969. *The Unbound Prometheus: Technological Change and Industrial Development in Western Europe from 1750 to the Present.* Cambridge: Cambridge University Press.

Lilley, Samuel. 1965. *Men, Machines and History.* rev. and enl. ed. New York: International Publishers.

Lockwood, William W. 1968. *The Economic Development of Japan: Growth and Structural Change.* Expanded ed. Princeton: Princeton University Press.

Maeda, Takeshiro. 1903. "Bōshokukōjō no Kikaiunten ni Dendōki o Mochiyuru no Riben ni tsuite." *Nippon Denki Geppō* 11: 15 March, pp. 3–7.

Mainichi Shinbunsha. 1972. *Mainichi Shinbun 100-Nenshi 1872–1972.* Tokyo.

Makino, Fumio. 1987. "Seishigyō ni okeru Dōryoku Sentaku." *Tokyo Gakugei Daigaku Kiyō, Dai-3-Bumon Shakai Kagaku*, vol. 39.

Maruyama, Kiyoyasu. 1956. "Nōson Suisha no Gijutsushi: Kita-Kantō ni okeru." *Kagakushi Kenkyū* 37: January and March, pp. 1–7.

BIBLIOGRAPHY

Marx, Karl. 1954. *Capital: A Critical Analysis of Capitalist Production.* vol. 1. Moscow: Foreign Languages Publishing House.

Matsumura, Shigetaro. 1923. "Bōsekikōgyō ni okeru Denryoku-Ōyō no Tokushitsu o Ronzu, I and II." *Denki Hyōron* 1: January and February, pp. 33–39 and 154–60.

Meade, Norman G., 1916. "Electric Drive in the Shoe Manufacturing Industry: Economies of Transmission, Dependable Service, Flexibility and Uniform Speed Among Advantages of Motor Operation." *Electrical World* 67: 25 March, pp. 708–09.

Meiji Kōgyōshi Hensan Iinkai. 1925. *Meiji Kōgyōshi, Kagakukōgyō Hen.* Tokyo: Kōgakukai.

—————. 1928. *Meiji Kōgyōshi, Denki Hen.* Tokyo: Kōgakukai.

—————. 1930. *Meiji Kōgyōshi, Kikai Hen.* Tokyo: Kōgakukai.

Meiji-Zen Nippon Kagakushi Kankōkai. 1973. *Meiji-Zen Nippon Kikai-Gijutsushi.* Tokyo: Nippon Gakujutsu Shinkōkai.

Minami, Ryoshin. 1965. *Tetsudō to Denryoku, Chōki Keizai Tōkei: Suikei to Bunseki*, vol. 12. Tokyo: Tōyō Keizai Shinpōsha.

—————. 1973. *The Turning Point in Economic Development: Japan's Experience.* Tokyo: Kinokuniya Shoten.

—————. 1976a. "The Introduction of Electric Power and Its Impact on the Manufacturing Industries: With Special Reference to Smaller Scale Plants." In Patrick 1976, pp. 299–325.

—————. 1976b. *Dōryoku Kakumei to Gijutsu Shinpo: Senzenki Seizōgyō no Bunseki.* Tokyo: Tōyō Keizai Shinpōsha.

—————. 1977. "Mechanical Power in the Industrialization of Japan." *Journal of Economic History* 37: December, pp. 935–58.

—————. 1981. *Nippon no Keizai Hatten.* Tokyo: Tōyō Keizai Shinpōsha.

—————. 1982a. "Water Wheels in the Preindustrial Economy of Japan." *Hitotsubashi Journal of Economics* 22: February, pp. 1–15.

384

—————. 1982b. "Mechanical Power and Printing Technology in Pre-World War II Japan." *Technology and Culture* 23: October, pp. 609–24.

—————. 1984. "Industrialization and Technological Progress in Japan." *Asian Development Review* 2, pp. 69–79.

—————. 1986. *The Economic Development of Japan: A Quantitative Study.* London, Basingstoke and New York: Macmillan Press and St. Martin's Press.

—————. 1987. "Nippon no Gijutsu Hatten: Senzenki no Gaikan." In Minami and Kiyokawa 1987, pp. 2–21.

—————, Ishii, Tadashi and Makino, Fumio. 1982. "Gijutsu Fukyū no Shojōken: Rikishokki no Baai." *Keizai Kenkyū* 33: October, pp. 334–59.

————— and Kiyokawa, Yukihiko, eds. 1987. *Nippon no Kōgyōka to Gijutsu Hatten.* Tokyo: Tōyō Keizai Shinpōsha.

————— and Makino, Fumio. 1983a. "Conditions for Technological Diffusion: Case of Power Looms." *Hitotsubashi Journal of Economics* 23: February, pp. 1–20.

————— and —————. 1983b. "Gijutsu Sentaku no Keizaisei: Men-orimono no Bunseki." *Keizai Kenkyū* 34: July, pp. 216–30.

————— and —————. 1983c. "Senzen-ki Men-orimono Gyō ni okeru Jun Rijunritsu to Dōryokuhi no Suikei." *Keizai Kenkyū* 34: October, pp. 364–70.

————— and —————. 1986a. "Choice of Technology: A Case Study of the Japanese Cotton Weaving Industry 1902–1938." *Hitotsubashi Journal of Economics* 27: December, pp. 12–33.

————— and —————. 1986b. "Seizaigyō ni okeru Gijutsu to Dōryoku: Senzenki Nihon no Nōson Kōgyō ni Kansuru Ichikenkyū." In *Ajia no Nōsōn Kōgyō*, ed. by Saburo Yamada. Tokyo: Ajia Keizai Kenkyūjo, pp. 45–92.

————— and —————. 1987. "Seishigyō ni okeru Gijutsu Sentaku." In Minami and Kiyokawa 1987, pp.43–62.

——————— and Ono, Akira. 1978a. "Yōso-Shotoku to Bunpairitsu no Suikei: Minkan Hiichiji Sangyō." *Keizai Kenkyū* 29: April, pp. 143–69.

——————. 1978b. "Modeling Dualistic Development in Japan." *Hitotsubashi Journal of Economics* 18: February, pp. 18–32.

——————. 1979. "Wages." In *Patterns of Japanese Economic Development: A Quantitative Appraisal*, ed. by Kazushi Ohkawa and Miyohei Shinohara. New Haven: Yale University Press.

——————. 1981. "Behavior of Income Shares in a Labor Surplus Economy: Japan's Experience." *Economic Development and Cultural Change* 29: January, pp. 309–24.

Mitani, Toru. 1930. *Saishin Seishigaku*, vol. 2, Tokyo: Meibundō.

Miwa, Shigeo. 1975. *Ishiusu no Nazo: Sangyō Kōkogaku e no Michi*. Tokyo: Sangyō Gijutsu Sentā.

Miyahara, Yoshihisa. 1950. *Mokuzai Kōgyōshiwa*. Tokyo: Rinzai Shinbunsha Shuppankyoku.

——————. 1956. *Seizai Kōgyō Hattatsushi: Ringyō Hattatsushi Shiryō*, vol. 44. Tokyo: Ringyō Hattatsushi Chōsakai.

Moriya, Fumio. 1948. *Bōseki Seisanhi Bunseki*. Kokyo: Nippon Hyōronsha.

Mumford, Lewis. 1934. *Technics and Civilization*. New York: Harcourt, Brace and Company.

Musson, A. E. 1976. "Industrial Motive Power in the United Kingdom, 1800–70." *Economic History Review* Second Series 29: August, pp. 414–39.

Nakagawa, Keiichirō ed. 1977a. *Nippon-teki Keiei*. Tokyo: Nippon Keizai Shinbunsha.

——————. 1977b. "Nippon-teki Keiei." In Nakagawa 1977a, pp. 9–48.

Nakamura, Takafusa. 1971. *Senzenki Nippon Keizaiseichō no Bunseki*. Tokyo: Iwanami Shoten.

——————. 1980. *Nippon Keizai: Sono Seichō to Kōzō*. Tokyo: University of

Tokyo Press.

Napier, Ron. 1981. "Nippon ni okeru Seizōgyō no Seisansei." In *Senkanki no Nippon Keizai Bunseki*, ed. by Takafusa Nakamura. Tokyo: Yamakawa Shuppansha, pp. 217–47.

Nippon Ginkō, Tōkei Kyokyu. 1966. *Meiji-Ikō Honpō Shuyō Keizai Tōkei*. Tokyo.

Nippon, Monbushō. 1962. *Nippon no Seichō to Kyōiku: Kyōiku no Tenkai to Keizai no Hattatsu*. Tokyo: Teikoku Chihō Gyōsei Gakkai.

Nippon, Ōkurashō. 1934–40. *Nippon Gaikoku Bōeki Nenpyō*. Tokyo.

Nippon, Ōkurashō, Insatsu Kyoku. 972. *Ōkurashō Insatsu Kyoku 100-Nenshi*, vol. 2. Tokyo.

Nippon Sen-i Kyōgikai, ed. 1958a. *Nippon Sen-i Sangyōshi, Sōron Hen*. Tokyo: Sen-i Nenkan Kankōkai.

——————. ed. 1958b. *Nippon Sen-i Sangyōshi, Kakuron Hen*. Tokyo: Sen-i Nenkan Kankōkai.

Nippon, Tsūshō Sangyōshō. 1961 and 1962. *Kōgyō Tōkei 50-Nenshi, Shiryō Hen*, vols. 1 and 2. Tokyo.

Nōgyō Hattatsushi Chōsakai, ed. 1954 and 1955. *Nippon Nōgyō Hattatsushi*, vols. 2 and 6. Tokyo: Chūō Kōronsha.

Noshiro Mokuzai Sangyōshi Henshū Iinkai, ed. 1979. *Noshiro Mokuzai Sangyōshi*. Akita: Noshiro Mokuzai Sangyo Rengokai.

Nōshōmushō Kōmukyoku. 1925. *Orimono oyobi Meriyasu ni Kansuru Chōsa*. Tokyo: Kōseikai Shuppanbu.

Odaka, Konosuke. 1972. "Shokugyō Kunren no Gendai-teki Kadai." *Kikan Gendai Keizai* 6: September, pp. 216–34.

Nōshōmushō Sanrinkyoku, ed. 1921. *Taishō 8-Nenmatsu Minsetsu Seizai Kōjō Ichiran*. Tokyo: Dai Nihon Sanrinkai.

Nōrinshō Sanrinkyoku, ed. 1935. *Mokuzai Kankei Kōjō Shirabe*. Tokyo: Dai

BIBLIOGRAPHY

Nihon Sanrinkai.

Ohkawa, Kazushi and Minami, Ryoshin, eds. 1975. *Kindai Nippon no Keizai Hatten: Chōki Keizai Tōkei ni yoru Bunseki*. Tokyo: Tōyō Keizai Shinpōsha.

————— and Rosovsky, Henry. 1965. "A Century of Japanese Economic Growth." In *The State and Economic Enterprise in Japan*. ed. by W. W. Lockwood. Princeton: Princeton University Press, pp. 47–92.

————— and Rosovsky, Henry. 1973. *Japanese Economic Growth: Trend Acceleration in the Twentieth Century*. Stanford: Stanford University Press.

————— *et al.* 1966. *Shihon Suttoku. Chōki Keizai Tōkei: Suikei to Bunseki*, vol. 3. Tokyo: Tōyō Keizai Shinpōsha.

————— *et al.* 1967. *Bukka. Chōki Keizai Tōkei: Suikei to Bunseki*, vol. 8. Tokyo: Yōyō Keizai Shinpōsha.

————— *et al.* 1974. *Kokumin Shotoku. Chōki Keizai Tōkei: Suikei to Bunseki*, vol. 1. Tokyo: Tōyō Keizai Shinpōsha.

Okamoto, Sachio. 1975. "Sōsetsu Bokkō-ki ni okeru Bōseki-kigyō to Dōryoku Shigen-Mondai Kanken." *Seinan Gakuin Daigaku Shōgaku Ronshū* 22: May, pp. 55–80.

Okumura, Shoji. 1973. *Koban, Kiito, Watetsu: Zoku Edo-Jidai Gijutsushi*. Tokyo: Iwanami Shoten.

Ono, Akira. 1986. "Technical Progress in Silk Industry in Prewar Japan: The Types of Borrowed Technology." *Hitotsubashi Journal of Economics* 27: June, pp. 1–10.

Osaka Fu. 1881–1898. *Osaka Fu Tōkeihyō*. Osaka.

Oshikawa, Ichiro *et al.* eds. 1960. *Chūshō Kigyō Kenkyū 1: Chūshō Kigyō no Hattatsu*. Tokyo: Tōyō Keizai Shinpōsha.

Ozaki, Shoichi. 1954. *Naganoken Sanshigyō Gaishi, Jō*. Nagano: Dai-Nippon Sanshikai Shinano Shikai.

Patrick, Hugh. 1967. "Japan, 1868–1914." In Cameron 1967, pp. 239–89.

388

——————— ed. 1976. *Japanese Industrialization and Its Social Consequences.* Berkeley and Los Angeles: University of California Press.

Rickards, A. E. 1914. The Production Problem in the Foundry and Machine Shop Industry." *Electric Journal* 11: April, pp. 216–19.

Robinson, Austin, ed. 1979a. *Appropriate Technologies for Third World Development.* London and Basingstoke: MacMillan Press.

——————. 1979b. "The Availability of Appropriate Technologies." In Robinson 1979a, pp. 26–44.

Rōdō Undō Shiryō Iinkai. 1959. *Nippon Rōdō Undō Shiryō, Dai 10-Kan, Tōkei Hen.* Tokyo: Rōdō Undō Shiryō Kankō Iinkai.

Rosenberg, Nathan. 1972. *Technology and American Economic Growth.* New York: Harper and Row.

Rosovsky, Henry. 1961. *Capital Formation in Japan: 1868–1940.* New York: The Free Press of Glencoe.

——————. 1966. "Japan's Transition to Modern Economic Growth, 1868–1885." In *Industrialization in Two Systems*, ed. by Henry Rosovsky. New York, London and Sydney: John Wiley and Sons, pp. 91–139.

Saigusa, Hirone. 1973. *Saigusa Hirone Chosakushū*, vol. 10. Tokyo: Chūō Kōronsha.

Sakai, Shozaburo. 1962. "Chūshō Keorigyō no Hattatsu." *Kenkyū 1—Chūshō Kigyō no Hattatsu*, ed. by In Ichiro Oshikawa *et al.* Tokyo: Tōyō Keizai Shinposha, pp. 105–60.

Sanpei, Takako. 1961. *Nippon Kigyōshi.* Tokyo: Yūzankaku.

Scott, Chas. F. 1915. "A Perspective Survey of Electricity in Industry." *Electric Journal* 12: January, pp. 6–10.

Sharlin, Harold I. 1963. *The Making of the Electrical Age From the Telegraph to Automation.* London: Abelard-Shuman.

Shimizukō Mokuzaishi Hensan Iinkai, ed. 1962. *Shimizukō Mokuzaishi.* Shimizu: Shimizukō Seizai Seikan Kyōdō Kumiai.

BIBLIOGRAPHY

Shinohara, Miyohei. 1949. *Koyō to Chingin.* Tokyo: Jitsugyō no Nipponsha.

—————. 1962. *Growth and Cycles in the Japanese Economy.* Tokyo: Kinokuniya Shoten.

—————. 1972. *Kōkōgyō. Chōki Keizai Tōkei: Suikei to Bunseki,* vol. 10. Tokyo: Tōyō Keizai Shinpōsha.

Shionoya, Yuichi. 1968. "Patterns of Industrial Development." In Klein and Ohkawa 1968, pp. 69–109.

Shiozawa, Kimio and Kawaura, Koji. 1957. *Kisei Jinushisei Ron.* Tokyo: Ochanomizu Shobō.

Shizuokaken Mokuzai Kyōdō Kumiai Rengōkai, ed. 1968. *Shizuokaken Mokuzaishi.* Shizuoka: Shizuokaken Mokuzai Kyōdō Kumiai Rengōkai.

Shōkōshō Kōmukyoku. 1934. *Honpō Naichi Kōgyō no Sūsei.* Tokyo: Shōkōshō Kōmukyoku.

Shores, E. 1916. "Individual Motor Drive for Flotation Machines." *Electric Journal,* 13: December, pp. 566–67.

Singer, Charles *et al.,* eds. 1954–58. *A History of Technology,* vols. 1–5. London: Oxford University Press.

Smith, G. F. and Kyle, Elmer L. 1915. "The Silk Industry in Northeastern Pennsylvania." *Electric Journal* 12: September, pp. 402–06.

Smith, Thomas C. 1959. *The Agrarian Origins of Modern Japan.* Stanford: Stanford University Press.

—————. 1965. *Political Change and Industrial Development in Japan: Government Enterprise, 1868–1880.* 2nd ed. Stanford: Stanford University Press.

Sonomura, Mitsuo. 1937. *Nōgyō Denka,* vol. 1. Tokyo: Kōgyō Tosho Kabushikigaisha.

Steinberg, S. H. 1959. *Five Hundred Years of Printing:* London: Faber and Faber.

Sueo, Yoshiyuki. 1980. *Suiryoku Kaihatsu Riyō no Rekishi Chiri*. Tokyo: Taimeidō.

Sugiyama, Shukichi. 1889. "Fuji Seishi Kaisha Kōjō no Gaikyō." *Kōgakukai Shi* 93: September, pp. 562–73.

Suzuki, Taira. 1936. "Denkikōgyō no Jūyōsei to Sono Kakuritsu." In *Kōgyō Chōsa Ihō*, ed. by Shōkōshō, Kōmukyoku. Tokyo: Kōgyō Chōsa Kyōkai, 14: pp. 91–92.

Suzuki, Tetsuzo. 1951. "Higashi Mikawa ni okeru Men-orimonogyō no Hatten." *Keizai Shirin* 19: January, pp. 103–34.

Takahashi Keizai Kenkyūjo 1941. *Nippon Sanshigyō Hattatsushi, Jō*. Tokyo: Seikatsusha.

Tamaki, Hajime. 1957. *Aichi Ken Ke-orimonogyō Shi*. Nagoya: Aichi Daigaku Chūbu Chihō Sangyō Kenkyūjo.

Tamura, Eitaro. 1943a. *Nippon Kōgyō Bunkashi*. Tokyo: Kagakushugi Kōgyōsha.

——————. 1943b. *Nippon Denki Gijutsusha Den*. Tokyo: Kagaku Shinkōsha.

Tamura, Nobuo and Asai, Y. 1901. *Binō Chihō Kigyō Torishirabe Hōkoku*. Tokyo: Tokyo Kōtō Shōgyō Gakkō.

Tanaka, Makoto, ed. 1950. *Enshū Yushutsu Orimono Shi*. Hamamatsu: Enshū Orimono Kōgyō Kyōdō Kumiai.

Tanaka, Tatsuo. 1916. "Kōjōdōryoku no Denka o Unagasu." *Denki No Tomo* 402: July, pp. 87–90.

——————. 1917. "Seitetsugyō no Dōryoku ni tsuite." *Denki No Tomo* 433: October, pp. 745–51.

Tanihara, Takeo, ed. 1958. *Men-sufu Orimonokōgyō Hattatsushi*. Tokyo: Nippon Men-sufu Orimonokōgyō Rengōkai.

Teikoku Tsūshinsha. 1928. *Nippon Sangyōshi, Jō*. Tokyo.

Temin, Peter. 1966. "Steam and Waterpower in the Early Nineteenth Century." *Journal of Economic History* 26: June, pp. 187–205.

Times Publishing Company. 1935. *A Newspaper History 1785–1935*. (Reprinted from *The 150th Anniversary Number of the Times, January 1935*). London.

Thorp, William L. 1929. "Horsepower Statistics for Manufactures." *Journal of the American Statistical Association* New Series 24: March, pp. 376–85.

Tokyo Dentō K.K. 1936. *Tokyo Dentō Kabushiki Kaisha Kaigyō 50-Nenshi.* Tokyo.

Tokyo Fu. 1881–89. *Tokyo Fu Tōkeihyō.* Tokyo.

Tokyo Shibaura Denki K.K. 1963. *Tokyo Shibaura Denki Kabushiki Kaisha 85-Nenshi.* Tokyo.

Toppan Insatsu K.K. 1961. *Toppan Insatsu Kabushiki Kaisha 60-Nenshi.* Tokyo.

Tōyō Bōseki K.K. 1953. *Tōyō Bōseki 70-Nenshi.* Osaka.

Tōyō Keizai Shinpōsha. 1935. *Nippon Bōeki Seiran.* Tokyo.

——————. 1950. *Shōwa Sangyōshi*, vol. 2. Tokyo.

Tsuchiya, Takao. 1954. *Nippon Shihonshugi no Keieishi-teki Kenkyū.* Tokyo: Misuzu Shobō.

Tsuda, Jisaku. 1925. *Orimono Jōshiki.* Tokyo: Sugiyama Shoten.

Tsukada, Fudo. 1937. *Tsuda-shiki Shokki Hatsumeisha: Tsuda Yonejiro.* Kanazawa: Kanazawa Shokkōkai.

Tsunekawa, Kiyoshi. 1916. "Kōgyōyō Dōryoku to shiteno Denki-Ōyō." *Denki No Tomo* 402: July, pp. 91–97.

Turvey, Ralph and Anderson, Dennis. 1977. *Electricity Economics: Essays and Case Studies.* Baltimore and London: Johns Hopkins University Press.

Uchida, Hoshimi. 1960. *Nippon Bōshoku Gijutsu no Rekishi.* Tokyo: Chijin Shokan.

—————. 1972. "Taishō Shōwa-shoki no Kagaku-kōgyō ni okeru Gijutsu-dōnyū to Jishu-kaihatsu." *Keiei Shigaku* 7: May, pp. 65–85.

—————. 1977. "Gijutsu Kaihatsu." In Nakagawa 1977a, pp. 131–58.

Umemura, Mataji *et al.* 1966. *Nōringyō: Chōki Keizai Tōkei: Suikei to Bunseki*, vol. 9. Tokyo: Tōyō Keizai Shinpōsha.

U.S., Census Office. 1902. *Twelfth Census of the United States, 1900*, vol. 7, part 1, *Manufactures*. Washington.

U.S., Department of Commerce, Bureau of the Census. 1913, 1923, 1928, 1930, 1933, 1942. *Census of the United States, Manufactures*. Washington.

Usher, Abbott Payson. 1954. *A History of Mechanical Inventions*. rev. ed. Cambridge: Harvard University Press.

von Tunzelmann, G. N. 1978. *Steam Power and British Industrialization to 1860*. Oxford: Oxford University Press.

Watto Tanjō 200-Nen Kinenkai, ed. 1938. *Zusetsu, Nippon Jōkikōgyō Hattatsushi*. Tokyo.

Yamaguchi, Kazuo. 1956. *Meiji-zenki Keizai no Bunseki*. Tokyo: *Tokyo Daigaku Shuppankai*.

Yamamura, Kozo. 1974. *A Study of Samurai Income and Entrepreneurship: Quantitative Analyses of Economic and Social Aspects of the Samurai in Tokugawa and Meiji Japan*. Cambridge: Harvard University Press.

—————. 1976. "General Trading Companies in Japan—Their Origins and Growth." In Patrick 1976, pp. 161–99.

—————. 1978. "Kikaikōgyō ni okeru Seiōgijutsu no Dōnyū: 1930-nendai Nippon Gaikō no Haikei-teki Yōin." In *Washinton-Taisei to Nichibei-Kankei*, ed. by Chihiro Hosoya and Makoto Saito. Tokyo: University of Tokyo Press, pp. 511–42.

Yamazaki, Hiroaki, 1969. "Ryōtaisenkanki ni okeru Enshū Men-orimonogyō no Kōzō to Undō." *Keiei Shirin* 6: July, pp. 33–79.

Yamazawa, Ippei and Yuzo Yamamoto. 1979. *Bōeki to Kokusai Shūshi, Chōki*

Keizai Tōkei: Suikei to Bunseki, vol. 14. Tokyo: Tōyō Keizai Shinpōsha.

Yasuoka, Shigeaki, ed. 1976. *Nippon no Zaibatsu.* Tokyo: Nippon Keizai Shinbunsha.

Yomiuri Shinbunsha. 1976. *Yomiuri Shinbun 100-Nenshi.* Tokyo.

Yoshida, Mitsukuni. 1974. *Kikai.* Tokyo: Hōsei Daigaku Shuppan Kyoku.

——————. 1977. *Zusetsu, Gijutsu to Nippon Kindaika.* Tokyo: Nippon Hōsō Shuppan Kyōkai.

——————. *et al.,* eds. 1968–76. *Oyatoi Gaikokujin,* vols. 1–17. Tokyo: Kashima Kenkyūjo Shuppankai.

Yuasa, Mitsutomo. 1972. "Gakkō-kyōiku to Sangyō Gijutsu." *Keiei Shigaku* 7: May, pp. 88–104.

Yui, Tsunehiko. 1977. "Edo-jidai no Kachi-taikei to Kanryōsei." In *Edo-Jidai no Kigyōsha Katsudō,* ed. by Mataji Miyamoto. Tokyo: Nippon Keizai Shinbunsha, pp. 173–99.

Zenkoku Sanrinkai Rengōkai. 1938. *Tenryūgawa Ryūiki Ringyō Keieichōsa Hōkokusho.* Tokyo: Zenkoku Sanrinkai Rengōkai.

INDEX

INDEX